Perceptions of Society in Communist Europe

Also available from Bloomsbury

The Holocaust in Eastern Europe: At the Epicenter of the Final Solution,
by Waitman Wade Beorn
Hungarian Women's Activism in the Wake of the First World War:
From Rights to Revanche, by Judith Szapor

Perceptions of Society in Communist Europe

Regime Archives and Popular Opinion

Edited by
Muriel Blaive

BLOOMSBURY ACADEMIC
LONDON • NEW YORK • OXFORD • NEW DELHI • SYDNEY

BLOOMSBURY ACADEMIC
Bloomsbury Publishing Plc
50 Bedford Square, London, WC1B 3DP, UK
1385 Broadway, New York, NY 10018, USA

BLOOMSBURY, BLOOMSBURY ACADEMIC and the Diana logo
are trademarks of Bloomsbury Publishing Plc

First published in Great Britain 2019

ISBN: HB: 978-1-3500-5171-3
         ePDF: 978-1-3500-5172-0
         eBook: 978-1-3500-5173-7

Typeset by Integra Software Services Pvt. Ltd.
Printed and bound in Great Britain

To my elder son, C., who was born when this project
took roots and is now an adult.
M.B.

Contents

Contributors

Muriel Blaive is Advisor to the Director for Research and Methodology at the Institute for the Study of Totalitarian Regimes in Prague. She is a sociopolitical and oral historian of communist and post-communist Czechoslovakia/the Czech Republic, placed in its Central European context.

Shawn Clybor received his PhD from Northwestern University. He is currently a history teacher at Dwight-Englewood School in New Jersey and manages a private collection of Czech avant-garde books and art in New York City. He has published on the political activism of the Czech avant-garde, 1920–1960.

Sonia Combe is Emeritus Research Associate at Centre Marc Bloch in Berlin. Her research interests focus on intellectuals in the former GDR and communist Europe, as well as the concentration camp experience under Nazism.

Martin K. Dimitrov is Associate Professor of Political Science at Tulane University in New Orleans. His research interests focus on the origins, evolution and demise of authoritarian regimes.

Adrian Grama is Postdoctoral Fellow at the Graduate School for East and Southeast European Studies, University of Regensburg, Germany, where he works on questions of social, economic and labour history in twentieth-century Eastern Europe.

Rosamund Johnston is a graduate student of Modern European History at New York University. Her research interests include sound studies, the history of broadcasting, migration and propaganda.

Marián Lóži is Researcher at the Institute for the Study of Totalitarian Regimes in Prague. He is also enrolled in the doctoral programme at the Institute of Economic and Social History at the Faculty of Arts, Charles University. His main area of interest is the history of the Communist Party of Czechoslovakia in the 1950s.

Jill Massino is Associate Professor of Modern European History at UNC Charlotte. She is co-editor (with Shana Penn) of *Gender Politics and Everyday Life in State Socialist Eastern and Central Europe* (Palgrave, 2009) and author of *Ambiguous Transitions: Gender, the State, and Everyday Life in Socialist and Postsocialist Romania* (Berghahn Books, 2018).

Libora Oates-Indruchová is Professor of Sociology of Gender at the University of Graz in Austria. Her research interests include censorship, cultural representations of gender in state socialism and post-socialism, gender and social change and narrative research.

Veronika Pehe is Marie Curie Fellow at the Institute of Contemporary History, Czech Academy of Sciences. Her work focuses on cultural memory, memory politics and the history of the economic transformation in East-Central Europe.

Molly Pucci is Assistant Professor of Twentieth-Century European History at Trinity College Dublin. She studies the history of communism, legal history and the history of policing in twentieth-century Europe.

Machteld Venken currently holds an Elise Richter Fellowship at the Institute of Eastern European History, University of Vienna. She studies European history, migration, border regions and children.

Acknowledgements

Even acknowledgements deserve a bit of historical contextualization. I am grateful to the Grant Agency of the Czech Republic for having funded the research project that led to this volume, entitled *Rulers and Ruled: Practical and Methodological Challenges in the Historicization of a Complex Relationship*, number 16-26104S. In fact, I am all the more grateful as I proposed it nine times in four different countries over fifteen years. The most amusing rejection is certainly the first one, delivered by the French Research Agency (CNRS) in 2001, for being 'unfeasible'. Thanks to the invaluable guidance of my PhD supervisor, Krzysztof Pomian, I never doubted that it was – but let this long journey be a message of hope for other scholars.

I thank my colleague at Charles University, Nicolas Maslowski, who encouraged me to persevere in my funding requests and was my original co-applicant for this project. I also thank my colleagues in the leading team of the Institute for the Study of Totalitarian Regimes in Prague, particularly Irena Fialková. Her help in organizing the conference that shaped this volume, as well as for shouldering many necessary and time-consuming tasks pertaining to the book, was priceless. I am grateful to Thea Favaloro at New York University Prague, who agreed to host this original conference and provided a wonderful academic environment – as well as legendary catering.

I cannot count myself fortunate enough that at mid-stage along this long journey, my then boss at the Ludwig Boltzmann Institute in Vienna, Thomas Lindenberger (curently director of the Hannah Arendt Institute in Dresden), and the then member of our Scientific Advisory Board, Dariusz Stola (curently director of the Polin Museum in Warsaw), significantly helped me fine-tune the project. The final version, which closely informs the conception of the present volume, owes much to them.

I would like to thank the contributors to of this book, who had to patiently endure a heavy-handed editor's endless requests. I am indebted to Shawn Clybor, Jill Massino, Veronika Pehe, Rosamund Johnston, Marián Lóži, Molly Pucci and Adrian Grama, as well as to Annina Gagyova, John Raimo, Thomas Lindenberger and Gérard-Daniel Cohen, for their critical remarks on my introduction and/or on my own chapter. Finally, I would like to thank Mark Trafford and Veronika Pehe for their excellent editing and proof-reading work. Rhodri Mogford and Beatriz Lopez at Bloomsbury Academic have been wonderfully efficient and pleasant to work with – may they be thanked, too.

Introduction

Muriel Blaive

The research project that led to this volume[1] departed from the relative absence of society as an object of analysis in the academic history of communism in Czechoslovakia, especially as compared to the former GDR and the former Soviet Union. Although Poland and Hungary, for instance, are much better represented as far as the social history of communism is concerned,[2] politicized patterns of interpretation tend to dominate in the countries of the whole region. The weaker representation of society was certainly caused by the impossibility for researchers to access crucial regime sources (notably the secret police files) until the late 1990s or even 2000s. I contend, however, that two other factors have played an important role: first, the reluctance in the national public spheres to confront the question of the popularity of the communist regimes, a reluctance that is intimately linked to the post-communist political project and its grand narrative of anti-communist resistance; second, the view on the communist past is all too often clouded by national perspectives. The invariable 'national exceptionalism' still prevents a systematic approach to understanding communism as an international social phenomenon. Many historians have dismissed the methodology worked out in German or Soviet studies on the pretext that their country is different. Yet Alf Lüdtke, who himself departs from the work of anthropologist James Scott,[3] shows that the communist regimes principally found a basis of legitimacy where their aspirations converged with the traditional values ('transcripts') of a nation.[4] Our volume points to such transcripts in each national case. That communist propaganda consistently attempted to adapt its content to each national context is a common characteristic and not a differentiating one.

Political science's failure in the 1990s to articulate a continuity between communism and post-communism was another source of inspiration. As simple as it may seem, the knowledge of the relationship of the people to communism before 1989 is the only way to understand their attitude towards the communist past after 1989. If there is little or no social-historical knowledge to be mobilized in order to analyse the pre-1989 attitudes, the necessary continuum between the pre- and the post-1989 period cannot be reconstructed. This is why 'memory' infiltrated social sciences and history and attempted to fill the void. Inspired by the memory turn of the Holocaust studies but disregarding its rich history, academic discussions on 'dealing with the past' or 'duty of memory' partly took the place of a painstaking, old-fashioned historical research. Social sciences and history often turned to activism and transformed 'memory' not only into an object of study but increasingly into a moral, if not institutional, necessity. But the ubiquitous presence of memory studies does little to refine the historical knowledge over this period. As historians and social scientists we are not invested with any 'duty of memory', but with a duty of history.

In East-Central Europe, the fall of communism and the return to democracy in 1990 eventually translated into the opening of the former communist regimes' archives. However, and apart from the case of East Germany, a country that was dissolved, the moral obligation to make documents accessible did not coincide with the need to understand and accept the communist past in the sense of a thorough *Vergangenheitsbewältigung*.[5] For such a process to happen it would have been necessary to document, on the basis of archival evidence, more than acts of communist terror and heroic anti-communist resistance. The way in which the citizens of communist countries might have individually and collectively accommodated themselves with the regime in power, or endowed it with a varying measure of legitimacy, would have been equally important. Instead, the memory policies in the region generally condemned the old regime while ignoring the issue of mass collaboration. A few prominent personalities in the political and cultural world were publicly exposed for their contacts with the secret police and served as scapegoats; meanwhile, post-communist states placed the emphasis on narratives that privileged repression and resistance.[6]

Naturally, how the people viewed their communist rulers, and vice versa, is difficult to reconstruct. At first glance, to question this relationship might even appear counterintuitive: How were people supposed to manifest their potentially negative opinions of their leaders in a dictatorship? Why should we give any credit to positive opinions? Why would rulers who had the armed forces and police at their disposal bother to take potential popular disapproval of their policies into account? How can we view the rulers and the ruled as having developed any kind of relationship, even a begrudging one, when everyday life was clouded by fear? How can we take the forms of compliance at face value when people felt largely compelled to act the way they did?

Beyond fear

In any history of communism focused on social processes rather than repressive policies, fear and its root causes, repression and violence, are the elephant in the room. Fear was a facilitator of political submission, and it defined to a large extent the relationship between the regime and the citizens it claimed to protect. But it is not only the people who feared the regimes, the regimes feared their people too. Accordingly, this volume's objective is to investigate the relationship between the rulers and the ruled, to deconstruct the power relations under communism.

We are fully aware that some lives were ruined, other people died or were killed and still others were imprisoned, sent to labour camps or deported. This violence did take place, and the victims deserve full recognition and compassion; they have all our authors' attention in this volume. Yet, it is important to state that the victims' pain should not confiscate the need for historical knowledge of these regimes and societies. While adequately factoring in repression and the fear it provoked, it is not the purpose of this volume to pursue a witch-hunt and assign responsibility for the implementation of the communist rule. We aim even less at establishing a would-be 'historical truth' – which is an artificial construct by nature regardless.[7] The legitimate pain that victims of communism, as well as their families and friends, have experienced must be clearly separated from our endeavour to understand how these regimes functioned on an everyday basis. This pain must not exempt us from pointing out the occasional successes of communist rule; it cannot serve to hide the conflict of loyalties between what people experienced as positive aspects of life under communism and the present, anti-communist political climate. Post-communist states have established institutions to pay tribute to the memory of victims and heroes, and this legitimate function must be clearly separated from that of historical research. Even though communism was a flawed, repressive system and democracy a better one, former communists were not all bad and new democrats are not all good. Most importantly, they are often one and the same people.

What has been often missing in the historical literature of communism on East-Central Europe (again, excepting the East German and Soviet cases), on the other hand, is a definition and epistemology of what constitutes both a victim and a perpetrator. A blanket rehabilitation led to a blanket condemnation – a striking feature of the Czech policy of dealing with the communist past, for instance[8] – neither of which can ever be fully accurate. Most of our chapters attempt to replace the 'systemic' with the 'individual', which is the only way to pass a fair(er) judgement on the behaviour of social actors. Ideally, no communist dictatorship should have come into being. Once it did, ideally people should not have collaborated. Once they did, at least they should not have lived a good life. But since they did, we have to understand why and how. Dismantling a certain tyranny of idealism concerning the past is in fact an evermore pressing task. Jan Tomasz Gross, the American historian of Polish origin, was nearly thrown in jail in Poland for having pointed to the extent of anti-Semitic crimes committed by Poles during the Second World War.[9]

As Veronika Pehe demonstrates in her chapter, the post-communist search for heroes, promoting positive models and the notion of a nefarious, repressive regime, has prescribed and manufactured a preordained historical narrative. Archival documents were used for purposes that were anything but strictly academic.[10] Just as was the case under communism, she points out that those who control the past think they control the present.

The rulers and the ruled

This is why in this volume we are studying the ordinary people, or at least keeping them as a strong component of our analysis. We are no more turning victimhood into resistance than we are celebrating heroes. Our objective is to show how 'conjunctures of hope and despair, doubt and relaxation had simultaneously existed, as two parallel realities'.[11] Not only do we endeavour to restitute a missing analytical dimension, we additionally wager that it is fruitful to study society from the point of view of regime archives. We want to study in our chapters how workers, functionaries, random ordinary people, politicians, intellectuals, listeners, viewers, children and academics interacted with the communist state in their everyday lives. This approach tells us, with all necessary caveats, not only about society and how it viewed the communist regimes in its multiple layers but about how regimes viewed society, and how both parties, privileging stability, individually and collectively tried to make the best from this unequal and uneasy relationship.

Indeed, the concept of modern dictatorship[12] leaves space not only for an undeniable degree of domination of the communist system but also for society's relative autonomy.[13] The enforcement of the communist domination system implied, according to the circumstances, resistance at the individual level but also compliance and tolerance.[14] A 'tacit minimal consensus'[15] (Thomas Lindenberger) was established between the people and the regime, and the notion of 'popular opinion'[16] (Paul Corner) becomes indispensable in this account if we are to understand the nature of this power relationship. Such a social-historical approach also gives us the opportunity to introduce into the equation the notion of 'Eigen-Sinn' or 'sense of oneself',[17] sometimes translated as 'agency', that is, that of small, autonomous spaces carved out by individuals in their own lives, away from the prying eyes of the regime.[18] Politics were to some extent 'privatized', providing individuals with strategies of avoidance, withdrawal and shutting down from the regime.[19] Sandrine Kott even speaks of the 'socialization of the state': 'The state machinery', she writes, 'functioned thanks to arrangements made within society. At every level, these arrangements were often actually informed, client-based relations.'[20] The communist state did not exert its power in a strictly top-down direction; on the contrary, it was penetrated by tensions and contradictory social and group interests, including in official institutions such as the Communist Party and the secret police.

Numerous studies of East German and Soviet communism have demonstrated that a permanent negotiation process was at play between the regime and society.[21] Communist authorities had to legitimize their domination and to keep the political and social situation under control. They were concerned with the approbation, or lack thereof, that the citizens, ordinary people or, in communist parlance, the 'workers, peasants and intellectuals', might have conferred on their policies. The violent protests that periodically emerged (the Hungarian 1956 revolution is an emblematic example) confirmed that stability was the most desirable state for regimes that maintained themselves by force – or by the threat of force. People accepted this rule on conditions which they themselves negotiated to some extent: 'I sign this paper, but you let my child go to university'; 'I write reports on this colleague but you promote me to the position which I deserve'; 'I join the Party but you let me buy this plot of land to build my house'; and so on. People sometimes even engaged in repressive policies, for instance by practising denunciation or by entering the workers' militia. To be sure, terror and state repression did play a crucial role in creating a particular atmosphere in which people felt entitled and even compelled to denounce their fellow citizens. But the regime lasted in time and was rooted in society only because the people themselves, willingly or not, contributed to perpetuating these repressive practices, contributed to their own domination. Moreover, small aspects on the everyday level that many of them viewed through a non-ideological lens (children participating in the Pioneers movement or families going to a mass gymnastic Spartakiáda event, for instance) significantly helped maintain and stabilize the regimes. Even people who hated the leadership or complained about the communist rule engaged in this particular form of everyday compliance. The result is that the border between the rulers and the ruled ran through each individual – or, as a person I once interviewed in the small Czech border town of České Velenice poetically put it: 'Where is the border between good and bad? It has always been blurred. Can we draw a thick line? It's not possible. Nothing is like this in life.'[22]

This socio-historical theoretical standpoint wrong-foots the 'totalitarian' characterization of the East-Central European communist rule: if we focus not on the mechanical conformity to rules and orders but on the realm of other forms of behaviour,[23] we see that these regimes might have been a dictatorship with totalitarian intentions but that totalitarianism in its narrow meaning is something which could hardly have been fully implemented, even less so for any longer period of time.

'Popular opinion' and the limits of dictatorship

In this volume, we employ the central concept of popular opinion to investigate the relationship between rulers and ruled. This concept, a methodological breakthrough of the past decade, was developed in Paul Corner's edited volume *Popular Opinion in Totalitarian Regimes: Fascism, Nazism, Communism*, published by Oxford University Press in 2009. While we leave aside the notion of totalitarianism, we do prefer 'popular opinion' to 'public opinion' for the analysis of one-party systems because, as Paul Corner emphasizes it, the latter 'carries suggestions of pluralistic debate within the public sphere of civil society', a concept which is 'hardly appropriate' for the cases that concern us.[24] However, because they were notions that were carved out and reflected upon for decades, public sphere and public opinion imply a level of objectivity and competence that does not characterize 'popular opinion'; on the contrary, popular opinion directly derives from the communist understanding of what the public was. To work on popular opinion thus amounts to working on, and within, a communist category, or one that was shaped by the communist practice. By putting ourselves in the social actors' shoes, we reconstruct the public sphere as a popular sphere, a nest from which we try to gauge the influence of communist rule on everyday behaviour. Although it might be difficult to quantify a phenomenon that was part and parcel of everyday life, popular opinion is thus a crucial tool in advancing historical research on dictatorships. Regimes were acutely aware of its importance, calling for multiple mood reports and opinion research, while analysing mail, letters of protest, and petitions, in addition to outright spying on their citizens. Incidentally, leaders also 'sought ways to instrumentalize popular opinion in their internecine conflicts' (Shawn Clybor).

It is perhaps the greatest paradox of communist regimes that while they devoted considerable resources to investigating the state of popular opinion, they failed to assuage it in the latter part of their lifespan, when they were in no position anymore to satisfy their populations' expectations in terms of standard of living. For a long time, their knowledge of popular opinion served as both a safety valve and a surveillance mechanism (Jill Massino); however, the more they perfected this knowledge, the less they were able to use it to their full advantage.

Our reference of choice for understanding how the regime tried to gauge popular opinion has been regime archives. These sources have often been dismissed as mindless propaganda, flawed or irrelevant, lacking authenticity and truthfulness. Our purpose is not to take them at face value but to deconstruct how the rulers operated in order to try and extract conformity from the ruled (Adrian Grama). In this sense, in combination with other types of sources and provided that they are submitted to a suitable source criticism, regime archives are invaluable. The ideological language that permeates them does not preclude the communication of genuine knowledge concerning the state of popular opinion. Quite the contrary, a realistic image of society does emerge from these documents in many cases (see in particular the chapters by Rosamund Johnston, Adrian Grama, Machteld Venken, Martin Dimitrov, Jill Massino and me).

Things were complicated: On the quest for boundaries

All the chapters in this volume analyse the bargaining power and strategies of the ruled, in all their diversity, but also of the rulers, in both parties' endeavours to negotiate the terms of this rule. Using Ministry of Information archives, Rosamund Johnston studies Czechoslovak radio listeners in the post-war period and their agency, namely their attempts at negotiating programme content with the communist authorities. Meanwhile, Adrian Grama is concerned, on the basis of regime archives, with workers in post-war Romania and their use of strikes to secure better living conditions. Marián Lóži studies regional party archives to illuminate the power practices of mid-level Stalinist functionaries after the communist takeover in Czechoslovakia and their sometimes despairing attempts to instil some order in the regions. Molly Pucci draws on secret police archives to analyse the role of the Czech secret police functionaries delegated from the centre for the same purpose: re-establishing order, as well as instituting a dignified and efficient operation of the dictatorship. Shawn Clybor introduces a hitherto forgotten Czechoslovak Stalinist musical and analyses its originally welcome criticism of the official ideology as can be retraced in the national archives. I study the behaviour of Czechoslovak society during the 1956 Hungarian revolution on the basis of secret police reports and show that the communist regime was monitoring popular opinion intensely in these crucial weeks – and it did manage to take the necessary measures to appease it. Martin Dimitrov goes on to explain, on the basis of party archives, how the Bulgarian Communist Party became acutely aware, in the 1950s and 1960s, of the necessity to properly assess and satisfy the consumer preferences of its population and to create the appropriate institutional tools. Sonia Combe's chapter examines, using secret police archives, the East German intellectuals who were simultaneously faithful to the party line but critical of it. Who was afraid of whom, she asks, because fear was shared by both sides. Of course, these intellectuals were quite removed from mainstream society; what we can derive from their behaviour regarding the society–regime relations is not entirely conclusive. However, Jens Gieseke's research into East German popular opinion has shown that the population kept a certain distance towards the regime while simultaneously appreciating certain values of the socialist society – equality, social justice. What ultimately mattered, as everywhere else, was the population's standard of living.[25]

Moving away from the period of Stalinist terror, the second half of the East-Central European communist regimes' lifespan was characterized by an even more obvious negotiation process between rulers and ruled. Machteld Venken analyses the way in which children's programmes on Polish television communicated the regime's values and historical reconstruction through a hit series that peaked in the 1970s. The authorities went so far as to poll children for their preferences so as to maximize the effect of communist propaganda. Libora Oates-Indruchová demonstrates, on the basis of the Czechoslovak Academy of Sciences archival material, that academic authors and editors entered a protracted negotiation process in the 1970s, in which ideology did not always play the main role and the search for academic quality sometimes did. Jill Massino offers a refreshing analysis of complaint letters addressed in the 1970s and 1980s to the Romanian leaders Nicolae and Elena Ceaușescu; she shows the full extent of the bargaining strategies adopted by the people at the bottom (including their occasional successes) and, by so doing, paints a complex portrait of Romanian society shortly before the fall of communism. Finally, Veronika Pehe deconstructs the fetishization and instrumentalization of the archival document, mostly for political purposes, in the post-communist period.

All of these chapters, despite studying different countries and time periods, portray the ruled as active social agents rather than passive recipients of the communist dictatorship. They reflect on the dichotomy between fear of the masses and popular consent (Adrian Grama). As already discussed, they show that complaints and grievances were often a safety valve (Jill Massino) rather than a destabilizing factor. They underline the importance of idealism, which went hand in hand with fear, opportunistic loyalty and particular egoistic interests. Moreover, several authors crucially emphasize that the very nature of complaints was based on an assumed, shared understanding of what socialist legality should be. To call for socialist legality was itself predicated on loyalty, or so the people hoped: their displayed loyalty allowed for the manifestation of their discontent, at least to some degree. Individuals learned to express themselves in the language of the regime (Stephen Kotkin's 'speaking Bolshevik').[26] In other words, appropriating the ideological world view of the regime allowed them to function within, not against, the normative framework established by party elite (Shawn Clybor). Let us never forget that, until almost the last day, people did not expect that the communist regimes would come to an end; they defined their survival strategies accordingly.

It is a tribute to this volume's endeavour to restitute the complexity of life under communism that all chapters point to the incessant quest for boundaries on the part of both the rulers and the ruled, as well as to the blurring of moral categories. Circumstances changed over time; individuals did, too. Behaviours evolved and might sometimes appear contradictory but they reflect the polymorphous shape of a dictatorship constantly seeking legitimacy. There are no ideal types here: on the contrary, cognitive dissonance reigns between desires and reality. Communist dictatorships learned how to tolerate, and indeed even encouraged, the hidden transcript of citizens so long as they respected the normative political and ideological boundaries of the public transcript.[27] The borderline between collaboration and resistance, constructive criticism and subversion, culture and politics is by no means easy to establish. Sonia Combe points to the intricate intertwining of conformism, freely consented submission, accommodation, acquiescence, blindness and sincerity.[28] By the same token, the traditional chronology of the communist rule in terms of crises (1948, 1956, 1968, 1977, 1980, 1981, 1986 and 1988) is seriously contested here. New continuities and discontinuities appear.

The role of mid-level, intermediate social actors, who moved information from top to bottom and vice versa, is another common feature of our chapters. Trade union delegates were often caught in the crossfire between violent workers and a violent regime and subjected to the pressure stemming from both superiors and workmates (Adrian Grama). Mid-level actors gathered feedback on how the policies were implemented on the ground (Molly Pucci). They served as the target of public criticism in order to get in the good graces of the centre (Marián Lóži). They cushioned the interaction between rulers and ruled, as in the case of communist, yet critical, intellectuals in the GDR (Sonia Combe). They also served as outlets for public frustration (Jill Massino): the people from 'below' could blame them while complaining to the highest leaders.

Last but not least, studying the regime from the bottom-up also allows us to paint the picture of a rule that was not only successful. The 'culture of Stalinism' (Molly Pucci) did not spread easily at first. In fact the situation was sometimes outright chaotic. The level of violence at the bottom led to the communist functionaries' fear (Adrian Grama). Heavily dysfunctional bureaucratic processes and domination instruments left these functionaries struggling to exercise minimal control (Marián Lóži). The rulers could not prevent people from listening to foreign broadcasts (Rosamund Johnston), they had no idea how to concretely implement a police dictatorship (Molly Pucci), they could not force even party intellectuals to support their Middle Eastern policy (Sonia Combe) and they admitted that the publishing situation had gone from 'unfavourable' to 'catastrophic' (Libora Oates-Indruchová).

A re-evaluation of the Slánský trial?

The clearest example that this volume can offer so as to illustrate the usefulness of studying regime archives in a bottom-up perspective, finally, is our almost unwitting discovery of a stunning new logic to the political and social usage of the Slánský trial in 1952 Czechoslovakia.[29] The current academic wisdom is that the Slánský trial was an epitomized expression of random, Stalinist terror under the guidance of Soviet 'advisors' sent by Stalin.[30] The public had no real role to play in this interpretation, apart from that of a passive recipient of blind terror, or alternatively as a semi-active anti-Semitic supporter.[31]

Marián Lóži's chapter suggests quite a different interpretation, which is backed by the context brought by Molly Pucci, Shawn Clybor and me. Lóži shows that the violence applied against (regional) Stalinist elite, a number of whom were present at the Slánský trial (notably, Brno leader Otto Šling), won a significant amount of popular approval and indeed was a request from the social actors from below. Some of the Stalinist elite under trial, pupils of Slánský's, had implemented a ruthless dictatorship at the regional level after 1948; in fact, they could be considered as small dictators of their own. They were thus blamed by popular opinion for not living up to Stalinist standards. Marián Lóži contends that what was essential for the functioning of the Stalinist dictatorship was its ability to achieve legitimacy rather than to implement violence. If so, we see that the Slánský trial was a way, among other dynamics at play, for the regime to regain popularity by deposing regional leaders and taking the dictatorship back under control for a more reasonable exercise of Stalinist rule. In other words, the trial attempted in a convoluted way to right some wrongs and it boosted the popularity of Stalinism – hence the regime's reluctance to relitigate it in 1956.

This is of course only the first step towards a new historical interpretation but, precisely like Wendy Goldman in the Soviet case, we can at least now claim that there seems to have existed a palpable logic to the terror, one in which social actors played a role at all levels.[32] The Slánský episode is but one example, albeit a spectacular one, that shows how our socio-historical approach of the political realm has yielded new and promising results. The other chapters follow suit and deconstruct a complex relationship between the rulers and the ruled, which brings the agency of ordinary social actors to the fore while exploring the more and less effective domination mechanisms of the representatives of power. As the editor of this collective volume, it has been my ambition, by offering such nuanced understanding, to contribute to a less polarized memory debate on what communism in practice has meant for generations of East-Central Europeans.

Notes

1   *Rulers and Ruled: Practical and Methodological Challenges in the Historicization of a Complex Relationship*, research project number 16-26104S supported by the Grant Agency of the Czech Republic (GAČR), of which I am the principal investigator. I thank GAČR for its support.

2   See, for instance, Katherine Lebow, *Unfinished Utopia: Nowa Huta, Stalinism and Polish Society*, 1949–1956 (Ithaca: Cornell University Press, 2013) for Poland, or Mark Pittaway, *The Workers' State: Industrial Labor and the Making of Socialist Hungary 1944–1958* (Pittsburgh: University of Pittsburgh Press, 2012) for Hungary.

3   James C. Scott, *Domination and the Arts of Resistance. Hidden Transcripts* (New Haven: Yale University Press, 1990).

4   Alf Lüdtke, 'La République démocratique allemande comme histoire. Réflexions historiographiques', *Annales* 53, no. 1 (1998): 1–39 (37).

5   Generally referring to Nazism, this term designates the overcoming of, coming to terms with, or coping with, the past.

6   For the Czech case, see the analysis of Françoise Mayer, *Les Tchèques et leur communisme* (Paris: EHESS, 2003), 10.

7   It is known at least since the work of French historian Marc Bloch and the *Annales* school that historical 'truth' is valid only in our time and place, i.e. that historians write from a specific viewpoint and in a specific social context, even when they use all methodological precautions and that what is the 'truth' today might become a contested interpretation tomorrow. Marc Bloch, *The Historian's Craft* (Manchester: Manchester University Press, 1954), 38.

8   See Muriel Blaive, 'The Czech Museum of Communism: What National Narrative for the Past?', in *Museums of Communism: New Memory Sites in Central and Eastern Europe*, ed. Steven Norris (Bloomington: Indiana University Press, 2018) [forthcoming]. See also Laure Neumayer, 'Integrating the Central European Past into a Common Narrative: The Mobilizations Around the "Crimes of Communism" in the European Parliament', *Journal of Contemporary European Studies* 23, no. 3 (2015): 344–363.

9   Associated Press, 'Princeton Professor Faces Three Years in Jail for Saying Poles Killed More Jews than They Killed Nazis', *National Post*, 14 February 2016, http://nationalpost.com/news/world/princeton-professor-faces-three-years-in-jail-for-saying-poles-killed-more-jews-than-they-killed-nazis (accessed 28 November 2017); Associated Press, 'Holocaust Scholar Questioned on Claim Poles Killed More Jews than Germans in War', *The Guardian*, 14 April 2016, https://www.theguardian.com/world/2016/apr/14/holocaust-scholar-questioned-on-claim-poles-killed-more-jews-than-germans-in-war (accessed 28 November 2017).

10 For a model of inflammatory usage of archival documents in a thinly disguised personal and political settling of accounts, see Karel Bartošek, *Les aveux des archives. Prague, Paris, Prague (1948–1968)* (Paris: Le Seuil, 1996). For other examples, as well as an excellent analysis of this failure to come to terms with the past, see Marci Shore, '"A Spectre Is Haunting Europe ..." Dissidents, Intellectuals and a New Generation', in *The End and the Beginning. The Revolutions of 1989 and the Resurgence of History*, eds. Vladimir Tismaneanu and Bogdan C. Iacob (Budapest: CEU Press, 2012), 465–493.

11 Lüdtke, 'La République démocratique allemande comme histoire', 8.

12 See Jürgen Kocka, 'The GDR: A Special Kind of Modern Dictatorship', in *Dictatorship as Experience: Towards a Socio-Cultural History of the GDR*, ed. Konrad Jarausch (New York: Berghahn Books, 1999), 17.

13 Konrad Jarausch, 'Au-delà des condamnations morales et des fausses explications. Plaidoyer pour une histoire différenciée de la RDA', *Genèses* 52, no. 3 (2003): 80–95 (84). Thomas Lindenberger, 'La police populaire de la RDA de 1952 à 1958. Une micro-étude sur la gouvernabilité de l'Etat socialiste', *Annales* 53, no. 1 (1998): 119–152 (121).

14 Ibid., 121.

15 Thomas Lindenberger, 'Tacit Minimal Consensus: The Always Precarious East German Dictatorship', in *Popular Opinion in Totalitarian Regimes: Fascism*, Nazism, *Communism*, ed. Paul Corner (Oxford: Oxford University Press, 2009), 208–222.

16 Paul Corner, ed. *Popular Opinion in Totalitarian Regimes: Fascism, Nazism, Communism* (Oxford: Oxford University Press, 2009).

17 'Eigen-sinn – Key term in Lüdtke's analysis of workers' everyday life, denoting wilfulness, spontaneous self-will, a kind of self-affirmation, an act of (re)appropriating alienated social relations on and off the shop floor by self-assertive prankishness, demarcating a space of one's own. There is a disjunction between formalized politics and the prankish, stylized, misanthropic distancing from all constraints or incentives present in the everyday politics of Eigen-Sinn. In standard parlance,

the word has pejorative overtones, referring to "obstreperous, obstinate" behavior, usually of children. The "discompounding" of writing it as Eigen-Sinn stresses its root signification of "one's own sense, own meaning." It is semantically linked to aneignen (appropriate, reappropriate, reclaim.)' See Alf Lüdtke, ed., *The History of Everyday Life: Reconstructing Historical Experiences and Ways of Life* (Princeton: Princeton University Press, 1995), 313–314. See also Thomas Lindenberger, 'Eigen-Sinn, Domination and No Resistance', in: Docupedia-Zeitgeschichte, https://docupedia.de/zg/Lindenberger_eigensinn_v1_en_2015 (accessed 1 March 2018); Thomas Lindenberger, Alf Lüdtke, ed., *Eigen-Sinn. Sprawowanie władzy jako praktyka społeczna* (Poznań: Wydawnictwo Nauka i Innowacje 2018).

18   See Thomas Lindenberger, 'Die Diktatur der Grenzen. Zur Einleitung', in *Herrschaft und Eigen-Sinn in der Diktatur. Studien zur Gesellschaftsgeschichte der DDR*, ed. Thomas Lindenberger (Cologne: Böhlau, 1999), 13–43.

19   Lüdtke, 'La République démocratique allemande comme histoire', 35.

20   Sandrine Kott, *Communism Day-to-Day. State Enterprises in East German Society* (Ann Arbor: The University of Michigan Press, 2014) [first edition in French 2001], 6–7.

21   For Germany, see, for instance, Mary Fulbrook, ed., *Power and Society in the GDR, 1961–1979. The 'Normalisation of Rule?'* (New York: Berghahn Books, 2009); Gareth Dale, *Popular Protest in East Germany, 1945–1989* (London: Routledge, 2005), as well as the works of Thomas Lindenberger, Alf Lüdtke, Konrad Jarausch, Paul Corner and Sandrine Kott quoted in this introduction. For Russia, see, for instance, Sheila Fitzpatrick, *Everyday Stalinism. Ordinary Life in Extraordinary Times: Soviet Russia in the 1930s* (Oxford: Oxford University Press, 1999); Wendy Z. Goldman, *Inventing the Enemy: Denunciation and Terror in Stalin's Russia* (Cambridge: Cambridge University Press, 2011); Stephen Kotkin, *Magnetic Mountain: Stalinism as a Civilization* (Berkeley: University of California Press, 1995).

22   Muriel Blaive, 'České Velenice, eine Stadt an der Grenze zu Österreich', in *Grenzfälle. Österreichische und tschechische Erfahrungen am Eisernen Vorhang*, Muriel Blaive and Berthold Molden (Weitra: Bibliothek der Provinz, 2009), 199.

23   See Thomas Lindenberger, 'Creating State Socialist Governance: The Case of the Deutsche Volkspolizei', in *Dictatorship as Experience. Towards a Socio-Cultural History of the GDR*, ed. Konrad Jarausch (New York: Berghahn Books, 1999), 125.

24   Paul Corner, 'Introduction', in *Popular Opinion in Totalitarian Regimes*, 2. However, Jens Gieseke's work shows that communist regimes tried to poll their societies' 'public opinion' in a classical way, too, particularly in the case of the East German Institute for Opinion Polling of the Socialist; Unity Party. See Jens Gieseke, 'Opinion Polling Behind and Across the Iron Curtain: How West and East German Pollsters Shaped Knowledge Regimes on Communist Societies', *History of the Human Sciences* 29, no. 4–5 (2016): 77–98. See also Klaus Bachmann, Jens Gieseke, ed., *The Silent Majority in Communist and Post-Communist States. Opinion Polling in Eastern and South-Eastern Europe* (Vienna: Peter Lang, 2018).

25   Jens Gieseke, 'Auf der Suche nach der schweigenden Mehrheit Ost. Die geheimen Infratest-Stellvertreterbefragungen und die DDR-Gesellschaft 1968–1989', *Zeithistorische Forschungen*, no. 1 (2015): http://www.zeithistorische-forschungen.de/1-2015/id%3D5182 (accessed 1 March 2018).

26   Kotkin, *Magnetic Mountain*, cited by Jill Massino.

27   See Scott, *Domination and the Arts of Resistance*.

28   Sonia Combe cites anthropologist Alexei Yurchak, who underlined that everyday
     practices routinely transgressed, reinterpreted or refused certain norms and
     rules represented in the official ideology of the socialist state. See Alexei Yurchak,
     Everything Was Forever Until It Was No More. The Last Soviet Generation (Princeton:
     Princeton University Press, 2006).
29   The show trial of the former Czechoslovak Communist Party general secretary,
     Rudolf Slánský, as well as thirteen co-defendants, for fabricated charges of espionage
     and treason, took place in 1952 in Prague. See Karel Kaplan, *Report on the Murder of
     the General Secretary* (Columbus: Ohio University Press, 1990).
30   Kaplan, *Report on the Murder of the General Secretary*. For an analysis of Kaplan's
     interpretation, see Muriel Blaive, *Une déstalinisation manquée: Tchécoslovaquie 1956*
     (Brussels: Complexe, 2005), 103–119.
31   Kevin McDermott, 'A "Polyphony of Voices?" Czech Popular Opinion and the
     Slánský affair', *Slavic Review* 67, no. 4 (2008): 840–865.
32   Goldman, *Inventing the Enemy*.

Part One

From Post-War to Stalinism

1

Secret Agents: Reassessing the Agency of Radio Listeners in Czechoslovakia (1945–1953)

Rosamund Johnston

'Eavesdropping, censorship, recording, and surveillance are weapons of power,'[1] writes Jacques Attali in his analysis of the political economy of music. 'At the heart of this apparatus,'[2] he continues, is 'the technology of listening in on, ordering, transmitting, and recording noise'.[3] In Czechoslovakia in the post-war and early communist period, Ministry of Information documents demonstrate how authorities experimented with every single one of Attali's 'weapons of power', though not uncontested and not without a degree of self-doubt. Indeed, in attempting to differentiate themselves from the recent Nazi past, Czechoslovak officials tied themselves in knots controlling and patrolling their citizens' listening practices.[4]

As well as techniques to maintain power, recorded sound and eavesdropping constitute for Attali 'the fantasies of men in power'.[5] And fantasies they most certainly were in post-war and early communist Czechoslovakia, marked by an acute shortage of tape recorders and nowhere near the official and technological capacity to detect every sound generated in and transmitted to Czechoslovak territory. In light of these shortcomings, the Czechoslovak authorities turned to negotiation with their listener-citizens. Through an analysis of the resultant bargaining between officials at the Ministry of Information and Czech and Slovak radio audiences, this chapter argues for a reappraisal of the agency of the allegedly 'passive' listener and complicates our understandings of domination practices in a nascent dictatorship. Radio listeners petitioned the Ministry of Information, using what they clearly understood to be legitimate and illegitimate listening practices, to extract concessions from officials.[6] Focusing on the elite discourses contained in these documents, furthermore, does not 'silence' non-elites as David Hopkin has charged; instead, I argue that such ministerial sources can be read to understand the bargaining power and strategies of those surveyed.[7]

This chapter examines debates surrounding Czechs' and Slovaks' radio listening habits in documents from the Ministry of Information between 1945 and 1953.[8] I argue first for an understanding of listeners as social agents, rather than passive recipients of sound, the etymologically related Czech terms *poslouchání* (listening) and *odposlouchávání* (eavesdropping) illustrating a repertoire of listening techniques historically available to the active listener. The chapter then explores the listening environment in Czechoslovakia during the post-war and early communist period. What was available to listen to, where, and when? Next, I turn to how listeners portrayed themselves and were presented in letters written to the ministry. These sources expose an official dilemma of whether to acknowledge, or not, the phenomenon of Western radio listening in Czechoslovakia during this period. Finally, I turn to representations, including self-representations, of the eavesdropper: debates surrounding the naming of the monitoring service and foreign radio transcripts evince the unease of those eavesdropping – as well as their clear technological advantage over the ordinary listener.

Eavesdropping versus listening: How audiences positioned themselves in political space

These reflections upon the agency of radio listeners in early Cold War Czechoslovakia were spurred by the recollections of one Polish radio listener, Ireneusz Haczewski, cited by historian Paweł Machcewicz in his monograph on Radio Free Europe's reception in Poland. Of his youth in Lublin in the 1950s, Haczewski recalled:

> A Phillips radio was one of the first pieces of furniture my father bought. I can remember our covered windows, the volume turned down low since we knew there were people who walked around outside and eavesdropped. The whole family huddled around this radio, as everyone tried to catch the words over the rattle of the jamming machine.[9]

In the scene depicted by Haczewski, his family listened to the radio, while state security informants eavesdropped outside.[10] But what was the essence of the distinction which Haczewski drew between eavesdropping and listening? The answer, in a word, was legitimacy. According to Haczewski, it was legitimate to tune into Radio Free Europe in one's own home and illegitimate to listen into that.[11] Poland's legal code in the 1950s begged to differ; it refuted the legitimacy of listening to Western radio programming,[12] but not the legitimacy of monitoring such behaviour and denouncing it.

In both instances of listening, a measure of secrecy remained essential. Haczewski's family hushed the volume of their radio set and covered their windows to avoid detection, while eavesdroppers had to conceal themselves in order to catch the Haczewski family in the act. Both parties had to pretend they were not listening, while operating on the assumption that the other one was. Both of the parties concerned were thus secret agents.

While the category of passive listener has long been a trope of linguists, and indeed the communications theorists behind Radio Free Europe's establishment,[13] this dichotomy between listening and eavesdropping (*poslouchání* and *odposlouchávání*) presents a good example of the political stance of the active listener at any given time. Whether one listened or eavesdropped depended on context and company. Puzzling out what constituted listening versus eavesdropping (and to whom) in the post-war and early communist years in Czechoslovakia furthermore complicates our understanding of the dynamics of power in a period frequently characterized as totalitarian in its forms of governance.[14]

The question of the sources

An analysis of radio listening in Cold War Czechoslovakia outlines the limits to surveillance. Despite jamming and other attempts to deter Western radio listening, successive Czechoslovak governments could not control the diffusion of foreign radio broadcasts on their territory. As a consequence, listening practices were negotiated between audiences and authorities. Surveillance is often discussed in terms of seeing;[15] this view is not so much wrong as it is partial. A study of aural forms of surveillance, which takes early communist radio as its central point of reference, enriches our understanding of the practice's mechanisms: radio renders audible the uneven ways in which power and surveillance were implemented in Central Europe during this period.[16] Surveillance staff did not live in isolation; on the contrary, they navigated the same dilemmas, rules and structures of secrecy as those they surveyed.

The sources used here date from 1945 until the demise of the Ministry of Information in 1953. Of course, the communist takeover happened in 1948 in Czechoslovakia, and so, at the state level, I am analysing sources generated under two different regimes. It is methodologically profitable, however, to understand communism as a regime that established itself institution by institution in Czechoslovakia, rather than overnight with the sudden resignation of non-communist coalition ministers in February 1948. Indeed, from the very first days of the Third Czechoslovak Republic in 1945, both the Ministry of Information and Czechoslovak Radio, which answered to the former, were firmly in the hands of the Czechoslovak communists, with party luminaries Václav Kopecký and Bohuslav Laštovička at their helms, and employees with 'rightist sympathies' promptly purged from both.[17] As historian Bradley Abrams has argued, 'the events of the hectic days of February 1948'[18] and political crisis have been overemphasized by Western scholars of Czechoslovakia. Consequently, it has been overlooked that the 'general atmosphere and charged political and social realities of the postwar era'[19] were incremental and sustained, reaching even beyond the communist seizure of power.

Rather than locating 'revolutionary changes'[20] in the events of February 1948, the sources I examine posit a revolution taking place on 5 May 1945 and unfolding over the years that followed. Ministry of Information documents, furthermore, display an extraordinary continuity of language and hostility to Western radio broadcasting into Czechoslovakia throughout the period 1945–1953. I argue, therefore, that it is relevant to emphasize the continuity of documents produced by the organizations studied here over the dramatic political changes taking place at the time of their creation. I opened with a Polish example rather than a Czechoslovak one, but it was not just the Haczewski family teasing out the difference between listening and eavesdropping at the period –

Czech and Slovak radio broadcasters and the highest echelons of the Czechoslovak government were as well.

The listening environment in Czechoslovakia from 1945 to 1953

Radio historian Eva Ješutová contextualizes the importance of the medium of radio in Czechoslovakia at the beginning of the Third Republic,[21] suggesting that 'the number of [state broadcaster Czechoslovak Radio's] listeners was higher than the number of those who read the daily press. On May 1, 1945, the authorities registered 1,083,208 radio license payers; by the end of 1948, this number had doubled (to 2,108,000)'.[22] The cost and size of contemporary radio receivers meant that one household would, in all likelihood, have only one set. Family members would have to reach a consensus on what to listen to, and listen together. We thus have to add to the millions of license payers many more who listened together with them to those same receivers. Oral history likewise suggests that group listening outside of the home was still common,[23] and Ministry of Information documents show that radio was broadcast and listened to collectively in factories.[24]

There were two Czechoslovak Radio stations with national coverage (Prague I and Prague II), as well as numerous regional stations (in particular in Czechoslovakia's strategically important border zones). As journalist and memoirist Josef Josten writes, stations broadcasting from outside of Czechoslovakia could be received by Czechoslovak transmitters as well.[25] The BBC, with its wartime prestige, broadcast in Czech and Slovak from London: Josten suggests that Czechs and Slovaks followed the station's English-language programming 'with almost religious fervour'[26] at the time of the communist takeover in February 1948. American Forces Network broadcast from Bavaria, and was also picked up by listeners in Czechoslovakia, as were Voice of America (broadcasting in Czech and Slovak), Radio Vatican, Radio Vienna and Radio Luxemburg.[27] In 1951, Radio Free Europe programming in Czech and Slovak elbowed its way onto the airwaves, quickly becoming a thorn in the flesh of Czechoslovak government officials, not least Information Minister Václav Kopecký.[28]

In listener polling conducted by the Ministry of Information both during the Third Republic and following the 1948 takeover, listeners invoked foreign stations as examples for, and ways to leverage, the state broadcaster. One listener petitioned the ministry in 1945 for more 'reports delivered naturally, like they are in the West'.[29] And post-coup, in October 1948, a listener told the Ministry of Information: 'Believe me, I'm always somewhat ashamed when I catch a foreign station (for example Vienna or Budapest) and I hear lots of beautiful arias from our operas, while here amateur brass music [kutálka] prevails.'[30] In December 1948, a third listener complained that 'a lot of us get up [early] and so we have to listen to foreign stations'[31] (as state broadcaster Czechoslovak Radio's programming only began at six o'clock in the morning). From polling, then, we can infer that a range of foreign stations in a number of foreign languages were audible to Czech and Slovak listeners, and also, in late 1940s Czechoslovakia, citizens actively discussed listening to foreign radio (perhaps using an appropriate language of shame or regret) in order to extract what they wanted from state broadcaster Czechoslovak Radio (in these instances, less brass music on air or programming at an earlier hour).

How should historians approach polling conducted in a nascent dictatorship? Czechs and Slovaks signed up to submit their opinions on radio output in regular written form to the Ministry of Information, having been encouraged to do so through radio announcements and adverts in the listings magazine *Náš rozhlas* (Our Radio). Both before and after the takeover, the ministry suggested it was working with hundreds of regular participants. Letters preserved by the ministry's polling division suggest a major incentive to participate came from the prospect of altering Czechoslovak Radio's output to one's own tastes. Judging by complaints the ministry received, it would appear that recruits were sorely disappointed in this. Households were also allocated a lottery number by which they were then identified. From this we can assume that prizes were an added incentive to encourage regular participation in polls.

Listeners often submitted their responses as a family identifiable by raffle number rather than individual name. And the Ministry of Information anonymized the responses it received yet further (prioritizing a respondent's occupation and gender). Polling files suggest that where unflattering feedback was garnered, the ministry generally applied its efforts to creating directives for Czechoslovak Radio, rather than dismissing the feedback. A poll on the broadcaster's news reporting sent to respondents in October 1948 found, for example, that 'those who consider foreign news to be better reproach the bias of Czechoslovak Radio's news most of all, but also its long-windedness, its repetition … the contrast between optimistic news and the grey reality … belated news, and the lack of attention paid to events abroad'.[32] The ministry did not seek to address all of these points (it notably did *not* criticize its bias), but subsequently recommended that Czechoslovak Radio's news team 'include the standpoint of other states on important events', as well as broadening foreign reporting more generally.[33]

In his analysis of Soviet radio, historian Stephen Lovell describes a 'pre-Cold War moment when it was possible to cite foreign radio with approval'.[34] Letters to the Czechoslovak Ministry of Information gained their force precisely because this was an emerging Cold War moment when voicing approval of foreign radio carried increased significance. Importantly, the Ministry of Information was not the secret police, and the same respondents may not have been so candid about their foreign listening preferences in an interview with law enforcement officers. But the point here is surely that interaction with the state took forms other than encounters with law enforcement alone in the early communist period, and, in engagement with the Ministry of Information regarding radio listening preferences, Czechs and Slovaks employed what they well understood to be unsanctioned practices precisely to force the hands of an elite.

Unlike in Haczewski's Poland, there was no law which banned listening to foreign radio in Czechoslovakia following the end of the war. In fact, a Ministry of Information document from 1945 discussed how radio broadcast from abroad may well introduce Czechs and Slovaks to ideas unfriendly to the state,[35] but that the Nazi-era ban on deliberate listening to foreign broadcasts should nonetheless be lifted 'in regard to the large-scale condemnation which was expressed towards this regulation'.[36] As historian Jan Rychlík notes in his analysis of Czechoslovak communist propaganda,

1945–1989, this legal state of affairs continued following the communist takeover: 'listening to foreign radio was not banned in Czechoslovakia and was not punishable',[37] he writes, 'because such a ban would resemble too closely Nazi measures during the Second World War when listening to foreign radio was punished by hard labour, or indeed death'.[38] Rychlík argues that a factor informing this decision was that wartime experience had proved that such a ban was ineffective; despite the risks of listening, BBC broadcasts had gained cult status by the end of the war.

Secret police documents show, however, that people could, and did, get in trouble for broadcasting Western radio stations in public places, or for talking about what they heard on Western stations. In the 1950s, discussing Radio Free Europe was often a move attributed to those accused of other crimes, and functioned as an aggravating circumstance, proving their treasonous intentions.[39] Regardless of the letter of the law, however, oral history suggests that some Czechs and Slovaks believed it was forbidden to listen to Western stations such as Radio Free Europe, and this belief surely must have affected their behaviour.[40] And importantly, punishment for listening to Western radio may not have taken criminal form, but such behaviour may have had professional repercussions if it ended up on one's personnel file. Instrumental in detection of any transgression were the hundreds and thousands of citizens listening vigilantly to their neighbours' radio habits.

While it comes from a later (and generally understood as gentler) period, a 1965 Radio Free Europe analyst's assessment summarizes the disconnect between legal statutes and social practice well: discussing the case of a bus driver demoted to the position of mechanic for tuning into Voice of America in his vehicle while working, the RFE analyst states: 'Though listening to "hostile" stations alone is not punishable, it is usually considered an aggravating circumstance at court hearings initiated for another offence. Subject to legal prosecution is "group listening" or dissemination of "hostile propaganda", which comes under the charge "inciting" (Para. 98 of the 1961 Penal Code)'.[41]

Prokop Tomek describes how this sort of punishment of listeners, refutation of content and jamming formed a trinity by which the Czechoslovak government set out to tackle Western radio broadcasting.[42] Tomek suggests that Czechoslovak security officials began discussing the prospect of jamming foreign broadcasts with their counterparts in neighbouring countries in 1950.[43] As Milan Bárta explains, jamming began in Czechoslovakia in 1952 and ceased in 1988 (despite extensive debates about the practice and a few days' pause at the time of the Soviet-led invasion of Czechoslovakia in 1968).[44] The jamming and refutation employed by Czechoslovak officials during this period operated on the very assumption that citizens did listen to Western radio stations. This point finds explicit articulation in the Ministry of Information documents studied below.

On listening: Letters to the Ministry of Information

A letter from the local branch of the Communist Party in Letovice, Moravia, to the Ministry of Information in September 1948 lamented the proclivity of the municipality's inhabitants to tune into Western radio. The discussion it provoked exposes the central official dilemma of whether or not to acknowledge such listening practices. The chair of the Letovice municipal committee, one Comrade Krejčí, complained to the ministry that 'a sizeable portion of our citizenry listens to our radio very rarely, the news not at all, and confines itself to foreign radio'[45] (the verb he used throughout was *poslouchat*, no matter the radio station, though here he referred to foreign radio listeners in a somewhat negative light, 'confining themselves' to such stations).

Krejčí suggested that Czechoslovak Radio should thus introduce a programme in which this 'fabricated, whispered propaganda'[46] would be overturned. Such a show would, he hoped, tempt foreign radio listeners to tune into Czechoslovak Radio and stick with the station thereafter. He added that a concise dismissal of foreign radio's lies on the Czechoslovak public broadcaster would furthermore help those working in public functions who 'really do not have time to listen to foreign radio for long enough, and who don't have the possibility of getting to know all their lies and the best arguments against them'.[47]

The Ministry of Information sought Czechoslovak Radio's advice on the matter: the latter claimed quite rightly that it was monitoring the situation closely (at this stage the broadcaster was indeed involved in transcribing foreign radio broadcasts). Radio staff argued that a programme of the type that Krejčí envisaged could, in fact, be dangerous, as it might 'alert listeners who up until then didn't listen to foreign news radio'[48] to the existence of these stations. The ministry assured the worried comrades of Letovice that Czechoslovak Radio would respond to the mendacious assertions made in international broadcasts on a 'case by case basis'.[49] This debate shows that months after the takeover, continued Western radio listening was acknowledged, and its ill effects were feared, but government officials walked a tightrope between denouncing such listening habits publicly (and thus affirming them), so the government itself ended up only whispering what it knew.

In this the ministry agreed with anthropologist Stefan Helmreich, who draws a distinction between listening and hearing and argues in 'An Anthropologist Underwater' that what is listened to, and what is heard, changes over time.[50] What is listened to, for Helmreich, is actively sought and tuned into by an audience, whereas what is heard is relegated to background noise. Technological advances can demote a sound that one previously strained to hear to the status of a background hum (the instance that he analyses concerns the sonar navigation systems of a submarine). The Letovice committee, meanwhile, understood the situation to have developed in quite the opposite direction; they argued that Western radio, which continued to broadcast after the war, was newly foregrounded and in ascendancy in September 1948.

The committee claimed that there was a wide spectrum of easily available listening choices, whereas we know from numerous Radio Free Europe reception reports at the Open Society Archives in Budapest that this was not the reality of the situation at all. Factors such as weather (in particular air pressure and sun spots) altered the audibility of Western radio broadcasts. Once introduced, jamming took place with different intensity in different places at different times of day.[51] A Radio Free Europe information item even suggested that a station's popularity was linked directly to the ease of its reception.[52] This means that listeners navigated an ever-shifting aural landscape, appraising radio broadcasts for their audibility as well as their content.

Another letter to the ministry from another municipal committee dated October 1948, meanwhile, made claims on the institution based upon the municipality's impeccable radio credentials.[53] The local branch of the Communist Party in Vokovice, Prague, asked the Ministry of Information to send a radio van and report on the opening of a new children's playground in the neighbourhood. It believed it was entitled to do so as those who built the playground fought for the Czechoslovak Radio building in 1945. It was bearing arms to defend, rather than listening to, Czechoslovak Radio which provided the basis of claims made to the ministry. But this letter exemplifies how Czechs and Slovaks, immediately following the takeover, invoked radio, and specifically the proper reverence towards Czechoslovak Radio, as a means of positioning themselves (favourably) in political space and extracting what they wanted (in this instance, radio coverage) from political elite. The idea that Czechs and Slovaks held loyalties to many and various stations lent force to the claims of stalwart radio allegiance made by Vokovice's political elite.

In these two cases, listeners articulated their habits to the authorities in order to extract certain concessions. For their part, authorities debated whether or not to acknowledge publicly listening practices of which they were aware. Having considered the way authorities reacted to claims made by the Czech and Slovak public, this chapter now turns to the ways that Czechoslovak officials understood the work of listening.

On eavesdropping: The practice of monitoring

Employees of different Czechoslovak ministries agreed unanimously that radio monitoring was invaluable at a meeting in January 1947. The monitor, Czechoslovak Radio, however, came under fire for the illegibility of some of its reports.[54] Those assembled (from the Ministry of Post, Foreign Ministry and Ministry of Information) went on to debate what this invaluable service should be called. The minutes report:

> It was also noted that the name 'odposlouchací služba' [which one could translate as 'monitoring service,' but 'odposlouchávat' also means listen-in or eavesdrop, as previously discussed] has an odious taste [odiosní příchuť] to it and it was recommended that another name should be found. It was agreed that the expression 'monitorovací služba' ['monitoring service'] should be recommended for use.[55]

Thus, a technocratic-sounding Anglicism was adopted as the title of the enterprise, and allusion to the pioneering role of the BBC in the transcription of foreign radio broadcasts was made.[56]

Salient in this document is the discussion of 'odposlouchací služba' having an 'odiosní příchuť', with the whiff of illegitimacy attached to the verb 'odposlouchávat'. Employees of different ministries agreed that they did not want to eavesdrop upon foreign radio, yet they found the transcripts produced by monitors to be of great use. The solution was a rebrand, and the shelter of a technocratic-sounding foreign borrowing. This was a decision taken at the highest level of government by delegates from a range of different ministries. Social stigma attached to *odposlouchávání* led ministry officials to call what they were doing something else.

Did this rebrand shroud the monitoring service in secrecy? Were its employees really eavesdropping all along under the guise of 'monitoring' foreign broadcasts? Not if we understand the techniques by which one listens to be bound to the social legitimacy of that listening. Arguably, the opprobrium with which one listens affects the way one does it: if one's job is endowed with a technocratic aura of expertise, rather than an 'odious flavour', this, assuredly, affects how one goes about it. In other words, there is a repertoire of listening techniques that one either chooses for oneself or is assigned, which affects the individual's very experience of listening. Meetings such as this, in which officials discuss what it was, in fact, that their employees were doing illustrate the lack of clarity and demonstrate the complexity of the work of listening.

The monitor's guilt and psychiatric health

At a very personal level, we find evidence of something akin to monitor guilt in one of the transcripts produced by the monitoring service in May 1952.[57] The Radio Free Europe programme *Listy domovu* (Letters Home) always started with an appeal made by the show's presenters to a section of the communist establishment. In this particular episode, the presenters addressed 'members of the monitoring service'[58] (referred to pejoratively as 'členové odposlouchávací služby'), whom they urged to 'listen carefully to our first letter'.[59] What followed was a playful exercise in addressing the monitor without seeming to. Presuming that the monitors listened on a regular basis to the entirety of the broadcast, the hosts addressed them in the vocative in the first part of the programme, before urging them to 'put down [their] headphones'[60] at a certain juncture, as 'the following letters weren't written for you'.[61]

The presenters attempted to persuade the monitors that they were intimately familiar with their techniques. Indeed they were; Radio Free Europe undertook exactly the same sort of monitoring of Czechoslovak Radio broadcasts. So as to convince the monitors that they were really addressing them, the presenters started by outlining in detail what they believed the monitors to be doing at that very moment: 'You carefully record every word of this programme, you slowly play back the tape, noting what is said and transcribing it.'[62] In an aural environment in which Czechs and Slovaks could tune into domestic and foreign radio broadcasts, only the monitors, as official surveillance staff, could record what they were hearing, which gave them a clear advantage. Tape recorders were few and far between in the late 1940s and early 1950s, meaning that monitors alone had the power to reproduce sound,[63] to take their own time and listen again to the evidence of radio broadcasts.[64] While radio broadcasts may have been periodically receivable by all, those employed by state surveillance thus had a decisive technological advantage.

Following a discussion of the monitors' daily activities, the presenters then appealed to the monitors' conscience: they insisted that much of the correspondence they would go on to broadcast was 'written to mothers'[65] and that 'it would be a big sin to break into the messages of people who love each other in order to determine the name of the addressee and the name of the sender'.[66] This guilt was compounded when the presenters further stated:

> somewhere in a small flat lives an abandoned mother, you want to put her in danger
> ... Somewhere lives an abandoned wife and her child doesn't know whether he
> is an orphan or whether he has a father. You want to put this woman in danger
> because her husband, who had to flee, sent her greetings and raised her spirits
> over the radio.[67]

Women were thus emotively invoked throughout by the show's presenters as particularly vulnerable Czechoslovak citizens. The figures of abandoned wives and mothers were used to underscore the message that members of the monitoring service preyed upon the weak. This charge was largely in keeping with Radio Free Europe's editorial line (audible in programmes such as *Dělnické vysílání*[68] – Worker's Broadcast – and the on-air speeches of Czechoslovak bureau chief Ferdinand Peroutka)[69] that one of the worst excesses of the communist government in Czechoslovakia was its supposed violence towards women.

And this appeal, it seems, largely worked. While a small section of the letter to the monitor is missing and annotated by the transcriber as 'about two sentences indecipherable',[70] the messages which followed (to which the monitor had been instructed to cease listening) are left practically untranscribed. The first message, as the presenters had just outlined, urged its recipient to take particular care of an émigré's mother. Following this statement, according to the monitor's annotation, 'a long section is indecipherable for technical reasons'.[71] Radio signal could be patchy of course, and endless reception reports stress that factors outside of broadcasters' control (be it weather, jamming or geography) could interfere with broadcasts, but in light of the thoroughness of transcripts which precede and follow this one, here arguably is a written manifestation of monitor guilt.

This would complicate the panopticon narrative of a surveillance state which derives its power through its ability to anonymously, dispassionately observe. As Steven Feld has argued, the notion of power being bound up with the ocular is partial and could be refined by considering how the aural fits into this too[72]: it is important in the letter to the monitor studied earlier that his or her behaviours are outlined, weight is lent to the claims the presenters make by the impression that they know what the monitor is doing through observation. But the monitor is chastised for abusing his or her power to listen – in this instance, according to the presenters, to eavesdrop on private correspondence. The monitor is encouraged to feel guilty for his or her surveillance work, and the transcript we are left with would suggest that the monitor did indeed feel guilty, ceasing as he or she did to write down much of the programme that followed.

Hence, in discussions of state surveillance, it remains to examine the reflexes and personal views of the monitor as an embedded social actor. As the previous example shows, such exposure could impact upon the form that surveillance itself took. If, as Haczewski suggests, there existed some sort of pressure to maintain the secrecy of listening, then calling monitors out for doing what they were doing presented one way in which to subvert their activity. That it was also possible to shame the monitor underlines that the surveillance official did not live outside of the society he or she surveyed, but navigated its dilemmas and rules similarly (albeit, as we have already discussed, with a marked technological advantage).

That sustained exposure to such dispiriting Western radio programmes could damage monitors' morale was indeed a concern for Czechoslovak government officials. More than once, the Ministry of Information voiced concern about the mental health of the monitors it oversaw. On 22 November 1948, ministry employees urged Information Minister Václav Kopecký to acknowledge the 'notable demands on the moral, political, and professional maturity of all employees, working in very difficult conditions'[73] in Czechoslovak Radio's monitoring service. In this document, disgust at Western news was not feigned; such broadcasts were recognized as taking their toll on monitors. Ministry officials understood Western broadcasts as capable of cumulatively eroding citizens' psychological well-being. Kopecký's expression of thanks would reward Czechoslovak Radio's monitors for their 'hard'[74] work and was meant to boost their morale sapped by Western broadcasts. Over and above ministerial recognition, the authorities were advised that better furniture for the monitors would be of key importance in preserving their physical and mental health.[75]

Conclusion

If we consider Czech and Slovak citizens and government officials as listeners, then we discover that domination practices in post-war and early communist Czechoslovakia were more complex and sophisticated than previously understood. People were open with the authorities that they listened to Western stations which regrettably exposed the inferiorities of domestic Czechoslovak broadcasting. Officials debated, meanwhile, the sorts of listening their monitor employees undertook and quite how legitimate that listening actually was. I have argued that these sources, which are predominantly institutional or commissioned by authorities, show us in fact how Czechs and Slovaks positioned themselves when speaking to those authorities. Czech and Slovak listeners in the post-war and early communist period knew themselves to be far from powerless. Together, these sources utterly refute the idea of listening as a uniform, and inherently passive, activity, which has long been the claim of communications theorists and linguists.

The social actors discussed in these sources may well be agents, but were they secret agents? Secrecy granted radio listeners and those who listened to them a bargaining tool in early Cold War Czechoslovakia. If no one was supposed to be listening to Western radio, nor to its audiences, then calling this practice out could, and did, shame the listener. We expose this conundrum most vividly through the value-laden claims of 'eavesdropping' permeating sources from the period. These documents show that Czechs and Slovaks negotiated with the authorities what exactly constituted private and public space. As such, they complicate our understanding of the loci and logics of social control.

This chapter has discussed the potential shame attached to forms of listening in the early Cold War – but it has barely touched upon the pleasure of such activities. The enjoyment of listening might indeed have been enhanced by the secrecy of the practice. It is certain that radio provided millions of Czechs and Slovaks with hours of happiness and entertainment during an epoch we often characterize as terrifying and joyless. Understanding the mechanics of this better constitutes, I believe, a fruitful future line of enquiry for the historiography of communism.

Notes

1   Jacques Attali, *Noise: The Political Economy of Music* (Minneapolis and London: University of Minnesota Press, 1985), 7.
2   Ibid.
3   Ibid.
4   The ideas in this chapter have been clarified through discussions with Gaurav Garg, Stefanos Geroulanos and Sujit Thomas, whom I thank for their input. I also thank participants at the conferences 'Sounding Czech: Towards an Aural History of Bohemia and Moravia' and 'Party, Security Services, and Government Archives in International Perspective: Perceptions of Society at the Top in East Central Europe, 1945–1981' for their feedback and ideas.
5   Attali, *Noise*, 7.
6   Foreign radio listening was, for example, evoked by listeners as an unfortunate only means of accessing forms of culture the post-war Czechoslovak state had committed itself to providing citizens – this will be discussed in more depth further down this chapter.
7   David Hopkin has argued that cultural historians' recent fixation on elite discursive practices has 'effectively silenced' non-elite; I propose here, on the contrary, that top-down, officially generated sources can be read to understand how non-elite positioned themselves in relation to state authorities, and understood their own negotiating power. For his concerns about the use of top-down sources, see David Hopkin, *Voices of the People in Nineteenth-Century France* (Cambridge: Cambridge University Press, 2012), 5.
8   The Ministry of Information was headed by communist Václav Kopecký from the spring of 1945 until its dissolution in 1953. Historian Justine Faure suggests that it was seen as a key ministry by the Communist Party when exile politicians assembled the caretaker cabinet which would run post-war Czechoslovakia in Košice in April 1945 – see Justine Faure, *Americký přítel: Československo ve hře americké diplomacie 1943–1968* (Prague: Lidové noviny, 2006), 49. The institution had been operative in the Protectorate of Bohemia and Moravia during the Second World War as the Ministerium für Volksaufklärung, which had ultimately answered to Joseph Goebbels in Berlin. Following the war, the institution continued to undertake coordinated, multimedia propaganda campaigns, though, as Erica Harrison helpfully points out, the term 'propaganda' in the mid-1940s did not yet have many of the pejorative associations it would go on to gain during the Cold War – see Erica Harrison, 'Radio and the Performance of Government: Broadcasting by the Czechoslovaks in Exile in London, 1939–1945' (PhD diss., University of Bristol, 2015), 22. The ministry oversaw nationalized film production, press censorship and the output of Czechoslovak Radio, among other tasks. Its operations were largely assigned to the Ministries of Education and Culture (with Kopecký becoming the head of the latter) in 1953.

9   Ireneusz Haczewski, cited in Paweł Machcewicz, *Poland's War on Radio Free Europe, 1950–1989* (Washington, D.C. and Stanford, CA: Woodrow Wilson Center Press, 2014), 5. Jamming was a means of interrupting foreign radio stations by broadcasting domestic programming or simply a steady signal on the same frequencies. The Czechoslovak Ministry of the Interior began this practice in 1952. For more on jamming, see the content that follows. A detailed analysis of jamming in Czechoslovakia during the communist period can be found in Prokop Tomek, 'Rušení zahraničního rozhlasového vysílání pro Československo', *Securitas Imperii*, no. 9 (2002): 334–367 and Milan Bárta, 'Přestaňte okamžitě rušit modré', *Paměť a dějiny*, no. 3 (2012): 45–54.

10   This account of the Haczewski family's listening habits was given to film director Maciej Drygas for his film *Głos Nadziei* (The Voice of Hope), about Radio Free Europe, in 2002. For more on Haczewski, see http://ireneusz.haczewski.pl/ (accessed 21 August 2017).

11   As historian Jonathan Sterne argues, innovation in sound reproduction technologies (such as the radio and the telephone) has, since the nineteenth century, become 'more oriented towards constructs of private space and private property. The construct of acoustic space as private space in turn made it possible for sound to become a commodity'. See *The Audible Past: Cultural Origins of Sound Reproduction* (Durham and London: Duke University Press, 2003), 24. Following Sterne's argument, the activity of listening to the radio was, by the time the Haczewski family did so in the mid-twentieth century, already coded private. Historically, lower rates of radio ownership and a tradition of group listening in Central Europe, however, suggest that further research is necessary into whether Sterne's findings (based on predominantly US sources) apply to the region.

12   In particular collectively, or should one decide to discuss the contents of the broadcasts with others. Both of these activities were punishable offences. See Machcewicz, *Poland's War on Radio Free Europe*, 52.

13   This trope was very much rejected by Mikhail Bakhtin, who wrote in the early 1950s (and edited in the 1970s): 'Still current in linguistics are such *fictions* as the "listener" and "understander" … These fictions produce a completely distorted idea of the complex and multifaceted process of active speech communication. Courses in general linguistics (even serious ones like Saussure's) frequently present graphic-schematic depictions of the two partners in speech communication – the speaker and the listener (who perceives the speech) – and provide diagrams of the active speech processes of the speaker and the corresponding passive processes of the listener's perception and understanding of the speech.' In *Speech Genres and Other Late Essays* (Austin: University of Texas Press, 2006), 68. Away from linguistics, the notion of the passive listener formed the bedrock of communications theorists Paul Lazarsfeld and Hadley Cantril's understanding of radio. Cantril and Lazarsfeld both served as US government consultants on psychological warfare in the late 1940s, which gave rise to the station Radio Free Europe, among other outcomes. For more on Lazarsfeld and Cantril's radio work, see Neil Verma, *Theater of the Mind: Imagination, Aesthetics and American Radio Drama* (Chicago: University of Chicago Press, 2012), 118–123. For more on Cantril and Lazarsfeld's role in psychological warfare campaigns, see Christopher Simpson, *The Science of Coercion: Communication Research and Psychological Warfare, 1945–1960* (New York and Oxford: Oxford University Press, 1996).

14   An interpretation of the years 1948–1989 as totalitarian, and thus resembling in important aspects of governance the Nazi occupation of the Czech lands during the Second World War, is a central premise of much research emanating from the Czech Institute for the Study of Totalitarian Regimes. With regard to radio, consider, for example, editor Jaroslav Pažout's suggestion in a volume recently published by the institute that both democracies and totalitarian regimes engage in propaganda, albeit in different ways. The volume then considers what the contours of totalitarian propaganda might be (see Jaroslav Pažout, ed. *Informační boj o Československo/v Československu (1945–1989)* (Prague: Ústav pro studium totalitních režimů, 2014), 7). Historians of communism such as Konrad Jarausch and Mary Fullbrook have offered a range of compelling reasons to view a 'totalitarian' understanding of the period with some circumspection. The risk of taking regime-generated sources too much at their own word, overestimating the centralization of power and overlooking social practices which built a regime's legitimacy from the bottom-up provide but three reasons why, I believe, historians might treat such a framework with some caution.

15   Perhaps most influentially so by Michel Foucault, who posits the panopticon of Jeremy Bentham's late eighteenth-century prison as emblematic of the way social control works in the modern period. Within the panopticon resides an anonymous, official observer, who can monitor what goes on around him/her with impunity. The obscurity offered by the panopticon allows the observer to come and go at will, but ensures that those within its line of vision behave as if the monitor were always there.

16   I am not arguing here that Foucault is wrong, but that privileging the ocular obscures some of the ways in which surveillance works, while a focus on the aural can bring these workings to the fore. Whether one can apply Foucault's understanding of power practices to state socialist countries is in itself a debate, spearheaded in particular by Laura Engelstein in 'Combined Underdevelopment: Discipline and the Law in Imperial and Soviet Russia', *The American Historical Review* 98, no. 2 (1993): 338–353. What Michel Foucault presents in *Discipline and Punish* is a helpful framework for reflecting on power, rather than a set of its exact coordinates in every situation. As such, his framework is a useful starting point for interrogating, rather than an exact description of the distribution of, power in communist Czechoslovakia.

17   For more on personnel changes at Czechoslovak Radio, see Eva Ješutová, ed., *Od Mikrofonu k posluchačům* (Prague: Český rozhlas, 2003), in particular the chapter 'Budovatelský rozhlas, 1945–1948', 183–234.

18   Bradley F. Abrams, *The Struggle for the Soul of the Nation: Czech Culture and the Rise of Communism* (Lanham: Rowman & Littlefield Publishers, 2004), 3.

19   Ibid., 3.

20   This is how émigré radio reporter Josef Josten describes the situation in *Oh, My Country* (London: Latimer House, 1949), viii. According to Abrams, such émigré accounts have moulded Western historians' telling of events.

21   The Third Czechoslovak Republic spanned from shortly before the liberation of Czechoslovakia at the end of the Second World War until the communist takeover in February 1948.

22   Ješutová, *Od Mikrofonu k posluchačům*, 191.

23   See, for example, Robert Budway, speaking to the National Czech & Slovak Museum & Library in 2011. Available online: http://www.ncsml.org/exhibits/robert-budway/ (accessed 22 January 2017).

24 See, for example, Národní archiv v Praze (National Archive, Prague; NAP).
    Ministerstvo Informací 1945–1953. Box 28. 'Zápis o schůzi … dne 4. ledna 1946',
    doc. 60293, 5 February 1946, in which ministry and Czechoslovak Radio employees
    moot the idea of playing more music during the day so as to boost the productivity of
    workers listening, they presume, in factories.
25 See Josten, *Oh, My Country*, 125.
26 Ibid.
27 Muriel Blaive, *Promarněná příležitost: Československo a rok 1956* (Prague: Prostor,
    2001), analysed secret police documents in order to understand Czechs' and Slovaks'
    foreign listening habits by the mid-1950s. She found that Czechs and Slovaks listened
    to all of the stations mentioned here, often voicing a preference for programming that
    was subject to less jamming (so, for example, Radio Vienna) over stations which were
    more thoroughly interrupted (such as Radio Free Europe). Her analysis of the foreign
    stations accessible to Czech and Slovak listeners can be found on pages 69–83.
28 See Václav Kopecký, *Proti kosmopolitismu jako ideologii amerického imperialismu*
    (Prague: Orbis, 1952), which constituted a diatribe against Radio Free Europe
    broadcasts. Kopecký claimed such broadcasts promoted 'cosmopolitanism', which
    he dubbed an 'American imperial ideology'. For details on the individuals and ideas
    involved in the creation of Radio Free Europe, see Robert Holt, *Radio Free Europe*
    (Minneapolis: University of Minnesota Press, 1958) or, for a monograph with a
    Czechoslovak focus, Prokop Tomek, *Československá redakce Radio Free Europe:
    Historie a vliv na československé dějiny* (Prague: Academia, 2015).
29 NAP. Ministerstvo Informací 1945–1953. Box 29. 'Studium posluchačů rozhlasu',
    doc. 60637, 29 September 1945. To understand the context of this remark, see David
    Vaughan, who reflects on the differences in American, British and Czechoslovak
    radio styles in the late 1930s in *Battle for the Airwaves: Radio and the 1938 Munich
    Crisis* (Prague: Radioservis, 2008).
30 NAP. Ministerstvo Informací 1945–1953. Box 29. 'Všeobecné poznámky z týdne od
    18. do 24. října 1948', doc. 65359, 13 November 1948.
31 · NAP. Ministerstvo Informací 1945–1953. Box 29. 'Ranní hudební relace Čs. rozhlasu
    – přehled poznámek', 11 December 1948.
32 NAP. Ministerstvo Informací 1945–1953. Box 29. 'Zvláštní průzkumová dotazníková
    akce …', doc. 65688. December 1 1948.
33 Ibid.
34 Stephen Lovell, *Russia in the Microphone Age: A History of Soviet Radio, 1919–1970*
    (Oxford: Oxford University Press, 2015), 135.
35 The Czechoslovak government was worried in particular about 'pirate Wehrwolf
    broadcasts', suspecting that former Nazi soldiers unwilling to accept the peace
    would play on the sympathies of Czechoslovakia's German minority using radio
    in the months after the war. NAP. Ministerstvo Informací 1945–1953. Box 24.
    'Osnova vyhlášky o nedemokratických předpisech z doby nesvobody', doc. 61527, 12
    December 1945.
36 Ibid.
37 Jan Rychlík, 'Komunistická propaganda v Československu 1945–1989 z tematického
    hlediska', in *Informační boj o Československu/ v Československu (1945–1989)*, ed.
    Jaroslav Pažout (Prague: Ústav pro studium totalitních režimů, 2014), 25
38 Ibid.
39 See, for example, the case of Josef Kuldan et al. which began in October 1953 and
    resulted in the sentencing of the defendants in December of that year. Kuldan and his

co-defendants were charged with transporting people and items across the border, and amassing arms with the intent to overthrow the government. While listening to Radio Free Europe does not appear as a crime for which they were sentenced, listening to the station is mentioned frequently throughout the interrogations, and the station is presented by both the interrogators and the interrogated as a catalyst for their crimes. See Archiv bezpečnostních složek (Security Forces Archive, Prague; ABS). V-PL, V-1178 (Skupinový spis státněbezpečnostního vyšetřování proti Josefu Kuldanovi a společníkům). In 1954, meanwhile, Rudolf Pešek et al. are accused of intentionally spreading foot and mouth disease in a collective farm near Chotěboř. Again here, the defendants 'confess' in interrogations that they were driven to and aided in their crimes by Radio Free Europe broadcasts. See V-HK, V-1182 (Skupinový spis státněbezpečnostního vyšetřování proti Rudolfu Peškovi a společníkům). Archiv bezpečnostních složek, Prague. Thanks to Prokop Tomek for alerting me to both cases.

40   These were Muriel Blaive's findings when conducting extensive oral histories in České Velenice. In-depth analysis of these interviews can be found in Muriel Blaive and Berthold Molden, *Hranice probíhají vodním tokem. Odrazy historie ve vnímání obyvatel Gmündu a Českých Velenic* (Brno, Barrister & Principal: 2009).

41   Open Society Archives, Central European University, Budapest. Records of Radio Free Europe/Radio Liberty Research Institute: Czechoslovak Unit: Information Items: Items [anonymized interviews], 1965–1965 to Items [anonymized interviews] 1968–1968. HU-OSA-300-30-13-1-1354/65. 'VOA Listener Sentenced', 3 September 1965.

42   Prokop Tomek, 'Rádio Svobodná Evropa a jeho československá redakce', in *Svobodně! Rádio Svobodná Evropa 1951–2011*, eds. Marek Junek et al. (Prague: Radioservis, 2011).

43   Tomek, 'Rušení zahraničního rozhlasového vysílání pro Československo': 334.

44   See Bárta, 'Přestaňte okamžitě rušit modré', 45.

45   NAP. Ministerstvo Informací 1945–1953. Box 30. 'Zahraniční rozhlas. Odpovědi Čs. rozhlasu', doc. 64315, 8 September 1948.

46   Ibid.

47   Ibid.

48   Ibid.

49   Ibid.

50   See Stefan Helmreich, 'An Anthropologist Underwater: Immersive Soudscapes, Submarine Cyborgs, and Transductive Ethnography', *American Ethnologist* 34, no. 4 (2007): 621–641.

51   See Machcewicz, *Poland's War on Radio Free Europe*, 50 or Tomek 'Rušení zahraničního rozhlasového vysílání pro Československo': 340.

52   Open Society Archives, Central European University, Budapest. Records of Radio free Europe/Radio Liberty Research Institute: Czechoslovak Unit: Information Items: Items [anonymized interviews], 1965–1965 to Items [anonymized interviews] 1968–1968. HU-OSA-300-30-13-1-440/66. 'RFE and Radio Luxemburg Fan Clubs in Czechoslovakia', 23 March 1966.

53   NAP. Ministerstvo Informací 1945–1953. Box 50. 'Vyslání reportažního vozu na slavnost KSČ ve Vokovicích', doc. 64755, 7 October 1948.

54   NAP. Ministerstvo Informací 1945–1953. Box 43. 'Monitorovací služba', doc. 60087, 15 January 1947.

55   Ibid.

56 In her history of Czechoslovak Radio, Eva Ješutová suggests that the BBC was
    the explicit paradigm for the broadcaster's nightly news as well. See Ješutová, *Od
    Mikrofonu k posluchačům*, 213.
57 NAP. Ministerstvo Informací 1945–1953. Box 1. Monitory 1952–1953. Monitoring
    Report, 25 May 1952.
58 Ibid.
59 Ibid.
60 Ibid.
61 Ibid.
62 Ibid.
63 Radio stations sometimes used the audio footage that they, or their monitors,
    recorded. Radio Free Europe, for example, broadcast excerpts from a speech made
    by Antonín Zápotocký in Brno in 1952 in several broadcasts, stunning Czechoslovak
    Radio monitors. See, for example, NAP. Box 1. Monitory 1952–1953. Monitoring
    Report, 26 May 1952.
64 Lubomir Dorůžka and Miloslav Ducháč discussed the state of sound recording in
    Czechoslovakia in the early 1950s in *Karel Vlach: 50 let s hudbou* (Prague: Ekopress,
    2003). They cited musician Jaroslav Kopáček, who said that particularly dexterous
    individuals could make 'primitive' electro-recordings of American Forces Network
    (which was 'easily audible' from its point of transmission in Munich). The recordings
    were made on old x-ray sheets. Kopáček stressed this was not an easy process, and
    that it was only real 'jazzophiles' who sought out such recordings, 120.
65 NAP. Ministerstvo Informací 1945–1953. Box 1. Monitory 1952–1953. Monitoring
    Report, 25 May 1952.
66 Ibid.
67 Ibid.
68 See NAP. Ministerstvo Informací 1945–1953. Box 1. 'Dělnické vysílání' in Monitoring
    Report, 26 May, 1952.
69 Ferdinand Peroutka was a prominent Czechoslovak journalist during the interwar
    period who spent much of the Second World War in Buchenwald Concentration
    Camp and then emigrated to the United States via Germany in 1948. In his inaugural
    speech as Czechoslovak section head on Radio Free Europe in 1951, he accused
    the communist system in Czechoslovakia of 'enslaving' women in the workplace
    which, in regime doublespeak he suggested, was referred to as women's 'liberation'.
    Thus, the cruelty or violence towards women that Peroutka identified hinged upon
    an understanding of their rightful place being in the home, a view which was by
    no means unanimous among Czechs and Slovaks at the time he spoke in 1951. See
    'Projev při zahájení vysílání Rádia Svobodná Evropa', in *Ferdinand Peroutka pro
    Svobodnou Evropu* (Prague: Radioservis, 2013), 10.
70 NAP. Ministerstvo Informací 1945–1953. Box 1. Monitoring Report, 25 May 1952.
71 Ibid.
72 See Steven Feld, 'Waterfalls of Songs: An Acoustemology of Place Resounding in
    Bosavi, Papua New Guinea', in *Senses of Place*, eds. Steven Feld and Keith H. Basso
    (Santa Fe: SAR Press, 1996).
73 NAP. Ministerstvo Informací 1945–1953. Box 43. 'Vyznamenání poslechové služby
    Čsl. rozhlasu p. ministrem informací a osvěty', doc. 65518, 22 November 1948.
74 Ibid.
75 See NAP. Ministerstvo Informací 1945–1953. Box 43. 'Zpráva o návštěvě v
    monitorovací službě Čsl. rozhlasu v Bubenči', doc. 61284, 22 March 1948.

2

Practices of Distance and Perceptions of Proximity: Trade Union Delegates and Everyday Politics in Post-Second World War Romania

Adrian Grama

Introduction: Beyond the Vichy analogy

Romania's transition to state socialism after the Second World War conforms to the infamous 'communist takeover' scenario that unfolded across Eastern Europe: brigading the communist and social-democratic parties together with various other political entrepreneurs, a Moscow-backed government imposed in March 1945 ended up organizing rigged elections in November 1946. Won by the communists, these elections produced a governing coalition which was quickly eaten up by the Romanian Communist Party, forcing the king to abdicate in December 1947 and instituting the Popular Republic of Romania the following spring. Historians' efforts to make sense of these events focused on the manifold tactics employed by the communists and their Soviet patrons in pursuit of political dominance between 1945 and 1947. For the first two post-war years, the brief experiment with 'popular front' coalitions was marked by the communists' colonization of key state institutions and the deployment of sporadic violence against political rivals, on both the Left and the Right. Consequently, the 'communist takeover' foreshadowed Sovietization, with the establishment of the Cominform in September 1947 signalling 'Stalin's growing conviction that East European states must conform to his own harsh methods of dictatorial rule'.[1] The benchmark year 1948 inaugurated the domestication of the Soviet blueprint in most spheres of social life, from the collectivization of agriculture and the erection of a police state to the etatization of industry and the remaking of the educational system.

Characteristically, 'takeover' narratives move onto the level of high politics – the domain of elite struggles over public resources – with only occasional incursions beyond the power dynamics that played into the control of state institutions. If the broader society is brought into this picture, it is less for its explanatory potential in illuminating the trajectory of these struggles and more for its importance in bearing witness to a regime of (foreign) occupation. On this understanding, the establishment of state socialism in Romania becomes a story of collaboration and opportunism, resistance and rebellion, accommodation and passivity. These categories compose an ethical test to be administered by the historian to a whole array of social groups and individuals, all to be summoned before a moral tribunal *in absentia*, their actions neatly separated between those that allegedly propped up the new regime and those that supposedly hindered, however ineffectively, its functioning. In what is still the classical work of this genre, exiled political scientist Ghiță Ionescu argued that the first post-war decade in Romania resembled the experience of the Vichy regime in France.[2] This suggestion allowed Ionescu to introduce a set of essentially moral categories to evaluate the range of attitudes Romanians supposedly adopted vis-à-vis the new communist authorities, distinguishing between a minority of opportunists and a passive majority that seldom engaged in acts of open resistance. According to Ionescu, those Romanians who chose to join the ranks of the Communist Party after 1945 were 'disgruntled factory workers, a sizable number of domestic servants, unemployed agricultural workers in the countryside, and in large numbers, the members of discontented national minorities', in addition to POWs returning 'already indoctrinated' from the Soviet Union and a good deal of former members of interwar fascist organizations.[3]

Written in the early 1960s, Ghiță Ionescu's book had a remarkable influence on recent Romanian historiography. The opening of the archives after 1989 and the possibility to delve deeper into the social context of the post-war period changed little of the original judgement. Nor was the overall framework of interpretation in any way challenged. The ferreting out of new evidence only reinforced the Vichy analogy, which remained the implicit model for historians exploring the second half of the 1940s and the 1950s: a puppet regime in Bucharest installed by the Soviets against which resistance had to be celebrated and collaboration disgraced. The subjects of retrospective historiographical humiliation were unsurprisingly the usual suspects already singled out by Ionescu himself: 'part of the industrial workers, some poor peasants, many members of some minorities, notably Hungarians, but also Jews and Armenians, some former members of the Legionary Movement, some military officers, state functionaries, intellectuals and very many lumpen (*elemente declasate*) from various social strata'.[4] To be sure, neither Ionescu nor contemporary historians go as far as to deny genuine feelings of support for the Communist Party among all these social and ethnic minorities. Yet most often these feelings are attributed either to self-deception or to the skilful manipulation of discontent on the part of Communist Party leaders. In this view, industrial workers in particular were susceptible to lend their allegiance to the Communist Party not out of conviction but rather due to the party's ability to fuel labour conflict through its industrial policies. For Ionescu, the cluster of policies adopted by the communist governments after 1945 was deliberately crafted to cause strife between management and workers.[5]

This chapter goes beyond current readings of the post-war period in Romania inspired by the Vichy analogy. Rather than asking what social groups joined the Romanian Communist Party after the end of the Second World War, I focus on the ways in which the party strived to extract conformity and exercise dominance over those among its members elevated to positions of influence in industrial milieux.

By narrowing the analysis on the figure of the delegate of the factory committee – politically active union representatives at the factory level – I show how workers had their own politics which sometimes aligned them with the Communist Party, yet most times went against the moderate approach encouraged by Communist Party and trade union leaders. In this context, I show how the delegate was often caught in the crossfire, being at the same time subjected to the pressure stemming from superiors and workmates. Following the trajectory of the delegates as they navigated the myriad constraints under which they were required to operate allows me to question the value of categories predicated on the collaboration/resistance conceptual pair. Instead of straightjacketing historical facts into this static and moral grid of interpretation, I find the notion of *Eigen-Sinn* more suitable to register and explain the range of activities, both oppositional and obedient, the delegates were engaged in (for a discussion of Alf Lüdtke's notion of *Eigen-Sinn*, see further down in this chapter). Moreover, grounded in thick descriptions of workers' everyday life, the concept of *Eigen-Sinn* has the merit of taking into account how those activities transformed over time: what seemed a legitimately conformist attitude in 1946 came to be seen as a form of disobedience by the end of the decade.

This chapter also asks a second question: How were the delegates' obstinate self-assertion of needs, interests and desires perceived at the top, among Communist Party and trade union leaders? Perceptions of unruliness and compliance as well as the supposed reasons that led delegates to act in a certain manner altered throughout the post-war period. Up until 1947, and as long as the communists shared control of the government and the trade union movement with the social democrats, the language used to interpret the delegates' misdeeds was derived from the semantic universe of the Third International. Notions such as 'anarcho-syndicalism', 'fascism' and 'backwardness' informed a limited yet flexible repertoire for classifying disobedience, soliciting conformity and enforcing allegiance. Beginning with 1948, however, these notions lost their appeal and slowly faded away from the everyday vocabulary Communist Party and trade union leaders used for framing the political *faits divers* of industrial life. This change reflected the new role assigned to the institution of the factory committee in the early years of 'popular democracy': no longer charged with containing strikes or other episodes of unrest as they had been during the immediate post-war epoch, after 1948 the delegates were given control over the distribution of welfare funds at the factory level and were charged with monitoring labour discipline on the shop floor. In this context, the polemic jargon of the Comintern was replaced by denunciations of embezzlement and libellous campaigns against infringements of socialist morality.

This chapter is divided into two section. In the first one, I reconstruct the fragmented biography of a union delegate whose trajectory within the Romanian Communist Party spans the first post-war decade. Departing from this example, in the second part I focus on the evolution of the factory committee as one of the key institutions that mediated the transition to state socialism in Romania and Eastern Europe more broadly. Finally, in the concluding remarks I argue for the need to approach the post-war period in terms of categories of interpretation and objects of analysis emancipated from the burden of contemporary memory politics.

'The fear of the masses'

Meet Tudor Anton: this name makes an appearance in the archives of Radio Free Europe in a note headed 'Communist Party: Inner Life' and based on scraps of information collected in 1951 from Romanian refugees arriving in a camp in Rome, Italy, allegedly 'partly confirmed by other sources'. Let us read closely the entire note:

> Tudor Anton, the president of the Labour Union of the '23rd August' factory (ex-Malaxa) in Bucharest was purged in the summer of 1951. Tudor was too friendly with the workers with whom he used to mingle freely. For this over-friendliness, he was accused at a union meeting of neglecting the duties entrusted to him by the Party. The accusation was made by the factory director Comrade Teodorescu who charged Tudor with being too friendly with the workers, drinking and taking motorcycle trips with them, thus wasting time that he might have used for the good of the Party. A group of workers protested against this accusation. They said that if Tudor rode around on a motorcycle he was always less fortunate than those who are riding around in luxurious cars. The fact is that President Tudor Anton was dismissed from the factory even though he was a communist and had attended the Party's leaders' school for six months. As a consequence of Tudor's dismissal, Radovici Constantin of 'bourgeois' origin and protected by Tudor in the factory, was also purged. In July 1951 he was accompanied to the factory by a member of the militia in order to pick up his belongings, which included a shop smock. Radovici was sent to Moldavia for a period of two months under the conditions of forced residence. In September 1951 he was officially dismissed from the factory.[6]

Note the involuntary tragic tone of this note: the dismissal of a highly trained communist could not but have involved some collateral damage, in this case the consequential purge of a 'protected' yet stigmatized fellow worker holding tight to his shop smock at the hands of the police. It is as if the insertion of the 'bourgeois' at the end of the story was meant to add depth and dignity to the already-unfortunate fate of the union leader. Tudor Anton's circle of friends was not, as it were, limited to drinking and motorcycling proletarian lads but could very well encompass the truly downgraded men such as Radovici – as long as they shared the space of the factory. This was a world turned upside down, or so it seemed from the shop floor: a carnivalesque display of inequality whereby some rode around in luxurious cars; workers were forbidden to freely enjoy their leisure time; union leaders were repressed for befriending workers; and the 'bourgeois' was paying the price of class origin. How, then, should we interpret the apparent contradiction between 'over-friendliness', trade union obligations and the duties placed upon Communist Party members?

We might proceed to unpack this conflictual triangle by way of retracing Tudor Anton's fragmented political biography, of which we will never know more than what has been preserved in the stream of paperwork issued by the Communist Party in and around Malaxa Works – Bucharest's largest metal factory. A skilled coppersmith of the locomotive section extolled for his craftsmanship in the pages of *Scânteia*, in September 1945 Tudor was one of the few secretaries of the Communist Party inside the plant: 'devoted, determined, brave, and energetic, defined by a low political consciousness yet responsible, trustworthy; an activist, with a collectivist outlook.'[7] In October 1945, Tudor was also a delegate of the factory committee, somebody whom the party was in urgent need of unmasking and expelling. Faced with an upsurge in labour unrest, the party concluded that the factory committee's delegates had lost their prestige and authority because workers understood that they had no say in matters of wages and provisioning. In this context, some of the delegates became 'vain' [*orgoliosi*] and cut themselves off from the masses [*s-au desprins de mase*]. Tudor Anton adopted the opposite attitude, one even more troublesome for the leaders of the Communist Party: 'There is an anarcho-syndicalist current of opinion in the locomotive section among leading communist delegates to place themselves at the forefront of the masses, lending their support to unpremeditated initiatives and breaking both union and Party discipline.'[8] Tudor was the 'anarcho-syndicalist' delegate of the locomotive section who, rather than opting to seclude himself from the workers, completely identified with their demands.

This was a risk inherent in the act of delegation: because the party claimed to represent the masses, it opened itself to instances when the masses could represent themselves through the party. In such cases, communist delegates of the factory committee such as Tudor were forced to decide: they could either side with their workmates and be accused of 'anarcho-syndicalism' or they could free themselves from their class binding and be accused of being 'vain'. For instance, in February 1946, Communist Party members at Malaxa Works 'let themselves get mobilized by the masses during an attempt to stop work. The moment they were enlightened [*lămuriți*] they adopted a just attitude and turned around the attempt to stop working into a demonstration of support for the factory committee and the Groza government.'[9] The hijacking of factory committee's delegates during protest outbursts was a permanent threat for the Communist Party. The preponderance of these actions at Malaxa Works throughout 1946 revealed how communist delegates dr[a]nk 'with the enemy' or how they felt 'hated' [*dușmăniți*] by workmates who reproached them for having made a pact with management. The physical proximity to one's co-workers and the duty to always confront their needs prompted violence, as was the case of comrade delegate Otto who 'struggle[d] against all the bandits [because] 240 men request[ed] his help on a daily basis'. As the report went: 'Fights break out when he is not there; he does organize meetings with these people, but it is all in vain: people are simple-minded, evil and drink. [...] [Comrade Otto] says beatings are good and that he was advised by the police to beat them up.'[10] Such violence could not be tolerated and was castigated under the euphemistic label of 'command methods'. In the words of one party official: 'This is not why we are communists; we have forgotten the party line, we are governed by old ways, we refuse to collaborate with those at the bottom. In trade union work we have to abolish command methods.'[11]

Drinking with one's workmates, being detested by them, listening to their complaints, befriending some, beating up others – this range of behaviours made up the web of reciprocities in which the delegate was invariably tangled up on the shop floor. This cluster of emotions and social relations – friendship and disgust, hatred and camaraderie – extended well beyond factory perimeters into a chain of interlocking social spaces: neighbourhoods and villages, pubs and canteens, tramway stops and train stations, sport fields and church parishes. The delegate, then, took to the shop floor a bagful of anxiety passed on by friends and foes at each and every juncture point on this chain. This anxiety of the delegate was dubbed in party reports 'the fear of the masses'. Take, for instance, the description of the western city of Timișoara in March 1946:

> Factory committees, made up of communist and social-democratic members, have become bureaucratized; a kind of fear of the masses trickles down from the county level party organization. Things went so far that even the secretary of the Timiș-Torontal communist county organization, comrade Stanciu Emil, wants to be back on the production line, arguing he cannot deal any more with the problems of working for the party. This fear of the masses, this fear of the workers – who are all angry over the difficult state of the economy – is due to our lack of political work.[12]

Or, take another party report detailing the situation in the southern Transylvanian town of Mediaș:

> Workers see trade unions as watchdogs (*cerberi*) of management. Our comrades in the unions speak a monotonous language, drafted on a simple model. Everywhere we can see the same fear of the workers, who are furious because they lack all sort of things. On many occasions, our own comrades behave as if we were the ones responsible for current economic hardships. [...] The fear of masses paralyzes our initiative.[13]

The 'fear of the masses' pushed many delegates back onto the production line and made some of the communist rank-and-file reject positions in the factory committees or even higher up the trade union hierarchy. In other cases, delegates bailed out by arguing that they worked and had no time for politics. This was Tudor Anton's strategy as well. In early 1947, 'he refused to fulfil the obligations he took on, arguing that he worked and had no time (with all our efforts we could not persuade him), thus exhibiting a complete lack of discipline; he blames the party for not understanding him; we propose to replace him [...]'.[14] One year later, Tudor was no longer a delegate of the Locomotive section of Malaxa Works but a mere party instructor, a significantly less demanding task that allowed him to carry on with the job and keep a relatively low political profile.[15] It took over three years for Tudor Anton to re-emerge as a representative of the workers. In March 1950, the president of the union was sacked on accusations of embezzlement.[16] Several weeks later, Tudor Anton was elected president of the factory committee. The factory newspaper portrayed his orphaned childhood, his entering Malaxa Works during the economic boom of the late 1930s and his early commitment to the Communist Party. In December 1950, he was also nominated to run for a seat in the local administration of a village near Bucharest.

Tudor's political career might have been cut short in the summer of 1951 as Radio Free Europe had it. Yet this was a trajectory intimately linked not merely with the Communist Party's 'inner life' but also with the evolution of the institution of the factory committee both within Malaxa Works and within the national trade union movement revived in the post-war period. This personal trajectory, as much as I could reconstruct it, shows the ways in which Tudor was simultaneously engaged in manoeuvring the distance between himself, 'the masses' and the party, abolishing it during work time in October 1945 when he was accused of 'anarcho-syndicalism', lengthening it in 1947 when he accused the party of lacking understanding for his condition and abolishing it again in 1951 during spare time when he was accused of 'over-friendliness'. This play on distance allowed Tudor to cast his copper in relative tranquillity and shelter himself from the combined claims put on him by his membership in the Communist Party and by the expectations of his workmates. It also allowed him to take an active, though perhaps less anxious, part in the activities organized by the party such as guarding the main gates of the plant during a Labour Day parade in 1949.[17] Tudor's constant negotiation of distance between peers and superiors in and out of the shop floor and up and down union hierarchy, as well as his oscillating commitments between working one's copper and working one's way through the ranks of the Communist Party, is what Alf Lüdtke has dubbed *Eigen-Sinn*.

Defined as 'the attempt to gain momentary distance from the expectations coming "from above" and "from nearby"', *Eigen-Sinn* is a relational concept that cuts across homogenizing binaries (support/opposition, resistance/accommodation, solidarity/ anomie) in order to reveal how everyday practices of distancing (*die Praktiken der Distanzierung*) might challenge, undermine, reproduce or consecrate patterns of domination and relations of power at the point of production and beyond.[18] In this view, the search for distance from workmates and foremen, from managers and militants or from the encroachment of trade unionism and the burden of party membership might end up in acts of mobilization but might also hinder or chip away at efforts towards collective expressions of dissent. For Lüdtke, *Eigen-Sinn* occurs at the interface between two entangled, mutually reinforcing historical processes: the politicization of the private and the privatization of politics. The first might be conceptualized as the expansion of organized mass politics, both at the level of the state (laws, policies, institutions etc.) and within the realm of civil society (political parties, unions, associations etc.). The latter falls within the purview of the localized, unregimented and frugal everyday and takes the form of relentless (re)appropriations of resources and opportunities made available or denied by the politicization of the private. Lüdtke grounds this historical dialectic in an underspecified, scantily alluded to drive to secure (and boost) the efficiency (*Tauglichkeit*) of labour power for generalized commodity production.[19] *Eigen-Sinn*, then, is not merely intended to map out disruptive practices in the social universe of industrial work – practices which might all too easily be miscataloged as *la perruque* – but rather to restore a degree of autonomy to the way in which workers make sense on their own of the multifarious, ever-changing regime of compulsions they find themselves subjected to at any given time: managerial hierarchy and the price of bread, wage systems and party meetings, union fees and starving children, labour law and the cost of a tram ticket, work-time and household chores, ties of class and delegation and so on.[20] Let us now turn to the question of the factory committee to see how workers and Communist Party leaders understood this institution.

The invention of 'anarcho-syndicalism'

The emergence of factory committees across post-war East-Central Europe was a remarkably uniform process, irrespective of these countries' trade union traditions and their diverse experiences of the war. For each case, as the German war economy collapsed and the Wehrmacht retreated, workers were able to organize themselves at the point of production well before the constitution of trade unions. Equally uniform was the initial reaction of the Communist Parties, which profited from the radicalism of the factory committees in their effort to expand their membership. It did not take long, however, for the same Communist Parties to launch an assault on the committees. By May 1945, Polish communists called for 'the increased and strengthened authority of the director, engineer and foreman' and condemned the committees for their 'anarcho-syndicalism'.[21] So too in Czechoslovakia: once the national trade union was set up in late 1945, factory committees drew increased attention for their alleged 'syndicalism'.[22] In each of these countries, laws were passed to regulate the prerogatives of the committees in order to re-establish shop floor hierarchy, limiting their power to matters of negotiations, banning all haphazard purges and dashing dreams of self-management, even in those enterprises abandoned by their former owners where workers kept production running on their own. While all these facts conjure a scenario of trans-bloc uniformity, there were notable differences as well.

In post-war Romania, factory committees mushroomed throughout the fall of 1944 as an outcome of the wartime alliance between the Communist and Social-Democratic Parties known as *Frontul Unic Muncitoresc* or FUM (United Workers' Front). From the outset, membership in the factory committee was premised on political allegiance rather than, as in Poland or Czechoslovakia, on lingering remnants of labour militancy from the interwar period. Established in April 1944, the FUM was supposed to monopolize all upcoming trade union activity and run it on a parity principle.[23] There were good reasons for this decision. Both parties had lost much of their working-class constituencies to home-grown fascism during the late 1930s and both were in urgent need to reorganize themselves as mass parties from the ground up. Rebuilding the network of trade unions and reorganizing the party required a conjoined effort, with the factory committee as the central pillar of this common platform. This strategy proved successful, at least for the first few months after the end of the war. By late 1945, one communist leader noted how the development of the trade union movement radically changed the social basis of the party: 'Whereas in the past the vast majority of our members in Transylvania and Moldavia were non-Romanian petty bourgeois, today we have over 85% Romanian Party members coming from heavy industry'.[24] This history of party enlargement was spectacular indeed, but it came at the price of de facto power-sharing within factories: enlargement spelled empowerment.

Much like in other East-Central European countries, the Romanian trade union law passed in late January 1945 specified that all employees could and had to organize themselves in factory committees of no more than thirty members elected by secret ballot.[25] Each committee would then propose a representative for the local trade union commission, which worked as an assembly of all the committees on a given territory.

These commissions would then be affiliated with a national branch union such as the Metal-Chemical Trade Union or the Mining Union, which in turn would be controlled from above by the General Confederacy of Labour (CGM). The commanding heights on this string – from the lowest to the highest – were shared within the FUM: an equal number of communists and social democrats would run the factory committees, the local trade union commissions, the branch unions and, finally, the central leadership of CGM. What resulted was an entangled hierarchy of supervision in which it was all too common for a rank-and-file delegate to take union issues to party meetings and party problems to union gatherings. The same law stipulated factory committees had no say in matters of administrative, technical or commercial undertakings, nor could they fire and hire on their own, all of which lay firmly with management. What they were allowed to do was to overview the 'professional interests' of the workers, a vague phrase which pushed CGM to issue its own explanatory note restating the law in a more comprehensible language.[26] Yet, it was precisely the explosive blend of party membership and union delegation that empowered the factory committees and turned them, in the derogatory words of a Communist Party leader, into a 'master in the factory' [*stăpân în fabrică*].[27]

There was no shortage of deprecating terms to describe the power factory committees exercised within factories. Already in May 1945 – two months after the appointment of the Groza government – party leader Gheorghiu-Dej was fretting in a state of awe over the so-called 'anarcho-syndicalist manifestations' of the committees: 'They disregard the unions and the CGM. How should we explain that in so many factories they still push for wage increases against the line set by the Confederacy? How is it still possible they end up organizing strikes?'[28] Nor was there a shortage of answers to this kind of puzzles. For party leader Vasile Luca, factory committees became 'surrogates of the owner' [*locțiitorii patronului*] and even 'super-owners' [*supra-patroni*] because delegates hunted 'fat' positions, indulged in 'business' and singlehandedly managed the provisioning of factory stores and the canteens.[29] In this context, many workers felt it was only normal to redirect their demands away from management towards the factory committee, a situation which put the party at risk. Luca indeed noted that this was a well-known set-up which communists should do well to remember: the desire to control factories happened in Germany and Austria following the First World War, a move he argued had been theorized by Karl Kautsky and one that paved the way for fascism and Hitlerism. Linking social democracy, the workers' council movement in Central Europe and Nazism was an ingenious gloss on the theory of 'social fascism' of the early Third International, of which Vasile Luca had been a venerable militant.[30] This political imaginary allowed Luca to time and again make the argument that:

> The origin of the conflict within factories has nothing to do with the fact that I do not love the social democrats or that they don't love the workers, but rather with the unhealthy struggle for positions which makes both the social democrats and communists take sides with one group (i.e. the workers) or another [...] We have to take away from the factory committees the opportunity for corruption provided by hiring and firing; they should not be able to do that; they should instead lead the

struggle of the workers. We cannot pursue workers' control [*control muncitoresc*] within a capitalist society; do not forget the experience of the factory committees in Germany and Austria. These committees ended up supporting the owners, and fascism more generally.[31]

Yet, neither the deployment of this rhetoric nor the enforcement of the trade union law of late January 1945 could address what Communist Party leaders understood to be the unquenchable, rebellious thirst of the factory committees. This problem became all the more acute by the end of the year, when the Communist Party had already recruited an extraordinary number of nearly 300,000 members only to see itself 'losing the masses'[32] in the wake of the strike wave that unfolded throughout October.[33] In spite of his Cominternism, Vasile Luca was not totally deprived of a modicum of common sense. In late November 1945, he noted that 'workers reason with the belly' and look up to the government to solve their most pressing needs.[34] Workers, however, were also reasoning with their senses and looked up to those in their proximity to provide them with better food at the canteen, clothes and footwear, firewood for the winter season and even to kindle their hopes for higher wages.[35] These were the delegates of the factory committee, be they communists or social democrats, men whom workers knew and had laboured along during the war, men whom they might have befriended over drinks or accompanied on the road to the factory and certainly men whom they could exert a certain pressure over at the risk of being punished for overstating their claims. Even the more experienced delegates, such as long-term union leaders of the interwar epoch, spoke of 'the discontent and unprecedented revolt of the workers'.[36]

The autonomy of the committees, then, was a consequence of the delegates succumbing to this exceptional pressure 'from nearby' in two complementary ways. They could either – as was said of the Jiu Valley delegates – fail to wield 'sufficient authority over the masses'[37] or – as with one president of the factory committee in the town of Făgăraș – seek 'to mischievously win the masses for his own personal goals'.[38] For the leaders of the Communist Party, it all amounted to one and the same thing, namely an open defiance of party and union directives:

> [I]t goes without saying that any action – pursued consciously or unconsciously – which threatens work discipline goes against the best interest of the employees, even when one might be led to believe the action was carried out with the aim of gaining rights for the workers.[39]

Many of the actions alluded to here were indeed strikes: short-lived, localized, flimsy and arguably hopeless events that were either genuinely carried out with the support of the factory committee (hence, 'consciously') or turned out rather impossible to be prevented by delegates (hence, 'unconsciously'). It was not necessarily the outcome of the strikes that worried most of the leaders of the Communist Party, but rather their ability to pose and expose the antinomy of representation on the basis of which the party grew as a mass organization. This explains why both the CGM and Communist Party leaders denounced the factory committees for having become 'political platforms', that is, instruments in the hands of 'demagogues' armed with a 'revolutionary phraseology' that used them as springboards for unrest:

> Where there are great difficulties and the employees are not clear on the objective causes which produced the economic difficulties of the country, they go on strike in order to secure their demands, disregarding the upper echelon of the trade union [...] CGM has made it explicit that one cannot use a strike to pursue demands; the strike has a reactionary character, now that the whole country needs to be reconstructed and all the citizens must sacrifice themselves. Given these conditions, those who want to go on strike are saboteurs of democracy and enemies of the reconstruction of the country.[40]

It was much easier when strikes or any other industrial conflicts that involved the factory committee could be proven to have been instigated or backed up by social-democratic delegates; in such cases, Communist Party leaders could mobilize an entire semantic arsenal centred on the notion of 'reaction'.[41] It was not that these delegates were more militant or more prone to engage in striking activity than the communist ones, but they often found themselves pushed to the forefront of protests by workers disenchanted with the perpetual play on distance the latter were engaged in on the shop floor. It was much more complicated when unrest was mounted or assisted by communist delegates, as it appeared to be the case with Tudor Anton at Malaxa Works throughout 1945. Such party members were directly compromising both the mass organization they helped build and the meaning of communism they embodied before the workers. Confronted with an even more severe upsurge in striking activity in 1946, the Communist Party resorted to a discursive repertoire nourished by a mix of local historical experience and Third International Marxism.

The mechanism at work here, one that was to be consistently employed by the Communist Party in its encounter with varying cases of labour unrest, aimed to put order into what William Sewell called the 'babble of cultural voices' or the 'semiotic sprawl'.[42] Sewell drew attention to the manifold ways in which large-scale cultural actors such as state institutions, political parties, churches or corporations – 'even in powerful and would-be totalitarian states' – strive not for the direct imposition of cultural uniformity, but rather employ strategies of 'organizing difference' whereby various cultural practices are marginalized, excluded or normalized with the goal of obtaining 'a certain focus on the production and consumption of meaning'.[43] In this sense, ordering meaning implied less of a conspicuous effort to impose a supposedly uniform 'communist' code of conduct on the rank and file – an effort which would have been logistically impossible anyway before 1948 – than the attempt to marginalize or even criminalize industrial practices considered to be at odds with party tactics at any given point in time. In the post-war field of labour relations, then, the codification of 'communism' as a cluster of rules of identification and self-identification of the rank and file was premised on the redefining and reordering of myriad locally embedded protests. Or, to put it differently, because the meaning of 'communism' was not textually given but rather socially mediated, every instance of labour unrest became a site of struggle over the politically accepted understanding of party membership.

Conclusion: Tudor's open-ended posterity

In October 1951, a denunciatory article was published by the Malaxa Works factory newspaper. The anonymous author of the article called upon management to intervene in the business of distributing the factory's social insurance budget, which was run exclusively by the factory committee. The president of said committee – one Tudor Anton – was accused of having overspent the money allocated for sickness leave by no less than 100%, a fact which was allegedly possible only because workers faked their illnesses and got away with it. Moreover, Tudor was allegedly in cahoots with the factory's medical doctors, who turned a blind eye on the vast numbers of workers on leave. Tudor Anton's removal, the article concluded, was imminent.[44] Such cases were not uncommon. Beginning with 1948, the factory committee was transformed from an institution geared towards containing workers' unrest to one entrusted to manage factory welfare and enforce labour discipline. This momentous change allowed for people like Tudor to preside over substantial financial resources, the distribution of which might have entailed episodes of favouritism. If, as the Radio Free Europe note discussed earlier shows, the general manager of the factory accused Tudor of 'over-friendliness' in his relations to fellow workers, it is plausible that the term stood for Tudor's discretionary will to allocate social insurance compensations to close comrades, perhaps first and foremost to those sharing his passion for motorcycles.

Was Tudor's case, all anachronisms aside, simply one of petty corruption? Was this communist locksmith a 'collaborator' with a foreign power and its puppet regime? Or was he rather engaged in some form of resistance, unknowingly sabotaging the establishment of socialism in the factories, first as an 'anarcho-syndicalist' in 1945 and then as a lenient president of the factory committee in 1951? Derived from the contemporary politics of memory, none of these historiographical categories can adequately explain the lived experience of people like Tudor Anton.[45] His life, much like many other individual trajectories marked by the post-war period in Romania and Eastern Europe more broadly, would be better served by a critical historiography that places at its core the notions of individual agency and domination practices. Tudor's oscillation between outright rebellion, muted support and full participation in the relations of power organized by the Communist Party at various points in time would reveal the panoply of actions that inform practices of domination. Once liberated from the penchant to classify the recent past in moral terms of victims and heroes, this historiography would be arguably more open to current concerns about oppression and the limits of emancipation.

What, then, would this historiographical liberation consist of? First, it would imply an effort on the part of historians to maintain distance from the demands put on the profession by various memory entrepreneurs and activists.[46] Ideally, this effort would be carried out in a language of scientific inquiry, evidence and explanation that would allow historians to reinforce the autonomy of their craft and militate for producing knowledge of the past that is neither immediately relevant for the public sphere nor easily appropriated by policymakers. For instance, exploring the dynamics of wages and prices during the 1950s may seem a topic of research far removed from the public debates over Romanian Stalinism, but it is no less crucial for understanding the overall trajectory of that decade.

Secondly, historians' search for the autonomy of their field of practice would entail their explicit concern to construe research objects and employ categories of analysis that do not fit easily within the prevailing narratives of public memory. One such example would be the Vichy analogy explored in this chapter, but the sheer range of heteronomous research topics and interpretations imported from the discourse of public memory into the historiographical field is much larger. Perhaps no other such topic has been more influential among Romanian historians than the question of 'anti-communist resistance', a research agenda formulated outside of the historiographical field by the outpouring of confessional literature after 1989 and the ensuing emergence of a landscape of public memory grounded in the glorification of political prisoners.[47]

Finally, in striving for autonomy vis-à-vis the entrepreneurs of public memory, historians will not abandon questions of morality altogether or renounce their concern with retrieving the stories of the victims of the recent past. As Jochen Hellbeck noted, the lines of division (and dispute) of the historiographical field in post-Soviet Russia and Eastern Europe will likely be drawn between 'more or less detached observers, between those who study the Soviet past from afar and those who personally experienced Soviet power or live on formerly Soviet soil and therefore have particular moral and political stakes in coming to terms with the Soviet legacy'.[48] In this context, it is only the autonomy of the historiographical field that may act as a buffer against the proximity of these 'moral and political stakes', thereby securing the modicum of distance the practice of history writing requires.

Notes

1   Mark Kramer, 'Stalin, Soviet Policy, and the Establishment of a Communist Bloc in Eastern Europe, 1941–1948', in *Stalin and Europe: Imitation and Domination, 1928–1953*, eds. Timothy Snyder and Ray Brandon (Oxford: Oxford University Press, 2014), 286.

2   Ghiţă Ionescu, *Communism in Romania, 1944–1962* (Oxford: Oxford University Press, 1964), 97.

3   Ibid.

4   Dumitru Şandru, *Comunizarea societăţii româneşti în anii 1944–1947* (Bucharest: Editura Enciclopedică, 2007), 14.

5   Thus, for Ionescu, one of the key industrial policies of the post-war era, namely the signing of collective labour contracts appears as 'another gambit designed to cause distrust between management and workers'. See Ionescu, *Communism in Romania*, 101. For how Ionescu's reading of the contracts mistook their outcomes with their causes, see the lengthy discussion in Adrian Grama, 'Labouring Along. Industrial Workers and the Making of Postwar Romania' (PhD diss., Central European University, Budapest, 2016), 185–200.

6   Open Society Archives, Central European University, Budapest. Records of Radio
      Free Europe/Radio Liberty Research Institute: General Records: Information Items.
      HU OSA 300-1-2-14134. 'Purges of Union President in "23rd August" Factory
      Bucharest', 17 January 1952.

7   Arhivele Municipale Bucureşti (Municipal Archives, Buchurest; AMB). Comitetul
      Municipal PCR Bucureşti, Comitetul Sectorului 23 August (Malaxa) al PCR,
      2/1945, 3. By September 1945, the Communist Party organization at Malaxa
      Works comprised 1631 members, less than 20 per cent of the total number of
      employees.

8   AMB. Comitetul Municipal PCR Bucureşti, Comitetul Sectorului 23 August
      (Malaxa) al PCR, 3/1945, 6-7.

9   AMB. Comitetul Municipal PCR Bucureşti, Comitetul Sectorului 23 August
      (Malaxa) al PCR, 8/1945, 7.

10   Ibid., 107. '[…] was advised by the police to beat them up' should probably be
      understood as follows: as a member of the Communist Party and a delegate of the
      factory committee, Dumitru Otto was in the habit of hunting down fellow workers
      allegedly engaged in various kinds of work 'on the side': repairing objects for private
      customers, employing the tools of the workshop for personal gain, appropriating
      all sorts of used and unused materials for home use, pilfering etc. ANR, MM,
      1044/1945, 42–44; MM, 1033/1946, 450. Comrade Otto would regularly hand these
      workers to the district police, where it is likely they were subjected to physical
      punishment. We might therefore suppose the police instructed Otto to beat them up
      on his own.

11   Ibid., 101.

12   Arhivele Naţionale ale României (National Archives of Romania; ANR). CC/PCR,
      Secţia Organizatorică, 112/1946, 22–23.

13   Ibid., 33.

14   AMB. Comitetul Municipal PCR Bucureşti, Comitetul Sectorului 23 August
      (Malaxa) al PCR, 11/1947, 1.

15   AMB. Comitetul Municipal PCR Bucureşti, Comitetul Sectorului 23 August
      (Malaxa) al PCR, 17/1948, 2.

16   Ibid., 38/1950, 256.

17   Ibid., 29/1949, 80.

18   Alf Lüdtke, 'Arbeit, Arbeitserfahrungen und Arbeiterpolitik. Zum
      Perspektivenwandel in der historischen Forschung', in his *Eigen-Sinn.
      Fabrikalltag, Arbeitererfahrungen und Politik vom Kaiserreich bis in den
      Faschismus* (Hamburg: Ergebnisse Verlag, 1993), 377 (my translation). Parts of
      this essay were translated in English as Alf Lüdtke, 'Polymorphous Synchrony:
      German Industrial Workers and the Politics of Everyday Life', *International
      Review of Social History*, no. 3 (1993): 39–84. The English version, however,
      obliterates the reference to 'distance': 'Eigensinn was the attempt to gain some
      welcome respite, at least for a few brief minutes, from unreasonable external (and
      shop floor) demands and pressures'.

19   Alf Lüdtke, 'Kolonisierung der Lebenswelten oder Geschichte als Einbahnstraße?',
      Das Argument 140 (1983): 536–542.

20   *La perruque* (the wig): established practices of the shop floor through which workers'
      appropriate time, tools and industrial waste for profitless fun (or for the sake of it),
      often labeled as 'theft' by those in power according to Michel De Certeau, *L'invention
      du quotidian. 1. Arts de faire* (Paris: Gallimard, 1990), 45–46.

21   Jaime Reynolds, 'Communists, Socialists and Workers: Poland 1944–48', *Soviet Studies* 30, no. 4 (1978): 516–520 (521).

22   Karel Kovanda, 'Works Councils in Czechoslovakia, 1945–47', *Soviet Studies* 29, no. 2 (1977): 255–269.

23   Ioan Chiper, 'Oragnizarea comitetelor de fabrică (23 August–Octombrie 1944)', *Studii. Revistă de istorie* 17, no. 4 (1964): 809–834. For an informative political history of the FUM written from the standpoint of the Communist Party, see Carol Niri, *Frontul unic muncitoresc în perioada 23 august 1944 – februarie 1948* (Bucharest: Academia de Științe Social-Politice 'Ștefan Gheorghiu', 1968).

24   ANR. CC/PCR, Organizatorică, 97/1945, 2.

25   *Monitorul Oficial* CXIII, no. 17, 21 January 1945, 419–424. The Polish law is discussed by Christoph Kleßmann, 'Betriebsräte, Gewerkschaften und Arbeiterselbstverwaltung in Polen (1944–1958)', *Jahrbücher für Geschichte Osteuropas* 29, no. 2 (1981): 185–214; the Czechoslovak one by Peter Heumos, 'Betriebsräte, Einheitsgewerkschaft und staatliche Unternehmensverwaltung: Anmerkungen zu einer Petition mährischer Arbeiter an die tschechoslowakische Regierung vom 8. Juni 1947', *Jahrbücher für Geschichte Osteuropas* 29, no. 2 (1981): 215–245.

26   For a case in point, see ANR, MM, 986/1945, 1–10.

27   ANR. CC/PCR, Organizatorică, 46/1945, 2.

28   ANR. CC/PCR, Cancelarie, 41/1945, 25.

29   Vasile Luca (1898–1963) was a leading member of the Romanian Communist Party and a key figure during the first post-war decade. In 1953, he was purged from the party, underwent a show trial and was finally imprisoned under accusations of mismanaging the Ministry of Finance. See Gheorghe Onișoru, *Pecetea lui Stalin. Cazul Vasile Luca* (Târgoviște: Cetatea de Scaun, 2014).

30   On the original context in which the theory of 'social fascism' was elaborated, see Silvio Pons, *The Global Revolution. A History of International Communism, 1917–1991* (Oxford: Oxford University Press, 2014), 69.

31   ANR. CC/PCR, Cancelarie, 113/1945, 24. See also ibid., 94/1945, 21. Here Luca argued that '[w]e should not make the mistake of believing that we can grab power through the factory committees as in Austria, by replacing the owner, because this is what led to National Socialism'.

32   This sentiment, already intensified by the struggles over the 'winter aid' in October, was further reinforced when a great number of workers turned up for the public celebration of King Michael's name day on 8 November 1945, an event that took place in many urban centres across the country; for a conventional narrative, see Petre Țurlea, *8 Noiembrie 1945* (Bucharest: Institutul Național pentru Studiul Totalitarismului, 2000).

33   This figure is given in ANR. CC/PCR, Cancelarie, 122/1945. It is important to note that out of these 300,000 party members only 47 per cent paid their membership fees regularly; ANR. CC/PCR, Cancelarie, 118/1945.

34   ANR. CC/PCR, Cancelarie, 107/1945, 10.

35   For a similar argument, see Jan De Graf, 'More than Canteen Control: Polish and Italian Socialists Confronting Their Workers, 1944–1947', *International Review of Social History* 59 (2014): 71–98.

36   ANR. CC/PCR, Organizatorică, 22/1945, 2.

37   ANR. CC/PCR, Organizatorică, 34/1945, 2. The report went on to note that the local Communist Party organization in the Jiu Valley was left to the 'locals', who, while

'devoted and zealous', could not control the masses because of a lack of 'political judgment' [*discernământ politic*].

38   ANR. CC/PCR, Cancelarie, 179/1945, 2.

39   'Cu prilejul alegerilor comitetelor de întreprindere. Între greşeli şi înfătuiri', *Scânteia* III, no. 418, 5 January 1946.

40   Gheorghe Apostol, 'Probleme actuale ale mişcării sindicale din România', *Scânteia* III, no. 416 (31 December 1945).

41   Much to his credit, Minister of Labour and social democrat leader Lotar Rădăceanu protested against attempts to portray his rank and file as 'reactionary' both privately – in letters addressed to Communist Party leaders – and publicly. For the first, see ANR. CC/PCR, Cancelarie, 154/1945. For the second, see Lotar Rădăceanu, 'Probleme actuale', *Revista Muncii* II, no. 15 (January 1947). Here Rădăceanu argues the issue of the so-called 'anarcho-syndicalism' was grossly exaggerated and required no special law to be contained. On the extraordinary figure of Rădăceanu, see Mihai-Dan Cârjan and Adrian Grama, 'Şerban Voinea/Lotar Rădăceanu', in *Plante Exotice. Teoria şi practica marxiştilor români*, eds. Andrei State and Alex Cistelecan (Cluj: Tact, 2015), 43–125.

42   William H. Sewell, Jr., 'The Concept(s) of Culture', in *Beyond the Cultural Turn. New Directions in the Study of Society and Culture*, eds. Victoria E. Bonnell and Lynn Hunt (Berkeley: University of California Press, 1999), 56–57.

43   Ibid.

44   'Activitatea Secţiei de Asigurări Sociale din Uzinele "23 August" trebuie îmbunătăţită', *Viaţa Uzinei*, no. 85, 17 October 1951.

45   For the politics of memory in contemporary Romania, particularly as it concerns the Second World War and the state socialist regime, see Maria Bucur, *Heroes and Victims. Remembering War in Twentieth-Century Romania* (Bloomington: Indiana University Press, 2009) and James Mark, *The Unfinished Revolution: Making Sense of the Communist Past in Central-Eastern Europe* (New Heaven, CT: Yale University Press, 2010).

46   For the notion of 'autonomy' in relation to various fields of knowledge, I follow the discussion in Pierre Bourdieu and Lutz Raphael, 'Sur les rapports entre l'histoire et la sociologie en France et en Allemagne', *Actes de la recherche en sciences sociales* 106, no. 1 (1995): 108–122. For the category of 'memory entrepreneurs' and the recent efforts to forge a pan-European public memory under the concept of totalitarianism, see Laure Neumayer, 'Integrating the Central European Past into a Common Narrative: The Mobilizations Around the "Crimes of Communism" in the European Parliament', *Journal of Contemporary European Studies* 23, no. 3 (2015): 1–20.

47   For a recent stocktaking of these developments, see William Totok and Elena-Irina Macovei, *Între mit şi bagatelizare. Despre reconsiderarea critică a trecutului, Ion Gavrilă Ogoranu şi rezistenţa armată anticomunistă din România* (Iaşi: Polirom, 2016).

48   Jochen Hellbeck, 'Of Archives and Frogs: Iconoclasm in Historical Perspective', *Slavic Review* 67, no. 3 (2008): 720–723 (722).

A Case Study of Power Practices:
The Czechoslovak Stalinist Elite at the Regional Level (1948–1951)

Marián Lóži

This chapter deals with the practices of legitimization and domination that prevailed in the Czechoslovak Communist Party (Komunistická strana Československa; KSČ) during the Stalinist period. Chronologically, it is situated between the years 1948 and 1951, at a time when the international and economic situation worsened due to the heavy pressure exerted by the Soviet Union. This atmosphere gave rise to a paranoid state of mind within leading party circles. The latter responded with heavy-handed persecution against individuals and groups of the so-called 'class enemy' at the central level, groups that gradually encompassed ever higher-ranking communist functionaries. As a consequence, the exercise of domination by the party centre and patterns of legitimization were significantly weakened.

These complex processes taking place in the centre also had their counterparts in the periphery at the provincial level of the party structure, namely in regions [*kraje*] and districts [*okresy*]. In this period, approximately 21 regional and 329 district party organizations of unequal size were spread out over the Czechoslovak territory.[1] Together, they constituted an intermediary level between party headquarters and grassroots party cells. This chapter is not primarily concerned with party regulations or official claims to absolute control. During the Stalinist period, bureaucratic processes and domination instruments were far from flawless; in practice, they often proved heavily dysfunctional. Obstacles were not overcome by systemic procedures, but through the effort of dedicated individuals and groups in positions of authority. They usually held the most important positions within local secretariats, either that of head or deputy head party secretary at the regional level. However, it was their individual attributes, not formal functions or prerogatives, that were essential for their mode of conduct. Studying these personalities in various regions and districts, I found a surprising number of analogous reputations, features and behaviours. I have included them here under the conjoint term 'Stalinist regional elite'.

These so-called elite implemented the central policy in their respective domains and exercised the day-to-day administrative duties. Their specific power practices served to concretely implement the Communist Party's domination. In the eyes of the local party functionaries, the rank-and-file members and even the society at large, they were considered to be in charge of practically everything. They built their own (sinister) reputation, which was much commented upon and criticized by various individuals and groups from the top to the bottom of the social structure. In a period of universal scarcity and fear of the next global war, they gradually became the focal point of an intra-party disgruntlement fomented by the centre's policy. Eventually, they were deposed under humiliating conditions and many of them even suffered repression. Some were in fact accused of belonging to the so-called 'anti-state conspiracy centre of former General Secretary Rudolf Slánský' and convicted in an infamous show trial or in related court cases. Their role was central to the instalment and legitimization of a Stalinist dictatorship. They were the first to put into effect and practice domination in a Stalinist fashion. Regional elite succeeded in their endeavours despite the unpopularity of Stalinist policies and of being personally associated with them. Subsequently, they were used as a focus point of popular resentment and as scapegoats exculpating the structure of the Stalinist dictatorship they helped establish.

By studying these Stalinist regional elite, we can thus reach a better understanding of the way the party functioned at the time. The long-established notion of 'total control' that the regime allegedly exercised through an omnipotent party machine and a conveniently deployed apparatus is, even in the Czechoslovak case, being gradually challenged. In this new historiography, the party administration is characterized as being problematic and even malfunctioning.[2] This is especially relevant for the Stalinist period, when it was in the process of (slowly) being put in place. Many local organizations were in a state of complete disarray or simply dormant,[3] while party secretariats lacked even the most basic overview of individual members.[4]

In an effort to better understand the true nature of this situation, I decided to switch scales and to turn from the centre to the periphery, from the systemic to the individual. My focus in this chapter is not only on the power practices and modes of conduct of the Stalinist regional elite in relation to the party centre but also on the local population during this period, including their actions, the context in which they operated and the latter's general significance and legitimization of the Stalinist dictatorship. In this way, I expect to reach a better understanding of the Stalinist dictatorship, its functioning and its acceptance within the wider public.

I follow three stages in my demonstration. First, I show how the Stalinist regional elite were perceived by a wide range of social actors. Their speeches and public statements were by no means neutral, but were the product of various motivations for whom idealism and the desire to help went hand in hand with fear, an opportunistic loyalty and particular egoistic interests. In addition, these statements were not always uniform. There were significant changes over time and noticeable voices of disagreement. However, at the time of their deposal or shortly thereafter, one mode of perceiving Stalinist regional elite gradually reached a level of almost absolute approval by both the central leadership, lower functionaries and the party rank and file: Stalinist regional elite were seen as the main culprits of all that was wrong with the system and universally despised.

This contemporary discourse, shared by both Stalinist regional elite and the people who tried to depose them, was, at least in intra-party circles, exclusively Stalinist. Indeed, it included verbal expressions and values such as the 'intensification of the class struggle', 'vigilance', 'criticism and self-criticism', the 'leading role of the working class', 'small dictators', 'planning', 'fake populism', 'listening to the voices from below' and so on. These terms played an essential role in formulating critical statements and voicing them in intra-party communications. I examine their more general implication for the legitimacy of the communist dictatorship.

Secondly, I focus on the material aspect of the Stalinist regional elite's peculiar reputation, as well as the context in which they operated. I study these elite within the party hierarchy, in the everyday conditions under which they had to exercise their duties. This empirical approach is necessary in order to conceive of Stalinist discourse and its legitimizing potential as a concrete rather than abstract phenomenon. It points to the domination practices of the Stalinist dictatorship on the regional level and to their nature and effectiveness.

Finally, I examine how the Stalinist discourse and Stalinist power practices interacted during one particular process – the deposal of the Stalinist regional elite. This discourse and these practices were promulgated by the party centre, but they quickly gained their own dynamics through the participation of various social actors at the regional level. The result was a significant haemorrhage in the ranks of the Stalinist regional elite and their almost universal condemnation. As such, it offers a relevant demonstration of the way the Stalinist dictatorship strived for legitimacy.

The baleful reputation of Stalinist regional elite

In the summer of 1950, Mikuláš Landa, the newly appointed head party secretary of the industrial region of Ústí nad Labem, is said to have visited the small mining town of Duchcov, which belonged to his administrative domain. As the story goes, instead of making a grand official entry, Landa disguised himself as a simple coal miner. With the rest of his temporary co-workers he then descended into the mines and worked a shift. When finished, he revealed his true identity, convened local functionaries and mercilessly berated the mine's deputy director in front of this audience as 'a slob, a Menshevik and a pimp'. The other functionaries were rebuked as 'idlers'. Landa's unexpected visit left the officials of Duchcov both perplexed and horrified. It was an experience to be remembered.[5]

This story, recounted by a local official, was just one example among many to show the arbitrariness of Mikuláš Landa's power practices, his dictatorial leanings, his disregard for proper conduct and his tendency to populist behaviour. Together, these elements represent the three facets of the negative reputation widely enjoyed by the Stalinist regional elite. I will describe them in turn and interpret their meaning regarding the legitimizing potential of Stalinist discourse.

First facet: The dictatorial practices of the regional Stalinist elite

Accusations of dictatorial conduct were quite common at the time. In fact, the recourse to dictatorship was presented as the main offence of the Stalinist regional elite, whether by lowly local functionaries or by powerful party dignitaries. General Secretary Rudolf Slánský himself complained at the 9th Czechoslovak Communist Party Congress in May 1949 that 'communists in various departments abuse their function in order to assume the authority to dictate and boss people around'.[6]

Stalinist regional elite were indeed criticized for resorting to various forms of dubious behaviour. They were allegedly prone to verbal abuse, including insults and threats. For instance, the head secretary of the Brno region, Otto Šling, was confronted in 1949 with a shortage of fodder for pigs and then with the subsequent killing of starving herds in the Znojmo district. His reaction was, according to delegates from the affected area, the following: 'he banged his fist on the table, threatened to send in the militia and green Antons [i.e. police cars], which he would drive in person and then arrest everybody'.[7]

The Stalinist regional elite were also accused of not choosing their direct subordinates within the ranks of respected functionaries in the assigned regions, hiring instead their personal followers who lacked any local legitimacy. Josef Stavinoha illustrates this trait. After he was transferred from Ostrava and appointed head secretary of the Olomouc region in spring 1948, Stavinoha supposedly brought in his original 'friends and collaborators'[8] and rewarded them with key positions in the regional party secretariat, thus disregarding candidates with local roots. The local candidates were the most affected and the most critical of these appointments.

Understandably, the relationship between these Stalinist elite and the local communist functionaries was also described as being quite strained. The deputy head secretary of the Pardubice region, Jiří Kotrch, was evaluated as being particularly aggressive in this regard. When visiting Vysoké Mýto, he reportedly forced the local head secretary and pre-war party member František Bartheldy to resign under humiliating conditions.[9] He then engaged in a particularly acrimonious conflict with the old comrade Pavla Šimonková. Their incessant quarrels in the regional bureau were so heated that she wanted to resign from her party functions, fearing that otherwise she would be fired from office under humiliating circumstances.

Otto Šling was seen as being very malicious in this regard. He was blamed for denouncing one of his opponents, Bohumil Ubr – another local communist and member of the Brno regional bureau – as an 'enemy of the Party' and for ordering the wiretapping of his phone.[10]

The Stalinist elite were perceived not only as ruthless dictators but also as individuals driven by their own interest, unbound by their belonging to the party administrative structure or their subordination to party headquarters. Their power practice was deemed unacceptable by the highest leadership of the party, as well as by party rank and file. It was considered brutal, vindictive and unpredictable. This criticism reflected the official discourse of the Stalinist period. The strong emphasis on 'comradely behaviour' and the detailed planning of actions were some of its important tenets, in direct opposition to strong-arm and haphazard dealings. This posed an interesting contradiction in that Stalinist regional elite were blamed for not living up to Stalinist standards: acceptance of the latter enabled the criticism of the former. Stalinist language was not only for the rulers but also for the ruled.

Second facet: A personalized exercise of power

This last point can be taken further. Stalinist elite were indeed also accused of blatantly disregarding established traditions and party rules. They allegedly dismissed the customary visits, demands and grievances addressed to regional headquarters and secretaries. For instance, Hanuš Lomský, head secretary of the Plzeň region, is reported to have reacted in the following way when a group of party members visited him, armed with complaints from local organizations, duly signed and stamped: 'I could not care less about stamps.'[11] Stalinist elite were thus charged with circumventing explicit party statutes. This happened, for instance, with Růžena Dubová, head of the organizational department of the Brno region and closest collaborator of Otto Šling. She was accused of instructing the screening committees to expel any unworthy member and to seize their party card. This provoked open criticism, insofar as only primary organizations were allowed to expel party members. Unimpressed by the commotion, Růžena Dubová bluntly stated: 'committees are allowed to seize Party cards, because they work with the authorization of the superior Party instances'.[12] Regional Stalinist elite were dismissive not only of lower party members but also of the very traditions and rules of the party.

The temerity of the Stalinist regional elite did not stop there. In some instances, they were charged with belittling the pinnacle of the party leadership, the chairman of the Czechoslovak Communist Party and president of the Republic, Klement Gottwald. This was considered a particularly severe offence. By the beginning of the 1950s, Gottwald's official cult had reached immense proportions. He was frequently quoted in papers and on the radio, and the biggest industrial enterprises were named after him. Even an entire town, the South Moravian city of Zlín, was renamed Gottwaldov after him. Gottwald's status is best summed up by the contemporary chant 'Stalin – Gottwald – Peace'.[13]

It was therefore considered shocking when the head secretary of the Tachov district, František Maťha, explained to party members awaiting admission into his office that he never let visitors in while working, since 'when I am in session, not even Gottwald is allowed to disturb me'.[14] But the worst accusation once again concerned Mikuláš Landa. He sent a celebratory telegram to President Gottwald in which he falsified details about the number of agricultural products bought from peasants. To party functionaries confronting him about the matter, Landa supposedly declared: 'It is not a sin to deceive Comrade Gottwald if it mobilizes the people'.[15] To the alleged sins of Stalinist regional elite was thus added yet another important charge: a strong disregard for established central authority and its leadership.

The Stalinist regional elite were also accused of ideological heresy. They allegedly ignored the ongoing class war against former exploiters and were willing to collaborate with individuals endowed with doctrinally problematic backgrounds. They even made them members of their immediate entourage. This was the case of Otto Šling. While implementing his agricultural policy, he relied on the Kuthan brothers, two former landowners who were later denounced as 'representatives of the capitalist order' and as 'typical exploiters'.[16] In the industrial sector, one of his collaborators was František Ryšánek, who had previously worked in the Baťa enterprises and practised as an independent businessman. Šling appointed him director of a large construction conglomerate that was established through the merger of 109 companies and that employed approximately 5,000 people.[17] He was even accused of establishing a veritable bond of partnership with Ryšánek. When the latter was arrested by State Security for the charges of theft and harassing employees, an infuriated Šling obtained his release. He apologized to him and appointed him back to his directorial position.[18] Šling was simply protecting his trusted aide. However, in the heated atmosphere of the 'intensification of the class struggle' it fostered the suspicion that he was in fact covertly defending class enemies. Allegations of this sort were typical of many Stalinist regional elite.

Finally, these elite were blamed for immoral and outright criminal conduct by enriching themselves through graft and theft. The Olomouc head secretary, Josef Stavinoha, was accused of buying an expensive car for a fraction of its price, under the pretext that it was in desperate need of repair.[19] Deputy head of the regional secretary in Brno Růžena Dubová supposedly obtained a luxurious automobile by sending its previous owner to a forced labour camp under a fabricated pretext.[20] Accusations and gossip related to cars were numerous at the time. Stalinist regional elite supposedly used their expensive vehicles to visit each other in their residences and wine houses, in whose cellars they spent many alcohol-fuelled nights. In the Brno region, a rumour circulated that 'comrades (were) driving their Tatraplan [high-class automobile reserved for privileged party and state functionaries] right into the cellars'.[21] It is not surprising that these allegations were a cause of special outrage among the population, given the state of universal shortage and deprivation.

All these allegations had one important element in common: they served to prove that Stalinist regional elite were trampling over everyone and everything that safeguarded what was deemed the proper manner of exercising domination. They were portrayed as something contradictory to established communist values, at once completely detached from proper norms of governance, yet holding almost diabolical power. This once again points to the binary structure of the Stalinist discourse, to the juxtaposition of Stalinist tenets and Stalinist elite. Many of the accusations were undoubtedly inspired by older, traditional values. This goes especially for customary gossip about stealing and self-indulgent ruling classes. However, they were still completely in accordance with Stalinist discourse, which was far from being alien to the Czechoslovak cultural context. In fact, it possessed more than one appealing aspect to disgruntled social actors who in turn filled their critical speeches and utterances with normative terms from its vocabulary. A Stalinist way of thinking thus permeated spaces of communication and became crucial in deciding what was legitimate and what was not, including Stalinist regional elite themselves.

Third facet: Populism at the regional level

A more peculiar variety of accusations against Stalinist regional elite concerned their so-called populism. They were blamed for bypassing proper mediatory channels of party administrative structure in order to establish themselves personally. Let us consider again the story of Mikuláš Landa's visit to the coal mines. Landa supposedly went down to work with the miners and then sharply criticized their superiors. It is not difficult to figure out why this stunt caused indignation among local functionaries: their leadership was usurped by a higher authority which they rightly deemed to be offensive. Their status, as a result, was significantly demeaned.

The individual who went the furthest in this respect was once again Otto Šling. Znojmo district functionaries complained that Šling, as head of a regional screening commission, visited their city and oversaw a large-scale review of leading district functionaries. It was not a secret procedure; on the contrary, the whole operation was carried out publicly. 'The screening was attended by 700 to 1,000 Party members daily and in the first days even by non-members and candidates of the Party … many functionaries from local and factory organizations [stated] that they watched it with great interest and that deemed it more entertaining than a theatre play.'[22] In front of this audience, Otto Šling and his collaborators posed district dignitaries blunt questions like 'People say that you are a womanizer. Is it true?' or 'Did comrade Vala bribe you with salami?'[23]

Charges of populism are significantly different from previous allegations of dictatorial leanings and improper conduct. For example, it is difficult to believe that populist tendencies, in their attempt to be liked by the people, would be seen as something negative. The head regional secretary in Olomouc, František Řezníček, was, for instance, praised for his visit to the Lipník factory, where he allegedly displayed a friendly attitude towards the local workers.[24] Strikingly enough, this praise was carried out by one of the factory's employees during a session of the regional committee where Řezníček faced harsh criticism from Alexej Čepička, the minister of defence who was also Klement Gottwald's son-in-law.[25] This scene has some interesting implications. For one, it proves that remarks about Stalinist regional elite could also be approbatory and positive. Of course, such remarks were in the minority, but they do offer a different perspective and show these elite to be caring champions of the people. On a more analytical level, the remarks point to the complexity of the contemporary discourse. In this case, one particular social actor used one of its core elements – highlighting the working-class status of a regional functionary – in order to defend him against the party centre. Far from being a simple tool for creating obedient subjects, the Stalinist discourse could become disruptive for the highest party leadership through an unchecked hierarchical flow of power. The relative importance of individual members (or groups) was not determined solely by their position within the administrative structure but also by their ability to speak the Stalinist language. This fact highlights the role of the party organism as a space of communication, where everybody – if respecting inviolable general rules – was able to present their complaints and to pass judgement.

Nevertheless, the predominant view of Stalinist regional elite was one of arbitrary despots with an insatiable appetite for power. They were not averse to coercion, abuse, demagogy or even criminal activities. On their rise to power, they viewed the complex social fabric of the local level as two evenly manipulable strata: the functionaries as prone to being intimidated by bullying; the common people as prone to being seduced by populism. This two-sided approach was to serve as their general strategy. The result seemed to be universal hatred against them displayed by each of the concerned groups. Stalinist regional elite also exhibited a surprising level of independence from the national party headquarters, which was reflected in their blasphemous statements regarding the highest leadership. Pushed to its extreme, this vision portrays Czechoslovakia as a loose conglomerate of autonomous local dictatorships, each controlled by a dictator or a group of dictators interested only in pushing their own particular agendas.

Fortunately for the Stalinist Party leadership, the legitimacy of the Stalinist discourse was not based solely on the perception of its regional elite. As noted earlier, the criticism of these regional elite was also articulated using values and expressions of the Stalinist discourse. These were shared throughout the party structure – by the central leadership, local functionaries and rank-and-file members. It is of course more difficult to assess what the rest of the population might have thought of the situation. It would be an exaggeration to claim that the rest of society was pervaded with the Stalinist discourse to the same degree as communists.

However, it would be equally preposterous to pretend that these two were separated by an impenetrable barrier. The KSČ was a mass party in the truest sense of the word. It was the largest Communist Party per capita in the whole Eastern Bloc. Historian Michel Christian has pointed out that this was not primarily due to mass recruitment among civil servants, but thanks to a distinctive implantation within the working class and to a lesser extent also in the countryside.[26] Therefore, the majority of the party members were simple workers and they faced the same worries as non-party members. They met with each other regularly and exchanged opinions. It is only logical that in this manner – a considerably more effective one than official means of propaganda –Stalinist discourse spread within the general population and exerted an indirect influence on popular opinion. Ordinary people and party members doubtlessly despised Stalinist regional elite equally.

Another important aspect of the Stalinist discourse is that the negative judgements regarding individual representatives *of* the system in no way hampered the belief *in* the system itself. This highlights one important aspect of the Stalinist discourse: its ability to transform potentially systemic criticism into a personal one. This is why the practice of scapegoating, classically associated with Stalinism, was so successful. In its ability to personalize blame, the contemporary discourse served as one of the main grounds for sanctioning the Stalinist dictatorship and the highest party leadership. Stalinist regional elite practised the same strategy, for a time with a modicum of success. Alas, their presence in the regional context was too visible to enable them to permanently shift the blame onto someone else (ideally their subordinates). Scapegoating was not an abstract undertaking, but was to a certain extent related to material reality. That partly explains why it in turn also hit (most notably in the personality of General Secretary Rudolf Slánský) the party centre. Extreme personalization of blame tends to ascend hierarchically, however.

Difficulties in exercising dictatorship

In this section I analyse why the Stalinist regional elite were so widely hated. This might appear unnecessary (given what I have described earlier), but one must be careful when evaluating accusations raised during the Stalinist period. By way of example, social actors turning on Stalinist regional elite pursued their own particular interests. They were either defending their position or seeking advantages. We must also bear in mind that by the spring of 1951, criticizing these elite was considered not only officially acceptable but even a desirable mode of conduct. So we cannot take these allegations at face value, even though to dismiss them completely would also be a mistake. Stalinist regional elite were criticized long before it was considered acceptable, and the charges were surprisingly similar throughout Czechoslovakia.

Yet the contemporary representation of Stalinist regional elite as villainous dictators capable of massive abuses of power was not always fair, nor indeed, in certain aspects, accurate. First, they were not independent authorities. They were selected by higher instances and, if considered unfit for their position, they were removed in the same manner. Absolute control over appointees was an established prerogative of the party centre, and it was never seriously contested at the time.

How can we thus reconcile the popular belief that Stalinist regional elite acted exclusively on their own initiative within their administrative prerogatives? I suggest that a more nuanced interpretation might be in order. The appointment of Josef Stavinoha to the party secretariat of the Olomouc region is a case in point. This decision, reached among the top party leadership, was considered normal at the time. It was Marie Švermová, the general secretary's deputy, who offered Stavinoha his new function. And it was General Secretary Rudolf Slánský himself who persuaded Stavinoha to take it. Yet, seen from Olomouc, the situation looked rather different. Apparently, Josef Zuzaňák, who was then regional political secretary, knew nothing of the transition. He refused to give Stavinoha any work and did not invite him to the sessions of the secretariat. It was a desperate Stavinoha, acting alone, who visited local enterprises and talked to the workers. It was only with great effort and the help of other employees of the secretariat that Stavinoha was finally able to establish himself.[27]

This example enables us to reconcile the apparent contradiction described earlier. The party centre evidently applied its prerogative to choose important regional functionaries. Yet it was Stavinoha himself who had to imbue his appointment with real meaning. I daresay that had he failed to do so the party headquarters would have deemed him incapable and replaced him with someone else. This shows the complexity of the relationship between the centre and the periphery and the importance of individual agency. The central leadership was clearly not exercising absolute control over its subjects. Stalinist regional elite, even those who accepted their subordinate position, had to behave and assert themselves independently if they wished to succeed. Simple deference to the party headquarters was not in itself sufficient. It is therefore clear that the Stalinist dictatorship relied to a certain degree on autonomy and personal practices of domination by its so-called elite.

This does not mean that Stalinist regional elite were left completely without guidance from the party hierarchy. For instance, the deputy head secretary of the Pardubice region, Jiří Kotrch, often informally met with the Central Instructor Marie Šplíchalová and on a few occasions even accompanied her back to Prague.[28] Deputy General Secretary Marie Švermová was also very active. She received selected regional secretaries on multiple occasions – Otto Šling and Mikuláš Landa, to name but a few – at her residence.[29] When Švermová was already under investigation by the State Security and publicly vilified, the head secretary of the Kraslice district, František Machálek, defended her at a Karlovy Vary regional committee session. He stated: 'Švermová touchingly took care of, and nurtured, head secretaries, she invited them into her apartment'.[30] He juxtaposed her sustained attention with the lack of interest demonstrated by the Party Central Committee.

This does not mean that Švermová – as one of the main charges brought against her claimed – created a faction hostile to the official leadership. That would have been impossible to carry out and it would certainly have never crossed Švermová's mind.[31]

Nevertheless, she apparently discussed with head regional secretaries vital policy issues and how to implement them. These encounters shared the characteristic of being conducted in an informal setting; they were strictly confidential and based on personal relations. It follows that Stalinist regional elite did not operate as independent figures, but rather considered themselves as essential players in the party networks. They behaved accordingly. If we wish to understand the true nature of the power structure, this context is of utmost importance. It demonstrates the extent to which relationships between central and peripheral actors were personal, thus pointing to the strong personal nature of the Stalinist dictatorship.

The second element which is important to consider is that the Stalinist regional elite had to work with mostly deficient subordinates. The reports dispatched by regional party headquarters lament both the quantitative and qualitative insufficiencies of the administrative personnel in the party. The latter's fluctuation was enormous. In district committees and apparatuses elected in the spring of 1950, half of the members and functionaries were newly appointed.[32] This tendency was even more pronounced at the regional level. No less than four-fifths of the regional committee members were replaced during the spring of 1951.[33] In regional apparatuses, the average employee lasted in an appointed function less than one year.[34] The agricultural department in the Pardubice region is a particularly striking case: in the summer of 1951, almost 90 per cent of its officials operating in political functions had to be dismissed because of their incompetence.[35]

With such a failure rate, it was only logical that the few who actually succeeded were overwhelmed with work. Even under Stalinism, competence had to count for something. It was not uncommon for one person to hold five and even ten different positions. The district functionary Jan Dluhoš complained bitterly during a screening in the Ostrava region in 1950 that 'he is so overwhelmed by all his positions (eighteen in total) that he cannot sufficiently concentrate on his work as a school and cultural officer … he is overburdened with functions which are related to each other. He is not satisfied with his work performance, because he cannot devote to it as much time as would be necessary'.[36] Dluhoš was just one among many. Understaffing and work overload were two typical burdens in regional secretariats.

It was under these conditions that the latter were supposed to engage in large building and agrarian projects that were to define the whole era. The Stalinist period was a period of intense industrialization and collectivization of agriculture, processes which were to literally transform the whole of society. Stalinist regional elite were endowed with the power to lead these megalomaniac endeavours. They were also required to supervise the construction of giant industrial enterprises, inspect grain requisitions as well as initiate the establishment of state-directed agricultural cooperatives, all with the help of the meagre administrative resources described earlier. The resulting discrepancy between ambitious tasks and the inadequate means to fulfil them was an ever-present phenomenon and a constant cause for concern.

Violence as a sign of weakness

This incongruity vividly manifested itself in the so-called Bílina incident during the 1950 harvest season. The head secretary of the Bílina district, Jaromír Tichý, decreed a universal labour duty and the absolute prohibition of alcohol in the entire area. In effect, 'every able man aged between 16 and 55 and every woman between 18 and 45, living or settled in the villages of the Bílina district ... were required to show up every day at 6 am ... [to] take their part in the harvest'.[37] At the same time, it was prohibited to dispense alcohol in every bar or inn.[38] The failure to comply with this ordinance was punishable by a fine of 100,000 crowns or by a three-month imprisonment.[39] The aim of the decree was simple: to accomplish a 'speedy completion of the harvest'.[40]

At first glance, such an order may appear like the expression of a purely dictatorial mind. In effect it was reprimanded and quickly revoked by the superior regional organization of Ústí nad Labem – headed at the time by Mikuláš Landa.[41] Secretary Tichý seemingly behaved like a ruthless despot, who viewed the local population as little more than disenfranchised serfs, enslaved to do his bidding. However, the situation was in fact more complex, insofar as the Bílina district secretariat was a sad sight to behold. With inexperienced staff (two head instructors and one personnel administrator were appointed only two weeks previously) and long left on its own without instructions, it struggled even to function.[42]

In these circumstances, an order that came from above to finish the harvest to counter what the office deemed an 'unacceptable deadline' proved to be the last blow.[43] The district functionaries strained themselves to the fullest in their attempt to accomplish this impossible mission. Yet the task ahead was too ambitious and the level of disorganization too high. The so-called 'volunteers', who were mostly workers sent from the city to help in the countryside for the duration of the harvest, were completely useless. They 'were stopping at the pubs, where they remained instead of working'.[44] Under these conditions, Secretary Tichý and his subordinates feared a complete failure, with severe repercussions for them. That is the context in which they decided to issue the fateful decree. It was not meant to exhibit their arbitrary power, but instead as a desperate measure to fulfil the central goals of the movement. It demonstrates that Stalinist elite were not necessarily driven by caprice or by the sense of their own omnipotence, but by arduous circumstances. Perceiving their position as volatile and the local society as recalcitrant, they acted accordingly.

This case is highly instructive for a proper understanding of how Stalinist dictatorship operated on the periphery. It would be pointless to deny its oppressive, even criminal nature. But the application of repressive practices was not always a sign of total control. Historian Muriel Blaive demonstrated that the scale of persecution in Czechoslovakia was by no means unique and cannot explain the long-term stability of the system.[45] I would add that on the periphery, the erratic and desperate nature of the repression paradoxically serves to demonstrate the weakness of a Stalinist dictatorship that maintained its domination on the regional and district levels through ad hoc procedures and haphazard violence.

The fall of the regional Stalinist elite

In this chapter's first section, I argued that the Stalinist discourse achieved a high level of acceptance among party functionaries, rank-and-file members and even society at large. In the second section, I pointed to the fact that the Stalinist dictatorship, in its show of domination was, at the periphery, rather fragile. In this third section, I show how these phenomena intersected and determined the legitimacy of the system during one particular chain of events, the fall of the Stalinist regional elite.

This process reached nationwide proportions with the deposition of Otto Šling, head secretary of the Brno region, in the fall of 1950. He was arrested by the State Security and branded a traitor. His denouncement was indubitably prepared in party headquarters, but initiated and accelerated by several party organizations in Šling's former administrative domain.[46] This process reflects the binary nature of the procedure, where both centre and periphery (regional actors) played an important role.

A critical period followed during which Stalinist regional elite faced harsh criticism and a rapid downfall. In retrospect it is quite fascinating to observe that they had initiated this process themselves, for it was they who related the Šling case to the state of affairs in their respective administrative domains.[47] The conduct of the Plzeň head secretary, Hanuš Lomský, was in this respect exemplary. At the October 1950 session of his regional committee, Lomský spoke extensively of Šling's 'dictatorial methods'.[48] He even used this opportunity to address deficiencies in his own administrative domain and criticized the 'absence of team spirit in the decision-making process', 'overlooking voices from below' [ignoring complaints from party rank-and-file] and the 'suppression of criticism'.[49] By resorting to typical phrases of the Stalinist discourse, Lomský undoubtedly hoped to get the approval of the party centre and sought to strengthen his own position within the regional organization. In the beginning it worked, and his speech was universally approved by the meeting's attendees.

However, the position of the Stalinist regional elite was fast deteriorating. During the winter and spring of 1951, they were flooded by a wave of criticism, as noted in the first section. At first, they naturally tried to defend themselves in partial admissions of guilt and vile attacks on already-fallen colleagues, emphasizing disputes they allegedly had with them in the past. For instance, the Ostrava head secretary, Vítězslav Fuchs, claimed that he had experienced his first clash with Otto Šling as early as in 1939.[50] Fuchs was thus trying to neutralize potentially dangerous liaisons that bound him to a would-be 'enemy of the people'. It did not work. Stalinist elite became the universal scapegoat for everything wrong in the system, and while some were already interrogated in the prisons of State Security, others resorted to anxious professions of faith or self-flagellation. Their despair was best summarized by the self-deprecation professed by deposed head secretary of the Pardubice region, František Jičínský: 'I never should have been Head Secretary ... I was not good enough ... I know that I am a bad communist.'[51] The fall of Stalinist regional elite was by no means a gentle procedure.

The party centre played an essential role in the matter. It disseminated official vocabulary and interpretations that were frankly hostile to these regional elite. The highest party leaders attacked them personally, as did officials sent from the centre to the periphery. If we also take into account the sinister task undertaken by State Security, it appears that the centre stood out as the only decisive force. Yet the contribution of regional actors should not be overlooked. The comparison between the depositions of Stalinist regional elite in two regions, Plzeň and Olomouc, is revealing in this respect. In Plzeň, the procedure was extensive and brutal. Local functionaries and party rank and file were not satisfied with Hanuš Lomský's mere arrest. They attacked several of his collaborators. In the end, no fewer than five members of the regional presidium, two employees of the secretariat and one member of the national parliament were ousted from their positions.[52] In Olomouc, on the other hand, the situation was completely different. Far from attacking the head regional secretary František Řezníček, local actors actually defended him.[53] He was eventually deposed anyway, but he was the only one in the regional power circles who met this fate. Without regional support, the campaign against the Stalinist elite lost its dynamic, which in turn reduced its impact.

With a few exceptions, the fall of Stalinist regional elite was a nationwide process in which a comprehensive range of social actors took part. It was generally perceived as a beneficial endeavour that purified the party. The indictment of Stalinist elite provided an explanation for the dire economic situation, the abhorrent power practices on the periphery and a general feeling of helplessness among party members. It provided an opportunity for individual voices to be heard. Finally, it offered an intelligible solution to accumulated problems strictly based on an individual, non-systemic basis. As such, the deposition of hated regional elite provided the Stalinist dictatorship with a significant source of legitimacy, a circumstance that was repeatedly recalled, for example, during the regional conferences of June 1951.

Most importantly, during the infamous Slánský show trial in November 1952, several fallen Stalinist regional elite appeared as co-defendants or witnesses, or their names were mentioned. This shows that the fall of these elite and the preparations of large-scale show trials of prominent communists were part of the same scapegoating technique. Its message was poignantly described by historian Peter Meyer: 'Not the party and the government, but wilful distorters of its policies, acting in the interest of expropriated capitalist and foreign imperialists, were guilty of the prevailing misery and oppression.'[54] At the same time, the presence of Stalinist regional elite during the

Slánský trial undoubtedly provided the whole undertaking with additional credibility. It would be an exaggeration to claim that their presence was the exclusive source of legitimacy for the trial but it did play an important role, especially on the regional level. The same applies for the system in general and its *modus operandi*. Instead of relying on pure administrative violence, the Stalinist dictatorship was able to generate consensus and obtain the necessary approval of the public. By punishing the Stalinist regional elite, the Stalinist central leadership was granted a relatively favourable popular opinion.

Conclusion

In this chapter, I have focused on three specific topics regarding Stalinist regional elite and their overall significance on the practices of domination and approval in the early communist dictatorship. First, I focused on the negative reputation of the elite with its three main aspects: criticism of dictatorial tendencies, selfish individualism and populism. I pointed out that these condemnatory judgements were expressed almost exclusively in terms of contemporary Stalinist discourse. The interpretation I offered for this apparent discrepancy stressed the importance of the discourse itself, which enabled regional actors to voice their discontent while still adhering to principal Stalinist values. At the same time, it was beneficial for the system since it explained deficiencies in strictly individual, non-systemic categories. This explains why the practice of scapegoating, so typical of the Stalinist dictatorship, functioned and even served as an instrument of popular approval.

In the second section, I focused on the sources of the universal disapproval suffered by Stalinist regional elite in the context of their rule. Stalinist elite clearly did not establish a firmly grounded, elaborate system of domination over their constituents. Theirs was more a body of ad hoc practices inspired by situational needs, as a result of the overall chaos that existed at the time. They were to implement a revolutionary transformation of both agriculture and industry, which was a distinct feature of Stalinist policy, while lacking basic administrative or organizational instruments. The result was pervasive anarchy and violence. It shows the discrepancy between the aims of the system and its resources, while revealing a general weakness of the Stalinist dictatorship in its everyday domination practices.

Finally, I studied the fall of the Stalinist regional elite. This demise was a joint endeavour of the party centre and of competing regional actors, giving the whole procedure nationwide proportions. The two groups were linked by a common use of the Stalinist discourse, which undoubtedly restored impaired ties between them and provided the system with a much-needed legitimacy. We can thus claim that the Stalinist dictatorship was not entirely based on violence and oppression. While violence and oppression were undoubtedly present and terrifying, instead of causing submission they produced resentment. The violence resorted to by Stalinist regional elite against local actors was almost universally hated and rejected.

On the other hand, the violence used against Stalinist elite won a significant amount of approval. But it is to be noted that it was a request from the social actors from below. It leads us to the general conclusion that what was essential for the functioning of the Stalinist dictatorship was its ability to achieve legitimacy rather than its ability to achieve violence per se. This legitimacy was reached mainly thanks to the Stalinist discourse, which provided various actors with instruments for voicing critical judgements of their immediate oppressors. At the same time, it conveniently rendered their actions strictly systemic. Social actors from below might occasionally criticize certain decisions or particular members of central institutions; however, this criticism was viewed as a safeguard and as the main source of a much-anticipated remedy. It was one of the key reasons why the Stalinist dictatorship in Czechoslovakia, however deficient and oppressive, never faced the serious threat of its own downfall and even enjoyed a marked level of popular support.

Notes

1   Jiří Maňák, *Proměny strany moci III: Početnost a složení pracovníků stranického aparátu 1948–1968* (Prague: Ústav pro soudobé dějiny AV ČR, 1999), 30.
2   Most recently and extensively in Michel Christian, *Camarades ou Apparatchiks? Les Communistes en RDA et en Tchécoslovaquie (1945–1989)* (Paris: PUF, 2016).
3   Václav Kaška, *Neukázněni a neangažováni: Disciplinace členů Komunistické strany Československa v letech 1948–1952* (Prague and Brno: Conditio Humana and Ústav pro studium totalitních režimů, 2014), 120–130.
4   Christian, *Camarades ou Apparatchiks?*, 100–104.
5   Národní archiv v Praze (National Archive, Prague; NAP). 1261/2/5, 41–254, *Ústí nad Labem – Kádrová práce*, 116.
6   *Protokol IX. řádného sjezdu Komunistické strany Československa* (Prague: Ústřední výbor KSČ, 1949), 153.
7   NAP. 1261/2/5, 74–408, *Brno – Kádrová práce*, 156.
8   Josef Bieberle, 'K politickým procesům (Olomoucký případ 1949–1950)', *Slezský sborník* 88, no. 3 (1990): 167–182 (172).
9   Karel Kaplan, *Dans les archives du Comité Central: 30 ans du secrets du Bloc soviétique* (Paris: Albin Michel, 1978), 34–35.
10 NAP. 1261/2/5, 74–408, *Brno – Kádrová práce*, 285.
11 NAP. 1261/2/5, 32–217, *Plzeň – Kádrová práce*, 133.
12 NAP. 1261/2/5, 74–408, *Brno – Kádrová práce*, 216–217.
13 NAP. 1261/2/33, 1489, *VII. krajská konference Komunistické strany Československa v Olomouci: Přerov, 1–3 June 1951*, 321.
14 NAP. 1261/2/33, 710, *Zpráva z okresní konference v Tachově*, 2.
15 Tomáš Hradecký, 'Hodnocení činnosti krajského tajemníka KSČ Mikuláše Landy pohledem regionálních politických složek z doby před procesem', *České, slovenské a československé dějiny 20. století* 8 (2013): 343–354 (351).
16 NAP. 1261/2/5, 74–408, *Brno – Kádrová práce*, 231.
17 Ibid., 190.
18 Ibid., 226–227.
19 NAP. 1261/2/5, 64–358, *Olomouc – Kádrová práce*, 44.
20 NAP. 1261/2/5, 74–408, *Brno – Kádrová práce*, 199.
21 Ibid., 242.

22   Ibid., 158.
23   Ibid., 159.
24   Zemský archiv v Opavě (Land Archive, Opava; ZA Opava), pobočka Olomouc, KV
     KSČ Olomouc, 16–19, *Zasedání pléna 1. 3. 1951*, 49.
25   Ibid., 66.
26   Christian, *Camarades ou Apparatchiks?*, 51–74.
27   Státní okresní archiv v Olomouci (State Regional Archive, Olomouc; SOkA
     Olomouc), Osobní fond Josef Bieberle, *Svědectví pamětníků, Josef Stavinoha*.
28   NAP. 1261/2/5, 54–315, *Pardubice – Kádrová práce*, 234.
29   *Rudé právo*, 4 April 1951, 3.
30   NAP. 1261/2/5, 37–235, *Karlovy Vary*, 274.
31   When Švermová testified before the rehabilitation committee years later, she put it
     thus: '… why should I have created a faction, what for?' NAP, KSČ – Ústřední výbor
     1945–1989, Praha – komise, 17–308, *Odpovědi s. M. Švermové na otázky komise z
     21.2. 1963*, 4.
32   Marek Pavka, *Kádry rozhodují vše!: Kádrová politika KSČ z hlediska teorie elit
     (Prvních pět let komunistické moci)* (Brno: Prius, 2003), 81.
33   Ibid.
34   Ibid.
35   NAP. 1261/2/5, 54–315, *Pardubice – Kádrová práce*, 409.
36   NAP. 1261/2/5, 69–385, *Ostrava – Kádrová práce*, 28.
37   NAP. 1261/2/5, 41–254, Ústí nad Labem – *Kádrová práce*, 90.
38   Ibid., 91.
39   Ibid.
40   Ibid., 90.
41   Ibid., 87.
42   Ibid., 94.
43   Ibid., 93.
44   Ibid.
45   Muriel Blaive, *Promarněná příležitost: Československo a rok 1956* (Prague: Prostor,
     2001), 187–205.
46   Kaška, *Neukáznění a neangažování*, 165–166.
47   The fall of Stalinist regional elite in 1950s' Czechoslovakia is strikingly similar to
     the destruction of Stalinist regional elite in the 1930s Soviet Union as described by
     historian Wendy Z. Goldman, *Terror and Democracy in the Age of Stalin: The Social
     Dynamics of Repression* (Cambridge: Cambridge University Press, 2007), 119–120.
48   Státní oblastní archiv v Plzni (State Regional Archive, Plzeň; SOA Plzeň), KV KSČ
     Plzeň, 27, *Zápis ze schůze KV KSČ 20. října 1950*, 1.
49   Ibid., 2.
50   ZA Opava, KV KSČ Ostrava, 29–35, *Zápis schůze krajského výboru KSČ, konané dne
     30. prosince 1950 v 8.30 hod. v sále sekr. KV KSČ v Ostravě*, 49.
51   NAP. 1261/2/5, 54–315, *Pardubice – Kádrová práce*, 333–334.
52   SOA Plzeň, KV KSČ Plzeň, 27, *Zápis schůze KV-KSČ, konané 11. března 1951 v 8
     hod. v Plzni*, 60; ibid., *Zápis krajského výboru, který se konal dne 21. dubna 1951 v
     Plzni*, 10.
53   ZA Opava pob. Olomouc, KV KSČ Olomouc, 16–19, *Zasedání pléna 1 March 1951*,
     49; 67–68.
54   Peter Meyer, 'Czechoslovakia', in *The Jews in the Soviet Satellites*, eds. Peter Meyer
     et al. (Syracuse: Syracuse University Press, 1953), 156.

4

Policing the Police: The 'Instructor Group' and the Stalinization of the Czechoslovak Secret Police (1948–1951)

Molly Pucci

On 12 April 1949, the instructor group, an elite counterintelligence unit, met to discuss problems communist leaders were facing in regional secret police offices. So far, few offices were acting on orders from Prague to establish surveillance networks on foreigners and the church, the two main targets of security operations.[1] Of concern was the outcome of the 'isolation campaign' [*akce isolace*], a Communist Party initiative in January 1949 to root out Western influence in Czechoslovakia through arrests, intimidation and surveillance operations.[2] So far, Prague had received no information on the campaign from most regional offices and only a little from three offices. The instructors were told to 'get the campaign in motion.'[3]

This meeting gives an unfamiliar picture of the Czechoslovak secret police force (StB) in 1949 that brings into question our common perception of StB officials as radical, uncompromising pursuers of the party's will. Judging by the discussions of the instructor group – a unit dispatched from the centre to ensure that lower-level offices carried out orders – this lack of compliance was less a question of resistance than of officials' tendency to ignore or react passively to orders from above. After the instructors toured regional and district StB offices between 1948 and 1949, the group discussed how those had evolved after the communist takeover in February 1948. When viewed from above, they ranged from zealous pursuers of the party line to shirkers of official duties.

The instructor group has largely been overlooked in the historical literature on the StB and early Stalinist era in Czechoslovakia. Studies of the establishment of communism focus largely on either the takeover of power in February 1948 or the show trials of prominent party officials in the 1950s. Most accounts of both eras are still written 'from above.'[4] Recently, scholars have begun to combine social and political history to explore how the Czechoslovak Communist Party (KSČ) rallied support from below, mapped onto local societies and drew on personal networks in their first years in power.[5] But there are as yet few studies of the 'intermediaries', the agents who moved information between the highest and lowest levels of the communist state administration.[6]

Likewise, there have been few studies of the aftermath of February 1948 – the disorder and chaos that the 'revolution' left behind. The date of the instructor meeting that opens this chapter, April 1949, signified in this sense a turning point in the history of the forces before the communists began to replace old officials and train new ones from the 'working class'. Even after the old officials were replaced, the compliance of lower-level StB offices with central orders was still dependent on local initiative. During the internal party terror in the early 1950s, instructors reported that central orders to build departments in order to root out Zionists, Trotskyites or bourgeoisie nationalists – the key divisions associated with the trial of Rudolf Slánský in November 1952 – were met with incomprehension and stalling in some regional offices.[7] This is a surprising observation in the institution that was supposedly an 'instrument of the class struggle' and whose members had been selected from the most fervent supporters of the new regime.

Most studies of the StB focus on either its organizational structure[8] or the biographies of its most prominent officials.[9] While historians, particularly those of the GDR, have begun to ask how secret police networks mapped onto local social networks, few have asked how the secret police incorporated and collected social feedback from an institutional perspective.[10] The instructors were, among other things, a way for the state to gather such feedback on how and whether policies had been implemented on the ground. Their reports from 1948 do not celebrate the successes or official narrative of the revolution. They contain sober reflections on its chaotic aftermath. It is unsurprising that historians have not studied this unit since the activities of the instructors were hidden from the public eye and appeared in no newspapers from the time. The instructors did not trumpet their actions from the rooftops, as Action Committees did after February 1948 or party newspapers did during the show trials of the 1950s.[11] According to the official instructions of the group, their task was to 'make suggestions' and 'advise' local offices, verbs that understated their importance.[12] And yet, in the Stalinist system, small groups of agents often had considerable (and frequently temporary) power to make changes outside of the public eye.[13] In Czechoslovakia, they were as central to the story of the consolidation of communist power as the figures on the front page of *Rudé právo*, the party daily.

In this chapter, I tell the story of the Stalinization of the StB in four section. First, I explore the evolution of the StB prior to the 1948 takeover. I argue that the communists did not have a monopoly on power in these structures before the takeover. Second, I examine the impact of the revolution on the StB and the corruption and disorganization in the institution that 1948 left behind. Third, I examine how communist leaders created the instructor group to collect information on and reorganize lower-level offices. Fourth, I provide a study of their notes, reports and discussions on the case of one regional office, the office of Liberec, between the end of 1948 and the middle of 1951 to explore how these changes were implemented in the Stalinist era.

Throughout, I argue that the communists' road to power was hardly as planned as totalitarian theorists often assumed and in fact it involved the participation of a considerable number of social actors. I also show how key campaigns were met with indifference and confusion outside of Prague. The show trial of General Secretary Rudolf Slánský in November 1952, moreover, was hardly met with a uniform reaction in the security force. It was pushed forward by members of the instructor group who had spent the past year helping to remake the StB into a Stalinist police force and who themselves would rise as a result of their participation in the investigations for the trial.

Documenting Stalinism

As Thomas Lindenberger has written of the People's Police (Volkspolizei) in the GDR, it is impossible to fully understand the communist state by only examining the texts of the central government. Documents were continually reformulated on their way to the desks of party leaders in Prague or Berlin. Police documents convey not only the 'truth' but also a mix of 'concealment and dramatization, mundane stocktaking and paranoid fixations, routine and improvisation, and varied methods of writing and behaving'.[14]

Instructors, who moved information from above to below, provide an alternative source of information on the internal workings of communist states. There were instructor groups in Poland and East Germany as well, suggesting their role in Soviet-style states more generally.[15] Because they worked outside the public eye, instructor reports contained surprisingly frank assessments on the limitations of communist power and the state's internal problems, including officials' lack of compliance, interpersonal struggles or incompetence. They discussed issues such as torture in StB offices,[16] corruption and theft by state officials[17] and the shortcomings of communist surveillance networks.[18] Their knowledge of these issues was based on personal observations they made after travelling to regional and district offices to study their activities and converse with local officials.

In Czechoslovakia, all instructors were trained operative agents. Several had been recruited from the field of counterintelligence. Counterintelligence officers did not assume that StB agents complied with orders out of ideological belief. They suspected that local agents covered up information, provided self-interested truths and hoarded resources for their own use. Since many instructors had been recruited from the working class, their files evinced prejudice towards older members of the forces, many of whom had been trained in the police forces of the First Czechoslovak Republic. This chapter draws on their reports from the period starting in 1948 to examine the messiness and disorganization that characterized the first years of the communist state in Czechoslovakia.

The StB before February 1948

Most accounts of the Czechoslovak takeover assume that the communists already controlled the secret police force in February 1948.[19] The communists, the argument goes, established a monopoly on key positions in the institution during the National Front era (1945–1948), including the position of minister of the interior. This picture overestimates communist control over the StB in February 1948 as well as the centrality of the StB to the takeover. Of course, as early as 1945, communist leaders did aim to place supporters in key security positions, from lower-level positions on national committees (i.e. local administrations) to the central office in Prague.[20] Between 1946 and the end of 1947, they managed to organize a network of intelligence agents called the ZOB II (an acronym for the intelligence branch of the regional security department – *Zemský odbor bezpečnosti*), which worked covertly for the party in regional offices of the National Front security forces.[21]

And yet, in contrast to security policy in other countries of Eastern Europe, which were governed by martial law (Poland)[22] or the law of military occupation (eastern Germany, Romania, Bulgaria, Hungary), security policy in the National Front was different. For one, it was subject to checks and balances in the National Parliament.[23] Seats on the 'security committee' in Parliament were distributed according to the results of the 1946 elections. The Communist Party had nine posts, the National Socialists (no relation to the Nazi Party) four, the People's Party four, the Social Democrats three and the Slovak Democratic Party four.[24] Non-communist political parties retained checks on major policies including the issue of political education in the forces, which was revoked after an opposition campaign in 1947.[25]

In the context of the post-war period, all political parties in the National Front, moreover, fought to secure state positions, including security appointments, for their members in order to win votes in the national elections. Starting in 1946, politicians, civic groups, national committees and private citizens rushed to secure promotions for as many supporters and acquaintances as they could. The general staff of the security corps (SNB) was deluged with the so-called 'interventions' – requests of political parties and civic groups to grant certain members of the security corps raises. Between October 1946 and April 1947, 683 interventions arrived at SNB headquarters. Of these, 296 were from political parties (95 from the Communist Party, 135 from the National Socialists, 23 from the People's Party and 43 from the Social Democrats).[26] Others were issued by civic organizations such as the Union for National Revolution (a partisan group), the Union for Liberated Prisoners and the Association for Czechoslovak Partisans.[27] An intervention by a prominent politician could grant a recruit officer status without the service normally required for it, a process that tied rank more to social connections and popular endorsement than training or education.

Communist attempts to increase the party's influence among rank-and-file StB officials, moreover, often met with difficulties. In January 1947, a police official who had joined the Communist Party tried to explain why so many security officials were joining the National Socialist Party, the communists' main rival.[28] He attributed this lack of respect to social class and age of the officials that the communists were recruiting as much as their party membership. He described a communist political education officer as 'a 21-year-old boy, from a non-military background, who, aside from the village in which he was born, has seen nothing and whose only life experience has been to graduate from a one-month political education course'.[29] He claimed that members of the National Socialist Party mocked communist political education officers: 'Look at what kind of leaders [the communists] have! They have no professionals! Look at who they sent us. People off the street, incompetents, work-shirkers, and inexperienced boys of doubtful moral qualities. They sent us those that represent themselves.'[30] A

Soviet report from June 1947 likewise expressed concern that the Czechoslovak Communist Party had insufficient control over state institutions. It specifically noted that although the KSČ had built an impressive party apparatus, its control over state institutions, including the Ministry of the Interior, was weak.[31]

Dissolving the state: Action Committees in the SNB

The communist coup in February 1948 only created more uncertainty about the loyalty and reliability of the institution by unleashing chaos in the force. On 21 February, communist leaders radically decentralized power to local offices to decide who to expel from its ranks. Rather than selecting agents through careful background checks, they devolved the authority for deciding who could serve in the new state to 'Action Committees'. Action Committees were revolutionary councils of communists and communist supporters that formed rapidly, and often spontaneously, in every area of state and civic life after the coup in February. While this story has been told elsewhere, its influence on the national security corps (SNB) is virtually unknown.[32]

The internal purge of the security forces began in March 1948.[33] This decree devolved control over personnel suggestions in the security forces, including firings, forced retirements and transfers, to local StB offices, Action Committees and security consultants (the head of security policy in local administration).[34] Since locals joined Action Committees on their own initiative and decided who to expel with little interference from the central government, the number of security officials they expelled differed in each place. According to reports, in Sedlčany, a district south of Prague, the security chief and the head of the national committee (similar to the position of mayor) had founded an Action Committee as early as 28 February and begun to fire security officials.[35] While communist leaders in Prague generally encouraged popular involvement in Action Committees, they appeared wary of unleashing a revolution in the armed forces. Security officials petitioned to ban them from the SNB since security was a military-style organization in which centralized control over personnel decisions was essential.[36] Action Committees in the SNB were not allowed to issue direct orders, in contrast to the extensive powers they were given in other institutions.[37]

The first instructions outlining the authority of Action Committees in the security forces repeated the decree governing the 'purge of public employees' that had been part of the retribution campaigns against wartime collaborators led by the National Front government in 1945 and 1946.[38] Two days after these instructions were issued, communist leaders expanded the authority of Action Committees to include dissent, the potential for future dissent and moral failings.[39] An addendum to the original decree specified that Action Committees consider four new categories of offences, including unreliability, incapability, incompetence and ineffectiveness.[40]

These charges went far beyond the original targets of the expulsions, which had been members of non-communist political parties. The charge of 'unreliability' applied to those discontented with the new political order and non-political charges such as working incorrectly, working superficially, engaging in 'passive resistance' or not keeping work hours. 'Incapability' related to 'any kind of personal shortcoming that may affect the administration of office', including sickness, negative habits, personal behaviour, character defects, drunkenness, gambling, an amoral lifestyle, arrogance or the careless acquisition of loans. 'Incompetence' described a lack of professional capabilities or experience. 'Ineffective' referred to someone whose work was insufficient, who left work randomly or who 'engaged in pointless activities'. Because of the scope of these charges, Action Committees could in practice fire whomever they wanted for any reason.

The concern that a purge of the security forces would disrupt discipline in the institution proved justified. Action Committees spiralled out of control. In an interview, Rudolf Slánský, the general secretary of the KSČ, warned that purges 'should not be abused to settle personal scores or for self-interested and dishonest goals'.[41] In an article titled 'How to Conduct a Purge', Antonin Zápotocký (the head of the Central Action Committee in Prague) explained to purge institutions that it was necessary to 'get rid of all personal interests, fits of vengefulness, and sadism' before doing so.[42] The demands that people rid themselves of their personal feelings only show that party leaders were aware that citizens were using the power granted by these committees to pursue personal aims.

A notice from March 1948 criticized Action Committees for firing border guards on duty without informing their superiors or giving a motive for doing so (apparently, this had not been a singular incident). It was difficult, the report explained, to replace border guards and it constituted a threat to national security when no one was guarding the borders: 'At the very least, such measures should be undertaken only in the most severe circumstances and after obtaining the approval of a border guard official.'[43]

In March 1948, security officials discussed the changes Action Committees had made in the forces.[44] The outcome looked different in each place, ranging from the removal of four members of the security forces in Ostrava to sixty-six in Most. Between February and June 1948, the number of Communist Party members in the military and security services doubled as compared with the period before February.[45]

This decentralization of authority had, as Slánský and Zápotocký realized, unleashed cases in which citizens had abused power and ignited social conflict. In Písek, the head of the security office demanded that all of the agents in his branch be transferred elsewhere.[46] A member of the Action Committee in Olomouc had a nervous breakdown and committed suicide.[47] In Liberec, four members of the Action Committee were arrested for theft. In several places, locals began to expel members of the German minority from the area.[48]

The reports sent to the central government from lower-level offices justifying the reasons for the expulsions were written in evasive language that makes it difficult to discern true motives. Officials employed the passive voice in reports ('twelve people were detained') or gave impossibly vague reasons for firing people ('negative views of the building of the state').[49] It is difficult to generalize about why people were fired or arrested during this period, although the warnings by communist leaders suggest how frequently personal motives stood behind supposedly 'political' purges. Whatever the reasons, it was left to local communities to decide. The takeover was not a top-down, bureaucratic campaign, but one that relied on mass mobilization and locals to purge their own ranks.

The aftermath of revolution: Disorder in the ranks

In May of 1948, security official Jan Hora, the head of the regional office of Prague, was tasked with observing district StB offices located in the Prague region in the aftermath of the revolution.[50] Hora was one of several 'old officials' who joined the KSČ with police experience from the First Czechoslovak Republic.[51] His first challenge was to find the office. Its location was, in his words, 'wretched'. It was situated haphazardly in at least six different buildings, none of which communicated with one another.[52] 'How, given this state of affairs, are the heads of [the security service] expected to run a united service and carry out oversight?' he lamented. Although he was not entirely sure, he *believed* that the Ministry of the Interior was located in five additional buildings: 'The location of the State Security service today is the result of its creation after the revolution. Out of necessity and circumstances, completely unplanned locations were searched out.'[53]

For months after February, chaos reigned. Rank-and-file party members, emboldened by their participation in Action Committees, continued to intervene arbitrarily in security appointments. At one point, Hora wrote, someone in the party had prohibited the security service from conducting investigations on foreigners. It was unclear why, where the order had come from or to whom the authority to investigate foreigners had gone. In one case, a party official had refused to approve two nominees for positions without giving a reason for doing so. The party member only vaguely accused the appointees of 'speaking out against the Party'. Hora continued: 'Out of interest I am noting that although I attend plenum meetings regularly, to this day I don't know whether these officials were accepted or not, or what type of statement they made against the party.'[54]

He noted cases of corruption in lower-level offices. In some cases, groups of relatives were in charge of security and party branches. In his words, 'unscrupulous characters in the Party' were abusing their power to 'demand restitution for supposed injustices' and attain political success.[55] Security agents had confiscated property from those they had arrested for use in local offices, including cars, typewriters and telegraph machines.[56] Hora noted that the communists had '[tolerated] different types of property theft carried out by members of the security corps, in most cases alongside abuse of office'.[57] Although, he admitted, 'it was necessary in the post-revolutionary era to overlook the punishment of such cases, it is not appropriate to pass by such things now'.[58]

Transforming the StB in the shadow of the upcoming Slánský trial

Given how decentralized these power struggles had been and the corruption that had resulted in many places, communist leaders in Prague did not always know who came to power at the lowest-level security offices or what they were doing. The first task of the instructor group was to collect information on precisely these issues. From the fall of 1948 to the end of 1949, the instructors travelled from Prague to lower-level offices to compile statistics on district and regional offices. Officially, their role was to advise lower-level offices in surveillance techniques and the recruitment of informers.[59]

Unofficially, their role was to report to the central authorities on who was in the office, which policing methods they were using, and to describe the location in which the offices were situated.

Most instructors had joined the Communist Party in or after 1945 and rose to prominent positions in the Stalinist StB in the 1950s. One of them, Antonín Prchal, became the deputy minister of the interior in 1951. Prchal had joined the Communist Party in 1945 through a partisan unit, the Revolutionary Guards. Prchal's personnel file described his talent for agent work and surveillance operations.[60] He had worked in the ZOB II, the communist intelligence network in the National Front. Another instructor was Milan Moučka. Moučka, similar to Prchal, rose to prominence in the later forces in part as a result of his work in the instructor group and the ZOB II. By April of 1953, he was appointed the head of the interrogation department of the StB.[61] He joined the Communist Party in May of 1945 after working as a carpenter and fought with Prchal in the Revolutionary Guards. He served as a chief interrogator during the investigations for the Slánský trial and was promoted to head of the interrogation department after the trial.

The instructor group was involved in implementing many changes in the StB. The first was to assist party members in a major recruitment campaign that began in December 1948.[62] Party members were tasked with recruiting around 8,000 new officials from factories and the armed forces to the security force. Next, the instructors' role was to check the recruits from a professional standpoint.[63] While it is not entirely clear what this meant, it seems from their later reports that it involved checking the age and class background of recruits to ensure that they would be 'reliable' members of the forces.

One meeting of the instructors focused on the issue of torture in regional StB offices. An official first raised the issue that agents were engaging in 'provocation', referring to a practice widespread in the StB in which agents pushed people to commit crimes in order to arrest them (entrapment). This conversation was one of the first that expressed concern with popular opinion of the service. The instructor noted that 'in the public [*mezi lidmi*] it is said that the StB is similar to the Gestapo'. Another responded defensively, accusing the first of 'generalizing'. 'On what are you basing this discussion of provocation? Only when such reports come from a large number of regions can we generalize.' A third lent support to the first opinion by admitting that 'during interrogations in regional offices, suspects are tortured in an unreasonable way given that the goal is to obtain reliable testimonies'. Incidences of torture were confirmed by two other instructors. One noted that he had witnessed torture in an office. When he protested such methods to local officials, he was accused of being 'too soft on the class enemy', showing that local agents were in some cases carrying out the centre's call for 'intensifying the class struggle' with more violence than necessary.[64]

In January 1949, the instructors met to discuss the issue of corruption.[65] Karel Černý, an old communist in charge of resource distribution and supplies in the forces, joined in.[66] They discussed the need for regional offices to establish oversight procedures over property confiscated from citizens who had been arrested or gone into exile. Černý agreed that agents should not be able to take property from people during a house search, commented on incidences of 'questionable morals in the services, and demanded that discipline be more strictly enforced and corrupt agents punished.

In early 1949, the instructors examined whether lower-level officials had built agent networks.[67] They ascertained that the latter only existed in five regions out of fifteen. Even there, they often functioned poorly. In some cases, lower-level offices were overly zealous in establishing surveillance networks. An office in Slovakia had, on its own initiative, created a department to oversee 'films and theatre'.[68] According to the instructors, this department was 'inappropriate' since it was not the task of the secret police to oversee culture.

They also introduced methods of centralized planning to the forces. Moučka noted in early 1949 the importance of pushing regional offices to 'plan' operations in advance rather than working on a case-by-case basis.[69] As is well known, planning was a key organizational principle of Stalinist institutions.[70] With respect to the secret police force, it changed the nature of security operations by making it possible to plan operations years in advance, a shift that involved the recruitment of long-term informers.

The instructors engaged in these and other micro-ways to change the way lower-level officials worked and to correct 'mistakes' in how offices were run. While the events of February 1948 were depicted as a revolutionary break, not least by the communists themselves, the instructors' activity points to the regime's efforts in the two years to follow to quietly ensure that the revolution had actually been carried out on the ground.

Case study: The regional office of Liberec

This section examines the case study of Liberec, a town in northern Bohemia previously populated by numerous 'Sudeten Germans'. According to the instructors, the office still had many police officials who had been trained before the Second World War.[71] Their reports reflect suspicion of the motives and intentions of these officials who had joined the party after February. After all, in the months following February, the Czechoslovak Communist Party had opened its ranks to millions of new members regardless of previous party affiliation, age, class background or occupation.[72] Mass recruitment made sense in the context of the National Front, where popular support in elections had translated into seats in Parliament and control over the political programme. The post-war policy of 'opening the doors of the Party' was halted after recruitment into the party waned and Stalin began to criticize the Czechoslovak communists in April 1948. He wrote that 'a Communist Party cannot and should not be an election apparatus adapted to Parliamentary elections and Parliamentary struggles'.[73] In December 1948, the KSČ momentarily halted new membership. Thereafter, members were accepted only on an 'individual basis' after background checks and multiple levels of bureaucratic procedure.[74]

Instructors' perception of 'loyalty' among StB officials centred, in this spirit, not on party membership but also on the social and professional criteria such as age and training introduced in this later period. In their notes and reports, instructors distinguished between old officials [*starší orgánové*] and newly recruited officials [*nově přijatí orgánové*], the former referring to StB officials who had been trained before the Second World War and the latter to those recruited to the forces after 1945.[75]

Instructors carefully studied the files of local agents and found that there were many continuities in personnel before and after February 1948. Some old officials had demonstrated their loyalty to the party by joining an Action Committee. One reported that a police official, Emanuel Šlene, had joined the police in the First Czechoslovak Republic and served in the Protectorate era.[76] Šlene had joined the Communist Party in March of 1948, an issue that raised a red flag for the instructor but did not require that he terminate his service in the StB. 'Although he joined the Party after February 1948', the assessment noted, 'he defended its interests and had a positive attitude towards the People's Democratic Republic during the events of February'.[77] Šlene was described as 'class conscious' since he had participated in a factory organization and an Action Committee, criteria that tied the concept of loyalty to social activism more than to party affiliation. Between October and December of 1948, officials were assessed for activism, loyalty and knowledge of party texts.[78] The instructor assigned to the case of Šlene concluded that was an 'old, experienced policeman' with thirty years of service and 'significant theoretical knowledge' of Marxist-Leninist literature.[79]

The file of another local official, Ladislav Madle, noted that he had served in the criminal police in Liberec in the First Czechoslovak Republic and joined the Communist Party in 1945. He had worked in the communist intelligence networks (the ZOB II) during the February takeover and, in the words of the assessment, 'held out, never wavered, and passed the test'.[80] Even so, he was not a member of the working class. Although he worked to strengthen the working class through activism, the instructor was concerned that none of the subordinates he selected for service in the office were workers, showing the way that these officials were expected to not only be of working-class background but also to apply class biases to recruitment and promotions.[81] Certainly, the instructors recruited new trainees to security courses on the basis of class background. The file of one new employee, Oldřich Prachař, stated that he had previously worked as a mechanic.[82] After February, he had joined the border guard regiments and served in the Liberec secret police office (StB). He had joined the party in December 1947.[83] The instructor assessed Prachař as 'young', 'immature' and 'non-descript', but a worker, pointing to the way class background was surpassing professional considerations.[84]

While initially there appeared to have been few tensions between older and younger officials in the office, this dynamic began to change when instructors transferred older agents from the forces and replaced them with younger ones. An instructor touring Liberec observed 'uncertainty and discontent among the so-called old members of the StB – those who joined security during the First Czechoslovak Republic or during the occupation – and who now were expected to be transferred to the uniformed services of the SNB'.[85] Across Czechoslovakia, StB officials not considered active or politically reliable were moved to less important positions in the economy, civil police and small factories.[86]

The trial of László Rajk in Hungary introduced more belligerent language to party meetings as it did across the Eastern Bloc.[87] The assertion that enemies had infiltrated the party was repeated in all regional StB offices, including Liberec, where officials gathered in October 1949 to 'assess the Rajk Trial' and set forth a more forceful programme of action to uncover enemies who had infiltrated the ranks of the party.[88] These meetings aired publicly the agenda instructors had implemented secretly for months, such as expanding agent networks and introducing a system of planning to the forces. Under the cover of the hysteria of the Rajk trial, the instructors removed the few remaining officials who had not embraced them: 'It is necessary to change the head of the First Department because he is incompetent and does not use any operative methods in his work.'[89] This campaign applied not only to Liberec. It was coordinated by instructors across the country.[90] In December of 1949, the instructors mentioned setting up listening devices in StB offices, suggesting that the suspicion and paranoia spread by the Rajk trial was leading also to new forms of internal surveillance in the communist state in Czechoslovakia.[91]

After 1950, instructors pushed forward campaigns to seek out enemies in the party. The Soviet advisors, who arrived in Prague in the fall of 1949, had introduced a new vocabulary to the force, including the anti-Semitic charge of 'Zionism'. This charge became the basis of investigations against Slánský and other prominent party officials of Jewish background.[92] The public reactions to these accusations were mixed. On the one hand, thousands of letters of support, many of which expressed anti-Semitic beliefs, poured into KSČ offices in Prague.[93] On the other hand, reports from lower-level StB offices demonstrate that even state officials found these charges incomprehensible. A report from September 1951 noted that few agents in Liberec understood the purpose of the units for investigating Trotskyites, enemies in the party, Zionists and bourgeois nationalists. These units had either not been created or were barely staffed: 'Trotskyites: this target has not yet been worked out, there has not been a list of Trotskyites drawn up in the region. Agents do not know how to work it out. Instruction is clearly necessary in this case.'[94]

The same was true of the 'unit for uncovering enemies in the Party': 'In this target there are two agents. Two files have been drawn up. It is clear that instruction is necessary.'[95] No one in Liberec knew what to make of the charge of Zionism: 'Zionists: this target has no agents and no files. Agents have no idea what to make of it. They lack even basic theoretical knowledge of Zionists. It is necessary to provide instruction because nothing has been done with respect to this target.'[96] Bourgeois nationalists were ignored: 'There are no agents working on this target and no files. Agents have no idea what to do because they are not clear on the issue of bourgeois nationalists. Instruction is needed.'[97]

In spite of the propaganda campaign surrounding these units and the enemy categories introduced by the Soviet advisors, many locals found these terms incomprehensible. Even the newly appointed agents, the young men the instructors had helped bring in from the working class, were in some cases not displaying unquestioning adherence to, or a deep-seated conviction in, the correctness of the party line.

Conclusion

By the time the first five-year plan in Czechoslovakia was interrupted in 1953 after the death of Stalin and due to the imminent collapse of the economy, the instructors had, together with communist leaders, rank-and-file party members and Soviet advisors, left in place an institution different than the one they had begun to inspect in the middle of 1948.[98] In only two years, the instructors had – at a manic pace – amassed information on the people, structures and policing methods of district and regional StB offices. They had shifted the organization of the secret police to a model of centralized planning, expelled officials trained before 1945 and recruited new officials into the service. As their activities show, our linear picture of how a communist security force was built in Czechoslovakia is incomplete. Local actors, such as Action Committees' members, played an important role in the political revolution in the force. Rather than imposing a clear-cut 'Soviet model', the Czechoslovak experience was also subject to different views on who should serve in the forces, whether older, experienced officials or younger members of the working class.

The role of the instructors in spreading the culture of Stalinism to lower-level secret police offices also brings into question the importance of communist ideology in driving forward the campaigns of violence in the late 1940s and early 1950s, which were neither uniformly realized nor pursued radically by every member of the secret police force. The main charges introduced in connection with what became the Slánský trial at the end of 1952 hardly met with enthusiasm or comprehension in all section of the communist state. In some cases, instructors pushed forward decrees, units and campaigns that not been embraced by the lowest levels of the services. The communists, recognizing local particularities, had tasked these elite agents to transform local offices in accordance with a different, more socially informed conception of revolution. The transformation of the StB into a Stalinist-style force required not only to change the political affiliation of state officials but also to replace them with officials from different social backgrounds, a social revolution encouraged or – if need be – compelled, from above.

Notes

1   Archiv bezpečnostních složek (Security Forces Archive, Prague; ABS), f. 310, a.č. 310-29-3. 'Zápis z porady instruktorů', 12 April 1949.
2   Milan Bárta, 'Akce "Isolace": Snaha Státní bezpečnosti omezit návštěvnost zastupitelných úřadů kapitalistických států', *Paměť a dějiny*, no. 4 (2008): 41–50.
3   ABS, f. 310, a.č. 310-29-3, l. 43. 'Zápis z porady instruktorů', 12 April 1949.
4   Karel Kaplan, *Short March: The Communist Takeover in Czechoslovakia 1945–1948* (London: C. Hurst, 1987); František Hanzlík, *Únor 1948: výsledek nerovného zápasu* (Prague: Prewon, 1997); Karel Kaplan, *Pět kapitol o únoru* (Brno: Doplněk, 1997); Václav Veber, *Osudové únorové dny 1948* (Prague: Nakladatelství Lidové noviny, 2008); Jiří Pernes, 'Únor 1948 jako významný mezník ve vývoji československé společnosti', in *Únor 1948 v Československu: Nástup komunistické totality a proměny společnosti*, eds. Jiří Kocián and Markéta Devátá (Prague: Ústav pro soudobé dějiny AV ČR, v. v. i., 2011), 17–21; Karel Kaplan, *Report on the Murder of the General Secretary*, trans. Karel Kovanda (Columbus: Ohio State University Press, 1990); Igor Lukes, 'Rudolf Slánský: His Trials and Trial', CWIHP Working Paper No. 50, 1–79; Bernd-Rainer Barth and Werner Schweizer, eds., *Der Fall Noel Field: Schlüsselfigur der Schauprozesse in Osteuropa* (Berlin: Basisdruck, 2005); Jiří Pernes and Jan Foitzik,

eds., *Politické procesy v Československu po roce 1945 a případ Slánský* (Brno: Prius pro ÚSD AV ČR, 2005).

5   Jiří Pernes, 'Mládež vede Brno: Otto Šling a jeho brněnská kariéra 1945–1950', *Soudobé dějiny* 11, no. 3 (2004): 45–46; Václav Kaška, *Neukáznění a neangažovaní. Disciplinace členů Komunistické strany Československa v letech 1948–1952* (Prague: Ústav pro stadium totalitních režimů, 2012); Michel Christian, *Camarades ou Apparatchiks? Les communistes en RDA et en Tchecoslovaquie: 1945–1989* (Paris: PUF, 2016); Jaromír Mrňka, *Svéhlavá periferie: Každodennost diktatury KSČ na příkladu Šumperska a Zábřežska v letech 1945–1960* (Prague: Ústav pro studium totalitních režimů, 2015); Marián Lóži, 'A Case Study of Power Practices: The Czechoslovak Stalinist Elites at the Regional Level (1948–1951)', in this volume.

6   One of the only studies of the instructors focuses on their role in an operation in 1950. Jan Kalous, *Instruktážní skupina StB v lednu a února 1950 – zákulisí případu Číhošt* (Praha: Sešit ÚDV, 2001).

7   ABS, f. 310, a.č. 310-14-2, 26. 'Zpráva o instruktáži na KV StB Liberec', 28 September 1951.

8   Igor Lukes, 'The Birth of a Police State', *Intelligence and National Security* 11, no. 1 (1996): 78–88; Jiřina Dvořáková, *Státní bezpečnost v letech 1945–1953* (Prague: Úřad dokumentace a vyšetřování zločinů komunismu, 2007).

9   Jiřina Dvořáková, 'Bedřich Pokorný – vzestup a pád', *Sborník Archivu Ministerstva vnitra*, no. 2 (2004): 233–279; Prokop Tomek, *Život a doba ministra Rudolfa* (Prague: Vyšehrad, 2009); Jan Kalous, 'Karel Černý – neznámý personální architekt Státní bezpečnosti', *Paměť a Dějiny*, no. 4 (2010): 70–79; Jan Kalous, *Štěpán Plaček – Život zpravodajského fanatika ve službách KSČ* (Prague: Ústav pro studium totalitních režimů, 2010).

10 Thomas Lindenberger, 'La police populaire de la RDA de 1952 á 1958', *Annales* 53, no. 1 (1998): 119–151; Sonia Combe, *Une société sous surveillance: les intellectuels et la Stasi* (Paris: Albin Michel, 1999); Jens Gieseke, ed., *Staatssicherheit und Gesellschaft: Studien zum Herrschaftsalltag in der DDR* (Göttingen: Vandenhoeck & Ruprecht, 2007); Duane Huguenin, 'Mutations des pratiques répressives de la police secréte tchécoslovaque', *Vingtième siècle: Revue d'histoire*, no. 96 (2007): 163–177. Françoise Mayer, 'Individus sous contrôle dans la société tchécoslovaque de 1945 à 1989', *Cahiers du CEFRES*, no. 32 (2012): 5–13.

11 Action Committees [*akční výbory*] were the revolutionary councils formed by the KSČ after the February coup in Parliament to expel non-communists from state and civic life and consolidate the communists' monopoly on political power. See Jaroslav Mlýnský, *Únor 1948 a akční výbory Národní fronty* (Prague: Academia, 1978).

12 ABS, f. 310, a.č. 310-14-2. 'Stručné směrnice pro práci instruktážního oddílu'.

13 On the tangle of such overlapping, and often short-lived, agent networks in the Stalinist state, see Niels Erik Rosenfeldt, *The 'Special' World: Stalin's Power Apparatus and the Soviet System's Secret Structures of Communication*, trans. Sally Laird and John Kendal (Kopenhagen: Museum Tusculanums Forlag, 2009).

14 Thomas Lindenberger, 'Der ABV im Text. Zur internen und öffentlichen Rede über die Deutsche Volkspolizei der 1950er Jahre', in *Akten. Eingaben. Schaufenster. Die DDR und ihre Texte: Erkundingen zu Herrschaft und Alltag*, eds. Alf Lüdtke and Peter Becker (Berlin: Akademie Verlag, 1997), 317.

15 Ibid. Stanisław Radkiewicz, the head of the Polish Ministry for State Security, discussed these groups in 'Materiały odprawy kierowników i zastępców kierowników WUBP oraz przedstawicieli wydziałów V, 28 March 1948', in *Dokumenty do dziejów*

PRL: Aparat bezpieczeństwa w latach 1944–1956, część 1 (Warsaw: Instytut studiów politycznych PAN, 1996), 72.

16   ABS, f. 310, a.č. 310-29-3. 'Zápis ze schůze', 9 January 1949.

17   ABS, f. 310, a.č. 310-29-3. 'Zápis ze schůze', 15 January 1949.

18   ABS Prague, f. 310, a.č. 310-29-3. 'Zápis ze schůze', 21 January 1949.

19   See Lukes, 'The Birth of a Police State', 78–88; Veber, *Osudové únorové dny 1948*.

20   ABS, f. 310, a.č. 310-21-21, unnumbered. 'Politické problémy národní bezpečnosti', 19 October 1946.

21   Dvořáková, *Státní bezpečnost*, 27–32.

22   Although this term has not generally been used to describe the legal state of Poland between 1945 and 1947, Polish military courts were in charge of sentencing civilians and 'combatants' (members of the Polish underground) during this period. According to Andrzej Paczkowski, 22,000 people were sentenced by military courts in Poland between 1947 and 1948. See Andrzej Paczkowski, *The Spring Will Be Ours: Poland and the Poles from Occupation to Freedom* (University Park: Pennsylvania State University Press, 2003), 234. These courts existed alongside hundreds of thousands of local officials in armed forces that included the State Security Service (MBP), Citizens' Militia, Reserve Citizens' Militia, Internal Security Corps and the Polish military, the 'Berling Army'. These forces, together with military tribunals, were the main source of repressive power in Poland after the majority of Red Army troops had departed from the country. As late as the period 1950–1953, military courts sentenced more than 9,500 people for belonging to 'illegal associations', showing that these courts continued to exert influence into the Stalinist era (Paczkowski, *The Spring Will Be Ours*, 246).

23   On security politics in Eastern Europe, see Krzysztof Persak and Łukasz Kamiński, eds., *A Handbook of the Communist Security Apparatus in East Central Europe* (Warsaw: Institute of National Remembrance, 2005); Liesbeth Van De Grift, *Securing the Communist State: The Reconstruction of Coercive Institutions in the Soviet Zone of Germany and Romania, 1944–1948* (Lanham: Lexington Books, 2012). On the politics of the National Front, see Karel Kaplan, *Národní fronta*.

24   ABS, f. 310, a.č. 310-65-26. 'Těsnopisecká zpráva o 3. schůzi ústavodárného Národního shromáždění republiky Československa', 8 July 1946.

25   Kaplan, *Short March*, 134.

26   ABS, f. 304, a.č. 304-78-1. 'Přehled intervencí a dotazů, zpracovávaných u ministerstva vnitra – hlavního velitelství SNB', 2 September 1947.

27   Ibid.

28   ABS, f. 310, a.č. 310-33-1. 'K politické situaci ve sboru SNB v Čechách', 14 January 1947.

29   Ibid.

30   Ibid.

31   This report was sent to Beria, Stalin, Malenkov and Zhdanov, 'Iz analiticheskoi zapiski zaveduiushchego sektorom OBP TsK VKPb PV Gulyaeva o polozhenii v Chekhoslovakii' (A note on the situation in Czechoslovakia), 22 July 1947, in *Vostochnaya evropa v dokumentach rossiiskikh arkhivov 1944–1953*, eds. T.V. Volokitina et al. (Moscow: Sibirski khronograf, 1997), 651–652.

32   Mlýnský, *Únor 1948 a akční výbory Národní fronty*; Kaplan, *Pět kapitol o únoru*; John Connelly, *Captive University: The Sovietization of East German, Czech, and Polish Higher Education, 1945–1956* (Chapel Hill: University of North Carolina Press, 2000), 127–129.

33 ABS, f. A14, a.č. A14-618. 'Osobní změny prováděné v souvislosti s očistou – řešení', 22 March 1948.
34 Ibid.
35 ABS, f. A14, a.č. A14-618. 'Okresní národní výbor v Sedlčanech: Návrh', 28 February 1948.
36 ABS, f. 304, a.č. 304-103-18. 'Dálnopisem na všechna oblastní velitelství SNB a místní velitelství SNB Praha', 27 February 1948.
37 ABS, f. A14, a.č. A14-618. 'Prozatímní opatření o služebním poměru zaměstnanců SNB odstraněných v rámci zaměstnanců očisty z veřejné služby', 2 March 1948.
38 ABS, f. A14, a.č. A14-618. 'Prozatímní opatření o služebním poměru zaměstnanců odstraněných v rámci očisty z veřejné služby', 1 March 1948.
39 In Czech, the term 'dissent' included the following actions: *negativní postoj proti systému lidové správy; ztotožňování se s názory reakčních politiků; negativní postoj proti znárodňování, proti instituci Revolučního odborového hnutí a ostatním revolučním vymoženostem; šíření pomluv o slovanských státech a jejich zařízeních; nelojální postoj vůči státu; provádění pasivní resistence; neodůvodněné nedodržování pracovní doby a podobné porušování služebních povinností zaměstnanců* (negative attitude towards the system of people's government; identifying with opinions of reactionary politicians; negative attitude towards nationalization, towards the institution of the Revolutionary Trade Union Organizations and other revolutionary achievements; spreading slanders about Slavonic states and their systems; disloyal attitude towards the state; carrying out passive resistance; an unsubstantiated breach of working hours and similar breaches in the professional duties of employees).
40 ABS Prague, f. A14, a.č. A14-618. 'Dodatek k oběžníku ministerstva vnitra ze dne 1. Března 1948', 3 March 1948.
41 Rudolf Slánský, 'O očistě, poslání tisku a růstu naší strany [interview]' (On the purge, the tasks of the press, and the growth of our party), *Rudé právo*, 7 March 1948.
42 Antonín Zápotocký, 'Jak provádět očistu' (How to Carry Out a Purge), *Rudé právo*, 11 March 1948.
43 ABS, f. S, a.č. S-557-4. 'Finanční stráž – zásahy akčních výborů národní fronty', 27 February 1948.
44 Ibid.
45 Jiří Maňák, Komunisté na pochodu k moci 1945–1948 (Prague: Studie ÚSD, 1995), 54.
46 ABS, f. S, a.č. S-557-4. 'Akční výbory a zákroky Sboru národní bezpečnosti', 2 March 1948.
47 Ibid.
48 ABS, f. MNB, a.č. MNB 11/4-104. 'Zápis o poradě přednostů zemských a oblastních úřadoven státní bezpečnosti země České a Moravskoslezské', 11 March 1948.
49 Národní archiv v Praze (National Archive, Prague; NAP), Ministerstvo vnitra – Nová registratura: 5582. 'Dodatek k oběžníku ministerstva vnitra', 10 March 1948.
50 Hoover Institution Archive (HIA). Jiří Šetina Collection, box 27, folder 2, non-paginated. Jan Hora, 'K problémům státně-bezpečnostní služby a bezpečnostní služby vůbec', 4 October 1948.
51 He was in the police between 1931 and 1939. Dvořáková, *Státní bezpečnost*, 60.
52 HIA. Jiří Šetina Collection, box 27, folder 2, non-paginated. Jan Hora, 'K problémům státně-bezpečnostní služby a bezpečnostní služby vůbec', 4 October 1948.
53 Ibid.
54 Ibid.

55   Ibid.
56   ABS, f. 310, a.č. 310-29-6. 'Zápis z porady konané v místnosti instr. oddílu', 15 January 1949.
57   HIA. Jiří Šetina Collection, box 27, folder 2, non-paginated. Jan Hora, 'K problémům státně-bezpečnostní služby a bezpečnostní služby vůbec', 4 October 1948.
58   Ibid.
59   ABS, f. 310, a.č. 310-14-2, s. 21. 'Stručné směrnice pro práci instruktážního oddílu'.
60   Jan Kalous, ed., *Biografický slovník představitelů ministerstva vnitra v letech 1948–1989* (Prague: Ústav pro stadium totalitních režimů, 2009), 151–153.
61   Petr Blažek et al., 'Tváře vyšetřovatelů Státní bezpečnosti', *Pamět a dějiny*, no. 4 (2012): 66–75 (73).
62   ABS, f. Zvláštní vyšetřování, a.č. ZV 4 MV 34, sv. 15, non-paginated. 'Stav a doplnění státně bezpečnostní služby', 20 December 1948.
63   ABS, f. 310, a.č. 310-29-3, l. 9. 'Zápis ze schůze', 9 January 1949.
64   Ibid, l. 12.
65   ABS, f. 310, a.č. 310-29-3. 'Zápis z porady', 15 January 1949.
66   Kalous, 'Karel Černý – neznámý personální architekt Státní bezpečnosti'.
67   ABS, f. 310, a.č. 310-29-3, l. 14. 'Zápis z porady', 21 January 1949.
68   Ibid, l. 18.
69   ABS, f. 310, a.č. 310-29-3, s. 25–26. 'Zápis ze schůzky instruktorů', 3 February 1949.
70   On planning in the Soviet secret police, see Paul Gregory, *Terror by Quota: State Security from Lenin to Stalin* (New Haven, CT: Yale University Press, 2009). On planning in the socialist system, see János Kornai, *The Socialist System: The Political Economy of Communism* (Oxford: Clarendon Press, 1992), 110–130.
71   ABS, f. 310, a.č. 310-14-2, s. 2. 'Činnost instruktáže KVStB Liberec', 5 July 1948.
72   Christian, *Camarades ou Apparatchiks?* 51–56.
73   'Spravka OVP TsK VKPb MA Suslovy: O nekotorych oshibkach Kommunisticheskoi partii Chechoslovakii' (On the mistakes in the Communist Party of Czechoslovakia), 5 April 1948, in *Vostochnaya evropa v dokumentach rossiiskikh arkhivov 1944–1953*, 831–851.
74   Jiří Maňák, *Proměny strany moci* (Prague: USD, 1995), 23.
75   ABS, f. 310, a.č. 310-14-2, l. 2 'Záznam o služební cestě u Z referatu Ostb Liberec', 1 July 1948.
76   ABS, f. 310, a.č. 310-14-2, s. 18. 'Untitled file for Emanuel Šlene'.
77   Ibid.
78   Marie Švermová, 'Prověřování zvýší bojovou sílu strany' (Verification Campaigns Raise the Fighting Power of the Party), *Rudé právo*, 12 September 1948.
79   ABS, f. 310, a.č. 310-14-2, s. 18. 'Untitled file for Emanuel Šlene'.
80   ABS, f. 310, a.č. 310-14-2, s. 47. 'OStB Liberec', 28 December 1948.
81   Ibid.
82   ABS, f. 310, a.č. 310-14-2, l. 13. 'Návrh do techn. kursu', 28 December 1948.
83   Ibid.
84   Ibid.
85   ABS, f. 310, a.č. 310-14-2, 68. 'Zpráva pro 01- Situační zpráva na KV-StB Liberec'.
86   ABS, f. 310, a.č. 310-33-13. 'Pokyny o zařazování pracovníků odvolávaných z funkcí při očistě stranického, státního a hospodářského aparátu', 9 July 1951.
87   George Hodos, *Show Trials: Stalinist Purges in Eastern Europe* (New York: Praeger, 1987), 59–72.

88 ABS, f. 310, a.č. 310-14-2, 5–6. 'Krajské velitelské shromáždění – hlášení', 29 October 1949.

89 ABS, f. 310, a.č. 310-29-3, 72. 'Zápis z porady instruktorů', 15 October 1949.

90 Molly Pucci, 'Security Empire: Building the Secret Police in Communist Eastern Europe' (PhD diss., Stanford University, Stanford, CA, 2015), 229–230.

91 ABS, f. 310, a.č. 310-29-3, l. 92. 'Zápis z porady instruktorů', 12 December 1949.

92 Kaplan, *Report on the Murder of the General Secretary*, 134.

93 Václav Brabec, 'Vztah KSČ a veřejnosti k politickým procesům na počátku padesátých let', *Revue dějin socialismu*, no. 3 (1969): 363–385; Kevin McDermott, 'A "Polyphony of Voices"? Czech Popular Opinion and the Slánský Affair', *Slavic Review* 67, no. 4 (2008): 840–865.

94 ABS, f. 310, a.č. 310-14-2, 25. 'Zpráva o instruktáži na KV StB Liberec', 28 September 1951.

95 Ibid., 26.

96 Ibid.

97 Ibid.

98 Jiří Pernes, *Snahy o překonání politicko-hospodářské krize v Československu v roce 1953* (Brno: Prius, 2000).

Part Two

From Stalinism to Real Existing Socialism

5

Constructive Complaints and Socialist Subversion in Stalinist Czechoslovakia: E.F. Burian's *Scandal in the Picture Gallery*

Shawn Clybor

Real existing socialism does not usually evoke the image of a singing party bureaucrat comparing his love for a shock worker to the joy of fulfilling production quotas. To the contrary, such a scene is so out of touch with reality that it is difficult not to laugh at its ironic absurdity. This was precisely the situation in the people's democracy of Czechoslovakia on 31 October 1953, when the Army Arts Theater (Armádní umělecké divadlo, or AUD) premiered its musical cabaret *Scandal in the Picture Gallery: A Comedy Developed According to the Party Line and With Special Insight into Today's Issues*.[1] Ostensibly the performance was a celebration of everyday life under Stalinist rule, but it served a dual purpose as a public airing of social, political and economic grievances with communist rule. Each of *Scandal's* ten acts and three musical numbers highlight various bureaucratic inefficiencies, misguided governmental policies, individual acts of greed and corruption, and inane political jargon, which are juxtaposed against a blindingly optimistic 'official' portrayal of everyday life.

The effect of *Scandal in the Picture Gallery* was electrifying for those disillusioned by the communist regime, including a teenage Václav Havel, who later drew upon the musical's absurd appropriation of socialist discourse for his first play *Zahradní slavnost* (The Garden Party, 1963).[2] Paradoxically, *Scandal* was also enthusiastically received

Portions of this chapter were presented at the conference 'Cultures of Grievance in Eastern Europe and Eurasia', organized by the Princeton University Programme in Law and Public Affairs, and the Programme in Russian and Eurasian Studies (8–9 March 2013). My deepest thanks to the organizers and participants of these events, especially Martin Dimitrov, Irina Grudzinska Gross and Sergei Oushakine for their thoughtful feedback and advice. Thanks also to those who have provided me with moral and logistical support, including Muriel Blaive, Jessica Brooks, Jacky Kuper and Francis Raška. Special thanks to the late Alena Mišková at the Masaryk Archive of the Academy of Sciences of the Czech Republic for providing me access to many of the materials used in this collection. The bulk of my research, conducted between 2007 and 2014, was funded by the US Department of Education's Fulbright-Hays Doctoral Dissertation Fellowship and the Buffett Institute at Northwestern University.

by political elite in the Communist Party of Czechoslovakia (Komunistická strana Československa; KSČ), including then president Antonín Zápotocký and Minister of Information Václav Kopecký. Less than a month after *Scandal* premiered – by which point the performance was running in more than a dozen theatres throughout Czechoslovakia – the KSČ Politburo proclaimed satire and cabaret humour compatible with the building of socialism. The party's enthusiastic response was short-lived, however; six months later the Politburo changed course and denounced *Scandal* as vulgar and dangerous. Within weeks the musical had disappeared from public life, if not from memory.

The bizarre legacy of *Scandal* as an inspiration to an emerging generation of dissidents *and* Communist Party elite reveals the complex boundaries between collaboration and resistance, constructive criticism and subversion, culture and politics. The 'regime' both tolerated and sanctioned *Scandal* even as it resonated with the general public as an expression of shared grievances against it. That the regime allowed this so-called communal satire [*komunální satira*] cannot be attributed simply to bureaucratic ineptitude or their inability to understand the joke. At the same time, it would also be an oversimplification to view the performance as an act of dissidence. This chapter will take as its point of departure the dual nature of resistance as both a discursive reinforcement and a subversive displacement, and will consider how the *Scandal* scandal reveals the problems and opportunities that cultural producers in Czechoslovakia faced when they attempted to express public grievances against the communist regime in the early 1950s. As a form of complaint *Scandal* operated according to (and indeed reinforced) the relevant norms of official ideology, constituting less a form of public resistance or dissent than a system-stabilizing complaint. What led to its downfall was not the content of its political critique, or even its public reception, but rather its effective appropriation of communist discourse at a time when certain party elite had grown increasingly sensitive to their inability to control this discourse.

Following closely the biographies of those who staged *Scandal,* and its critical reception, I attempt to provide an explanation as to how and why Stalinist cultural producers could both reinforce and subvert the regime in which they participated. I then provide a general overview of the performance – which has never been translated into English and is almost completely unavailable in Czech – supplemented with close readings of several key scenes and musical numbers. Following this analysis, I consider more broadly how political instabilities determined the fate of *Scandal,* which at first benefitted from and later fell victim to power jockeying in Moscow between Beria, Malenkov and Khrushchev, and their web of clients in the Czechoslovak Politburo. This offers a new perspective on regional political instabilities in the Eastern Bloc in the early years of the so-called de-Stalinization. My larger argument is thus that communist political elite sought ways to instrumentalize popular opinion in their internecine conflicts, which in turn created space for the articulation of discontent. In this way, political discontent served as a useful (albeit unpredictable and dangerous) political tool for the creation of a new political consensus following the deaths of Stalin and Klement Gottwald in Czechoslovakia.

Scandalous methodology: Art of resistance and system-stabilizing complaints

Since 1989, Eastern European historical scholarship has focused a considerable amount of attention on the relationship between communist political elite and everyday people – in no small part to better understand the durability (and demise) of communism as a political system. The work of anthropologist James Scott has played a central role in this historiography.[3] Although Scott does not focus in specific on Eastern Europe, historians have appropriated his methodological focus on the practice of political domination as discursive 'public transcripts' that political elite impose upon their subjects.[4] According to Scott, the gestures, speech and practices that are excluded from these public transcripts via repression or censorship do not necessarily disappear, but oftentimes survive as a suppressed 'hidden transcript' in which those who are dominated continue to express themselves 'freely'.[5] By appropriating and expanding upon Scott's methodology, our understanding of political elite in state-socialist dictatorships has long since evolved beyond the classical 'totalitarian' model in which political domination was seen as utterly repressive and absolute. To the contrary, most scholars now agree that communist dictatorships learned how to tolerate, and indeed even encouraged, the hidden transcript of everyday citizens so long as they respected the normative political and ideological boundaries of the public transcript. The key, according to Scott, is that everyday people enjoy the space to 'freely choose' their path in certain matters – no matter how illusory this freedom may be, or how limited the space. Once they do, they become more willing to conform to political domination.[6] This process of *normalization*, as Mary Fulbrook calls it, required the participation of everyday citizens in the seemingly non-ideological institutions, activities and organizations of communist dictatorships.[7] An acceptance or embrace of the public transcript was not required.

Although expedient in the short run, the strategy of communist political elite to allow for an equilibrium between public and private transcripts proved risky and ultimately unsustainable. As Barbara Falk has noted, the offstage discursive practices of everyday citizens ruptured into the public transcript in the late 1980s, and the results were revolutionary.[8] But are hidden transcripts truly an autonomous discourse that outlived and ultimately defeated the repressive mechanisms of communist dictatorships? Scott has suggested that they are – because the parameters of the official discourse determine what must be relegated to the hidden transcript, the official discourse is both constitutive and 'ontologically prior'.[9] Ironically, this point somewhat undermines Scott's central argument that dominant and everyday discursive spheres exist as bifurcated and parallel poleis. In his study of Soviet *samizdat*, Serguei Oushakine argues that offstage 'oppositional discourse' shares the 'symbolic field with the dominant discourse', and thus cannot exist 'outside or underneath' this discourse in the manner that Scott's public/private distinction implies.[10] To the contrary, Oushakine demonstrates that the politically destabilizing dynamic of dissent in the USSR, at least until the late 1970s, rested not in its rejection of the public discourse, but in its ability to mirror and extend this discourse. This was a 'terrifying mimicry' of the public transcript, or 'mimetic resistance', that was subversive not because of its rupturing potential as autonomous free speech (in the model of liberal thinking), but because it created a 'structural noncorrespondence between the dissidents' (subordinate) social location and the type of (authoritative) discourse they borrowed and tried to master'.[11]

While Oushakine offers a more fluid understanding of dissent as both rupture and mimesis, he focuses primarily on a discourse that exists in a clearly delineated alternative social location – the realm of *samizdat*.[12] But how can we account for resistance that is articulated in an 'official' capacity from *within* the official framework of a dominant public transcript? If and when such an articulation occurs, how is it possible to distinguish between a primary source of articulation and an alternative social location? Such distinctions are easy to parse when they involve political elite who invoke official government discourse and oppositional figures who exist outside that discourse, but what about the divisions *between* opposing factions of political elite? Local party functionaries could (and did) challenge the discourse of central authorities, just as cultural producers could (and did) challenge party functionaries. Indeed, according to Marcin Kula, 'the world under communism did not divide into "society" on the one side and "power" on the other. Rather there existed a continuum. Even members of the Political Bureau might find themselves thinking and speaking with the pronoun "them," as in us against them'.[13]

Our understanding of oppositional discourses in communist states and the relationship between party elite and everyday people is further occluded by our conceptual vocabulary. Scholars tend to employ terms such as 'resistance' and 'dissent' to describe a broad spectrum of complaints and grievances, but the assumption is that any form of complaint, no matter how mundane, is fundamentally destabilizing to communist dictatorships. The reality was often quite different – hidden transcripts could also reinforce and stabilize communist domination. This is why party elite in the Soviet Union and Eastern Europe from the 1960s onwards sought to unearth and understand their citizens' preferences with public opinion surveys. They even tolerated, if not *encouraged*, complaining, so long as these complaints were officially authorized or remained off the public transcript.[14] According to Martin Dimitrov: 'This decision is driven by practical concerns for regime preservation: information allows for governance problems to be identified when they are still manageable and do not threaten to lead to regime instability'.[15] In other words, challenges to communist political rule served a positive and regime-stabilizing function – they allowed the regime to better understand citizen preferences and, when necessary, to make adjustments to its ideology and political rule.

Scandalous performance: Satirizing the terror

Although *Scandal in the Picture Gallery* premiered more than a decade before communist elite began gauging citizen preferences with rigorous and standardized polling, in several important respects it served a similar function as an officially tolerated articulation of grievances that appropriated the public transcript of the communist dictatorship during the 'Stalinist era'. The performance was the collaborative product of two prominent and outspoken satirists: the playwright Václav Jelínek (1920–1982) and the theatre director Emil František (E.F.) Burian (1904–1959). Jelínek was a social worker and municipal bureaucrat who became a radio producer at Czechoslovak State

Radio (Československý rozhlas) after 1945. The communist seizure of power in 1948 had a positive impact on his career trajectory – amid party-led purges he became director of the station's central advisory council. Among his many responsibilities, he produced the weekly radio broadcast '15 Minutes with Antonín Zápotocký' – a series of 'fireside chats' with the prime minister and later president. While working as a radio producer, Jelínek began writing plays and screenplays, and became chief editor of the satirical illustrated publication *Dikobraz* (Porcupine) in 1954. E.F. Burian was a multitalented singer, composer and dramaturge who founded the experimental avant-garde Theater D. During the interwar era, Burian had been a prominent avant-gardist and a devout communist, although he enraged many of his friends and comrades with an outspoken criticism of Stalin in 1938. He was also an outspoken anti-fascist and openly criticized Hitler and the Gestapo after the German occupation of Prague in 1939. He was arrested for his provocations in 1941 and spent the next four years in concentration camps. After surviving a death march to the North Sea, he returned to Prague a defiant communist hardliner. His outspokenness irritated party functionaries, who repeatedly tried to purge him from public life. He survived the Stalinist era, however, thanks to the intervention of several high-powered admirers, which included President Gottwald. To avoid losing his theatre, Burian joined the Czechoslovak army, became an honorary lieutenant and rebranded Theater D as the 'Army Arts Theater' (Armádní umělecké divadlo; AUD).[16] *Scandal* would become his first and only smash hit of the communist era.

Scandal begins by simultaneously reinforcing and undermining its titular claim to provide 'special insight into contemporary issues'. Even before the curtain rises, an announcer notifies the audience over the PA that the show has been cancelled. To explain this decision, the playwright walks up the aisle and clambers onto the stage, where he nervously mumbles an explanation to an increasingly raucous and noisy crowd. The announcer begins relaying this nonsensical muttering over the PA so it can be better heard and translates his grunts into an articulate apology. According to the playwright, as translated over the PA, *Scandal* has been cancelled because it addresses topics that are 'simply too serious for tomfoolery'.[17] Instead, in the spirit of realism, random people off the street have been asked to come onstage and re-enact scenes from their everyday lives. After each re-enactment, the playwright will lead a question-and-answer session that will allow audience members to 'express themselves'.[18] The joke, of course, is that the entire scene is scripted: the announcer, the playwright and the raucous audience members are all actors, just as the ten scenes to follow and the 'everyday people' performing them are all scripted. From the very beginning, the idea of 'reality', whether the performance itself or the everyday life it claims to depict, is completely undermined. It is a reality that is both mediated and opaque: the 'playwright' is an actor who speaks nonsense that must be 'translated' through a PA system by a disembodied voice of another actor to an audience that has been infiltrated by actors. During an era of rehearsed show trials and intense media censorship, the performance's reality was in fact *no less real* than the public sphere of Stalinist Czechoslovakia. Both presented a falsified version of reality in the framework of a fictionalized performance as if they were objectively happening. The resulting non-correspondence is precisely what makes *Scandal* so effective as satire: it reveals the flaws underlying official ideology through ostensibly uncritical adherence. Given the conceptual complexity of this endeavour, one can only wonder if the occasional audience member took the performance at face value and spoke freely during the question-and-answer sessions – the final transformation of falsehood into reality.

At several key moments, the social and political criticism underlying the performance breaks through its own crust of mediated reality. In the second act, entitled 'Hallelujah, We Have a Bureaucrat!' a man visits a technology exhibition, at which his tour guide introduces him to a robotic office worker that belches out meaningless communist jargon such as 'we must collectively determine the answers to the great problems that stand before us'.[19] The visitor politely interrupts the robot to ask about a new model of automatic dishwasher. When the tour guide feeds the request into the robot, it continues to babble:

> I maintain without slogans and without vague statements: many problems still stand before us. Indeed, we must understand the question and the various angles of its underlying causes. Nevertheless, we discussed the issue at length and we can be glad that, at the end of the day, we have occupied ourselves with its various perspectives. Finally, I am building, I am building, I am building, I am building.[20]

As the curtain drops, the guide searches frantically for the robot's power switch and yells: 'Where's the power on this thing? Cut the power! Everything about it is exhausted!'[21] The 'it' is left ambiguous – it could signify the robot, the robot's lingo or the entire scene – because the moment the curtain drops, an overeager plumber runs onstage to promote his local business, a deliberate attempt to change the subject by an actor pretending to be an everyday citizen. The endless drone of false reality thus maintains control of the proceedings: neither the 'robot' onstage, nor the 'plumber', nor the 'audience' (both real and fake) are allowed to veer from the official script of Stalinist discourse.

How radical was the performance? Although satire was extremely rare in Stalinist Czechoslovakia, the genre enjoyed a long, if complicated, history in the USSR that stretched back to the earliest years of the Bolshevik Revolution.[22] The idea of a specifically 'socialist' form of satire solidified with the rise of socialist realism in the 1930s: the goal was to provide constructive criticism that contrasted individual vices and flaws against the ideals and achievements of Marxism-Leninism. In other words, satire could point out flaws in Soviet society, but it did not expose these flaws as systemically linked to political, economic or ideological structures. In this regard, *Scandal* was not atypical. For example, in the first act, 'On Account of My Wife', a local party bureaucrat and his wife attempt to scare their neighbours into giving away their all-inclusive vacation certificates by casually mentioning avalanches, bear attacks and dangerous waters. The scheme backfires, however, when their neighbours embrace their trips as an opportunity to overcome their fears and try something new.[23] Similarly, in the third act, 'Before They Caught Him', a lazy family brags about the illnesses they faked to take time off work for a pig roast. As they laugh about their fake maladies, they turn to their neighbour, who showed up uninvited and complained about a headache. 'So, what brought you here then, your headache?' they ask him. He responds: 'Nope. Surveillance. Checking up on people who call in sick.'[24] In the sixth act, 'The Certain Party Man', a party activist is going through personnel files in search of someone to become the manager of an auto plant. After weighing several candidates closely, he realizes that maybe a woman should become the manager, because after all they are just as capable as men. He immediately calls his mother to tell her the good news: 'No more unemployment for you!'[25]

What makes *Scandal* exceptional compared to Soviet satire is not that it illuminates the corrosive effect of individual selfishness, corruption and nepotism on socialist society; but rather, at a more implicit level, it suggests that state socialism itself has corroded individual behaviours. In the fourth act, 'Speak Not of the Unknown', the young author Kadeřábek must seek permission to publish an article celebrating the Czechoslovak Army. His boss Comrade Poplašný is the division chief at the party's personnel office, infamous for its role in investigating party members during the show trials. The scene begins with a distraught Comrade Poplašný looking around for his desk, filled with 'sensitive state secrets', which has mysteriously gone missing. Meanwhile, Kadeřábek enters the office and hands him a copy of his article, which, he explains, depicts simple country life. Unimpressed, Poplašný demands to know if the villagers are portrayed as 'manly'. Taken aback, Kadeřábek responds cautiously that they are, as far as he can tell. Poplašný demands to know if he explicitly wrote this. Kadeřábek responds that while it is peripheral to the story, he certainly implies it. Sceptical, Poplašný skims through the article until he finds a passage that describes a military convoy winding through the mountains and glistening in the afternoon sun. He begins to point out the mistakes:

> There are several shocking revelations here. For example, this part: 'The wheels of the heavy troop transport …' See! You cunningly revealed that troop transports are heavy. How cunning you are to signal to your readers this sort of thing. And here, this part about the motor of a 'silver bird' buzzing overhead? What precisely does that mean, anyway? … Just as I'm asking now, so too will your readers demand to know. And there you are, shoving it in their face that airplanes are flying overhead.[26]

Kadeřábek protests that he intended no harm. Scoffing, Poplašný describes various incidents during which individuals had committed similar mistakes. Each of his stories reveals sensitive state secrets, including plans for a future hydroelectric dam, the location of military fuel depots and research into the new synthetic material 'Eutinbal'. Now quite nervous, Kadeřábek insists that he knows nothing about dams, depots or Eutinbal. Poplašný responds that if only he could find his desk, he would show off the documents to prove they are real.

In an attempt to shift the discussion away from state secrets, Kadeřábek mentions that he has a photograph of the troop transport in question and had planned to publish it with the story. Poplašný explodes with anger:

> Show me this picture! Have you gone mad? A picture! Of a heavy troop transport! Filled with soldiers! … Where exactly did you come upon this photograph? Were you prowling around military convoys with a camera or something? Is that it? You speak up right this moment … how'd you get this picture? Did you steal it from someone?[27]

Kadeřábek sputters: 'The picture ... my ... uh ... my friend gave me the picture.' Poplašný demands the name of this 'criminal' and 'every member of his circle'. As it turns out, Kadeřábek's friend had photocopied the image from a popular Soviet magazine. Poplašný immediately backpedals: 'Oh. I see. Ha. Well, I was just testing you. Look, one must always be vigilant. One must always be alert. So anyway, go on and print the picture. Just make sure you explain where you got it.'[28] The scene ends when a maintenance crew enters the office with Poplašný's missing desk, which they took by mistake. Poplašný begins digging through the drawers and realizes something is missing: a brochure for the new office coffee machine. Kadeřábek exclaims: 'Christ! What if that brochure falls into the wrong hands?' Poplašný, amused at Kadeřábek's naivety, responds: 'Do not fear, my dear boy. It was only a *copy* of the brochure. The original is in my steel safe! One must always be vigilant!'[29] As the curtain falls, the actor who plays Poplašný steps forward and criticizes the playwright for revealing important secrets onstage, especially the secret synthetic compound 'Eutinbal', which 'every small child knows' is not real. He quips: 'It's called Pertonal.'[30]

Typical of socialist realism, this scene is built upon a binary opposition between two character types: on one side is the journalist Kadeřábek, a cautious idealist who submits an article that is humorously inoffensive; on the other side is the paranoid and paternalistic bureaucrat Poplašný, who makes haphazard decisions for almost unfathomable reasons. Ostensibly, the scene is a criticism of Poplašný for his incompetency; however, the real target of the satire is something much deeper: the malevolent and coercive force of fear. Although he has done nothing wrong, Kadeřábek fears that his work will be censored and that his safety could be at risk. By the end of the performance, his fear has intensified to the point of hysteria. Poplašný is similarly consumed by fear. Although his missing desk, a photograph from a Soviet magazine and a stolen instruction manual seem like trivial concerns, to him they are matters of great existential importance. The humour of the scene is thus rooted in the absurdity of both characters' paranoia, but no matter how misplaced this paranoia may be, it is presented as the logical result of forces beyond their comprehension or control. In this regard, *Scandal* is deeply subversive: it moves beyond a superficial criticism of individual flaws to critique the deeper structural forces that generated and perpetuated Stalinist terror.

Scandalous context: Clean and official

The absurdity of life for individuals who are trapped within bureaucracies is a common theme in Czech literary works by Hašek, Kundera, Havel and Kafka (if one can count him as 'Czech'), among many others. What makes *Scandal* unique, however, is that it premiered in an acutely repressive climate and received a curiously positive response from political elite. While it might be tempting to argue that the performance was an early (indeed too early) result of 'de-Stalinization' in the months following Stalin's death, such an interpretation is not plausible for two reasons. First, *Scandal* premiered at the height of the terror in Czechoslovakia, not after its conclusion. Unlike Poland and Hungary, where Stalin's death led to an immediate relaxation, if not an outright reversal, of Stalinist policies, the party line in Czechoslovakia maintained a relatively steady course into 1956 and (in certain respects) beyond.[31] Second, although it inspired an emerging generation of dissidents, key members of the party elite authorized and defended the performance, including many of Stalin and Beria's most trusted allies in Czechoslovakia. Foremost among them was the head of the Czechoslovak Army and Minister of Defence Alexej Čepička, who occupied a unique position as the only cabinet minister to report directly to the Soviet Politburo. This arrangement was a matter of Soviet state security. In a rare exception to the pattern established in other Eastern European countries, the Red Army left Czechoslovakia shortly after the conclusion of the Second World War. When the Cold War intensified, Stalin viewed the speedy build-up of the Czechoslovak Army and the ideological consolidation of its commanding officers as top priorities to defend against Western military intervention. Minister Čepička believed arts and culture would aid in this ideological consolidation, and to fulfil his vision he lavishly funded film studios, artists and theatres, including E.F. Burian's AUD, where *Scandal* first premiered.[32] Because this expansive military-industrial complex answered directly to Moscow, it functioned almost completely outside the control of the Czechoslovak Party leadership. As a result, Burian and Jelínek were not required to submit their script to the Czechoslovak Theatre and Literary Agency and Prague National Committee for approval, and did so only after months of political wrangling, at which point the performance had already become a smash hit.

Party periodicals made no direct mention of *Scandal* when it first premiered in October 1953, perhaps due to uncertainties as to how, or whether, to respond. Although I was unable to locate in the archives any private discussions regarding the play prior to its release, there are several clues that editors and critics anticipated a controversy. On the same day that *Scandal* premiered, the weekly newspaper *Literární noviny* (Literary News) – the official mouthpiece of the Czechoslovak Writers' Union – published 'Vulgarity does not make satire effective', a half-page criticism of Jelínek's productions at Czechoslovak Radio.[33] That such a lengthy criticism of a relatively minor literary figure surfaced on the same day as the premier of *Scandal* cannot be a coincidence. The editorial staff at *Literární noviny* most likely decided to hedge their bets: if the party leadership responded to *Scandal* favourably, then no one could claim that they had criticized a sanctioned performance; conversely, should the party launch a campaign against the performance or its author, then no one could claim that they had failed to anticipate Jelínek's 'unfriendly attitudes'. This decision proved wise. President Zápotocký attended an early showing of *Scandal* and commended it on his weekly radio show in an interview with Jelínek (still his producer). *Literární noviny* cautiously responded the following week with a half-page article by a third-string critic (conveniently, the big names did not posit official opinions), which acknowledged for the first time that the performance was selling out.[34] This was an understatement. According to correspondence with military officials in AUD archives from April 1954, Burian began reneging on his contractual obligation to allot free tickets to soldiers on leave because the performance was already booked for months in advance.[35] According to the review, the play's success came from its satirical take on 'abuses, bad habits, backwardness, inflexibility, bureaucratic mentalities, slovenliness, and character flaws; not from some distant time in the past, or in some faraway land, but the flaws that manifest themselves today, at this very moment, in our very midst'.[36] This positive assessment was followed by a reassurance that although 'rumours' were circulating that the play would 'shut down', the AUD would be increasing the number of weekly showings. The article concluded: 'Jelínek's play is a lesson for all authors that it is possible to offer a healthy criticism that is both clean and official. If a criticism has the proper intentions, one need not cower from it'.[37]

The party's ambivalent public response reflected behind-the-scenes conflicts over political realignments in Moscow that hardly deserve the appellation 'de-Stalinization', but nevertheless reflect subtle shifts that would have seismic ramifications over the following years. In July 1953, the Soviet Politburo (more specifically Beria and Malenkov) made it clear to their loyalist Zápotocký that certain hard-line positions of the KSČ leadership were no longer acceptable. The following month, the Czechoslovak Politburo introduced to the Central Committee a list of proposals and reforms that for the first time acknowledged in writing that certain dynamics of their economic and political policies had been flawed. Hardliners in the leadership, led by the recently appointed party secretary Antonín Novotný, refused to ratify the list; instead, they continued to insist that any failures that had occurred since 1948 were due to individual error and flawed implementation.[38] This conflict, in turn, was amplified by ongoing struggles within the Soviet Politburo, where shifting alliances resulted in Beria's execution in December 1953 and Malenkov's forced demotion in February 1955. Replacing them as party leader was Nikita Khrushchev, who backed Novotný over Zápotocký as Gottwald's successor.

When *Scandal* premiered, the Czechoslovak Central Committee was thus divided in its loyalties. On one side were those who supported Beria, and later Malenkov, and remained publicly loyal to Stalin while calling for reforms. On the other side were those who backed Khrushchev and blamed political and economic failures on the individual corruption of Beria, Malenkov and, ultimately, Stalin himself. It was precisely this divide that explains the meteoric rise and disappearance of *Scandal*. In general, the party leaders who backed Beria and Malenkov spoke positively of the performance and used it as a pretext to call for greater leniency towards political satire, caricature and humour. Those who backed Khrushchev, on the other hand, condemned the performance as a vulgar attack against the People's Republic and demanded that it be cancelled. This division was explicitly clear at a meeting of the Central Committee in December 1953, at which leading members of the Politburo laid out their visions for the so-called 'New Course' reforms in cultural politics. First to speak was Novotný, who criticized satire as dangerous and warned against the 'harmful disdain of our intellectuals'.[39] Next spoke Minister of Information Václav Kopecký, a long-time ally of Beria and Malenkov, who defended satire, cabaret humour and operettas as compatible with socialist realism. Although both men publicly declared that they were in 'complete agreement', the stark difference in their positions was obvious.[40]

By spring 1954, Novotný and his circle of supporters had gained the upper hand in the Central Committee, and their former opponents either closed ranks behind them or distanced themselves from the emerging power centre (among this latter group were Čepička and Zápotocký). *Scandal* became an early casualty of this shifting power constellation. The turning point came in April 1954 with a speech by Novotný that denounced satire for hiding 'the danger of slander against our humanist state'.[41] The party leadership immediately pivoted to follow the new line, and the following week the president of the Czechoslovak Writers Union published an article in *Literární noviny* that accused *Scandal* of 'mocking the achievements of our socialist system'.[42] More than a dozen productions of *Scandal* running throughout Czechoslovakia closed over the following two weeks, forcing several theatres to refund hundreds of advance tickets. Burian at AUD defiantly refused to remove the piece from his repertoire, a decision that no civilian authority had the power to countermand since he answered directly to the army.[43] The Ministry of Defence quietly backed Burian's decision, although Čepička chose not to comment on the affair to avoid a public confrontation. Outraged, Novotný's office appealed to the Soviet embassy, which forced Čepička to shutter the performance.[44] The consequences of Čepička's defiance became clear two years later, when in the wake of Khrushchev's Secret Speech, he was branded a 'Czech Stalin' and purged from the Ministry of Defence. Because Čepička's nearly invulnerable political status was the result of Stalin's patronage, his downfall is easy to mistake as an early sign of the Stalinist 'thaw' in Czechoslovakia. I would argue, however, that it was not his loyalty to Stalin that doomed him so much as his refusal to follow the emerging party line after Stalin's death. His liberal attitudes towards culture, including his support for *Scandal*, reflected – and quite possibly factored into – these conflicts.

Scandalous conclusion

During the final act of *Scandal in the Picture Gallery*, the 'author' returns to the stage and dares the audience to discuss the play and its meaning among themselves. He asks them to be precise, critical and judgemental in their opinions, but to remember that the play was shown to people in high positions, and they approved. When the author is done speaking, the cast joins him on stage and sings:

> *Criticism shouldn't have to be*
> *Criticism shouldn't have to be*
> *Criticism shouldn't have to be personal*
> *Let's save that for when we argue drunkenly*
> *And completely unconstructively*
> *That's not what we're doing here today.*
> *… Let criticism battle our mistakes*
> *Let criticism battle our mistakes*
> *Battle our mistakes, battle for the people*
> *Everywhere, against the rubbish that arises*
> *And for progress, on the great road before us*
> *But in the meantime, leave us the hell alone.*[45]

Through its supposed authentic portrayal of scenes of everyday life, *Scandal* embraced communist ideals and criticized communist praxis in a manner not dissimilar to Soviet socialist realism in the late 1930s. Unlike Soviet propaganda, however, *Scandal* was not vetted by party censors or formulated by party bureaucrats. Jelínek and Burian enjoyed the creative space, no matter how exceptional that space might have been, to feel as if they were 'freely' appropriating the ideological world view of the regime, and then sharpened it into a biting critique. What is important, however, is that the performance functioned within, not against, the normative framework established by party elite in the early 1950s. As a result, it does not fit readily into categories such as 'propaganda' and 'dissidence'.

Ultimately, *Scandal* was the happenstance result of political instabilities that created an unparalleled opportunity for an articulation of grievances from an alternate social location within the regime itself. Perhaps it also offers a glimpse of what communism might have looked like in Czechoslovakia had it been Beria or Malenkov, as opposed to Khrushchev, who emerged victorious from the leadership struggles that followed Stalin's death. Perhaps, even further, it was the memory of *Scandal* that served to remind true believers that socialism with a 'human face' was capable of allowing public criticisms, a core belief shared among many of the anti-Novotný ex-Stalinists who became Prague Spring reformers in the 1960s.[46] Leaving aside these counterfactuals, it bears repeating that a number of leading political figures, including the president, minister of defence and minister of information not merely tolerated *Scandal*, but openly and actively enjoyed it as a healthy expression of 'constructive' attitudes. In this regard, their rhetoric regarding the necessity of free and spontaneous socialist criticism was more than hollow propaganda. It was only once their opponents outmanoeuvred them that they agreed to ban the performance, because they did not dare to publicly defy the myth of party solidarity to defend their beliefs. Nevertheless, the impact of their initial support cannot be overestimated on individuals such as Burian at AUD, who until his death in 1959 continued to insist that what he did with *Scandal* demonstrated the true potential of socialist realism to express artistic experimentation and public discontent.[47] In other words, at a time when many of his colleagues had long since abandoned socialist realism, it was the man who staged the most subversive performance of the 1950s who remained an unrepentant true believer. And for those who remembered his *Scandal,* he represented a glimmer of hope that underneath the ossifying leadership of Novotný and his 'hardliners', there were other comrades who could take a joke.

Notes

1   The performance is extremely rare. Although it was never published, a limited number of manuscript copies were submitted to the Czechoslovak Theater and Literary Agency, which read and approved all theatrical performances. Such materials are deposited in the collections of the Ministry of Information and Enlightenment in the National Archive (Národní archiv); however, the exact location of the performance is not catalogued and is thus unknown. Moreover, because the Army Arts Theatre was subordinate to the military, the performance was not submitted to the Prague National Committee (municipal government), and

is therefore not available in the Prague City Archives. To date, I have been able to locate two copies of the performance. The first is a carbon copy of the performance in E.F. Burian's personal archive, which is part of the 'Divadlo E.F. Buriana' collection at the Czech Literary Archive (Památník národního písemnictví). The second is a manuscript copy printed for the Ministry of Information and Enlightenment, which is currently a part of my personal collection. A digitized copy of the playbill is available online: Václav Jelínek, 'Skandál v obrazárně', Jihočeské divadlo – Archiv, https://www.jihoceskedivadlo.cz/archiv/porad/1063-skandal-v-obrazarne (accessed 3 June 2017).

2   Zdeněk Hořínek, 'Absurdní paraboly v hrách Václava Havla' [Absurd parables in Václav Havel's plays], *Divadelní noviny*, 9 January 2012, http://www.divadelni-noviny. cz/absurdni-paraboly-vhrach-vaclava-havla (accessed 5 May 2017).

3   German historiography in particular has played a key role in the spread of Scott's ideas, which emerged in the work of Konrad Jarausch on Nazi Germany, and were then applied to the GDR in Thomas Lindenberger, ed., *Herrschaft und Eigen-Sinn in der Diktatur: Studien zur Gesellschaftsgeschichte der DDR* (Cologne, Weimar, Vienna: Böhlau 1999), and Czechoslovakia by Muriel Blaive 'Discussing the Merits of Microhistory as a Comparative Tool: The Cases of České Velenice and Komárno', *East Central Europe* 40, no. 1–2 (2013): 74–96.

4   James Scott, *Domination and the Arts of Resistance* (New Haven: Yale University Press, 1990), 20–21.

5   Ibid., 2–5.

6   Ibid., 109–110.

7   Mary Fulbrook, 'The Concept of "Normalisation" and the GDR in Comparative Perspective', in *Power and Society in the GDR, 1961–1979: The Normalisation of Rule?* ed. Mary Fulbrook (New York: Berghahn Books, 2009), 27–28.

8   Barbara J. Falk, 'Resistance and Dissent in Central and Eastern Europe: An Emerging Historiography', *East European Politics and Societies* 25, no. 2 (2011): 318–360 (321).

9   According to Scott, 'By definition, we have made the public transcript of domination ontologically prior to the hidden, off-stage transcript'. See Scott, *Domination and the Arts of Resistance*, 111. To make this argument, Scott cites explicitly from Michel Foucault's analysis of the technology of domination in *Discipline and Punish* and the impossibility of the 'exteriority of resistance' in *The History of Sexuality*. See Michel Foucault, *Discipline and Punish: The Birth of the Prison*, trans. Alan Sheridan (New York: Vintage Books, 1979); and Michel Foucault, *History of Sexuality. An Introduction*, vol. 1, trans. Robert Hurley (New York: Vintage Books, 1980), 95.

10   Serguei Oushakine, 'The Terrifying Mimicry of Samizdat', *Public Culture* 13, no. 2 (2001): 191–214 (192). Oushakine's argument parallels Theodor Adorno's 'Cultural Criticism and Society', in which Adorno argues that 'cultural criticism shares the blindness of its object'. See Adorno, 'Cultural Criticism and Society', in Theodor Adorno, *Prisms*, trans. Samuel Weber and Sherry Weber (Cambridge: MIT Press, 1982).

11   Oushakine, 'The Terrifying Mimicry of Samizdat', 204.

12   Ibid., 192.

13   Marcin Kula, 'Poland: The Silence of Those Deprived of Voice', in *Popular Opinion in Totalitarian Regimes: Fascism, Nazism, Communism*, ed. Paul Corner (New York: Oxford University Press, 2009), 150.

14   See Brad Abrams, 'Consumption and Political Legitimization in East-Central Europe: The Czechoslovak Case', paper presented at the conference 'The End and the Beginning: The Revolutions of 1989 and the Resurgence of History', Washington,

D.C., 9–10 November 2009; Martin Dimitrov, 'Tracking Public Opinion Under Authoritarianism: The Case of the Soviet Union Under Brezhnev', *Russian History* 41, no. 3 (2014): 329–353; Martin Dimitrov, 'What the Party Wanted to Know: Citizen Complaints as a "Barometer of Public Opinion" in Communist Bulgaria', *East European Politics and Societies and Cultures* 28, no. 2 (2014): 271–295.

15   Dimitrov, 'What the Party Wanted to Know', 291.

16   For a more thorough overview of E.F. Burian and AUD in the 1950s, see Shawn Clybor, 'Laughter and Hatred Are Neighbors: Adolf Hoffmeister and E.F. Burian in Stalinist Czechoslovakia, 1948–1956', *East European Politics and Societies* 26, no. 3 (2012): 589–615.

17   Jelínek, *Skandál v obrazárně*, 3.

18   Ibid., 4.

19   Ibid., 17.

20   Ibid., 17–18.

21   Ibid., 18.

22   Prominent Soviet functionaries and cultural producers including Anatolii Lunacharskii, Mikhail Bakhtin and Sergei Eisenstein defended the genre as necessary, although the forms it should take were a matter of ongoing dispute. For a brief overview, see Serguei Oushakine, '"Red Laughter": On Refined Weapons of Soviet Jesters', *Social Research* 79, no. 1 (2012): 189–216.

23   Jelínek, *Skandál v obrazárně*, 5–12.

24   Ibid., 27–28.

25   Ibid., 53.

26   Ibid., 35.

27   Ibid., 36.

28   Ibid.

29   Ibid., 37.

30   Ibid., 38.

31   Muriel Blaive, *Promarněná příležitost. Československo a rok 1956* (Prague: Prostor, 2001).

32   For a more in-depth background into how the Czechoslovak Army funded and protected culture, especially film, in the 1950s, see Alice Lovejoy, *Army Film and the Avant-Garde: Cinema and Experiment in the Czechoslovak Military* (Bloomington: Indiana University Press, 2015). For a more general study of Alexej Čepička and his involvement in the Ministry of Defence, see Jiří Pernes, Jaroslav Pospíšil, and Antonín Lukáš, *Alexej Čepička. Šedá eminence rudého režimu* (Prague: Brána, 2008).

33   dl, 'Vulgarita nedá satiře účinnost' [Vulgarity Does Not Make Satire Effective], *Literární noviny* 2, no. 44 (1953): 2.

34   J. Strnad, 'Poplach se skandálem' [Alarmimg Scandal], *Literární noviny* 2, no. 46 (1953): 2.

35   'Dopis Burianovi', Památník národního pisemnictví (National Literary Archive; PNP), *E.F. Burian*, sig. B/1–100, inv. č. 531.

36   Strnad, 'Poplach se skandálem', 2.

37   Ibid.

38   Jiří Knapík, *V zajeti moci: kulturní politika, její systém a aktéři 1948–1956* (Prague: Libri, 2006), 222–225.

39   Ibid., 226.

40   Ibid., 226–227.

41   Ibid., 237.

42 Ibid.

43 Jindřich Černý, *Osudy českého divadla po druhé světové válce: divadlo a společnost, 1945–1955* (Prague: Academia, 2007), 395.

44 A similar fate befell Pavel Kohout's play *September Evenings* (Zářijové noci). See Pernes, Pospíšil, and Lukáš, *Alexej Čepička,* 232.

45 Jelínek, *Skandál v obrazárně,* 89.

46 Antonín Liehm, for example, co-founded his journal *Kulturní politika* with none other than E.F. Burian in 1945. Liehm was fired in 1950 because of his connections to Vladimír Clementis, who was hanged during the Slánský trials, and later became a leading proponent of the Prague Spring. After the Warsaw Pact invasion, he emigrated with his wife to Paris.

47 As late as 1958, he continued to publicly proclaim: 'I support Socialist Realism!' E.F. Burian, 'Nechtít pohnout kupředu uměním, ale společností: několik kapitol z úvodního slova k divadelnímu semináři v Karlových varech', *Kultura,* no. 3 (1958): 2.

6

Perceptions of Society in Czechoslovak Secret Police Archives: How a 'Czechoslovak 1956' was Thwarted

Muriel Blaive

The events of 1956 around the world are well documented – by all standards, it was a remarkable year. On the European front, public opinion, pundits and believers were shaken by the twentieth Congress of the Communist Party of the Soviet Union (CPSU) that took place in February 1956. On the last day of the Congress, CPSU First Secretary Nikita Khrushchev delivered his famous Secret Speech in which he denounced Stalin's crimes and dictatorial behaviour. The terror initiated by Stalin, he now revealed, had devastated not only the population but also the Soviet's higher instances and most powerful authorities, such as the presidium members.[1] These revelations constituted a significant impetus for the demonstrations that took place in June, then in October in Poland and for an outright anti-communist revolution in October–November in Hungary.

But what was actually going on at that time in the third communist country of Central Europe, lying between insurrectionary Poland and Hungary?

The absence of events in 1956 Czechoslovakia

Since the opening of communist-era archives in the 1990s, we can summarize the answer to the previous question in a few words: no events of real significance.[2] Of course, it is now documented that the Second Writers' Congress, which took place that year in April, saw two poets, Jaroslav Seifert and František Hrubín, courageously criticize party policy in cultural matters.[3] Also that month, students publicly presented resolutions in which they demanded better study conditions and the abolition of censorship. A traditional student street parade, Majáles, was allowed to take place that year for the first time since 1946. It permitted, in both Prague and Bratislava, a humorous ventilation of students' frustrations about communism in practice.[4] A small proportion of rank-and-file party members shocked by the revelation of Stalin's crimes, mainly among the Prague intelligentsia, called for a party congress (0.5 per cent of local party organizations, representing 1 per cent of party members).[5] And finally, there was a hint of criticism concerning the Czechoslovak Stalinist leader Klement Gottwald's so-called 'cult of personality', pronounced at a Central Committee meeting in March 1956 by the Czechoslovak Communist Party leader, Antonín Novotný. The architect of the collectivization of agriculture, the lesser-known Slovak apparatchik Július Ďuriš, was even more outspoken.[6] Gottwald, like Stalin, had died in 1953 but, unlike its Soviet counterpart, the Czechoslovak leadership did not seize this chance to change course.

The existing historiography has long emphasized that this conservatism was the result of fear or cowardice. Marián Lóži's chapter in this volume suggests a completely different explanation: it is probable that Czechoslovak Communist Party General Secretary Rudolf Slánský and his Stalinist peers had been sacrificed in 1952 in a major show trial in order to both terrorize *and* appease popular opinion – which did not appreciate these 'small dictators'.[7] If we pursue this logic, the failure to rehabilitate the Slánský trial victims in 1955–1956 was no expedient dictated by a general reluctance to implement any post-Stalinist change. On the contrary, it becomes the continuation of an active policy to try to satisfy those segments of popular opinion that mattered most to the regime (namely, the workers). To reaffirm that small dictators would not be rehabilitated, while quietly freeing those who had survived the show trials, can, in this perspective, be read as a continuous attempt to convince the population that the Czechoslovak Communist Party was standing for a form of 'socialist legality' and for what its leaders conceived of as a reasonable exercise of the dictatorship of the proletariat. This is certainly consistent with the rest of Communist Party policy in the 1953–1956 period, which was largely devoted to improving the living standards of the population – at least of those segments that were not associated with the former economic elite. Of course, such a policy was only a complement to the regime's primary resort: repression, or the threat thereof.

Unsurprisingly then, none of the potential catalysts of revolutionary criticism in 1956 received any collective support. Neither the writers nor the students massively supported the few in their midst who were willing to go further and seriously challenge the regime. No one greeted Ďuriš outside the conference hall after he declared: 'Comrade Gottwald knew how to be threatening after 1948 and he restrained more and more the collective leadership of the Presidium.'[8] Had a big crowd turned him into a hero by cheering him and showing him unrestrained support, a Czechoslovak Imre Nagy or Władysław Gomułka could have been born then and there.

Instead, what was actually happening in Czechoslovakia in October–November 1956, as revolutionary days were overwhelming Poland and Hungary? What was the population thinking and why did it collectively stand aside? This chapter presents the answer that Czechoslovak citizens themselves provided at the time, as secretly recorded by the secret police (Státní bezpečnost or StB). These files are not personal files (either of collaborators or of people placed under surveillance) but general information files on the mood of the population. The StB, and in particular the thousands of functionaries working in its third section, in charge of the 'Fight Against the Internal Enemy',[9] compiled a dense collection of reports about the population and its feelings in October and November 1956. The information was mostly collected by their informant network – secret collaborators who were recruited among the general population and who factually reported on what they heard.

Even as early as January 1947, before the communist takeover, these collaborators were considered 'the most important information source' by the StB: 'Collaborators are recruited in all layers of the nation so that we have a faithful picture of reality at all times and in all domains.'[10] Some 28,412 of them were active at the end of 1956, of which approximately a quarter might have worked for 'political counter-espionage', that is, around 7,000 of them.[11] They conducted their spying activity for the most part unnoticed, simply listening in or participating in conversations in the workplace, in shops, on the street and in pubs. Reports are usually a few pages long; in the more professional districts they often include the full name of the incriminated citizen and even their address – indicating serious police background work. Northwest Bohemian agents (Ústí nad Labem, Liberec, i.e. the former Sudetenland) were particularly meticulous in this work. Two elements were of special interest to the police: the subject's political affiliation (past and present) and socio-economic category (profession).

How to interpret StB reports?

As hinted earlier, the structure of the political police has been extensively described in the Czech case, but has been much less the object of an interpretative analysis than in the German and Soviet cases. The figure of the 'collaborator', in particular, remains quite unexplored. The volume edited by Sándor Horváth, Péter Apor and James Mark, *Secret Agents and the Memory of the Everyday Collaboration in Communist Eastern Europe*, although dealing with most post-communist countries, does not contain any chapter dedicated to the Czechoslovak StB.[12] Yet, how collaboration affected ordinary people and how the latter internalized the informants' presence and their overall impact on society are 'questions vital to an understanding of life in the dictatorship'.[13]

Popular opinion was the only public opinion that the communist dictatorships could afford: there was no free public sphere and certain opinions could land a citizen in jail, but the population did, of course, have an opinion on the rulers and on the rule. This opinion is anything but trivial, as Paul Corner shows:

> having suppressed all the channels that permitted genuine and spontaneous communication between regime and citizens, (the regimes) then became frightened by the silence and set up spy networks in order to find out what the people were really thinking. The extent of these spy networks ... is an indication of the importance that the regimes themselves gave to the monitoring of public opinion – an importance related not only to the ever present need to suppress dissent but also to the search for legitimacy in the eyes of the people which all regimes aimed to achieve.[14]

By starting from the realities of everyday life, the bottom-up approach centres on the individual rather than the system and follows their 'forms of adjustment and modes of self-defence'. Speech, be it in public or in private, was one of them. And even in the most stringent dictatorship, the individuals held on to their ability to express themselves – in this sense, they never became 'merely a passive subject of authority' but retained 'some real space for action and reaction'.[15] This investigation of social support was first inspired by the revisionist school in the 1970s, notably by Sheila Fitzpatrick, on the premise that 'political regimes generally satisfy some social interests and rarely survive by force alone'.[16]

Of course, secret police documents must never be approached as the promise of a fantasized 'historical truth'. As French historian of the USSR Nicolas Werth wrote: 'While analysing a police report one must always sort between the expectations and the demands of the rulers, but also between their representatives' own vision, the typologies they had to learn ... and the prevailing explanatory schemes repeated over and over again'.[17] One must decipher and weigh the communist jargon in the reports. The designation 'enemy of our popular democracy' might describe a citizen busy doing grocery shopping; rushing into stores was indeed considered a hostile gesture by the regime in times of crisis, a concession to the 'enemy propaganda' that predicted an impending regime collapse.

These reports also give us an insight into the 'subtle nature of control'[18] that the secret police inflicted on their population. East German studies have provided a new methodological model: 'Rather than seeing East German history through the lens of top-down "blanket surveillance", historians began to explore dominance (Herrschaft) as a social practice. Sense of one's self (Eigen-Sinn) often collided with the regime, causing both sides to compromise'.[19] Thomas Lindenberger even inverted the classic 'boundaries of dictatorship' description to 'dictatorship of the boundaries', in which social actors became active in defining the limits of the rule. Pursuing stability occasionally meant for the regime 'reach[ing] out to the population, whether in the form of allowing rock concerts for youth, more freedom to the cultural sphere for writers and artists, or allowing renegade church leaders to continue initiatives that were not in line with state policy'.[20]

Serious methodological precautions are required to study a presentation that is the product of a double bias: the police pursued their own interests (repressing any form of dissent, as well as burnishing their image to their superiors), while the population was wary of the police. But this bias is rather easily exposed so it can be factored in:

1. The StB functionaries who recruited informants usually exhibited a certain personality type, prone to supporting an authoritarian approach; in the 1950s, most of them were certainly still staunch believers in communist ideology.
2. They wrote for the benefit of their superiors. As such, they tended to exaggerate the 'good feelings' of the population. A typical result is the almost obligatory statement in any report that pertains to the 'massive approval by the population of the Central Committee's policy'. The vagueness of such statements suffices to discard them as reliable information.
3. Another constant feature is the doctoring of the functionaries' and/or informants' absence of real activity in the hope to give an active impression. Numerous reports, especially in Slovakia, thus concern ill-defined groups of people, for

instance 'the workers of such-and-such factory', 'the employees of such firms' or even 'the vast majority of the citizens in our district', who allegedly 'support the government on this or that policy'. The author spends a minimal time writing his report and probably expects to procure maximum satisfaction to his superiors. Such reports are unverifiable; they tell us more about their author than about the population's mood.

4. On the other hand, the search for real or imaginary opponents (the 'enemy' in contemporary vocabulary) might have led them to exaggerate the danger represented by individual actions. An innocent joke told at a pub after too many beers could become an 'attempt at sabotage'. However, the exact description of the would-be subversive activity allows us to replace it in its context – and assess that it is usually much less of a genuine opposition to the regime that these agents might have pretended it was.[21]

5. Finally, one central element of discourse is a strategy of silence: absolute silence concerning Khrushchev's Secret Speech; silence on the victims of political repression and the Slánský trial. Any element that would question the rulers' personal responsibilities was put aside to the profit of less compromising discussions of a few acknowledged regime shortcomings (for instance, shortages). In this, the reports faithfully reflect the official policy followed in 1956: turn the page and do not look back; do not turn the 'lessons of the twentieth Congress' into a pretext for unsettling questions about the past; allow criticism only if it respects the previous two points.

Beyond these biases, the reports also reflect all sorts of whimsical rumours that circulated among the population. The most absurd is a notice from Liberec that people were rushing to buy vinegar to shield themselves against the nuclear bombs that they feared would soon hit them.[22] So how can we profit from this mass of reports while keeping a critical mind? It is only possible by corroborating them with other sources: reports from competing institutions, especially the Communist Party but also the regular police, interviews made by Radio Free Europe at the time, the reports from the French and American embassies in Prague, the official media, the media published abroad by Czechoslovak exiles, Western media, as well as interviews that I carried out with 1956 witnesses in the mid-1990s.[23] The elements emphasized here are the common characteristics that appear in all sources. They are relatively homogenous throughout the Czechoslovak territory and their input was apparently taken at face value by the authorities – or at least I could not find suggestions that they were contested in any way.

In the relationship between rulers and ruled, it is not only the rulers' role that must be re-evaluated. Sarah Davies reminds us that while dealing with popular opinion it is time to 'get away from the totalitarian insistence on the atomised, voiceless masses ... Clearly, along the continuum from active consent to active resistance/dissent were a range of heterogeneous positions'.[24] The range of behaviours was rarely absolute, and opposition to one aspect of the regime policy did not preclude support for other aspects – an observation valid for authoritarian regimes in general.[25]

Czechoslovakia in 1956

Our comparative dimension, together with an extensive knowledge of the historical context, allows us to infer a few points: first and foremost, the vast majority of the Czechoslovak public was shocked by the violence of the Hungarian insurrection. All sources confirm this in almost identical terms, even when they are as ideologically divergent as the official Czech press and Radio Free Europe.

Second, the StB informants played an effective mediating role between the rulers and the ruled, as a hinge between the state apparatus and a society that fulfilled its informational purpose by relaying popular concerns from the bottom up – this doubtlessly is one of the keys of the regime's stability all the way until 1989.

Third, the presence of the same informants, as well as of StB functionaries, also effectively conveyed the limits of the dictatorship to the rest of the population in a top-down direction. Their presence helped to clarify the rules in maintaining the balance of the system of domination. Certain dissonances with the official policy and narrative were tolerated as long as they remained vague: for instance, hoping that the regime would soon collapse or the admiration of Czechoslovak citizens for the Western world.

We can hence speak like historian Sandrine Kott of a 'socialization of the state'. The rule of the Communist Party must be analysed as an exchange, however unbalanced, between those who exerted power and those who were submitted to it, but were by no means devoid of any resources. In this Foucauldian view, the subject becomes a (begrudging) social actor of the domination mechanism.[26]

Once the limits were known and accepted, the people did indeed participate in the equilibrium of rule. On the one hand, the StB reports reveal the conforming strategy of the population to the official linguistic repertoire and their acceptance of certain symbolic representations of the regime, such as the red star. In fact, they even 're-appropriated' the propaganda, made it 'work for their own purposes, selected those aspects of it which corresponded with their own beliefs, while rejecting others.'[27] On the other hand, the reports show that official propaganda also internalized certain cultural and even nationalist elements that pleased the public ear. In this way, a form of social contract was born in which both parties sent certain signals of social collusion to the other side and found a common language. Values at the top and at the bottom thus did not necessarily clash. On the contrary, Inkeles and Bauer observe in *The Soviet Citizen* (as cited by Sarah Davies) that 'there is a general marked congruence between popular values and the goals the system purports to pursue'. The conflicts, concludes Davies, 'emerge only when the regime fails to implement these values.'[28]

In 1956, there was no conflict. This chapter's main argument is that the lack of protest, or what some contemporary actors coined the passivity of the Czechoslovak population, only concealed its absence of major disagreement with the communist regime, as well as a form of approval for the benefits it had to offer; most people wished for the hasty demise of communism and the return of democracy, but their standard of living meant they had something to lose and were therefore not prone to taking risks.

StB files on 1956

I first had access to these documents in Hungary in 1994 in the archives of the Hungarian Ministry of Foreign Affairs – long before they were made available in the Czech Republic. Indeed, post-1989 Hungary and Czechoslovakia had exchanged their secret police files on 1956 in Czechoslovakia and 1968 in Hungary. I photocopied them extensively, and in this chapter I still use the Hungarian archival classification. A few thousand pages of documents on Czechoslovakia in 1956 were divided into eleven files, the first of which came from the Czechoslovak Ministry of Foreign Affairs, the next nine from the Ministry of the Interior and the last from the Central Committee. This chapter mostly deals with the nine files coming from the Ministry of the Interior. As mentioned earlier, their aim was to account for the mood of the population.[29] The officials feared that the Hungarian revolution or the Polish events might lead the Czechoslovak population to try to overthrow the regime.

Authorities at all levels intuitively conceived of these reports as genuine public opinion polls, although they of course never bothered to reflect on the methodological assumptions this would entail. The reports bear varying titles from day to day and from district to district, suggesting a lack of centralized orders. Some bear no title, while others are simply called 'Situation', 'Reactions to the Hungarian Events', 'Reactions among the Population to World Events' and so on. But many, probably more than half of them, use some variation of the term(s) 'public opinion' and/or 'polling': 'Investigations of the Population's Public Opinion', 'Investigations of the Population's Public Opinion in Relation to the Events in Poland and Hungary', 'Remarks on the Public Opinion Poll', 'Polling of the Reaction to the Polish Events', 'Polling of the Reactions to the Latest Events' and so on. The StB functionaries clearly shared the collective, unspoken belief that they were 'polling public opinion'. The reports' significance is magnified by the fact that their most fervent reader was none other than First Secretary Antonín Novotný.[30]

I review first of all the so-called 'cultural' argument that was one of the main explanatory schemes invoked at the time, both by pundits abroad and at home: it would be in the nature of Czechs and even Slovaks not to act in any violent way, and that is allegedly why nothing happened in Czechoslovakia in 1956. However, and this is the second part of my argument, the people who did not support the communist regime appeared quite capable of violent actions. Furthermore, there was a genuine expectation among the population and even many officials that the regime was about to collapse and democracy was to return. Why then did the regime not collapse? It is mainly, as we see in the last and fourth part, due to the relatively high standard of living of the population.

The red star issue

What were the Czechoslovak citizens talking about as the battle was raging in the streets of Budapest? They had concerns of a very different nature than their fighting neighbours; one of those was the fate of the red star, the archetypal communist symbol.

Red stars adorned public buildings, as well as locomotives or busses, for instance. In their April Resolutions, the students had already demanded that they be taken down, just as they had demanded that the Soviet anthem not be played anymore at the end of the daily radio and TV broadcasts.[31] Symbols of Soviet domination and of a detested regime for some, token of stability and progress for others, the red stars were vested with a particular significance in 1956, especially as regards the tense relations between Slovaks and Hungarians.

The reports tell us that the manager of a Slovak mechanical factory said, while 'more or less laughing', that a Czechoslovak locomotive had been attacked on the Hungarian side at the border station of Komárno in order to dismantle its red star.[32] A railway worker confirmed that he had also been coerced into taking down the red star from his locomotive when he crossed into Hungary.[33] A Czechoslovak citizen back from Hungary described the fact that the *Red Star Hotel* in Budapest had just been rechristened the *National Hotel*, a piece of information sufficiently important in his eyes to appear in prime position in his report.[34] A mason ended up in jail for having criticized the wearing of a red star by a train conductor and for having promised to him that it would soon be torn off his clothes as was happening during those days in Hungary.[35]

The red star issue busied the minds of a group of travellers during a trip to Hungary. They had gone to Lake Balaton on vacation and found themselves stranded in Budapest on 23 October 1956, at the time when the revolution broke out. According to written accounts, most of them were terrified and secluded themselves in their hotel while awaiting a chance to go home – very few went out to see what was going on. According to several testimonies, the women were crying and the participants in the excursion were so nervous that they kept their national flag cautiously displayed on the hotel tables at which they sat to kill the time.[36] Bitter comments followed the refusal of the Czechoslovak embassy to secure their repatriation. The travellers did not seize this unexpected chance to flee to the West: only two out of the fifty-three passengers (members of the Hungarian minority in Slovakia who had relatives in Budapest) refused to go back to Czechoslovakia.[37] A long justification seemed necessary to each of the participants interviewed by the StB upon return in order to explain why the driver took down the red star from their bus and replaced it with a white flag.[38]

The subjective impression left by the debriefings back home (tone, vocabulary, expressed disgust at the Hungarian revolutionary violence) is very similar to that of other contemporary sources (newspapers, newsreels, interviews led by Radio Free Europe, reports from the French and the American embassies). We cannot know, on the basis of these police archives, if the people who claimed to support the regime really did support it, but it is clear that they went to great pains to have the regime believe so. In terms of collective mobilization – or absence thereof – it amounts to the same.

It appears that a large number of these travellers belonged to the Hungarian minority in Slovakia; if it is any indication, I could find mention of only seventy-two arrests among Slovak Hungarians throughout the Hungarian revolution (mostly for having sung the Hungarian national anthem while inebriated).[39]

Discussing the passivity of the Czechs

Why would Czechs and Slovaks be so concerned with protecting communist symbols? Interestingly enough, a majority of the population and among them, many a communist, anticipated that the regime would soon come to an end. Some expected the collapse would take place within five days, others the following week, others still before the end of the year. But not many people believed this regime was there to last.

Philosopher Jan Sokol was an apprentice in the 1950s. He befriended an older worker. One day, the latter took him to a hangar and revealed to him his secret plan against the communist regime: he was building, piece by piece, a moving van. He put all his love into this handiwork, the vehicle's bodywork was smooth and polished, the paint shining and new. A bemused Sokol asked him why he was doing this. The answer was instructive: 'It's very simple! When it breaks out, people will want to move! I will be ready and in two hours, I am out in the street.'[40] Getting ready to move the communists out and the expropriated people back into their homes, this man was preparing for the return of democracy.

The StB, the secret police, took a poll in a Slovak town that revealed that 70 per cent of the people expected the regime to come to an end soon.[41] This figure is consistent with other reports and testimonies. A number of small citizens were even preparing to reopen their small businesses once democracy was re-established. A former Slovak Hungarian merchant had already bought a house in his small town's main street to settle his two sons. One was to open a hairdressing salon and the other a drugstore.[42] Czech medical doctors were also looking forward to reopening their private practices.[43] A barman pictured himself at the head of his future coffee house.[44] Others exasperated officials with their attitude; a miner, for instance, allegedly walked around all day smiling and 'picturing to himself the overthrowing of the regime'.[45] Political prisoners also expected the imminent collapse of the regime. Eduard Goldstücker, the first ambassador to Israel and communist leader who was imprisoned until the end of 1955, recounted that the jailed democrats had spent their time discussing how much the Americans would give them as compensation for each day spent in jail; they were also preparing a list of future government ministers.[46]

In official ranks, the celebration of two anniversary dates was expected to provide an unwelcome opportunity for trouble: the creation of Czechoslovakia on 28 October[47] and the Great October Revolution on 7 November.[48] Police units were put on maximum alert. But the political activism of the population appeared feeble: according to historian Jiří Pernes, a group of people had prepared a demonstration on Wenceslas Square for 28 October; but because the weather changed for the worse and it started to rain, no one attended, not even the organizers.[49]

The Politburo archives hold another recap report from the Ministry of Interior concerning the so-called 'anti-state activities' of students.[50] A few of them were accused of storing weapons and explosive bullets, preparing to attack policemen and spreading subversive periodicals. In reality, this 'enemy activity' seems to have consisted mainly of listening to Radio Free Europe and criticizing the regime in closed circles. Out of the thirty-five people cited, thirty-four already were under arrest.[51] Everything was under control.

Few people were willing to openly defy the regime. While they expected the regime to fall soon, they were not personally prepared to fight to bring this about. One of the favourite scenarios circulating among the populace smelled of oranges. Jan Sokol describes it as follows: 'We used to say, the Americans have a special gas, they will release it overnight, and in the morning we will wake up, there will be an orange smell and the Americans will be here. You can imagine how revolutionary the mood was!'[52]

American diplomats had also heard of the orange gas scenario and wrote the following telegram to Washington:

> On June 18 (the Czechoslovak newspaper) Mlada Fronta carried article endeavoring ridicule rumor current in Czecho(slovakia) that Am(erican)s will liberate Czecho(slovakia) July 10 and that preceding their arrival there will be smell of oranges in the air which lethal for all except for those who immediately suck lump of sugar. Those who do so will fall asleep for two days and wake up 'in the Am(erican) paradise of freedom'. According article rumor originated ... from 'fiction re smell of oranges put out by V(oice)O(f)A(merica) itself'.[53]

Nor were they amused by their long-term impression that the Czechoslovak population was defeatist and unwilling to do anything more than await the return of the American army.[54]

The American diplomats were annoyed for good reasons; this reference and other similar cases show that Voice of America, as well as Radio Free Europe and probably other Western channels, were not immune to propagating baseless rumours and gossip. It confirms, as Rosamund Johnston's chapter in this volume shows, that the Czechoslovak population did listen to them; but it also relativizes the quality of these Western broadcasts, which at times led the populations to believe false news, for instance the imminent intervention of the American army in Hungary.[55]

Meanwhile, in his 'Observations on the Limpness of the Czechoslovak People', Ambassador Briggs made in his unique, flowery style reference to

> the early impression reported therein that notwithstanding widespread opposition to Communist domination, the citizens of Czechoslovakia do not appear to be the stuff from which revolutions are made ... The foregoing is not to say that the Czechs are unpatriotic or incapable of resistance, but that their resistance appears to be of a passive, slow-burning nature, consistent perhaps with the circumstances of their history during the past three centuries, but producing few seeds likely to sprout as dragon's teeth into an army capable of throwing off their present slavery.[56]

The Czechs and Slovaks secretly recorded by the StB in 1956 could not have agreed more. As a former Czech merchant expressed it, he personally would not want to dirty his hands, 'others would do it'.[57] According to a Slovak colleague, the system was to collapse by itself 'just like a house of cards'.[58] A worker from a chemical factory judged that the Czechs were 'too cowardly' to act like in Hungary.[59] Yet another worker thought that the Czechs would be the last ones to break away from the Soviets because they were 'opportunists' and did not want to risk anything.[60] A former shopkeeper and an employee viewed the Czechs as 'old grandmas' as opposed to the Hungarian 'lads'.[61] A railroad worker said he had heard on the Swiss radio that the Czechs, as a 'cultured' nation, would be among the last to get rid of communism.[62]

We can find the harshest criticism of this Czechoslovak aloofness in a Swiss newspaper, as reported by the French embassy:

> The *Journal de Genève* Bonn correspondent has no qualms about speaking of a genuine 'moral treason' of the Czechoslovak people, who are making the best of the Soviet tutelage as they had of the Nazi occupation. Mr Georges Blum claims that even the Prague government was surprised by the conformism of Czech opinion during the recent events. During a demonstration of faithfulness to the Soviet Union, the Soviet Ambassador, Mr Grishin, was allegedly cheered by 250,000 demonstrators. 'Prague remains the last bastion of Stalinism', concludes this journalist.[63]

Please let someone else do the job

This 'national character' stereotype even permeated the relations between Czechs and Slovaks and served to justify contradictory opinions, be it the passivity of the Czechs, the passivity of the Slovaks or the alleged hazardousness of would-be 'hot-blooded people', that is, Slovaks in the eyes of the Czechs and Hungarians in the eyes of the Slovaks. The most extravagant rumours were circulating, all confirming that things were about to start. In Slovakia, people were saying that arms and munitions were already being distributed to the Czechs but that their own secret police forces were holding the situation too tightly for the Slovaks to join them.[64] A haulage contractor assured his colleagues that the atmosphere was starting to 'rot' in the Czech lands and the people over there were rebelling.[65] A Slovak citizen coming back from a trip deemed the atmosphere in Brno 'chaotic'; according to her, people were saying that Slovakia was about to break away from the 'historical provinces' and they were convinced that a new world war was about to break out and a monetary devaluation would take place.[66] A former high-ranking functionary thought that things could break out in Bratislava but that it would first begin in the Plzeň region, before getting to Ostrava and then to the border region with Slovakia.[67]

The Czechs did not want to be outdone. A former soldier, who had fought on the Western front during the Second World War, was convinced that the troubles had already started in Slovakia and that 'it would soon begin', a hope shared by the two persons he was speaking to.[68] A social security employee, who doubted the 'Czech worker' could get interested in anything but his 'well-being' and 'the contents of his plate', nevertheless thought that 'something' could happen in Slovakia.[69] A peasant was expecting 'things' to begin any day, but first in Slovakia since he judged the Slovaks to be 'more courageous' than the Czechs.[70] A Slovak member of the Communist Party who was working in the Czech lands was already rejoicing about the upcoming restoration of the Slovak state, unless Slovakia 'reattach itself to Hungary' and a 'structure similar to the former Austria-Hungary' be revived.[71] A doctor judged that nothing could happen in the Czech lands, for the 'workers' were 'doing too well'; however, he thought the 'Communists' feared that something might break out in Slovakia as the Slovaks were known to be 'hot-blooded'.[72] And a so-called 'kulak', disappointed by the outcome in Hungary after the second Soviet intervention, was pinning all his remaining hopes on the 'troubles' and the 'riots', which he thought had just broken out in Slovakia. He formulated a positive opinion on the Slovaks' greater ability to act and deemed them 'less indifferent' than the Czechs.[73]

If some Czechs, who harboured hostile feelings towards the communist regime, counted on the Slovaks to take the initiative of an open resistance movement, others, more supportive of communism, displayed on the contrary ill feelings and nagging suspicions of Slovak separatism. A technician in a big industrial complex thus feared that the Slovaks would try to take advantage of the Hungarian situation to break away from the Czechs; according to him, the Hungarians had always had a big influence on the Slovaks and knew how to 'impress' them.[74] A restaurant employee declared that the Slovaks were as 'vicious' as the Hungarians and it would not be hard to lead them to 'ill-considered provocations'.[75] A coal miner, who did not belong to any political party, assessed that the Slovaks were 'hot-blooded' and unreliable since, for them, '[wartime fascist leader] Tiso was the greatest, in his time everyone was doing fine and everyone held this period in esteem'.[76] According to a priest, if 'something' were to happen, it would begin in Slovakia; one could always go there but with no assurance of coming back alive.[77]

The opinion expressed on the Hungarian and Polish situation allows us to gauge the feelings towards the regime: hostile to the Poles and the Hungarians, favourable to the regime; favourable to the Poles and the Hungarians, hostile to the regime. In these archives, approximately 80 per cent of the testimonies that expressed sympathy for the Hungarians also hoped that communism would soon come to an end in Czechoslovakia. A similar proportion of those who expressed their disgust at the spilled blood, the would-be 'bestiality' of the Hungarians (the contemporary expression) or violence in general simultaneously manifested their support for the regime. Testimonies concur on the fact that the image of Hungarian communists or secret police functionaries hanging from Budapest lamp posts dissuaded people, even those who were unhappy, from rebelling against the communist regime. The following letter from a wife to her conscript husband posted in Slovakia, seized during a control of the post, appears particularly representative:

Olina B. wrote to Antonín B. from Liberec: Hungary wants to take back Slovakia to recreate Greater Hungary. I am so afraid for you, afraid that you will be sent to war and that we are separated, maybe forever. Even if there are many problems here, many shortfalls, we are doing quite well and I would not want us to get into a fratricidal fight like in Hungary. Mommy also says that the worst would be if we started to fight among ourselves. You know how much I hate to go to meetings but yesterday we went there to discuss the international situation. A gentleman spoke about his children, about war, he said he had a baby that was only a few weeks old, that he would have to resign himself to war, rationing, bombs, and people applauded him. We had tears in our eyes. I think, and I realized that anew yesterday, that even if we all, including me, are dissatisfied, we would go and defend our Republic weapon in hand.[78]

Hostile feelings towards the Hungarian revolution

One of the other reasons why part of the Czechoslovak audience, after an initial favourable feeling, failed to entirely sympathize with the Hungarian revolution is because it was shocked by the violence of the insurrection. A Czech conscript wrote to his mother that the Hungarians were 'so vicious' that they could be mistaken for 'wild beasts' or 'SS men'. According to him, certain 'fascist elements' had killed guards and carried their heads around on pikes. His conclusion was: 'Either they will get me or I will get them. We are all watching the border with these thoughts in mind.'[79] From two workers' point of view, the Hungarian revolutionaries were 'clearly fascists' in view of their 'brutality'. The two were hoping that the borders were going to be hermetically sealed, so that no 'criminal' could escape to the West.[80] A former shopkeeper claimed in a pub in front of many people that considering what the 'members of various gangs' had committed in Hungary, a 'real barbarism', it was high time to 'concretely speak' of 'hanging and other punishments of the counter-revolutionaries'.[81] A former functionary of the Socialist-National Party wondered privately how the Hungarians could 'murder in such a brutal way'. He prayed that God 'keep us from something similar happening here'.[82] A priest remarked that he could not approve of the 'fratricidal chaos' reigning in Hungary and that the 'bestialities perpetrated over there' did not 'ask for comment'.[83] The wife of a man who had been jailed for 'stealing national property' stigmatized the 'counter-revolutionary putsch in Hungary' for its 'savagery'; she displayed her support for the Red Army's intervention.[84]

A former member of the Socialist-National Party opined that every sensible person had to condemn the 'bestiality of the reactionary forces on innocent victims' in Hungary. However, he was thanking in his mind the said 'reaction' for having 'shown its true face', adding that it would henceforth not be possible anymore to find anyone who would 'like to go back to the old days'.[85] A coal miner also criticized the 'bestiality' which presided over Hungary and explained that, in contrast to his past habits, he was now closely following the news since the 'Czechs' security' was at stake. He expressed his belief that the 'capitalists' were about to strike them, just like the Germans, and beseeched God not to let them come back to Bohemia because they would 'kill us all'.[86]

The communist functionaries' unpopularity

At the same time, the reports also show multiple expressions of bitterness or even aggression towards representatives of the regime. This latent hostility focused on the fate kept in store for communists and functionaries in the event of a sudden regime overthrow. A brochure, seized during an inspection of the mail in Slovakia, called for the 'death of judeo-bolshevism' and the hanging of the 'red dogs'.[87] A worker belonging to the Hungarian minority in Slovakia, whose 'Hungarian blood' was 'boiling', was preparing to hang the 'dirty communists' on acacias.[88] In a Czech tavern, a group of 'reactionary oriented' persons complained about the lack of trees on which they could hang the communists.[89] A worker urged his colleagues to finish as fast as possible the construction of a hoist to use it as a hanging device for the communists.[90] Another had prepared a candelabrum for the same purpose.[91] During the beetroot harvest, a galvanized peasant woman (a so-called 'kulak') declared to the assembled company that her cousin the butcher had already prepared the hooks on which to suspend the communists and slit their throats.[92] As for the inhabitants of Lesenice, they discussed among themselves the order in which the local functionaries would be hanged in case of a regime overthrow like in Hungary. The first ones were to be the mayor, the leader of the local Communist Party organization and the head of production at the local co-op.[93] In any case, many people insisted they would be the 'first' to assassinate the communists.[94]

In this context, it is not surprising that representatives of the communist regime felt rather nervous. Some, like a medical doctor, decided to 'keep a low profile' until the situation quieted down.[95] Others, like a priest, feared they would be excommunicated for having 'collaborated with the communists'.[96] Others still, like a functionary, worked on installing bars on his window because according to him, 10,000 functionaries had been killed in Hungary and he feared for his life.[97] A former member of the Communist Party was terrified by what he believed to be a pending regime change, as he thought even former members would be assassinated.[98] A shop manager urged a bookstore sales assistant to stop 'compromising him' by sending him 'political literature' and recommended she stop selling any as 'it could break out here before dawn'.[99]

Zdeněk Kopecký's testimony is coherent with this representation of the situation in the country. As a former democrat who was in prison in 1956 during the Hungarian revolution, he noticed that the wardens seemed to have 'lost faith in the Soviet Union'. Several of them were verbally assaulted while going to work in the morning with threats like 'just wait, the same will happen to you as in Hungary, you will all be hanged or shot'. One prison guard even turned to one of his fellow prisoners who was cleaning the corridors and asked him: 'Listen Krejčí, is it true that you will all hang us when it breaks out?'[100]

The importance of the standard of living

The example of the people who did not support communism shows that the reluctance to use violence was not actually an issue. If one looks back on the first years of the communist regime and remembers that 10,000 people took to the streets of Brno in 1951 because their Christmas bonuses had been curtailed,[101] or that the monetary devaluation of 1953 caused riots in Plzeň,[102] the 'anti-violence cultural component' pales in comparison to the socio-economical argument. Czechoslovaks indeed had no reason to become violent. After the 1953 downfall, the economy was on the rise. The American diplomats noticed the extent to which the regime was willing to compromise with the population on this matter after 1953, increasing the tempo of price reductions, salary raises and other efforts to keep the shops well supplied.[103] According to US academic experts, the pre-war standard of living was recovered around 1955 – as opposed to the end of the 1950s in Poland and supposedly 1963 in Hungary. Besides, the pre-war level was significantly higher in Czechoslovakia.[104]

American diplomats noticed how this apparent harmony between the regime and the population translated into unexpected aspects of everyday life. They ironically dubbed the return of Santa Claus at Christmas 1956 'the event of the year' (more precisely the return of Saint Nicholas, the cultural equivalent of Santa Claus for Central European countries – even though he comes earlier in December). According to the disillusioned diplomats, the disappearance of the Soviet Father Frost, whom the regime had attempted to impose on the country in the previous years, was yet another concession to the population after lowering prices and keeping the shops well stocked. The objective, of course, was to prevent the propagation of the Polish and Hungarian situation: 'We can thus claim without exaggeration that the Hungarian revolt brought about the demise of Father Frost.'[105]

The economic expert of the French embassy confirms that the shops had been 'better and better supplied' since 1955 and that the products' quality was 'improving', that employees' birthdays and name days were celebrated with wine and pastries at work, the population was better groomed, the automobile traffic had densified to the point of creating a few traffic jams at the end of weekends and the population had a few savings. He concluded even before the 1956 Hungarian revolution and the show of inertia on the Czech side: 'These various aspects tend to prove that the population is not "unhappy."'[106]

The Czechoslovak citizens themselves were very much aware of their privileged economic situation as an explanation of the calm prevailing in their country. If their standard of living was much higher than in Poland or Hungary, was it worth fighting? A so-called 'kulak' was of the opinion that this regime was 'bad' but no, it was not worth trying to fight like in Hungary.[107] A priest preferred 'a bit of repression' to 'glory on dead bodies' in the streets and in the fields.[108] A small landowner commented that freedom of speech would not help him in any way if it meant he had nothing to eat anymore.[109] One of his colleagues proclaimed that the Czechs had a higher standard of living than the Poles and the Hungarians, and that they had as well more culture, which is why the situation was different in their country.[110]

To a wide majority, these material assets appeared substantial enough to deter them from any inconsiderate action and they put up with the regime while awaiting better days – especially since they believed that the communist regimes would all soon fall.

Conclusion

Most Czechs and Slovaks would have favoured democracy over communism; they were looking forward to the impending demise of the communist regime; but they did acknowledge its credentials in terms of welfare and well-being, and chose to profit from them in the meantime. To paraphrase Ian Kershaw on the Bavarian population during

Nazism, the 'muddled majority' were neither full-hearted communists nor outright opponents. Their attitudes betrayed all at once 'signs of ideological penetration and yet show the clear limits of propaganda manipulation'.[111] Mainly, they followed their economic interest.

Moreover, the StB reports indicate that the 1956 events strengthened the hold of the Communist Party on society. Prior to and after the communist takeover, its influence had been prominent, indeed massive; in 1946, party leader Klement Gottwald had scored a large victory and the Czechoslovak Communist Party was the most popular actor on the democratic political front, earning 38 per cent of the votes. By the end of 1948, it was congregating in its ranks 2.5 million members, that is, no less than one Czechoslovak adult out of three, that is to say, and this is never emphasized enough, more than 49 per cent of the active Czech population.[112] In relation to its population, the Czechoslovak Communist Party had twice as many members as in Hungary and almost four times more than in Poland.[113] If it certainly does not mean that there were as many convinced communists, it does point to the fact that there were as many people who were willing to pretend, at least to a certain extent, to support the regime.

If such a high proportion of the adult population was enrolled into the Communist Party and if we additionally take into account the 150,000 or so persons who are said to have been, at one point or another, collaborators of the secret police (StB) between 1948 and 1968,[114] we must conclude that the communists had concentrated impressive power in their hands. The system self-sustained this so-called 'popular support': when one became a party member, one was under a considerable amount of pressure to support its policies. Members had to attend demonstrations, 'voluntary' socialist brigades and militant meetings, or even to 'offer' extra working hours for causes like the Korean War or the fight against American barbarism.[115] Fear, opportunism and conviction were the mixed feelings that constituted the cement of a finely supervised 'popular enthusiasm'. Despite the purges that affected the Czechoslovak Communist Party like all other communist parties, its membership rate remained far higher than that of other 'popular democracies'.[116] In 1962, Czechoslovakia still had 17.8 per cent of its adult population enrolled, against 7.6 per cent in Poland and 7.1 per cent in Hungary.[117]

Vice versa, these reports unquestionably show that the official propaganda successfully instrumentalized certain cultural and even nationalistic traits.[118] This is especially true for the Czechs, with their traditional emphasis on egalitarianism and their tendency to national self-definition in terms of 'culture'. If there is anything like a Czech reticence to use violence, communist propaganda embodied it.

Finally, the out-and-out divergence of interests between the Czechoslovak, Polish and Hungarian societies in 1956 could not be better illustrated than by the fact that during the few revolutionary weeks in Hungary and Poland, the support for the communist regime in Czechoslovakia was mingled with an expression of patriotism. The Hungarians and the Poles were fighting to redeem their national consciousness at the expense of a communist regime perceived as the symbol of Soviet domination; by contrast, despite its dictatorial attributes and its definite unpopularity, the Czechoslovak communist regime was awarded a new legitimacy.

As hinted earlier, the 1956 events, or lack thereof as far as Czechoslovakia was concerned, established for decades to come the basis of what we may now coin an unspoken, but effective, 'reasonable exercise of the dictatorship of the proletariat'. In 1952, the regime led by Klement Gottwald had explicitly distanced itself from the worst excesses of Stalinism by hanging Slánský and his peers. After the 1953 monetary reform disaster, seizing the opportunity provided by the new Soviet post-Stalinist policy, it reaffirmed its commitment to satisfy workers, as well as larger strata of the population, in economic, cultural and recreational matters. Now, in 1956, it exhibited a certain tolerance for dissenting popular opinion as long as it remained vague and abstract – while ruthlessly nipping in the bud anything resembling concrete opposition. These characteristics were to define the exercise of the communist dictatorship all the way until 1989. The rulers and the ruled had come to a certain *modus vivendi* – predicated on an excellent knowledge of the state of popular opinion by the rulers, itself the result of a considerable level of popular collaboration with the secret police.

To paraphrase Wendy Goldman on denunciations, these practices of domination were not the doing of a 'system' but of concrete people, of a broad popular participation.[119] Bringing to the fore the 'human agents of terror' might make it a 'history without heroes'[120] but it is describing a profoundly human behaviour.

Notes

1   See 'Khrushchev's Secret Speech', *Encyclopaedia Britannica*, 2011, https://www.
     britannica.com/event/Khrushchevs-secret-speech (accessed 29 September 2017).
2   My PhD thesis, *Une déstalinisation manquée. Tchécoslovaquie 1956* (Brussels:
     Complexe, 2005), was challenged on this point by Jiří Pernes and Kevin McDermott,
     who are both intent on a more dramatized vision of 'crisis', if not 'resistance', on the
     part of the population in their reading of the regime archives in 1956; however, their
     works barely yielded any element lending credence to a different approach. See Jiří
     Pernes, *Krize komunistického režimu v Československu v 50. letech 20. století* (Brno:
     CDK, 2008); Kevin McDermott and Vitězslav Sommer, 'The "Club of Politically
     Engaged Conformists"? The Communist Party of Czechoslovakia, Popular Opinion
     and the Crisis of Communism', *Cold War International History Project,* Working
     Paper No. 66, 2013; Kevin McDermott and Klára Pinerová, 'The Rehabilitation
     Process in Czechoslovakia: Party and Popular Responses', in *De-Stalinising Eastern
     Europe: The Rehabilitation of Stalin's Victims After 1953*, eds. Kevin McDermott and
     Matthew Stibbe (Basingstoke: Palgrave Macmillan, 2015).
3   See Muriel Blaive, 'Le parcours du "rapport secret" en Tchécoslovaquie et les
     ferments de contestation nés du XXème Congrès', in *Une déstalinisation manquée*,
     35–54, for the specific case of the writers 47–48.
4   Ibid., 48–52.
5   Ibid., 45–47.
6   Ibid., 61.
7   Kevin McDermott does show that Slánský was massively unpopular among large
     sections of the population. See his article 'A "Polyphony of Voices"? Czech Popular
     Opinion and the Slánský Affair', *Slavic Review* 67, no. 4 (2008): 840–865.

8   Ibid.
9   The third section of the Ministry of Internal Affairs was dedicated to 'political counter-espionage' and 'fought against the internal enemy', updating the list of 'illegal organizations and anti-state groups'. See František Koudelka, *Státní bezpečnost 1954–1968. Základní údaje* (Prague: Sešity ÚSD, vol. 13, 1993), 19. For a general presentation of the StB, see Karel Kaplan, *Nebezpečná bezpečnost* (Brno: Doplněk, 1999), as well as numerous articles in the journal *Paměť a dějiny* published by the Institute for the Study of Totalitarian Regimes and accessible online here: http://old.ustrcr.cz/cs/pamet-a-dejiny-2016#pad3-2016 (accessed 29 September 2017).
10   Jan Frolík, 'Nástin organizačního vývoje státobezpečnostních složek sboru národní bezpečnosti v letech 1948–1989', *Sborník archivních prací*, no. 2 (1991): 447–510 (481).
11   Koudelka, *Státní bezpečnost*, 52–53.
12   The book includes only a chapter comparing the Czech and Slovak memory institutes, written by a Slovak historian. See Martin Kovanič, 'Institutes of Memory in the Slovak and Czech Republics – What Kind of Memory?', in *Secret Agents and the Memory of the Everyday Collaboration in Communist Eastern Europe*, eds. Sándor Horváth, Péter Apor, and James Mark (London: Anthem Press, 2017), 81–104, as well as one chapter on intellectuals at the Faculty of Arts by Matěj Spurný, Katka Volná and Jakub Jareš.
13   Gary Bruce, *The Firm. The Inside Story of the Stasi* (Oxford: Oxford University Press, 2010), 145.
14   Paul Corner, 'Introduction', in *Popular Opinion in Totalitarian Regimes: Fascism, Nazism, Communism*, ed. Paul Corner (Oxford: Oxford University Press, 2009), 3.
15   Ibid., 5.
16   Sheila Fitzpatrick, 'Popular Opinion in Russia Under Pre-War Stalinism', in *Popular Opinion in Totalitarian Regimes*, ed. Corner, 18.
17   Nicolas Werth, 'Une source inédite: les *svodki* de la Tchéka-OGPU', *Revue des études slaves* 66, no. 1 (1994): 17–27 (26).
18   Bruce, *The Firm*, 2.
19   Ibid., 8.
20   Ibid., 8. Such an everyday life approach to the secret police must, of course, not lead in any way to a whitewashing of the regime: the 'state-society relationship was not one between equals'. Ibid., 12.
21   In his volume comparing regular police and secret police reports in East Germany, Thomas Lindenberger has also shown that secret police (Stasi) reports tended to emphasize and exaggerate the 'danger' posed by certain individuals, particularly rebellious youth, while the regular police (Volkspolizei) saw them for what they were: harmless teenagers. See Thomas Lindenberger, *Volkspolizei. Herrschaftspraxis und öffentliche Ordnung im SED-Staat 1952–1968* (Cologne: Böhlau, 2003).
22   Külügyminisztérium levéltár (Ministry of Foreign Affairs archives, Budapest; KML). Liberec, 4 November 1956, XXXII – 16, III, 1, 93.
23   See Blaive, *Une déstalinisation manquée*.
24   Sarah Davies, *Popular Opinion in Stalin's Russia. Terror, Propaganda and Dissent 1934–1941* (Cambridge: Cambridge University Press, 1997), 6.
25   Ibid.
26   Sandrine Kott, *Le communisme au quotidien* (Paris: Belin, 2001), 16–17. For another example of a Foucauldian study of power relationships at the micro-level, see Stephen

Kotkin, *Magnetic Mountain. Stalinism as a Civilization* (Berkeley: University of California Press, 1995), 23.

27 Davies, *Popular Opinion in Stalin's Russia*, 193–184.

28 Ibid., 185.

29 Especially in the citation of these sources, this chapter repeats large extracts from my volume *Une déstalinisation manquée*, as well as from the following article: Muriel Blaive, 'La police politique en action: les Tchécoslovaques et la révolution hongroise de 1956', *Revue d'histoire moderne et contemporaine* 49, no. 2 (2002): 176–202.

30 See Koudelka, *Státní bezpečnost*, 138.

31 See the testimony of one of the student movement leaders, Michael Heyrovský in Muriel Blaive, *Scénario du film '1956, le rendez-vous manqué de l'histoire'* (Prague: Cefres, 1997), 12. This 60-minute documentary film, realized in 1996 by Jan Šikl and entitled *1956. Promarněná šance aneb Návrat Ježíška do Československa*, features many testimonies on the 1950s in Czechoslovakia. It can be viewed on YouTube: https://www.youtube.com/watch?v=2KFr7GGRdPM&t=8s (accessed 15 October 2017).

32 KML. Nitra, 29 October 1956, XXXII – 16, III, 3, 17.

33 KML. Nitra, 30 October 1956, ibid., 24.

34 KML. Bratislava, 4 November 1956, XXXII – 16, IV, 2, 192.

35 KML. Nitra, 22 November 1956, ibid., 65.

36 KML. Nitra, 30 October 1956, XXXII – 16, III, 4, 35–36.

37 KML. Nitra, 29 October 1956, ibid., 14–15.

38 KML. Ibid., 14–30.

39 See the recap report: KML. Nitra, 22 November 1956, XXXII – 16, IV, 2, 58–66.

40 KML. Nitra, 29 October 1956, XXXII – 16, III, 4, 14.

41 KML. Hlohovec, 2 November 1956, XXXII – 16, IV, 2, 232.

42 KML. Nitra, 7 November 1956, XXXII – 16, III, 3, 60.

43 KML. Ústí nad Labem, 5 November 1956, XXXII – 16, IV, 5, 15–16.

44 Ibid., 20.

45 Ibid., 11.

46 See Blaive, *Scénario*, 5.

47 KML. Nitra, 3 November 1956, XXXII – 16, III, 3, 46, or Bratislava, 26 October 1956, XXXII – 16, II, 3, 35.

48 KML. Nitra, 4 November 1956, XXXII – 16, III, 3, 51, or Nitra, 22 November 1956, XXXII – 16, III, 4, 66.

49 See Blaive, *Scénario*, 16.

50 Národní archiv v Praze (National Archive, Prague; NAP). Politbyro ÚV KSČ, Fond 02/2, sv.126, aj.162, l.7, Bod 15/a, 'Zatčení několika skupin studentů, kteří se dopustili trestné činnosti', com. Barák, 28 December 1956.

51 See Blaive, *L'année 1956 en Tchécoslovaquie*, 130–132.

52 See Blaive, *Scénario*, 13.

53 U.S. Embassy, Prague. Records of the Foreign Service Posts of the Department of State, Czechoslovakia. Classified General Records, 1945–1957. 1950–1952; 570.3 to 670.51. Box 23. Entry UD 2378-A. Telegram sent to: secstate. 20 June 1952. VOANY (Voice of America New York), Johnson, RG 84.

54 NAP, Declassified E. O. 11652 ou E. O. 12356, LM 85 film 1, Report from Prague, 9 February 1950: 'Visit of Mrs. Briggs to Mrs. Beneš, Widow of President Beneš', 1.

55 See Miklós Mólnár, *De Béla Kun à János Kádár. Soixante-dix ans de communisme hongrois* (Paris: FNSP, 1987), 234; Robert Holt, *Radio Free Europe* (Minneapolis:

University of Minnesota Press, 1958), 194–195; Sig Mickelson, *America's Other Voices. Radio Free Europe and Radio Liberty* (New-York: Praeger, 1983), 98–99.

56   NAP. Declassified E. O. 11652 ou E. O. 12356, LM 85 film 1, Report from Prague, 2 May 1950: 'Observations on the Limpness of the Czechoslovak People', 1–2.
57   KML. Ústí nad Labem, 7 November 1956, XXXII – 16, IV, 5, 100.
58   KML. Nitra, 3 November 1956, XXXII – 16, III, 3, 50.
59   KML. Ústí nad Labem, 30 October 1956, XXXII – 16, III, 1, 33.
60   Ibid., 38.
61   KML. Jihlava, 1 November 1956, XXXII – 16, III, 1, 46, or Ústí nad Labem, 5 November 1956, XXXII – 16, IV, 5, 21.
62   Ibid., 13.
63   Archives of the French Embassy, Prague. Box 353, TS 5.3.1 Procès, Dépêche de Berne n°3201, 'Attitude du peuple tchécoslovaque', 21 December1956, French Ambassador in Switzerland Etienne Dennery.
64   KML. Nitra, 2 November 1956, XXXII – 16, III, 3, 43.
65   KML. Nitra, 5 November 1956, ibid., 57.
66   Ibid., 209.
67   KML. Bratislava, 26 October 1956, XXXII – 16, II, 3, 33.
68   KML. Ústí nad Labem, 30 October 1956, XXXII – 16, III, 1, 30.
69   Ibid., 39.
70   Ibid., 42.
71   KML. Liberec, 5 November 1956, XXXII – 16, IV, 5, 37.
72   KML. Ústí nad Labem, 7 November 1956, XXXII – 16, IV, 5, 103.
73   KML. Pardubice, 8 November 1956, ibid., 128.
74   KML. Ústí nad Labem, 30 November 1956, XXXII – 16, III, 1, 38.
75   Ibid., 91.
76   KML. Ústí nad Labem, 7 November 1956, ibid., 104.
77   KML. Ústí nad Labem, 20 November 1956, ibid., 282.
78   KML. Liberec, 4 November 1956, XXXII – 16, II, 3, 97–98.
79   KML. Liberec, 2 November 1956, XXXII – 16, II, 3, 58.
80   KML. České Budějovice, 4 November 1956, ibid., 79.
81   KML. Olomouc, 4 November 1956, ibid., 102.
82   KML. Jihlava, 5 November 1956, XXXII – 16, IV, 5, 41.
83   KML. Ústí nad Labem, 6 November 1956, ibid., 66.
84   KML. Ústí nad Labem, 7 November 1956, ibid., 101.
85   KML. Ústí nad Labem, 9 November 1956, ibid., 150.
86   Ibid.
87   KML. Nitra, 31 October 1956, XXXII – 16, III, 3, 32.
88   KML. Nitra, 22 November 1956, XXXII – 16, III, 4, 61.
89   KML. Jihlava, 1 November 1956, XXXII – 16, III, 1, 48.
90   KML. Jihlava, 6 November 1956, XXXII – 16, IV, 5, 75.
91   KML. Liberec, 7 November 1956, ibid., 110.
92   KML. České Budějovice, 6 November 1956, XXXII – 16, IV, 5, 59.
93   KML. Ústí nad Labem, 16 November 1956, ibid., 239.
94   KML. Ústí nad Labem, 5 November 1956, ibid., 4, and 20.
95   KML. Ústí nad Labem, 5 November 1956, XXXII – 16, IV, 5, 16.
96   Ibid., 17.
97   Ibid., 20.
98   Ibid., 22.

99   KML. Ústí nad Labem, 5 November 1956, XXXII – 16, IV, 5, 29.
100   See Blaive, *Scénario*, 16.
101   See Jiří Pernes, 'Dělnické domonstrace v Brně v roce 1951', *Soudobé dějiny* 3, no. 1 (1996): 23–41.
102   See Blaive, *Une déstalinisation manquée*, 90–93. For the latest research on this topic, see Jakub Šlouf, *Spřízněni měnou. Genealogie plzeňské revolty 1. června 1953* (Prague: FF UK, 2016).
103   See National Archives and Records Administration (NARA). General Records of the Department of State, 1955–59, File 749.00/10–156, Box 3300, Report from the American Embassy in Prague, 13 December 1956.
104   See George R. Feiwel, *Poland's Industrialization Policy: A Current Analysis Sources of Economic Growth and Retrogression* (New York: Praeger, 1971), 230–231 et 261, as well as Thad P. Alton, ed., *Personal Consumption in Hungary, 1938 and 1947–1965* (New York: Research Project on National Income in East Central Europe, 1968), 22–23.
105   NARA. Archives of the Department of State, General Records of the Department of State, 1955–59, File 749.00/10–156, Box 3300, Report from the American Embassy in Prague, 13 December 1956. For the record, Father Frost was back in 1957 and did not disappear for good before the Prague Spring eleven years later.
106   Archives of the French Embassy, Prague. Box 357, file 29b, 30, 'Evolution de l'économie tchécoslovaque au cours de l'année 1955', 21 September 1956, 33–34.
107   KML. Olomouc, 4 November 1956, XXXII – 16, III, 1, 102.
108   Ibid., 102.
109   Ibid.
110   Ibid., 103.
111   Ian Kershaw, *Popular Opinion and Political Dissent in the Third Reich: Bavaria 1933–1945* (Oxford: Clarendon Press, 1983), viii.
112   See Jiří Maňák, *Komunisté na pochodu k moci 1945–1948* (Prague: Studie ÚSD, 1995), 57. For updated figures and a brilliant analysis of the Czechoslovak and East German communists between 1945 and 1989, see Michel Christian, *Camarades ouapparatchiks? Les communistes en RDA et en Tchécoslovaquie 1945–1989* (Paris: PUF 2016).
113   See Blaive, *Une déstalinisation manquée*, 152.
114   See Koudelka, *Státní bezpečnost*, 68.
115   See, for instance, Rosemary Kavan, *Freedom at a Price: An Englishwoman's Life in Czechoslovakia* (London: Verso, 1985), 68.
116   In 1954, for instance, the Polish United Workers' Party counted 1,296,938 members while the Czechoslovak Communist Party, for a total population inferior by 50 per cent counted 1,489,234 members. See Branko Lazitch, *Les partis communistes d'Europe 1919–1955* (Paris: Les îles d'or, 1956), 96 and 110.
117   See Jan F. Tríska, 'Czechoslovakia and the World Communist System', in *Czechoslovakia Past and Present I*, ed. Miloslav Rechcígl (The Hague: Mouton, 1968), 376. Because of the extreme difficulty, at the time, of gaining access to reliable sources, the membership figures mentioned earlier are possibly not completely accurate. Nevertheless, they give us a sufficient estimate for us to be able to establish a comparative pattern and they were overall confirmed by the recent work of Michel Christian, *Camarades ou apparatchiks? Les communistes en RDA et en Tchécoslovaquie 1945–1989* (Paris: PUF, 2016).

118   A similar trend was unveiled in the Soviet case, what Stephen Kotkin coins the
        'partially intersecting dreams' between the regime and the population. See Kotkin,
        Magnetic Mountain, 23. Paul Corner speaks of 'shared values' in his 'Introduction',
        in *Popular Opinion in Totalitarian Regimes*, ed. Corner, 8–9.
119   Wendy Z. Goldman, *Inventing the Enemy: Denunciation and Terror in Stalin's Russia*
        (Cambridge: Cambridge University Press, 2011), 1–2.
120   Ibid., 20.

7

Crises and the Creation of Institutions for Assessing Popular Consumption Preferences in Communist Bulgaria (1953–1970)

Martin K. Dimitrov

Communist regimes exemplify the concept of a 'shortage economy'.[1] The standard interpretation is that these regimes did not aim to satisfy the consumption preferences of the population,[2] ruling instead through repression of the masses.[3] This received wisdom has been challenged both by early scholarship that emphasized the decline in repression within post-Stalinist regimes[4] and by subsequent studies of the socialist social contract,[5] which argued that citizens would remain quiescent for as long as the regime provided them with stable access to jobs, housing, welfare benefits and, importantly, consumer goods.

The collapse of communist regimes led to an archival revolution that allowed scholars to assess the validity of arguments that were made without access to primary sources. Recent archival studies have confirmed the insights of the earlier literature concerning the importance that communist regimes attached to satisfying the consumption preferences of the population.[6] Research on 'welfare dictatorships' has validated Václav Havel's astute observation that late socialism 'has been built on the foundations laid by the historical encounter between dictatorship and the consumer society'.[7]

This chapter complements the findings of the recent literature on consumption by focusing on two interrelated questions that allow us to shed light on the political logic of socialist consumption. It addresses the following puzzles: When do communist regimes start paying attention to the consumer preferences of the population, and how do they find out what these preferences are? This reflection allows us to shed light on the origins of the institutions that supplied the top leadership with information about popular opinion. The chapter engages with this issue by focusing on the case of communist Bulgaria. It relies primarily on the rich collections of the Central State Archive (TsDA) and the State Security Archive (AMVR and KRDOPBGDSRSBNA-M). The study contributes to the literature on welfare in autocracies,[8] as well as to the rapidly expanding literature on durable authoritarianism.[9]

This chapter is chiefly concerned with how unanticipated crises may lead to the creation of institutions that can supply the leadership with information on brewing discontent. As I have argued elsewhere,[10] communist regimes distinguish between overt (visibly expressed) and latent discontent. In the view of communist regime insiders, overt discontent stems from unaddressed latent discontent.[11] In turn, frustrated consumption preferences are a key trigger of latent discontent.[12] In this understanding, which emerged gradually as communist regimes survived and learned from various unexpected crises, establishing institutions for assessing consumer discontent (and using the information they collected to defuse this discontent) was essential for maintaining regime stability.[13]

This chapter argues that a confluence of domestic and international crises in the first half of 1953 forced the Bulgarian party-state to focus on placating unrest by satisfying the consumption preferences of the population. The period from the second half of 1953 until 1962 was characterized by an increased awareness (strengthened by the 1956 events in Hungary and Poland) that assessing and satisfying popular consumption preferences can form the wellspring of regime stability. The closure of the Lovech camp in 1962 marked the end of de-Stalinization and the definitive transition to a low-repression equilibrium that enabled the creation of the institutions needed for the systematic collection of information on popular discontent in general and on frustrated consumer preferences in particular. The most useful mechanism for evaluating consumer preferences was the analysis of information that was voluntarily transmitted to the regime through citizen complaints. The institutions for assessing popular discontent were largely in place prior to 1968, but the Czechoslovak crisis helped convince the leadership that the information on consumption preferences they generated had to be proactively used to prevent expressions of system-destabilizing mass discontent similar to those that emerged in the GDR and Czechoslovakia in 1953, in Poland and Hungary in 1956, and following the August 1968 invasion in Czechoslovakia. This chapter argues that although domestic political processes also played a role in sensitizing power-holders in Bulgaria to the importance of attending to popular consumption preferences, the main impetus came from the external crises that beset various countries in the Eastern Bloc between 1953 and 1968.

Part I: A growing awareness of consumption preferences, 1953–1962

By 1953 the Bulgarian Communist Party had overseen nearly a decade of harsh repression that had allowed it to identify and neutralize the most serious organized threats to its rule. In adopting a Stalinist governance model, however, the party and State Security had ignored popular consumption preferences. In the very rare cases when consumer demands were reflected in party or State Security reporting, they were presented as instances of enemy activity.[14] As this part of the chapter will demonstrate, the death of Stalin in March 1953 unleashed pent-up discontent in Bulgaria and elsewhere in the Eastern Bloc. This discontent forced the Bulgarian leadership to contemplate a new, less-repressive governance model that relied on better information and attended to the consumer expectations of the population.

The decade between March 1953 and the end of 1962 marked a new type of governance in communist Bulgaria. However, as we shall see, the ongoing presence of small-scale opposition to the regime prevented a complete transition to a low-repression equilibrium. The cyclical flare-ups of repression in the 1950s meant that levels of fear remained relatively high and precluded the establishment of institutions that could systematically monitor consumer preferences and respond to them prior to their expression as overt discontent. Although they signalled welcome change, measures to satisfy popular consumption expectations prior to 1962 remained reactive and episodic.

Unanticipated crises in the Eastern Bloc

The political vacuum created by the death of Stalin on 5 March 1953 resulted in a wave of worker strikes throughout the Eastern Bloc. In Bulgaria, laid-off tobacco workers in Plovdiv went on strike on 3–4 May 1953, protesting unemployment.[15] There were also strikes organized by textile workers in Khaskovo and preparations for a strike in the Maritsa textile plant in Plovdiv later in 1953.[16] In Czechoslovakia, the strike wave began when thousands of workers in the Škoda factory in Plzeň protested on 1 June 1953 the higher food prices that had resulted from a currency redenomination.[17] Additional strikes took place in various cities in Bohemia and Moravia.[18] Largest in scale, the East German strike wave came last. It started on 17 June 1953 in Berlin and engulfed fourteen of the fifteen provinces [*Bezirke*] of the GDR. Up to one million East German workers were protesting the increase in prices for staples, which was announced at the same time when higher work norms and lower pay for industrial workers were introduced.[19] Part of the reason for the larger size of the German uprising was that the border to West Berlin was still open and citizens believed in the possibility of a German reunification. The uprising was quelled with the help of Soviet troops which led to the killing of dozens of protesters.[20]

These instances of unrest had several commonalities. One is that in the GDR and Bulgaria they came as a surprise for the party and for State Security, both of which lacked the sophisticated institutions needed for evaluating the popular mood and for producing accurate warnings of trends in latent discontent that may lead to the rise of overt discontent.[21] The second commonality was that lacking those institutions of anticipatory governance, the East European regimes reacted to the surprise eruptions of discontent in the same way – namely, by deploying brute and sometimes deadly force. The final similarity is that the long-term response of power-holders to these episodes of regime crisis consisted of a two-pronged strategy of consumer concessions and establishing institutions that could help improve access to information. We should clarify that protests transmit information about popular discontent, but they also threaten regime stability. For this reason communist regimes needed to develop institutions that allowed them to detect latent discontent prior to its expression as overt discontent. These institutions (most effective of which is the analysis of citizen complaints) allow for the routinized collection of information on popular discontent and for stable anticipatory governance, in contrast to the ad hoc retrospective governance that was resorted to following surprise mass eruptions of discontent like the ones that occurred in the GDR or Bulgaria in 1953.

Consumer concessions

Consumer concessions were expressed primarily through a lowering of prices in the weeks and months following the strikes. In Bulgaria, the key concessions involved forgiveness of unfulfilled procurement targets for various agricultural goods, as well as improving the quality and lowering the price of bread.[22] Both of these measures were consistent with popular expectations, as revealed through rumours registered by the party in the summer of 1953.[23] Other policies involved the payment of compensation to small owners of property nationalized in 1947–1950 and reducing the tax burden imposed on craftsmen and itinerant peddlers [*ambulantni turgovtsi*].[24] The remaining concessions that came in response to the protests of 1953 were unveiled in early 1954, when the leadership announced its goals for the second five-year plan. In January, general secretary of the Bulgarian Communist Party Vulko Chervenkov proclaimed that the chief task for the second five-year plan was the rapid improvement in the standard of living of workers. Specifically, as in all the other countries of the bloc, starting with the Soviet Union (Malenkov), this included higher salaries, price reductions and increases in the quality and variety of consumer goods.[25] The details of these promises were further clarified in the draft directive of the Sixth Party Congress, which took place in March 1954. This document outlined ambitious targets for improving the well-being of ordinary citizens by raising the quality and variety of food products, shoes and apparel, as well as by increasing the amount of housing stock and enhancing the quality of municipal services.[26]

Another round of policies aimed at improving the standard of living were unveiled in 1956, just like in Czechoslovakia.[27] At the April Plenum, the party initially announced a lowering of prices and an increase in salaries and pensions, as well as a two-hour reduction of the Saturday working hours.[28] Further details on the increase in salaries were provided in December 1956, following the events in Poland and Hungary earlier that year.[29] By the end of 1956, Bulgaria had instituted pensions for members of collective farms (this did not occur in the Soviet Union until 1964), had limited the state procurement targets and raised the procurement prices for agricultural goods, had increased the amount of the monthly child subsidy and had lowered the price of food in workplace canteens.[30] These policies were consistent with popular concerns, as communicated to the leadership through anonymous leaflets,[31] citizen letters[32] and in a report prepared by Khristo Radevski, who at the time was chief secretary of the Union of Bulgarian Writers.[33] A report by Prime Minister Anton Iugov explicitly acknowledged the role of the Polish and Hungarian events in stimulating regime efforts to improve the standard of living and to eliminate unemployment.[34] The cumulative effect of the policies implemented in 1953–1956 was to send a strong signal that the party took the consumption preferences of the population seriously.

These measures reflected a new understanding that popular discontent was directly linked to frustrated consumption preferences, as revealed by an October 1956 instruction to the heads of the provincial offices of the Ministry of the Interior, which drew their attention to the activation of the enemy contingent, whose members were emboldened by 'certain difficulties in the provision of bread' and called for anti-regime activities similar to those in Poland and Hungary.[35] Western diplomats had a similar understanding of the connection between consumption and discontent. According to an August 1957 report of British Ambassador Richard Speaight, the new policies reflected decisive government efforts to deflect calls for political liberalization through material concessions.[36]

The available evidence indicates that, at least as far as big cities were concerned, there occurred a rapid improvement in the quality and variety of consumer goods immediately after 1956.[37] The opening of the Central Department Store [*Tsentralen universalen magazin* or TsUM] in 1957 in Sofia stood as a concrete physical manifestation of the new emphasis on consumption. Western diplomats noted the relative abundance of goods in the capital. In a report from August 1957, Ambassador Speaight observed that the availability and variety of goods in the stores had improved by comparison with the previous year.[38] In a November 1960 report, his successor Ambassador Lincoln noted that communist rule had led to an improvement in the standard of living.[39]

State Security and Western diplomats reached identical assessments of the political effects of improved access to consumer goods. According to State Security, regime efforts to enhance the quality of food served in worker canteens, to raise salaries and to increase the number of paid vacation days were very popular.[40] State Security opined that the cumulative effect of these policies was increased loyalty to the regime, which made it harder for foreign intelligence service to recruit informants in Bulgaria.[41] British Consul Mark Heath similarly remarked in a 1962 report that the increase in consumer goods had reduced the level of popular discontent.[42] The agreement between British diplomats and Bulgarian State Security analysts about the regime-sustaining effects of policies aimed at promoting consumption is remarkable.

However, consumption preferences could not be consistently satisfied outside the capital and a few of the largest cities. In the second half of the 1950s and early 1960s, the party and State Security noted numerous instances of consumer dissatisfaction. In the cities, securing an apartment remained a major source of discontent.[43] In rural areas and small cities, shortages of various staples (and even of bread) occurred.[44]

Improved access to information

The ongoing incidence of overt discontent throughout the 1953–1962 period highlights the importance of information gathering aimed at detecting latent discontent prior to its transformation into an overt one.[45] This information allows for proactive, anticipatory governance. In the absence of such information, governance remains reactive, haphazard, ad hoc and geographically uneven.

Therefore, the second long-term strategy in response to the events of 1953 involved efforts to use better information gathering to prevent the rise of future crises. As far as the Communist Party was concerned, this meant that the Central Committee required lower-level party offices to send weekly reports analysing the popular mood and enumerating instances of excessive violence.[46] With regard to State Security, the need for improved information gathering meant conducting a thorough assessment of the quality of its informants.

In an attempt to increase the quality of the collected information, in November 1953 the Bulgarian Politburo took the unusual step of issuing an order to State Security to reduce the size of the informant network by one-third and to stop the 'harmful practice of indiscriminate recruitment of informants'.[47] This decision was made in light of a report to the Politburo by the minister of the interior, which stated that indiscriminate recruitment had lowered the overall quality and effectiveness of the informant network.[48] Following the Politburo decision, all informants were evaluated and those whose work was deemed unsatisfactory were excluded from the secret police ranks over the course of the following year.[49] The clean-up was so extensive that in some areas of Bulgaria up to half of the existing informants were terminated. As I have argued elsewhere,[50] the archival records reveal that citizens were recruited through two main channels: blackmail and voluntary cooperation. A concern that too many informants were recruited through blackmail was expressed as early as 1946; for example, one State Security report stated that 'we need to learn how to recruit through more flexible methods ... open blackmail is naturally not always an effective method'.[51] Nevertheless, an assessment of the informant network in 1950 indicated that 54 per cent of its members were still recruited through blackmail.[52] Efforts to increase voluntary cooperation continued throughout the 1950s; most effective in this regard were instructions to use blackmail only in exceptional cases.[53] What was even more important for increasing voluntary cooperation was a general decline in repression.

A relaxation of repression favours better information gathering. Although the general 1953–1955 trend pointed towards such relaxation, the Communist Party was not yet ready everywhere to make a complete switch to a new type of governance under a low-repression equilibrium. Several signs point to the ongoing presence of significant dissent. One was anti-communist leaflets and slogans in Bulgaria, which were detected before 1953 as well, but became more numerous after the strike wave began; these leaflets (some of which were produced domestically and others dropped by planes and air balloons flying over the country) provided information to Bulgarians about the events in the Eastern Bloc and urged them to follow the example of their Czechoslovak, East German, Hungarian and Polish brethren.[54] The second trend was that although no new *goriani* armed resistance groups emerged after the first half of 1953, remnants of the movement and its sympathizers persisted until 1955.[55] Finally, after a brief hiatus in 1951–1954 (instituted in response to peasant riots), forced land collectivization resumed in 1955, which led to renewed sporadic acts of resistance.[56] For these reasons, the Polish and Hungarian upheavals of 1956 provided a welcome pretext for a domestic crackdown on dissent in Bulgaria; in justifying its actions retrospectively, the party claimed that had it not authorized harsh repression, Hungarian-style developments could have occurred in Bulgaria as well.[57] State Security used the 1956 events as a justification for expanding the size of the so-called 'enemy contingent' [*vrazheski kontingent*] to include gypsies and vagrants [*lumpeni*] and for focusing on members of the intelligentsia, youth and students.[58] The reopening of the Belene camp at the end of 1956 marked the beginning of an intensification of repression in 1957–1959 that allowed the party to complete the task of identifying and eliminating small groups and individuals opposed to the regime.

By the start of the 1960s, three factors had converged, enabling a transition from mass repression to surveillance and targeted repression. The first was that the size of the enemy contingent was becoming known. One measurable indicator of the ability of State Security to establish control over it was the fact that the only serious threats to the regime in the 1956–1968 period came from party insiders, rather than from regime enemies outside the party: one was the Kufardzhiev-Varon letter to the Central Committee in 1960, another Gorunia's attempted pro-Maoist coup in 1965 and the third was Doktorov's 'second centre' in the struggle against Zhivkov.[59] All three were internal party splits that reflected the rise of factionalism but did not stem from broader social opposition to the regime. This means that State Security had successfully neutralized the opposition through continuous surveillance and selective repression.

Although the process of cataloguing different groups of opponents started as early as 1947,[60] it could not be completed until two other factors were in place: technical sophistication and a high-quality informant network. Surprisingly considering the paucity of resources, by the 1950s State Security in Bulgaria acquired access to state-of-the-art surveillance technology that was used for telephone tapping, audio and even video surveillance.[61] These technologies were added to the more traditional methods of human surveillance and mail control, thus giving State Security considerable information about oppositional activities.[62] However, the main improvement that enabled the transition to surveillance was the enhanced quality of the informant network, which made it possible for the regime to keep abreast of its political opponents.

Harsh repression gradually declined in the second half of the 1950s. In part, this reflected the elimination of organized opposition to the regime (*goriani*, underground resistance groups sent from outside the country etc.) and in part the improved access to information. One statistic is revealing: out of the total of 23,531 individuals who were sent to labour camps between 1944 and 1962, only 3,352 account for the 1956–1962 period.[63] Although arrests were still conducted (e.g. against the so-called 'hooligans' in 1958),[64] State Security was reorienting itself towards surveillance and selective repression (those who were sent to the camps were not always incarcerated for political reasons). By 1962, a single internment camp remained (in Lovech), but the Politburo decided to close it down after determining that repression there was unnecessarily harsh.[65] The closure of the camp marked Bulgaria's transition to a mature post-Stalinist stage of political development, in which repression was used sparingly, even if the State Security apparatus continued to expand in size and to actively monitor the population. In this, Bulgaria resembled the other countries of the communist bloc.[66]

Part II: Establishing institutions for the systematic assessment and satisfaction of consumer preferences

Three developments in the 1960s made possible the systematic assessment and satisfaction of consumer preferences in Bulgaria. One was the expectation of an improvement in the standard of living, which was created by the broad package of social services and consumer goods that the leadership promised at the 1962 and 1966 party congresses and in the wake of the 1968 Czechoslovak events. Unfortunately, universal delivery on these general promises was impossible under conditions of pervasive shortages that were characteristic of all countries in the Eastern Bloc.[67] The creation of sophisticated institutions that could provide detailed assessment of latent discontent could therefore be used to guide the selective provision of consumer goods, which was the most efficient way for the regime to meet its commitments to the population.

However, the institutions for the collection of information could only operate successfully when a third development took place: namely, levels of fear had to be sufficiently low for citizens to be willing to express their consumption preferences through routine channels such as complaints (rather than by engaging in protests) without concern for retribution. The 1960s were characterized by a general decline in repression, which culminated with the 1968 revision of the Criminal Code in Bulgaria. In sum, by the late 1960s, a comprehensive system for evaluating and responding to consumer preferences had been put in place. The final impetus for institution building was provided by the Prague Spring, which had two effects. One was to convince power-holders to use the information that was being collected to engage in anticipatory governance. The other was to consolidate the socialist social contract, which involved contingent consent based on the satisfaction of consumer preferences.

This part of the chapter first reviews the promises made by the regime, then describes the institutions created for assessing citizen preferences and, finally, discusses the impact that the decline in repression had on information transfer.

Commitments to improved consumption

The 1960s in Bulgaria are notable for the explicit promises that the regime made to increase the standard of living of the population. At the Eighth Party Congress in 1962, Todor Zhivkov declared that the main concern of the party was to keep in mind the growing material needs of the population and to make efforts to satisfy them.[68] The leadership reported that an increase in personal income and in the consumption of foodstuffs, textiles, shoes and furniture had occurred over the previous decade.[69] The congress promised a further growth of income, as well as improvements in the provision of municipal services and the availability of consumer goods. A key goal was to increase the expenditure of the social consumption funds, which were used to finance free medical care, kindergartens and nurseries, free education, stipends for students, old-age pensions, annual leaves and subsidized vacation packages.[70] These plans were reiterated at the Ninth Party Congress in 1966. The party made a commitment to avoid raising prices (and to lower them whenever possible), to improve the availability of durable goods (TVs, washing machines, refrigerators, vacuum cleaners, furniture and cars), to increase the expenditures of the social consumption funds and to speed up housing construction.[71] Another key commitment was to gradually adopt a five-day workweek.[72]

The next round of policies aimed at improving consumption was announced in 1968. The timing of these measures was not random. Although some of the relevant decrees were drafted prior to 1968, the events in Czechoslovakia sped up their official promulgation.[73] The Prague Spring and the subsequent August 1968 Warsaw Pact invasion demonstrated the fragility of socialist regimes by showing that political liberalization would not be tolerated by Moscow, thus elevating to an even higher level the importance of buying popular support through increased consumption. In particular, several sets of policies were implemented in 1968. Some targeted specific groups. For example, the party aimed to improve the standard of living of students by raising their stipends, increasing the number of spots in student dormitories, decreasing the price of meals in student canteens and constructing new vacation homes for students.[74] In addition, old-age social pensions for individuals over seventy without labour service were introduced.[75] Efforts were also made to placate the general population by decreasing the prices of some food items (poultry, cow's milk *kashkaval*, fish), limiting the exportation of eggs and wheat and increasing the volume of imported meat, canned fish, olives and coffee.[76] The final policy was adopted in November 1968, when the Central Committee instructed the people's councils, that is, the local administration, to devote significant efforts to increasing the availability of services (even when they were provided by private craftsmen), to supply logistical support for the construction of new housing, to improve the quality of municipal services (transportation, postal services and various public utilities), to control the quality of customer service in stores and to facilitate raising the standard of health care and education.[77]

In sum, the 1962 and 1966 party congresses and the policies implemented in 1968 created extensive expectations for significant improvements in the standard of living of the population.

Institutions for assessing citizen preferences

In the 1960s, several entities were created with the explicit goal of assessing popular preferences. One was the Sociological Group at the Central Committee (*Sotsiologicheska grupa kum TsK*), which was established in 1967; in 1970, this group was integrated into the newly created Information-Sociological Centre of the Central Committee. Another was the Centre for Sociological Youth Research (*Tsentur za sotsiologicheski izsledvaniia na mladezhta*), which was created by the Komsomol (DKMS) in 1968. In addition, various newspapers (*Rabotnichesko delo, Sturshel*) and magazines (*Mladezh, Zhenata dnes*) conducted surveys of their readers.[78] Another newly established avenue was the Central Information-Analytical Service (*Tsentralna informatsionno-analitichna sluzhba*, or TsIAS) at State Security. It was charged with aggregating information that was collected through various types of sources; as repression declined in the 1960s, State Security began to pay more attention to tracking popular preferences, including those about consumption. The third channel for collecting information were the informants (*informatori*) within the grass-roots party organizations (*purvichni partiini organizatsii*), which were expected to send monthly reports to the county party organizations; in turn, the county organizations sent reports to the provincial party offices; finally, the provincial party committees informed the Central Committee.[79] The available archival evidence indicates that by the 1960s, the party had begun to pay systematic attention to identifying and satisfying citizen consumer preferences.

The decline in repression and the transfer of information

In the mature post-Stalinist system, massive arrests and imprisonment were used infrequently. As Minister of the Interior Angel Solakov reported at a Central Committee plenum in 1967, the number of individuals who engaged in 'enemy activity' declined ninefold between 1955 and 1966, in part as a result of the improvement in the material well-being of the population,[80] but also certainly because like in every other bloc country people who opposed communism realized that the regime was there to stay and resigned themselves to that new reality. This decline in the incidence of 'political crimes' led to a very important change: when a new Criminal Code was promulgated on 15 March 1968, it no longer listed neutralizing enemies of the people as a goal of criminal punishment.[81] As the following graph demonstrates, over time, there was a general softening of repression.

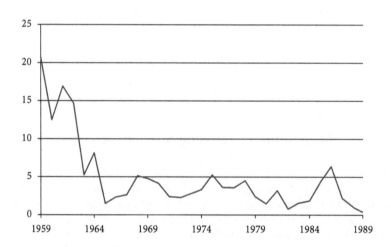

Number of Individuals Prosecuted for Crimes against the People's Republic, 1959–1989 (per million people). Source: Martin K. Dimitrov, based on figures from Durzhavno upravlanie za informatsiia pri Ministerski suvet/Glavno statistichesko upravlenie, *Prestupleniia i osudeni litsa*, 1969–1990.

The decline in repression in the 1960s allowed State Security to reorient some of its vast information-gathering resources towards assessing and responding to consumer discontent. Although indicators of this reorientation are more easily identified for the period after 1970, we can mention two signs dating back to the 1960s. One concerns the increasing frequency of reports on popular dissatisfaction that resulted from the shortage of consumer goods.[82] Of course, such reports were previously generated by State Security during crisis moments in the 1950s; what is remarkable about the reports from the 1960s is that they were produced during normal times, thus signalling that the monitoring of consumer discontent was becoming a routine task for State Security. The second trend was the use of the capacity of Scientific-Technical Intelligence to solve some consumption problems. It is relevant that as early as 1966, State Security aimed to alleviate consumer goods shortages through the acquisition by Scientific-Technical Intelligence personnel of the formulae needed to manufacture on a mass scale various chemical and pharmaceutical products.[83]

Unsurprisingly, the Communist Party devoted more extensive resources than State Security to monitoring and responding to consumer discontent in the 1960s. In 1965, the Central Committee Department of Trade and Food Industry informed the Politburo about problems in the production of household necessities (ranging from glassware to toys and haberdashery) and the provision of various services.[84] In the same year, Politburo members received copies of a report on the political mood prepared by the Sofia City Party Committee, which indicated significant dissatisfaction as a result of problems in the allocation of housing, the poor quality of transportation and periodic food shortages in the stores in outlying districts; residents of the capital also complained about air pollution.[85] In 1967, the Organization Department of the Central Committee issued a report on the political mood that documented citizen dissatisfaction with the poor quality of durable goods and meat shortages.[86] Frustration about the scarcity of spring lamb was especially severe, due to a widespread rumour that lamb was being exported to Greece and Italy.[87] In 1969, Politburo members received a report from the Industrial-Economic Department of the Central Committee on the remaining unresolved problems with the provision of municipal services.[88] These examples testify to the attention that the party paid to tracking and responding to popular consumer preferences. In comparison to the 1950s, when widespread consumer dissatisfaction led to large strikes and numerous riots, consumer discontent in the 1960s appeared more limited in scope and thus more manageable.

The 1960s also saw a new emphasis on the importance of complaints for assessing and satisfying citizen consumption preferences. At the Eighth Party Congress in 1962, the head of the Central Control and Audit Commission reported that most complaints were about housing and job allocation, although citizens also highlighted problems in transportation, trade, the supply of utilities and the provision of welfare assistance.[89] At the Ninth Party Congress in 1966, the Central Control and Audit Commission reiterated the importance of providing a timely response to complaints and clarified that they allowed the party to monitor the political mood of citizens.[90] In 1968, municipal councils were instructed to radically improve their complaints work. The party issued an express prohibition that complaints be adjudicated by the authorities against which citizens complained.[91] Overall, the regime tried to reassure members of the general public that they should not fear retaliation for complaining. As I have argued elsewhere, the effect of these measures was felt in the 1970s and early 1980s, when the analysis of citizen complaints was widely used to engage in anticipatory governance.[92]

Conclusion

This chapter has analysed the origins of the institutions for collecting information on citizen consumption preferences in communist Bulgaria. It has argued that the establishment of these institutions came in response to external and internal regime crises that occurred between 1953 and 1968. The crises of 1953 (the domestic strikes and the protests in Czechoslovakia and the GDR) forced power-holders in Bulgaria to make concessions in the area of consumption. The new emphasis on producing consumer goods that the post-Stalin Soviet leadership articulated also played an important role.

However, the Polish protests and the Hungarian Revolution in 1956 impacted the decision-making calculus of Bulgarian leaders in more complex ways. On the one hand, they reaffirmed the importance of responding to already-existing and visible discontent with further consumer concessions. At the same time, they led to a new spike in state violence, thus obstructing the inchoate progress towards a decline in repression that would have allowed the regime to transition from ex-post governance (which focuses on the management of overt discontent) to ex-ante governance that aims to identify and address latent discontent prior to its transformation into overt discontent.

The chapter argues that the gradual decline in the use of harsh repression throughout the 1960s allowed power-holders to respond to the crisis of August 1968 differently: namely, in contrast to their reaction in 1956, they decided that instead of intensifying repression, they would base their rule on a combination of selective repression and contingent consent that rested on the satisfaction of consumer preferences just like elsewhere in the Eastern Bloc. The institutions for the collection of information, which were fully operational by the end of the 1960s, were essential for identifying and managing consumer frustrations prior to their transformation into overt discontent.[93] The utility of the Bulgarian case lies in giving us an example of why a communist regime would prefer to evaluate consumption preferences through voluntarily provided information (rather than through protests). The routinized voluntary transmission of information through citizen complaints allowed the Bulgarian regime to engage in anticipatory governance in the 1970s and the early 1980s. This model was successfully implemented until Bulgaria experienced an economic crisis starting in 1983–1984. This crisis called into question not only the responsiveness to citizen consumption preferences that was essential for anticipatory governance but also the stability of the entire political system as well.

Notes

1   Janos Kornai, *The Socialist System: The Political Economy of Communism* (Princeton: Princeton University Press, 1992).
2   Carl J. Friedrich and Zbigniew K. Brzezinski, *Totalitarian Dictatorship and Autocracy*, 2nd rvsd. ed. (Cambridge: Harvard University Press, 1965).
3   Hannah Arendt, *The Origins of Totalitarianism* (New York: Harcourt, Brace, 1951); Friedrich and Brzezinski, *Totalitarian Dictatorship*; Bruce Bueno de Mesquita, Alastair Smith, Randolph M. Siverson, and James D. Morrow, *The Logic of Political Survival* (Cambridge: MIT Press, 2003).
4   Alexander Dallin and George W. Breslauer, *Political Terror in Communist Systems* (Stanford: Stanford University Press, 1970).
5   Alex Pravda, 'East-West Interdependence and the Social Compact in Eastern Europe', in *East-West Relations and the Future of Eastern Europe: Politics and Economics*, eds. Morris Bornstein, Zvi Gitelman, and William Zimmerman (London: George Allen and Unwin, 1981), 162–187; James R. Millar, 'The Little Deal: Brezhnev's Contribution to Acquisitive Socialism', *Slavic Review* 44, no. 4 (1985): 694–706; Peter Hauslohner, 'Gorbachev's Social Contract', *Soviet Economy* 3, no. 1 (1987): 54–89; Linda J. Cook, *The Soviet Social Contract and Why It Failed: Welfare Policy and Workers' Politics from Brezhnev to Yeltsin* (Cambridge: Harvard University Press, 1993).
6   Mark Landsman, *Dictatorship and Demand: The Politics of Consumerism in East Germany* (Cambridge: Harvard University Press, 2005); Lewis H. Siegelbaum, *Cars for Comrades: The Life of the Soviet Automobile* (Ithaca: Cornell University Press, 2008); Paul Betts, *Within Walls: Private Life in the German Democratic Republic* (New York: Oxford University Press, 2010); Paulina Bren and Mary Neuburger, eds., *Communism Unwrapped: Consumption in Cold War Eastern Europe* (New York: Oxford University Press, 2012); Diane Koenker, *Club Red: Vacation Travel and the Soviet Dream* (Ithaca: Cornell University Press, 2013).
7   Konrad Jarausch, ed., *Dictatorship as Experience: Towards a Socio-Cultural History of the GDR* (New York: Bergahn Books, 1999); Václav Havel, *The Power of the Powerless* (Armonk: M. E. Sharpe, 1985), 38.
8   Cook, *The Soviet Social Contract*; Stephan Haggard and Robert R. Kaufman, *Development, Democracy, and Welfare States: Latin America, East Asia, and Eastern Europe* (Princeton: Princeton University Press, 2008); Tomasz Inglot, *Welfare States in East Central Europe, 1919–2004* (New York: Cambridge University Press, 2008); Linda J. Cook and Martin K. Dimitrov, 'The Socialist Social Contract Revisited: Evidence from Communist and State Capitalist Economies', *Europe-Asia Studies* 69, no. 1 (2017), 8–26.
9   Beatriz Magaloni, *Voting for Autocracy: Hegemonic Party Survival and Its Demise in Mexico* (New York: Cambridge University Press, 2006); Jason Brownlee, *Authoritarianism in an Age of Democratization* (New York: Cambridge University Press, 2007); Steven Levitsky and Lucan A. Way, *Competitive Authoritarianism: The Origins and Evolution of Hybrid Regimes in the Post-Cold War Era* (New York: Cambridge University Press, 2010); Valerie J. Bunce and Sharon Wolchik, *Defeating Authoritarian Leaders in Postcommunist Countries* (New York: Cambridge University Press, 2011); Milan W. Svolik, *The Politics of Authoritarian Rule* (New York: Cambridge University Press, 2012).

10   Martin K. Dimitrov, 'Tracking Public Opinion under Authoritarianism: The Case of the Soviet Union under Brezhnev', *Russian History* 41, no. 3 (2014): 329–353.

11   Martin K. Dimitrov, 'What the Party Wanted to Know: Citizen Complaints as a "Barometer of Public Opinion" in Communist Bulgaria', *East European Politics and Societies and Cultures* 28, no. 2 (2014), 271–295.

12   Ibid.

13   Martin K. Dimitrov, *Politicheskata logika na sotsialisticheskoto potreblenie* (Sofia: Ciela Publishers, 2018).

14   Arkhiv na Ministerstvoto na vutreshnite raboti (Archive of the Ministry of the Interior; AMVR), f. 1 op. 1 a. e. 802 l. 1–12 (27 July 1951).

15   AMVR, f. 1 op. 1 a. e. 2922 l. 5 (1953).

16   Arkhiv na Komisiiata za razkrivane na dokumenti i obiaviavane na prinadlezhnost na bulgarski grazhdani kum Durzhavna sigurnost i razuznavatelnite organi na Bulgarskata narodna armiia – M (Archive of the Committee on Access to and Disclosure of Documents and Announcing the Affiliation of Bulgarian Citizens with State Security and the Intelligence Services of the Bulgarian National Army – M; AKRDOPBGDSRSBNA-M), f. 13 op. 3 a. e. 579 l. 6 (1953).

17   Muriel Blaive, *Une déstalinisation manquée: Tchécoslovaquie 1956* (Brussels: Complexe, 2005), 90–93.

18   Ivan Pfaff, 'Weg mit der Partei!' (Down with the Party!), *Die Zeit*, 22 May 2003, http://www.zeit.de/2003/22/S_86_Vorspann_Pilsen (accessed 12 April 2017).

19   Christian F. Ostermann, ed., *Uprising in East Germany, 1953: The Cold War, the German Question, and the First Major Upheaval Behind the Iron Curtain* (New York: Central European University Press, 2001).

20   The exact number of victims is still not certain but the German government places it at fifty-five. See https://www.bundesregierung.de/Content/EN/Artikel/2017/06_en/2017-06-17-gedenken-17-juni-1953_en.html (accessed 17 July 2017.)

21   AMVR, f. 1 op. 1 a. e. 2811 (1954); Armin Mitter, 'Die Ereignisse im Juni und Juli 1953 in der DDR', *Aus Politik und Zeitgeschichte*, no. 5 (1991): 31–41.

22   Vladimir Migev, *Kolektivizatsiiata na bulgarskoto selo (1948–1958)* (Sofia: Universitetsko izdatelstvo 'Stopanstvo', 1995), 163–165; Vladimir Migev, 'Nasiliia, reformi i kompromisi: Kum vuprosa za otrazhenieto v Bulgariia na krizisnite protsesi v suvetskiia blok (1953–1981 g.)', in *Istoriiata – profesiia i sudba: Sbornik v chest na 60-godishninata na chlen-korespondent d. ist. n. Georgi Markov*, eds. Vitka Toshkova, Vasilka Tankova and Nikolai Poppetrov (Sofia: Tangra TanNakRa, 2008), 550.

23   Tsentralen durzhaven arkhiv (Central State Archive, TsDA), f. 1B op. 15 a. e. 585 l. 2–7 (17 July 1953).

24   Vladimir Migev, 'Za Aprilskiia plenum – 1956 godina i za liberalizatsiiata na rezhima v Bulgariia prez 50-te i 60-te godini na XX vek (Opit za istoricheska eseistika)', *Istoricheski pregled* LXV, no. 1–2 (2009): 187–199 (193).

25   TsDA, f. 1B op. 5 a. e. 131 l. 51–58 (19 January 1954).

26   TsDA, f. 1B op. 5 a. e. 131 l. 25–50 (25 February–3 March 1954).

27   Blaive, *Une déstalinisation manquée*.

28   Evgeniia Kalinova and Iskra Baeva, *Bulgarskite prekhodi 1939–2005* (Sofia: Paradigma, 2006), 133.

29   TsDA, f. 1 op. 5 a. e. 239 (4 December 1956); Valentin Aleksandrov, *Ungarskata revoliutsiia 1956: Vutreshnopoliticheski i mezhdunarodni aspekti* (Sofia: Voenno izdatelstvo, 2007), 164.

30   Migev, 'Nasiliia, reformi i kompromisi', 552–553.

31   TsDA, f. 378B op. 1 a. e. 757 (9 November 1956).

32   TsDA, f. 378B op. 1 a. e. 748 (10 November 1956); TsDA f. 378B op. 1 a. e. 748 (17 November 1956).

33   TsDA, f. 1B op. 7 a. e. 1778 l. 1–2 (15 November 1956).

34   TsDA, f. 317B op. 1 a. e. 135 l. 4–34 (7 December 1956).

35   AKRDOPBGDSRSBNA-M, f. 1 op. 1 a. e. 3780 l. 1–3 (29 October 1956).

36   Dimitur Dimitrov, *Suvetska Bulgariia prez tri britanski mandata (1956–1963): Iz arkhiva na Foreign Office za subitiia i lichnosti v Bulgariia* (London: BBC, 1994), 19.

37   Elitsa Stanoeva, 'Organizirane na sotsialisticheskata turgoviia v Bulgariia (1954–1963): doktrinalni protivorechiia i mezhduinstitutsionalni naprezheniia', *Sotsiologicheski problemi* XLVII, no. 1–2 (2015): 111–133.

38   Dimitrov, *Suvetska Bulgariia prez tri britanski mandata*, 17–18.

39   Ibid., 76.

40   AMVR, f. 1 op. 1 a. e. 61 l. 1–31 (23 June 1959).

41   Ibid.

42   Dimitrov, *Suvetska Bulgariia prez tri britanski mandata*, 120.

43   TsDA, f. 1B op. 15 a. e. 702 l. 33–42 (4 May 1957).

44   AMVR, f. 1 op. 5 a. e. 79 l. 12–13 (26 September 1962).

45   For a more detailed treatment of this point, see Martin K. Dimitrov and Joseph Sassoon, 'State Security, Information, and Repression: A Comparison of Communist Bulgaria and Ba'athist Iraq', *Journal of Cold War Studies* 16, no. 2 (2014): 4–31.

46   Migev, *Kolektivizatsiiata na bulgarskoto selo*, 163. As Migev argues, the period of intense peasant unrest in 1951 also resulted in demand for regular reporting: in March 1951, both the provincial party committees and State Security were required to issue daily reports on popular unrest (ibid., 124).

47   Politiburo Decision 'On the Activities and Tasks of the Ministry of the Interior and the Organs of State Security', 21 November 1953. TsDA, f. 1B op. 64 a. e. 185, l. 9.

48   TsDA, f. 1B op. 64 a. e. 185 (8 November 1953).

49   AMVR, f. 1 op. 5 a. e. 40 (30 March 1955).

50   Dimitrov and Sassoon, 'State Security, Information, and Repression'.

51   AKRDOPBGDSRSBNA-M, f. 1 op. 1 a. e. 219 l. 1–7 (7 September 1946), at l. 2.

52   AKRDOPBGDSRSBNA-M, f. 13 op. 1 a. e. 616 l. 2–20 (11 January 1951), at l. 13.

53   AKRDOPBGDSRSBNA-M, f. 1 op. 11 a. e. 49 l. 60–81 (20 June 1962), at l. 66.

54   TsDA, f. 1B op. 24 a. e. 125 (1953); TsDA, f. 1B op. 24 a. e. 126 (1953); TsDA, f. 1B op. 24 a. e. 159 (1954); TsDA, f. 1B op. 24 a. e. 162 (1954); TsDA, f. 1B op. 24 a. e. 221 (1956).

55   See documents reproduced in *Gorianite: Sbornik dokumenti*, t. 2 (1949–1956) (Sofia: Durzhavna agentsiia 'Arkhivi', 2010). The *goriani* armed resistance groups were small in size (typically fewer than ten members). The total number of participants in these underground resistance groups is estimated to have been about 5,000.

56   See documents reproduced in *Durzhavna sigurnost i kolektivizatsiiata (1944–1959): Dokumentalen sbornik* (Sofia: KRDOPBGDSRSBNA, 2015).

57   Durzhaven arkhiv-Sofia (State Archive, Sofia), f. 3B op. 13 a. e. 2 l. 92–96 (1957).

58   AKRDOPBGDSRSBNA-M, f. 1 op. 2 a. e. 312 l. 21–26 (1957).

59   Dimitur Ivanov, *Politicheskoto protivopostaviane v Bulgaria 1956–1989 g.* (Sofia: Ares Press, 1994), 10–44; Mikhail Doktorov, *V skhvatka s oktopoda: 'Vtoriiat tsentur' v borbata sreshtu zhivkovistite, 1965–1968 g.* (Sofia: Ares Press, 1993).

60   AKRDOPBGDSRSBNA-M, f. 1 op. 1 a. e. 377 l. 137–139 (1947); AKRDOPBGDSRSBNA-M f. 13 op. 1 a. e. 795 l. 1–15 (12 March 1951), at l. 1.

61 On telephone tapping and audio surveillance, see AKRDOPBGDSRSBNA-M, f. 1 op. 11 a. e. 22 l. 383–393 (7 February 1955); on video surveillance, see AKRDOPBGDSRSBNA-M, f. 1 op. 11 a. e. 48 l. 224–239 (26 May 1962).

62 On these methods, see AKRDOPBGDSRSBNA-M, f. 1 op. 11 a. e. 31 l. 274–295 (6 May 1957); AKRDOPBGDSRSBNA-M, f. 1 op. 11 a. e. 31 l. 165–173 (19 February 1957).

63 Penka Stoianova and Emil Iliev, *Politicheski opasni litsa: Vudvoriavaniia, trudova mobilizatsiia, izselvaniia v Bulgariia sled 1944 g.* (Sofia: Universitetsko izdatelstvo 'Sv. Kliment Okhridski', 1991), 101.

64 The 21 January 1958 Politburo decision authorizing State Security to conduct arrests of 'hooligans' is reprinted in Stoianova and Iliev, *Politicheski opasni litsa*, 155.

65 The 5 April 1962 Politburo decision is reprinted in Stoianova and Iliev, *Politicheski opasni litsa*, 169–177.

66 Duane Huguenin, 'Youth, the West, and the Czechoslovak Secret Police: Immaturity or Ideological Diversion?' *Vingtième Siècle: Revue d'Histoire* 1, no. 109 (2011): 183–200; Sandrine Kott, *Le communisme au quotidien: Les entreprises d'Etat dans la société est-allemande* (Belin: Paris, 2001); Thomas Lindenberger, *Volkspolizei: Herrschaftspraxis und öffentliche Ordnung im SED-Staat 1952–1968* (Cologne: Böhlau, 2003).

67 On the shortage economy, see Kornai, *The Socialist System*.

68 *Osmi kongres na Bulgarskata komunisticheska partiia (5 noemvri–14 noemvri 1962 g.) (Stenografski protokol)* (Sofia: Izdatelstvo na Bulgarskata komunisticheska partiia, 1963), 72–73.

69 Ibid., 71–72.

70 Ibid., 73–74.

71 *Deveti kongres na Bulgarskata komunisticheska partiia (14 noemvri–19 noemvri 1966 g.) (Stenografski protokol)* (Sofia: Izdatelstvo na bulgarskata komunisticheska partiia, 1967), 74–81.

72 Ibid., 80.

73 Vladimir Migev, *Prazhkata prolet '68 i Bulgariia* (Sofia: Iztok-Zapad, 2005), 285.

74 Ibid., 255.

75 Nina Dimitrova, 'Rolia na sotsialnite uslugi v Bulgariia v perioda 1944–1989 g.: Trudoviiat kolektiv kato razshireno sotsialistichesko semeistvo', in *Da poznaem komunizma: Izsledvaniia*, ed. Ivailo Znepolski (Sofia: Ciela Publishers, 2012), 255.

76 Ibid., 262–263.

77 *Miastoto i roliata na narodnite suveti v sistemata na sotsialnoto upravlenie (reshenie na Tsentralniia komitet na Bulgarskata komunisticheska partiia, 27 noemvri 1968 g.)* (Sofia: Izdatelstvo na Bulgarskata komunishticheska partiia, 1968), 9–17.

78 Stoian Mikhailov, *Sotsiologiiata v Bulgariia sled Vtorata svetovna voina* (Sofia: M8M, 2003), 44–47; Migev, *Prazhkata prolet '68 i Bulgariia*, 276–277; Kristen Ghodsee, 'Pressuring the Politburo: The Committee of the Bulgarian Women's Movement and State Socialist Feminism', *Slavic Review* 73, no. 3 (2014): 538–562 (549).

79 Migev, *Prazhkata prolet '68 i Bulgariia*, 169.

80 TsDA, f. 1B op. 34 a. e. 52 l. 1–112 (1967) (cited from Veselin Angelov, *Strogo sekretno: Dokumenti za deinostta na Durzhavna sigurnost [1944–1989]* [Sofia: Simolini, 2007], 512).

81 Martin Kanushev, 'Postoianen nadzor i infranakazatelnost: bulgarskoto nakazatelno pravo prez perioda 1957–1969 godina', *Sotsiologicheski problemi* XLI, no. 3-4 (2009): 175–199.

82   AMVR, f. 1 op. 5 a. e. 80 (1963) is representative of this trend.

83   TsDA, f. 1B op. 34 a. e. 52 l. 1–112 (1967) (cited from Angelov, *Strogo sekretno*, 527).

84   TsDA, f. 1B op. 91 a. e. 1060 (1965).

85   TsDA, f. 1B op. 91 a. e. 1431 l. 1–11 (1965), l. 7–11.

86   TsDA, f. 1B op. 91 a. e. 1437 l. 6–10 (1967).

87   Ibid., l. 6.

88   TsDA, f. 1B op. 91 a. e. 1118 (1969).

89   *Osmi kongres na Bulgarskata komunisticheska partiia*, 175–179.

90   *Deveti kongres na Bulgarskata komunisticheska partiia*, 126.

91   *Miastoto i roliata na narodnite suveti v sistemata na sotsialnoto upravlenie*, 17.

92   For more on this point, see Martin K. Dimitrov, 'Zhalbite na grazhdanite v komunisticheska Bulgariia', in *Da Poznaem Komunizma*, ed. Znepolski, 167–226; Dimitrov, 'What the Party Wanted to Know'.

93   For more details on how these processes unfolded in the 1970s and 1980s, see Dimitrov, 'What the Party Wanted to Know'.

8

Who Is Afraid of Whom? The Case of the 'Loyal Dissidents' in the German Democratic Republic

Sonia Combe

According to the dominant view – shared by laypersons and pundits alike – fear and resignation were the main factors that contributed to the stability of Soviet-style societies.[1] The first part of this chapter accordingly deals with the concept of fear. Based on a comparison between the Stasi (political police) files and the records of the Writers' Union in the German Democratic Republic (GDR), two quite different sources, this part aims to demonstrate that fear was shared both by the political establishment and by the citizens, albeit in different measures and with an evolution over time. During my past research in the Stasi files, I showed that these archival materials tell us more about the organization of repression, its goals, its practices and the security obsessions of the rulers than about the people under observation.[2] Two specific moments in GDR history give credence to this thesis: June 1967, with the media treatment of the Six-Day War, and November 1976, when the popular singer-songwriter Wolf Biermann was deprived of his citizenship.

In the second part, I draw attention to the social agents that the rulers most feared. I introduce a category of intellectuals that tends to be ignored by scholarly literature: the so-called *linientreue Dissidenten*[3] (loyal dissidents), who were positioned as a pivot between the rulers and the ruled. As representatives of this social category, I focus on the scientist Jürgen Kuczynski and the writer Christa Wolf, both members of the SED.[4] They were not trusted by the country's rulers but they were moral authorities who were highly respected in the country. I argue that the deconstruction of the way this social category operated provides a clue to understanding the stability of the East German regime until its collapse in 1989 – when fear decisively switched sides.

The contingencies of establishing communism in a non-nation state

I focus on the GDR not only because it is the country where I conducted my fieldwork in the 1980s – a privilege I share with ever fewer colleagues – but also because the negotiation between rulers and ruled, the analysis of which is at the core of this volume, was a necessity that was even more vital there than in any other Eastern Bloc country. The reason for this is rather obvious: the GDR was not a nation. It was only a small part – actually the smaller part – of a nation. Despite the commendable efforts of communist ideology, an East German identity or, for that matter, an East German nation was never successfully created. Indeed, Germans from the Eastern and Western parts of the country shared the same language and the same cultural heritage; and in Germany, ever since Johann Gottfried Herder (1744–1803), this has been considered a defining characteristic of the national identity.

As a consequence, and as opposed to all the other members of the Eastern Bloc, leaving the country was hardly synonymous with emigrating for its citizens: those who departed simply landed in another part of Germany that congratulated them, at least after the Wall was erected, provided them with ID papers straightaway and helped them to resettle. Moreover, they encountered no difficulty with the language, could easily find a job, study or send their children to school. They were praised as victims, sometimes even as heroes, no matter what their reasons to leave the eastern part of the country might have been in the first place, and they always deserved, or so it was thought, good treatment. If we compare this situation to that experienced by citizens from other socialist countries, the difference is quite striking. Competing with West Germany for its entire lifetime, the GDR had to struggle to keep its skilled people from running away, threatened as it was by a shortage of manpower. The building of the Berlin Wall in August 1961 was the brutal answer to this conundrum. Still, the GDR was in a unique situation and, in that sense, was and remained the weakest link of the socialist chain.

This particular situation largely predetermined the relationship between the rulers and the ruled in the country. The existing research in the Stasi files on the relationship between the intellectuals and the state in particular shows that institutional violence declined after the erection of the Berlin Wall. Physical punishment (torture and imprisonment) progressively disappeared and was replaced by psychological violence, in particular by the knowledge that one could be observed at any time, and all the time. Christa Wolf described in her book *Was bleibt* (What Remains) the state of mind resulting from this form of violence.[5] In a somewhat paradoxical way, however, the closing of the Berlin Wall resulted in a higher degree of internal freedom – including freedom of speech. The complexity of the state surveillance apparatus led to an apparent contradiction: the more it was watched by the Stasi, the more East German society became permissive.[6]

Establishing a chronology of East German socialism

The two events that support this claim occurred in the period that has been dubbed 'late state socialism',[7] when traditional styles of repression declined and were replaced by global surveillance. Introducing the concept of 'late state socialism' was important in the history of German communism because insufficient consideration has traditionally been given to a chronological differentiation of the communist regimes. The historiography usually distinguishes two periods: the first one ends with

Khrushchev's Secret Speech at the twentieth congress of the Soviet Communist Party in February 1956 and the second with the final collapse of communism in 1989 – or 1991 for the USSR. Until 1956, fear and enthusiasm for the new order coexisted. In the second period, the prevailing social behaviour has been described as one of accommodation.[8]

The American historian of Hungarian descent István Deák, on the other hand, also distinguishes two distinct periods, but with the first one ending only in 1963.[9] As far as the GDR, but also other countries, are concerned, we also have to take into account the Soviet invasion of Prague in 1968.[10] In any case, with the notable exception of Romania, which took a reverse path and increased repression after 1968, we cannot possibly compare the 1950s – even the late 1950s – in any of the Soviet Bloc countries with the two last decades (1969–1989). We can agree that 'late state socialism' starts at different periods according to the local context, but that the abandonment of massive physical punishment is a common and decisive turning point in the second phase of communist rule.

'The Tango Player'

Political and social historians are often reluctant to refer to literary works. They question the academic value of this type of source. Yet there is hardly any better description of the Prague Spring's influence on East German society than that present in *Der Tangospieler* (The Tango Player),[11] a novel by Christoph Hein. The author tells the story of a character named Dallow, a historian working at Leipzig University who comes home after being released from jail. He had been sentenced to twenty-one months of imprisonment because of certain lyrics. As an amateur pianist in a band, he had indeed played a fateful song that told the story of 'an old man who led the country'. This was enough for the Stasi to recognize a reference to Walter Ulbricht, the first secretary of the SED and president of the country, and to indict him for 'desecrating the president', an offence whose punishment was consistently enforced in communist countries, as opposed to Western Europe where it slowly fell into disuse. Coming back to Leipzig after his release, Dallow discovers that this tango song is now played everywhere. He thus realizes that he has been sentenced for a crime that is no longer a crime. In less than two years, the situation has greatly evolved.

From that point onwards, in the 'late state socialist' period as defined by starting in 1968 or 1969, the traditional form of repression involving jail sentences became sporadic in the GDR. If at all, it now affected only young, anonymous rebels, who were sentenced to jail, then sent to West Germany against hard currency – the FRG indeed paid hefty sums of money (70,000 deutschmarks per head) to secure their release and transfer to the West.[12] The task of negotiating their release and their transfer fell to the Lutheran Church.

While enjoying a substantial rise in the standard of living together with the decline of classical-style repression, and as the citizens adjusted to the communist regime and vice versa, fear progressively faded away, especially among the most critical minds. Many intellectuals (especially writers), although supportive of the political establishment, started to speak out after the Soviet military intervention of Prague in August 1968. Their attitude had evolved over the years. During the uprising of 17 June 1953, many of them had supported Walter Ulbricht's regime. In fact, they supported the rulers because they were afraid of the mob howling in the streets: it reminded them of the masses cheering Hitler and the Nazis only a few years previously.[13] In the GDR, to use the term 'the people' (*das Volk*) had become highly unpopular. The ambivalence of East German intellectuals is well illustrated by Bertolt Brecht's famous joke in his 1953 poem 'The Solution', written after the 1953 uprising, asking whether it 'would not be easier for the government to dissolve the people and elect another?'[14] However, for the most part the intellectuals had remained loyal to the government. This did not prevent them from exerting a newly found critical pressure after 1968.

Cross-checking the Stasi files with the records of the Writers' Union in the late state socialist period

I evoke in this section two events, the reactions to which will serve as useful indicators of the difference of attitude between the Stasi and the intellectuals.[15] The first case took place in June 1967 during the Six-Day War in the Middle East, a year before the Warsaw Pact military intervention in Prague. As is well known, this third Arab-Israeli War provoked a change in Soviet policy towards the Middle East and its support of an ever more aggressive attitude towards Israel.

Initially supportive of Israel at the time of its founding in 1948, the USSR soon transferred its support to the Arab states. This shift became notorious in the Soviet discourse against Israel from that moment onwards. It was especially prominent during the Stalinist show trials of the early 1950s, notably with the Slánský trial in Prague and its narrative of 'anti-Zionism' (in effect, anti-Semitism).[16] On 31 May 1967, and while the issue of the war was still uncertain, *Neues Deutschland*, the SED's newspaper, displayed on its front page the following headline: 'Republik empört über imperialistische Anschläge in Nahost' (Country Indignant about Imperialist Attacks in Middle East). Reporting on the hostilities, the East German press resorted to a vocabulary against Israel with a virulence unmatched after the National Socialist period. The way the media (TV, radio and newspapers) criticized Israel did indeed leave a lingering stench of anti-Semitism. Consequently, the Stasi could almost immediately observe in its reports on intellectuals within the Writers' Union that more than a few of them confessed to feeling uneasy; they even spoke of 'the return of the repressed'. This was especially evident in the case of one of the most famous writers at the time, Stephan Hermlin.[17] According to his Stasi file, he was thought to believe that anti-Semitism was still present in the GDR, and that evidence of this could be found in the way the media reported about the Middle Eastern conflict.[18]

This diffuse feeling of unease is quite possibly the reason why *Neues Deutschland* tried to launch a campaign featuring Jewish personalities condemning Israel. The daily newspaper tried in vain to mobilize famous East German Jews for its cause. In the Stasi files, as well as in the archives of the SED members in the Writers' Union,[19] personalities such as Anna Seghers, Stephan Hermlin, Stefan Heym and others –

the most prominent writers of Jewish origin in the GDR – a report can be found. According to this report, we can reconstruct the unfolding of events as follows: on 8 June 1967, *Neues Deutschland* tried to get in touch with these writers in order to publish a statement from 'East-German citizens of Jewish origin' condemning 'Israel's aggression against the Arab states'. The first writer the editors reached was Stephan Hermlin. He answered that he had to think about the matter and would give his agreement later. As soon as he hung up the phone, he called Anna Seghers. We do not know the details of their conversation, but we can easily figure it out. Contacted in turn by the newspapers, Anna Seghers did not answer the phone. Her secretary explained to the *Neues Deutschland* journalists that Seghers was at home but wished not to be disturbed. Stefan Heym was then called but unfortunately he was in a hurry on his way to La Charité, East Berlin's biggest hospital, and he would call back after his appointment – except that he never did. The editors had to call him again. His wife was apologetic but he hadn't come home yet, although it was late – unfortunately too late at a certain point to put his name at the bottom of the declaration which had to be published in the morning edition. The same happened with Anna Seghers and Stephan Hermlin. As to the most important personality of the Jewish world in the GDR at that time, Arnold Zweig,[20] *Neues Deutschland* did not even try to get in touch with him: they knew he would not accept.

The declaration was published on 9 June 1967 on page 2. With one or two exceptions, the signatories were quite unknown (Carlheinz von Brück, Wolfgang Frankenstein, Kurt Goldstein, Lea Grundig, Siegbert Kahn, F.K. Kaul, Franz Loeser, Ernst Reifenberg, Elizabeth Thierfeld and Gerry Wolf).

An anecdote that Stefan Jerzy Zweig, known as the 'Child of Buchenwald', personally recounted to me is worth noting here.[21] As a boy, Zweig had been rescued by German political prisoners in Buchenwald. He had spent his youth in Israel and had been invited by the East German film company – the famous DEFA – to study in the GDR, where he stayed for a few years. Upon hearing how the East German radio reported on the Israeli Army in 1967, which was decidedly reminiscent of the German radio reporting on the Red Army in 1943, he decided to complain to Helene Weigel, a 'non-Jewish Jew'[22] (Isaac Deutscher) and the widow of Bertolt Brecht. As such, she was a person whom the Politburo did not wish to alienate. She supposedly picked up her phone, called the head of Radio Berlin International, the international broadcaster of the GDR, and complained in turn. As from the following day, according to Stefan Jerzy Zweig, the tone of the radio was perceptibly curbed.

State authorities were faced with a similar conundrum a year later, when they demanded that university students and academics support the Warsaw Pact invasion in Prague in order to publish an equivalent declaration. We now know that the refusal to publicly support the Soviet policy did not lead to sanctions; on the other hand, the public denunciation of the invasion did land many a protester in jail, while life became more difficult for a writer like Rainer Kunze, who left the party as a sign of protest.[23] As mentioned earlier, the 1968 Prague events were a turning point as concerns the behaviour exhibited by many people who had, until then, supported the regime.

The Wolf Biermann case or how fear switched sides

The Wolf Biermann case is quite famous. The expulsion from the GDR of this singer-songwriter, popular among urban intellectuals and the cultural world, occurred in November 1976. Biermann was a young, committed communist when he defected from Hamburg in West Germany to the GDR in 1955, but soon his non-conformist views alarmed the East German establishment and he became blacklisted. He was prevented from giving public concerts, so he famously organized parties in his own apartment, in the prime real estate sector of Chausseestrasse in Berlin, where he also recorded his famed protest songs.[24] He was under permanent Stasi surveillance but otherwise led a rather uneventful life. In November 1976, as the most beloved East German dissident in the West, he was invited to give a concert in Cologne. Against all expectations he was authorized by the regime to cross to West Germany. However, immediately after his concert and while he was still abroad, the East German authorities seized this opportunity to deprive him of his citizenship. As a result, he was not allowed to come back to East Berlin.[25]

This decision gave rise to righteous indignation among famous East German writers. It is to be noted that their prime reaction was not fear, but indignation – or indignation more than fear, as it were. In both Germanies, stripping anyone of their rights has the irresistible power to evoke the Nazi regime, a time period when the Third Reich massively deprived anti-fascists and emigrating Jews of their citizenship. The popular personalities Christa Wolf and, again, Stephan Hermlin (who might have been less known than Christa Wolf abroad but who was highly respected at home) launched a petition against this decision. It was signed by thirteen members of the Writers' Union, as well as by over a hundred people outside it. Inside the Union, the minutes of several sessions, as well as the Stasi files of the protagonists, testify to a raging conflict concerning this petition. Both sources coincide on this matter, which is a rare occurrence.[26]

The Biermann affair had thus become a scandal. Most members of the Writers' Union disagreed with the regime's decision but the real reason for the conflict lay elsewhere and is worth underlining: the initiators of the petition had informed a Western press agency of their action instead of addressing it to the Politburo. By doing so, they doubtlessly intended to signal that they had lost any hope of secretly negotiating with the authorities, as had been the case before. Requiring secrecy is a very powerful form of control. From that turning point onwards, the relationship between the regime and its writers was one of suspicion from both sides. Writers had breached the system.[27]

As a consequence of this disobedience, the Stasi increased its surveillance efforts over the petitioners. A peek into the archives of the Hager office – Kurt Hager was responsible for culture at the Politburo – reveals that the political establishment hesitated between two policies: distribute awards to some of the writers in order to prevent them from becoming dissidents and divide the profession; and blacklist them, that is, ignore their publications, prevent them from being published and force them to choose between having to wait for publication and emigration. Such was the extent of the considered range of punishments; at no point did the authorities envisage a more severe form of retribution. In fact, we can infer from similar situations that the members of the political establishment certainly underwent an internal conflict, a struggle between hardliners and pragmatic decision-makers.

At any rate, this hesitation and the final decision to give up traditional and more sinister forms of punishment was evidence of the establishment's own mounting fear – while the fear of what looked increasingly like a civil society below them was declining.

Negotiation as a necessary power practice that undermines power

Only by paying due attention to the archives of the Writers' Union it is possible to understand that this institution cannot be reduced to the status of the Communist Party's go-between, as claimed by the anti-communist narrative. The same statement could be made for other institutions like feminist organizations. I refer here to an ongoing debate about the feminist agenda under state socialism. In the spirit of the Cold War, the conventional wisdom was that all aspects of everyday life in the Soviet regimes were decided within the Communist Party and Politburo, and no decision-making power belonged anywhere else. If we deny any agency and influence to women, writers, trade unionists or leaders of any other social institution, we fail to understand the complexity of the relationship between society's top and its bottom, between the rulers and the ruled.[28]

After the consolidation of the communist regime's power, negotiation spaces between the regime and the population had to be carved out in order to maintain stability. In 1975, the GDR passed a law entitled *Gesetz über die Bearbeitung der Eingaben der Bürger* (law on the treatment of citizens' petitions). To a certain extent, the rulers knew they had to take a step back and allow some initiative from the bottom-up. However, we can observe that without the threat of repression, the Stasi was no longer efficient. It could only unearth, observe and report on critics within the institutions. By 1989, the secret police was in the position to know everything, but no longer in the position to do anything against the regime's opponents. At this point, we can safely claim that the Stasi was more afraid of the people than the people were of the Stasi.

Between loyalty, compromise and voice:
Albert Hirschman revisited

Let us finally focus on the personalities the rulers were most afraid of: the writers and intellectuals – at least before the authorities realized, in the course of the 1989 fall, that their existence as elite was threatened by the population itself.[29] The Stasi was able to identify public, and sometimes private, 'deviations' in thinking as compared to the regime's tenets, as well as to keep track of ideological disagreements – independently of the fact that it was also inclined, in a well-established institutional practice, to amplify or invent them if necessary, in order to service its own aims (which would be another chapter in the long story of the communist domination practices).[30]

The characterization 'critical but friendly to the regime' was often applied to intellectuals who were members of the Communist Party but that the authorities did not trust. The discussions led by Stasi agents with academics and university professors who agreed to collaborate with them paradoxically reveal the extent of the potential for anyone to express disagreement. In a way, it can even be claimed that such discussions constituted an opening of sorts for the freedom of expression. It often happened that the informer expressed his criticism without restraint. To be sure, fear governed society in the years of the regime's stabilization (what Mary Fulbrook has coined the 'normalization of the rule'),[31] but when the memory of the Berlin Wall's erection faded away, fear's intensity diminished.

The intrinsic weakness of dissent in the GDR remains beyond doubt, especially compared to its extent in Poland and Hungary. Only individual opposition existed in the GDR (that of Wolfgang Harich, Robert Havemann or Stefan Heym),[32] at least until, as we saw, the revocation of Wolf Biermann's citizenship in 1976 led to the first collective action among intellectuals in the form of a petition. This action probably also opened the path to the pacifist movement that developed in the 1980s. But how can we account for its weakness for so many decades? Wider-ranging questions also come to mind: To what extent can the specific national contexts and their different constraints explain the diametrically opposite attitudes of intellectuals in Hungary and Poland, compared to East Germany? Would it be possible to establish a typology of intellectual protests, ranging from open dissent (Charter 77 in Czechoslovakia, even though the movement was very limited in number, or the Solidarity movement in Poland) to 'internal emigration' with the known practice of circles or half-secret communities (such as the group around the review Poiski in the Soviet Union)?

The majority of the East German intellectual elite who did not emigrate to the West until 1961 openly supported the project of building a socialist society – without necessarily agreeing with all the details of its realization. Even if we exclude from consideration all those who remained communists (either as party members or as believers) after their experience in a Gulag or in a prison, the attitude of the majority of these intellectual elite remains hard to interpret, even for scholars who wish to avoid the traps of an irrelevant dichotomy.[33] Few among the intellectuals who remained communists after 1961 have spoken up publicly, even after the repression became milder and was replaced by surveillance. The two events we have mentioned in this context (the response to the Six-Day War and Wolf Biermann's expulsion) show how difficult it was for them to break the silence.

Different degrees and roots of loyalty to the system must be distinguished here: conformism, freely consented submission, accommodation, acquiescence, blindness and sincerity. The opening of the archives, even if it has provided unequal access to the sources in the different post-communist countries, the amount of autobiographical writings since the collapse of the Soviet Bloc, the publication of previously censored manuscripts, the availability of correspondence and the many collections of eyewitness accounts, all facilitate the study of a whole range of behaviours within the last generation of East-Central European communists and non-communist citizens. Alexei Yurchak's book on 'the last Soviet generation' provides us with an answer of sorts:

The Soviet system produced tremendous suffering, repression, fear and lack of freedom, all of which are well documented. But focusing only on that side of the system will not take us very far if we want to answer the question posed by this book about the internal paradoxes of life under socialism. What tends to get lost in the binary accounts is the crucial and seemingly paradoxical fact that, for great numbers of Soviet citizens, many of the fundamental values, ideals, and realities of socialist life (such as equality, community, selflessness, altruism, friendship, ethical relations, safety, education, work, creativity and concern for the future) were of genuine importance, despite the fact that many of their everyday practices routinely transgressed, reinterpreted, or refused certain norms and rules represented in the official ideology of the socialist state.[34]

As I already mentioned, leaving the country for an East German citizen, especially an intellectual, did not entail the same consequences as for any other East-Central European intellectual. The East Germans could hold on to their most important work instrument – their native tongue. Since emigration was possible when one disagreed with the regime even if this was not always easy, the potential for protest greatly diminished. In his famous interpretive pattern – *exit/voice/loyalty* – that he retroactively applied to the GDR shortly after the fall of the Berlin Wall,[35] the American sociologist Albert Hirschman explained how leaving (the 'exit') diminished the expression of dissent (the 'voice'): 'A recurring theme of my 1970 book was the assertion that there is no pre-established harmony between exit and voice, that to the contrary they often work at cross purpose.' Quoting his own work, Hirschman goes on: 'The presence of the exit-alternative can atrophy the development of the art of voice.'[36]

The majority of the studies that departed from Hirschman's work were interested in the voice/exit alternative more than in loyalty.[37] Some East German intellectuals did choose exit (Arthur Kantorowicz, Ernst Bloch, Hans Mayer).[38] Still, the majority of those who had embraced communist Germany at the end of the war and who had decided to stay kept silent in the name of their loyalty to its ideology. My hypothesis is that this attitude, in fact the attitude of the entire first generation of post-war communist intellectuals, has contributed to preventing the birth and development of later dissidence in East Germany. Given its prestige as opponents of Nazism and thanks to its moral and intellectual impact, this generation of communist intellectuals and founding fathers transmitted its behaviour (silence) down the line to the next generation of intellectuals of whom Christa Wolf was a prominent member.

We thus have to distinguish between three generations:

1. The generation of the founding fathers, including the political personnel and the intellectual elite who opted for the GDR in 1949, who had come back from their exile in the USSR or Western countries during the Nazi period (Bertolt Brecht, Jürgen Kuczynski, Anna Seghers), or were anti-fascist survivors of the Nazi extermination camps;
2. The generation born and socialized under the Third Reich, which developed a political conscience under the communist regime (Christa and Gerhard Wolf, Wolf Biermann);

3. The generation born and socialized in the GDR (*Hineingeborenen*). Their representatives, who eventually did break the silence, were to be found in the pacifist and feminist movements of the 1980s (Bärbel Bohley, Ulrike Poppe, Roland Jahn).

The first generation influenced the second, but the second largely failed to keep a hold on the third. The aura of the anti-fascists was already fading out, which is why this third generation managed to 'leave' and speak out. That is how, twenty years after the publication of his book *Exit, Voice and Loyalty*, Albert Hirschman could analyse the evolving relationship between exit and voice that was confirmed by the events taking place in the GDR in fall 1989: 'Here exit (out-migration) and voice (protest demonstrations against the regime) worked in tandem and reinforced each other, achieving jointly the collapse of the regime.'[39]

A heuristic oxymoron

The oxymoron *linientreue Dissidenten* (loyal dissidents), which was also the title of Jürgen Kuczynski's autobiographical narrative (the choice of his editor),[40] reflects the position and attitude of this social group towards the regime. It suggests a form of tension that translated into a somewhat inconsistent behaviour. We could also opt for the characterization used by the Stasi, 'critical but friendly to the regime', but it does not reflect the double constraint (faithfulness to the party line vs. holding on to their critical mind) that communist intellectuals structurally experienced. Besides, even if the intellectuals generally remained loyal to the party, the examples of the Six-Day War and of the Wolf Biermann affair show that some nevertheless did break the silence, thereby raising the fear level in the rulers' ranks. What is at stake here is the construction of an ideal type of 'loyal dissident' around characteristics derived from the common experience of the first two generations: their engagement against National Socialism and their choice in favour of the GDR for the first; their loyalty to the founding fathers and to the anti-fascist legacy for the second.

The Christa Wolf cohort (i.e. the second generation) opened their eyes to the monstrosity of the Nazi regime when they became teenagers, then young adults. Henceforth, as Christa Wolf often explained it herself, they could not conceivably rebel against the founding fathers – even if the consequence of this attitude was facing what Leon Festinger has dubbed 'cognitive dissonance', that is, the obvious inadequacy between expectations, wishes and social reality.[41] They were so devoted to the communist ideal that they silently endured the absence of freedom of speech and movement, as well as censorship and surveillance. The loyalty involved in this posture becomes obvious when we study the minutes of the Akademie der Künste meetings; in this closed circle, we can see that these intellectuals did criticize the regime's policy and they did complain about censorship. But they kept an outwardly supportive front. Besides, they genuinely disliked West Germany, which they saw as a country in which the old Nazis had come back to power after a short stint in jail. As is well known, justice might have been more lenient towards the former dignitaries of the National Socialist regime in the Federal Republic than in the GDR as the Americans rapidly became more interested in the fight against world communism than in denazification.[42]

If we sum up the characteristics of these 'loyal dissidents', we come up with the following portrait:

1. They were no bureaucrats (apparatchiks). Opportunism or careerism was not among their dominant/prevailing qualities.
2. They were cultivated Marxists, often party members. They were no party intellectuals in the dogmatic sense, but intellectuals within the party.
3. When they expressed disagreement, they did it exclusively within the party, or they addressed their grievances directly to the ruling circles without giving them unwanted publicity.

The following and last characteristic is the most crucial one. As is the case with every ideal type, it does not completely match reality but is rather a heuristic, indicative notion. Although it applies to some degree to every segment of society, no other social category exhibits it to the same degree. Let us first concentrate on what this special quality is not. The loyalty of the 'linientreue Dissidenten' does not derive from conformism in thinking, nor in their adaptive capacity – these behavioural patterns can be found in every society, in dictatorships as well as in democracies. Similarly, the ratio of dissidence to faithfulness to the party line is at variance from one person to another. Born at the end of the nineteenth or the beginning of the twentieth century, the first generation exhibited party discipline and committed sacrifices to satisfy communist rituals (self-criticism, struggle for reintegration in the party in case of exclusion). This trait distinguished them from the 'believers' (what Hannah Arendt described as the 'ex-communists'), for whom the party was a substitute for the church and who became opponents once they were excluded.[43]

What is, then, the defining characteristic of the loyal dissidents? The following questions might help us bring the final touch to their portrait:

1. Is it a German national characteristic? Is it a communist characteristic, involving the habit of 'Stalinist obedience'? Is it a German-communist characteristic, involving both national character and 'Stalinist obedience' or *habitus*?
2. To what extent does this characteristic contribute to explaining not only the weakness of the dissidence but also the longevity and stability of the East German regime, as well as the internalization by the population of the values promoted by the official narrative (allegiance to the founding social project)? This internalization of values could be observed throughout the forty years of existence of the GDR. All the way until the fall of 1989, it successfully masked the contradiction between the escape ('exit') and the speaking up ('voice') – at least before this status quo's final implosion.
3. But also: could one see in the loyal dissidents a coterie – a specific group – whose decision to remain silent outside the party bounds could be related to a form of collective defence, as defined by sociologists such as Erving Goffman?[44]

These questions remain open. It might be useful here to distance ourselves from the so-called East German *Sonderweg*, that is, its exceptionalism or special path[45] – an analogy to the notion of the German *Sonderweg* that is usually described in relation to the catastrophic event of Nazism as a phenomenon supposedly reflecting unique German flaws in character (this characterization was attributed by historians like Léon Poliakov or A.J.P. Taylor and many others).[46]

On the other hand, we might compare our East German intellectuals to non-German communist figures who also seem to have possessed the aforementioned characteristics. We could mention, for instance, György Lukács (1885–1971), the famous author of *History and Class Consciousness* (1923)[47] in Hungary, and Adam Schaff (1913–2006) in Poland. Both were philosophers, cultivated Marxists and members of the Communist Party, and both wanted to be readmitted after they were excluded. In their own ways, both chose a form of inner exile. It will be remembered that Lukács refused to intervene publicly during the Soviet intervention in Czechoslovakia in August 1968, but sent a personal letter to Hungarian president János Kádár, while Adam Schaff refused to emigrate during the wave of official anti-Semitism in Poland but accepted a temporary invitation to teach at an Austrian university. If Schaff, as opposed to Lukács, never founded a school of thinking bearing his name, it is to be noted that he nonetheless strongly influenced the loyal dissidents in East Germany, as well as in other countries.

Conclusion

The country where the loyal dissidents doubtlessly exerted the strongest influence on society remains East Germany. This is so not only because, as often argued, the German Communist Party was stronger in interwar Germany than in any other East-Central European country, apart perhaps from Czechoslovakia. This might be true, but the same can be said for West Germany. The difference is that as opposed to the Federal Republic, the GDR was ruled by people who had struggled against Nazism. Whatever hardship they may have gone through (prison, camp, exile), and even for those who had not been great heroes, they had spoken out – unlike the majority of the German population, east and west alike. In this context, in their role as mediators between the rulers and the ruled and as long as the aura of the founding fathers remained strong, the 'loyal dissidents' prevented the building of an opposition in the GDR. This may not have been their intention, but the fact is that their presence erected a *cordon sanitaire* of sorts between the people (*Das Volk*, a reference to the 1989 demonstrations' epic slogan 'Wir Sind Das Volk')[48] and the decision-makers.

The intellectual elite's silence under communism also goes a long way to explain the absence of resonance of the so-called 'third way' – an intellectual, alternative movement that would have proposed a form of socialism 'that one would not want to escape from' – I am quoting Christa Wolf's famous talk on Alexanderplatz in Berlin on 4 November 1989.[49] This belated call for a third way came much too late. Fear had definitively switched sides: the powerless citizens' fear of the regime had turned into the powerless regime's fear of its citizens. The 'loyal dissidents' had no more role to play and the regime collapsed practically overnight. Socialism was no more.

Notes

1   See Hubertus Knabe, *Die Mörder sind unter uns* (Munich: Propyläen Verlag, 2007). This view was also popularized by Václav Havel in his famous essay 'The Power of the Powerless'. The essay is accessible online: http://vaclavhavel.cz/showtrans. php?cat=clanky&val=72_aj_clanky.html&typ=HTML (accessed 1 March 2018).

2   Sonia Combe, *Une société sous surveillance. Les intellectuels et la Stasi* (Paris: Albin Michel, 1999). See also Sonia Combe, 'Figures de l'officier traitant à travers les archives de la Stasi', *Cultures et Conflits* 53, no. 1 (2004): 99–112.

3   Jürgen Kuczynski, *Ein linientreuer Dissident. Memoiren 1945–1989* (Berlin: Aufbau-Verlag, 1992).

4   *Sozialistische Einheitspartei Deutschlands* or Socialist Unity Party, that is, the East German Communist Party.

5   Christa Wolf, *Was bleibt* (Berlin: Aufbau, 1990), translated into English under the title *What Remains,* by Heike Schwarzbauer and Rick Takvorian (New York: Farrar, Strauss, & Giroux, 1993).

6   Combe, *Une société sous surveillance.*

7   See Alexei Yurchak, *Everything Was Forever Until It Was No More: The Last Soviet Generation* (Princeton: Princeton University Press, 2006).

8   See Thomas Lindenberger, 'Die Diktatur der Grenzen. Zur Einleitung', in *Herrschaft und Eigen-Sinn in der Diktatur. Studien zur Gesellschaftsgeschichte der DDR*, ed. Thomas Lindenberger (Cologne: Böhlau, 1999), 13–43.

9   Istvan Deak, 'Scandal in Budapest', *New York Review of Books*, 20 September 2006.

10 For a discussion of the periodization of late state socialism, see Pavel Kolář, *Der Poststalinismus: Ideologie und Utopie einer Epoche* (Cologne: Böhlau, 2016), 7–14.

11 Christoph Hein, *Der Tangospieler* (Berlin: Aufbau-Verlag, 1989). *The Tango Player*, translated into English by Philip Boehm (Evanston: Northwestern University Press, 1994).

12 See Gareth Dale, *Popular Protest in East Germany, 1945–1989* (London: Routledge, 2005), 87.

13 Combe, *Une société sous surveillance.*

14 Bertolt Brecht, *Buckower Elegien, 1953. Ausgewählte Werke in sechs Bänden*. Dritter Band: Gedichte 1. (Frankfurt: Suhrkamp, 1997), 404.

15 The Writers' Union records (Schriftsteller Verband) are accessible in two places: at the Akademie der Künste (Academy of Arts) in Berlin and at the Landesarchiv in Berlin – Büro Hager (National Archive, Berlin – Hager Office). The Stasi files are located in the different offices of the Bundesbeauftragten für die Stasi Unterlagen (BStU), the Federal Commissioner for the Records of the State Security Service of the former GDR.

16 See Karel Kaplan, *Report on the Murder of the General Secretary* (London: I. B. Tauris & Co., 1990).

17 BStU, Berlin. Mfs AIM 2173, Stephan Hermlin.

18 Ibid.

19 Landesarchiv Berlin. Magistrat. Abteilung Kultur C Rep 121 (1963–1974).

20 Arnold Zweig (1887–1968) was a famous contemporary German writer who emigrated to Palestine during the period of the Third Reich. After the war, he came back to East Germany and became the Head of the Akademie der Künste (Academy of Fine Arts).

21   Personal interview with Stefan J. Zweig in Vienna, February 2013. For a wider view of this project, see Sonia Combe, *Une vie contre une autre. Echange de victime et modalités de survie dans le camp de Buchenwald* (Paris: Fayard, 2014).

22   See Isaac Deutscher, ed., *The Non-Jewish Jew and Other Essays* (Oxford: Oxford University Press, 1968).

23   Rainer Kunze, *Deckname 'Lyrik.' Eine Dokumentation* (Frankfurt: S. Fischer Taschenbuch, 1990).

24   See his album *Chausseestrasse* 131 (1968).

25   Many volumes have been written on Wolf Biermann's case. Recently he published his autobiography: Wolf Biermann, *Warte nicht auf bessere Zeiten! Die Autobiographie* (Berlin: Propyläen, 2016).

26   See Stephan Hermlin's Stasi file (mentioned earlier), Christa Wolf's Stasi file (Mfs HA XX/7), as well as 'Protokolle der Sitzungen des Schriftsteller Verband der DDR', and the 'Protokolle von Sitzungen von Grundorganisationen der SED, Akademie der Künste, Berlin', C Rep 904–079/097 (1968–1976), C Rep 121 (1974–1989).

27   Stiftung Archiv der Parteien und Massenorganisationen der DDR im Bundesarchiv, Berlin (Foundation Archives of Parties and Mass Organisations of the GDR in the Federal Archives; SAPMO). Büro Hager. DY30 IV A et B. See also Eva Patzelt, *Un haut fonctionnaire est-allemand aux prises avec l'intelligentsia (1963–1989). Kurt Hager face aux écrivains Volker Braun, Stefan Heym, Helmut Sakowski et Erwin Strittmatter* (Paris: L'Harmattan, 2014).

28   Krassimira Daskalova, 'Audiatur and altera pars: in response to Nanette Funk' in 'Ten Years After: Communism and Feminism Revisited', *Aspasia* 10, no. 1 (2016): 102–168.

29   We may recall how the Stasi head, Erich Mielke, whose stubbornness was legendary, addressed the East German Parliament on 13 November 1989 in a famous – and pitiful – shout: 'Ich liebe Euch doch Alle' (But I love you all). The speech can be found on YouTube: https://www.youtube.com/watch?v=1XBEqyu5Mck (accessed 27 November 2017.) See his biography on the website of the DDR Museum in Berlin: https://www.ddr-museum.de/en/blog/archive/i-love-i-love-all-all-humans-erich-mielke-biography (accessed 27 November 2017).

30   See Sonia Combe, ed., *Archives et écriture de l'histoire dans les sociétés post-communistes* (Paris: La Découverte, 2009).

31   Mary Fulbrook, ed., *Power and Society in the GDR, 1961–1979. The 'Normalization of Rule'?* (New York: Berghahn Books, 2009).

32   Wolfgang Harich (1923–1995) was a philosopher who was arrested and sentenced to twelve years in prison for conspiracy against the regime. Robert Haveman was a chemist and a critic of socialism. He endured house arrest from 1976 to his death in 1982. Stefan Heym (1903–2001) was a writer and critic of the regime, who endured censorship and surveillance (but not prison or house arrest.)

33   Here it must be admitted that the reshaping of memory after the fall of the Berlin Wall is often a screen that may alter the representation of the past.

34   Yurchak, *Everything Was Forever Until It Was No More,* 8.

35   Albert Hirschman, *Exit, Voice and Loyalty. Responses to Decline in Firms, Organizations and States* (Cambridge: Harvard UP, 1970). Albert Hirschman, 'Exit, Voice and the Fate of the GDR: An Essay in Conceptual History', *World Politics,* 45 (1993): 173–202.

36   Hirschman, 'Exit, Voice and the Fate of the GDR', 176.

37   See Steven Pfaff, *Exit-Voice Dynamics and the Collapse of East Germany: The Crisis of Leninism and the Revolution of 1989* (Durham: Duke University Press, 2006).

38   Arthur Kantorowicz (1899–1979) was an academic who left the GDR in 1957; Ernst Bloch (1885–1977) was a philosopher and the author of *Prinzip Hoffnung* (translated into English under the title *The Principle of Hope*), published in three volumes between 1954 and 1959, who left the GDR just before the erection of the Berlin Wall in August 1961; Hans Mayer (1907–2001) was a literary scholar who emigrated to West Germany in 1963.

39   Hirschman, 'Exit, Voice and the Fate of the GDR', 177.

40   Kuczynski, *Ein linientreue Dissident.*

41   Leon Festinger, Henry W. Riecken, and Stanley Schachter, *When Prophecy Fails* (Minneapolis: University of Minnesota Press, 1956), 25.

42   Frederick Taylor, *Exorcising Hitler: The Occupation and Denazification of Germany* (London: Bloomsbury Publishing, 2011), 277.

43   See Hannah Arendt, 'The Ex-Communists', *Commonweal* 11 (1953): 595–598. Festinger, Riecken, and Schachter, *When Prophecy Fails*, 23–55.

44   Erving Goffman, *The Presentation of Self in Everyday Life* (Garden City: Anchor, 1959).

45   Catherine Epstein, *The Last Revolutionaries* (Cambridge: Harvard University Press, 2003); Axel Fair-Schulz, *Loyal Subversion. East Germany and Its Bildungsbürgerlich Marxist Intellectuals* (Berlin: Trafo, 2008).

46   See, for instance, AJP Taylor, *The Course of German History* (London: Hamish Hamilton, 1945), 213.

47   For the English translation, see Georg Lukács, *History and Class Consciousness: Studies in Marxist Dialectics* (London: Merlin Press, 1971).

48   See the article 'Monday Demonstrations in East Germany', *Wikipedia*, https:// en.wikipedia.org/wiki/Monday_demonstrations_in_East_Germany (accessed 27 November 2017).

49   Christa Wolf, 'A Speech in East Berlin', *The New York Review of Books*, 7 December 1989. The speech can be watched on YouTube: https://www.youtube.com/ watch?v=gr1MffkSttI (accessed 27 November 2017).

Part Three

From Real Existing Socialism to the End – and Beyond

9

Did Communist Children's Television Communicate Universal Values? Representing Borders in the Polish Series *Four Tank-Men and a Dog*[1]

Machteld Venken

Recent research has revealed how foreign television shows being broadcast in Warsaw Pact countries formed a transnational communication space in Cold War Europe.[2] This chapter goes one step further and argues that the shows made in the West that were also broadcast in the Polish People's Republic inspired domestic television producers to create their own children's series on behalf of the state-controlled television station. The producers managed to reconcile the seemingly contradictory aims of producing a show modelled on examples from the West while meeting the regime's expectations. In this chapter, I focus on the script of the series *Czterej Pancerni i Pies* (Four Tank-Men and a Dog),[3] first aired in 1966.

The series succeeded in transposing into the Polish context a mixture of popular television genres imported from the United States and Western Europe. By analysing how this series was judged and adapted for propaganda aims, I reveal how the historical imagination of the nation was negotiated. Moreover, I situate how and why this representation was so willingly consumed by children in Poland and throughout the Soviet Bloc (the show became one of Poland's most popular cultural export products). The regime thus largely (albeit not entirely) imposed a propagandistic version of past events.

My analysis focuses on the representation of borders in the series. In modern statehood, power has been linked to border control. Moreover, Hannah Arendt has argued that in totalitarian regimes, objectivized enemies are more important than ideology.[4] Border zones constitute an ideal physical space where these enemies can be staged in cultural productions. It should not come as a surprise, then, that scenes taking place at the border are given considerable attention in *Four Tank-Men*.

Conceptualizing (children's) television shows

Historical shows have been conceptualized in different ways in Western and East-Central European television. By the late 1960s, the genre had become a key concept in Anglo-Saxon film theory.[5] It has also since gone on to become a tool to research children's television shows produced in the West.[6] According to the *Collins English Dictionary*, 'genre is a particular type of literature, painting, music, film, or other art form which people consider as a class because it has special characteristics'.[7] Essential to a genre, moreover, is that it consists of socially agreed-upon codes and conventions that evolve over time as they incorporate, respond and adapt to production techniques, marketing strategies and the expectations of the audience.[8] Mass media products reproduce what has previously met with viewers' enthusiasm, while introducing something new in order to maintain interest. Borrowing from their viewers' world, genres, it has been observed, serve as ideological reproductions of the capitalist system.[9] Ideology should be understood here as a process of making sense of society in which rulers, sponsors, producers and child viewers are all involved.[10]

In studies both on children's television during communism and on communist cultural products for children in general, historians use the concept of propaganda as the central prism for analysis.[11] Propaganda distinguishes itself from other types of ideological inflection by influencing the attitude of the audience through deception instead of persuasion. Censorship organs were often set up in communist countries to screen, alter or veto audiovisual productions.[12] As it is aiming to reveal rather than understand, however, such research tends to present a simplistic opposition between regime and society.[13] The existing literature on children's television does not include genre as a key concept of analysis and therefore gives the impression that propaganda and genre are two mutually exclusive categories of analysis. This chapter shows that the aims and techniques of propaganda and genre could function in a creative tandem, feeding off each other, and eventually melting into each other so as to become almost indivisible.

Television watching in Poland

Four Tank-Men was an immensely popular hit show during communism and beyond, and it won the 1995 Polish public broadcasting television station (TVP) award for the most popular series ever.[14] Viewers have consistently praised this children's series more than they have any series made for adults. Therefore, if we are to understand everyday communist society, turning our lens on children's television is essential. We need to analyse young viewers as not only passive but also active consumers of communist culture.

Poland experienced a spectacular baby boom; by the mid-1960s, 25 per cent of the population was attending school.[15] This configuration had an influence on the emergence of televised youth culture. The Polish broadcasting industry was from its creation in 1952 monopolized by the Communist Party, but its socialist realist template resulted in a disgruntled audience.[16] In 1956, the new leader Władysław Gomułka and his administration understood that by making television attractive, they could implement their ideological aspiration to exert control over a standardized culture. The latter had the potential to spread among all strata of the population and break down elitist culture. Broadcasting coverage grew rapidly over the years, from 10,000 viewers in Warsaw at the end of 1955 to 78 per cent of the whole Polish population having access to a TV in 1967.[17] By the end of the 1960s, watching television had become a favourite pastime of the masses, including children and youngsters.[18] In remote villages, for example, people either gathered together in order to watch television or, alternatively, shied away from social activities if a television was available at home.[19] In 1967, a study conducted in Poland revealed that only 15 per cent of adolescents did not aspire to have their own television.[20]

The territorial context in post-war Poland

The most popular children's series *Four Tank-Men and a Dog* featured the adventures of a tank crew fighting in a military unit within the Polish First Army, often referred to as the Berling Army.[21] In 1944, this army was composed in the Soviet Union and was put under the supervision of the Red Army. The series followed its path from Siberia to Berlin in 1944 and 1945.[22] When it was broadcast in the late 1960s, it was already obvious that it falsely represented Polish borders. The 1956 Polish protests had shown that, while communism had utterly failed to win the population over despite its slogans on modernization and social progress, the possibility of finding any way out of Soviet hegemony was just as unrealistic.[23] For the sake of a relative autonomy, it was crucial to tolerate the communist regime and to keep the Polish borders in place. The inherent dilemma of preserving Polish national identity through the acceptance of Soviet hegemony was something Polish citizens needed to live with.

Censored cultural productions often focused on Poland's borders in those years. The country had geographically shifted in 1945, gaining 103,788 square kilometres in the west while losing 214,200 square kilometres in the east. Post-war Poland encompassed the territory between the Oder and Neisse rivers in the west and the Bug River in the east.[24] Official narratives presented the Polish post-war border at the Bug as the historic Polish-Soviet border and deliberately glossed over the memory of the recent past in the region east of the river (which had been part of the Polish Republic in the interwar period).[25]

The Polish-German borderline, on the other hand, was depicted as uncertain and contingent; fear was manufactured over what propaganda dubbed 'German revisionism'.[26] The Oder–Neisse borderline had been defined at the Potsdam Conference in 1945, pending an international peace treaty. Said treaty never materialized, and while the Polish People's Republic signed a bilateral agreement with East Germany on the acceptance of this border already in 1950, it did not reach a similar bilateral agreement with West Germany until December 1970.[27]

A seemingly unsafe Polish-German border, however, was a motivational tool in securing Poland's place on the geopolitical map. Gomułka himself called the Polish People's Republic 'a kind of Slavic bastion', an *antemurale Slavorum*, fighting against an expansionist West.[28] His words aimed to legitimize the Polish authorities. Together with their Soviet friends only, they could defend the population in the case of conflict.

The Polish broadcasting corporation

The regime found in the rapidly growing broadcasting industry a new means of disseminating its message. Polish broadcasting was controlled by state officials but was negotiated with film directors, scriptwriters and actors, as well as with viewers. Defining together what messages could be broadcast, television professionals became co-designers of national education.

Polish broadcasting started to air a permanent children's programme in 1957. Television producers were in a position to pay more attention to education and entertainment than before the protests against Soviet hegemony in October 1956, which resulted in a liberalization of the regime,[29] thanks to which educational programming without specific propaganda content, such as the series *Zrób to Sam* (Do it yourself), in which children were taught how to make things (such as a bird table), were launched.[30] By the 1960s, however, the children's show supply saw an increase in series with a sharper propagandistic message.[31] Just as teachers adjusted their teaching to include fear of potential German revisionism, and just as children's authors produced manuscripts addressing nationalist ideology, so too children's television programmes were required to play their role.[32] Television series made it easier for children to develop emotional bonds and their episodic nature was more effective at serving propagandistic aims.[33]

That change in focus resulted from a new Resolution of the Central Committee on Cinematography of 1959–1960, which restricted anew television producers' freedom and enforced ideological convergence upon them. It also prescribed a more stringent selection of foreign shows.[34] Control was institutionalized in a Commission for the Evaluation of Scripts (Komisja Ocen Scenariuszy), and from 1967 onwards in a Programme Council (Rada Programowa). These organs focused on the way the Soviet Union and Germany were depicted and evaluated the socialist didactic value of productions.[35] When a 1962 questionnaire sent out by the Polish television broadcasting station to viewers all over Poland showed that a majority of respondents wished for a reduction in the amount of talk shows and an increase in the amount of sports, movies and fictional programmes,[36] state officials opted to prioritize entertainment as a channel for propaganda.[37] Additional funds were devoted to the production of fictional television shows underpinning Gomułka's nationalist ideology.[38] The Resolution and the work of the Commission for the Evaluation of Scripts overshadowed cultural production and led to artists' conformism.

A hunger for fiction had initially lured viewers to imported and dubbed productions made in the West, but by the mid-1960s, Polish productions were becoming increasingly popular. They managed to transpose to a domestic context what had been attractive for Polish viewers in such shows. Fiction made it possible to play with the meaning of propagandistic messages. In addition, whereas socialist realism had prescribed the heroization of collectives and had reduced the role of individuals, producers now featured individual experiences against the backdrop of a historical setting.[39] Viewers could see themselves in these heroes, or project their dreams onto them, which led to their identification with the state-approved characters.[40]

With the increasing political influence of both army and ex-combatants, an ideology of power in which patriotism and military tradition were foregrounded[41] began to be featured in audiovisual productions. Polish movies for adults often presented a soldier courageously undertaking military actions, fulfilling his obligations in the name of patriotism and often finding himself in extreme situations. With only his innate sense of justice to guide him, he would find the right path to serve the motherland.[42]

An emblematic series: *Four Tank-Men and a Dog*

Four Tank-Men and a Dog depicted Second World War events with a myriad of historical mistakes, but supported a narrative that gave meaning to Polish nationalist ideology. The scripts were based on a book by Janusz Przymanowski.[43] The story reminds me of the English best-seller *Three Men in a Boat (To Say Nothing of the Dog)* from 1889, Jerome K. Jerome's humorous account of a boat journey on the Thames that colourfully depicts subversive leisure-time activities. The book was first translated into Polish in 1912 and was reprinted regularly, but Przymanowski never referred to it as a source of inspiration.[44]

One can easily recognize codes and conventions from several television genres in the series: road movies, comedies and historical war movies, with some of the fighting scenes not out of place in a Western. Just as would happen in a road movie, the show features a vehicle transporting a group of close male friends from point A (the Soviet Union) to point B (Berlin).[45] As is the case with comedies, the amusing escapades and jokey banter the protagonists enjoy challenge the demands of realism.[46] Just like in historical films, the content is portrayed as authentically as possible, aiming to glorify the national heritage on screen.[47] The television series also shares the iconography of a war movie: large-scale battles alternate with individual stories of heroism; while the protagonists are at the heart of the action, the enemy is portrayed as an impersonal other.[48] Most of all, however, *Four Tank-Men* resembles a Western. The main character gets the better of his enemies by outsmarting them, and he achieves justice for his home country on his journey civilizing the West.[49] A reason for the Western genre's success in America lay in the fact that viewers were fascinated with the concept of the frontier, which was imagined as a place for an encounter between civilization and the wilderness, between the East and the West. It has even been argued that 'the characteristics of the American intellect – restless energy, practical expediency, exuberance, and individualism among them – are the product' of that encounter.[50]

The archetypical children's Western *Zorro* started to be broadcast in Poland in the early 1960s.[51] In 1964, the head of Polish television programming, Stanisław Stefański, even worried that too many children's series made in the West, such as *Robin Hood* and *Zorro*, were being broadcast in the country, leading to a proliferation of what he called the 'ideal of the American hero'.[52] The Zorro symbol, a capital Z, started to appear on apartment walls and fences.[53] The popularity of this series indicated that the repetition of similar codes and conventions in a domestic children's series could be just as successful. By depicting upbeat skirmishes between easily recognizable good and bad guys, *Four Tank-Men* helped heal a nation traumatized by the Second World War. When in 1968 a journalist asked a little boy what he considered his favourite scene, the boy answered: 'When the Pole punches the Kraut, and when Szarik [Little Grey One – the dog] steals a sausage from the Germans.' The journalist commented: 'In Polish movies, usually we are the ones who are punched and it is our sausage that gets stolen.'[54]

The main protagonist, first tank-man Janek Kos, is a good-looking Polish orphan from Gdańsk who is wandering the globe, searching for his father's grave.[55] The latter fell in the Westerplatte battle in September 1939, while his mother died when their house was set on fire. In Siberia, Janek finds a little dog and the two become an inseparable pair. A viewer might fall for the illusion that Gdańsk was Polish before the war, or was inhabited by a majority of Poles, and that the city was taken over by Germans after Poles heroically battled them at Westerplatte. In reality, Gdańsk was in the interwar period a free city under the auspices of the League of Nations, and Poles accounted for a minority of the town's population.

Moreover, Janek's fictional search for his father is less innocuous than it might appear. The series glosses over the estimated 200,000 Poles who, like Janek, fled the German-occupied territories towards the east in the autumn of 1939.[56] Having crossed the German-Soviet demarcation line, they were deported to Siberia by Soviet authorities, as the latter were afraid of potential German spies.[57] The fictional main character links the symbolic meaning of Westerplatte as a memory site of Polish heroic resistance to the (only partly represented) experience of Polish citizens who found themselves in Siberia during the Second World War. Although his search for his father's grave in Siberia was not strictly accurate, historically speaking, it is precisely this narrative that made him a highly popular television hero.

In Siberia, Janek also meets the second tank-man, the Georgian character Grigorij, not too coincidentally a countryman of Stalin's. After their exchange, they come to the following conclusion: '[This is] my war, your war, our war, one war', a sentence that skates over unpleasant questions about the 1939 Soviet invasion of Poland, while accentuating Soviet-Polish friendship.

The third tank-man is Gustlik. Raised in the German-Polish borderlands, he knows German, and this ability will soon prove useful. Any fears this might have prompted regarding his loyalty to the Polish cause are allayed by his having been born by the Vistula, a river often depicted as the Polish nation's symbol.[58]

Scriptwriter Konrad Nałęcki's characters resort to half-truths, deliberate vagueness and repetition of the 'Westerplatte trope' in order to catch children's attention. A look at the Commission for the Evaluation of Scripts' orders shows that these half-truths, vagueness and repetitions were entirely suggested by the scriptwriter, which indicates that he was well aware of how he ought to present content in order to get past the censors.[59] As Nałęcki was present at the Commission's meetings, this is no surprise. He knew the identity of the people who would be evaluating his script and could anticipate their wishes.[60]

Last in line in the crew is tank commander Jarosz Olgierd (a difference with Przymanowski's book, where the Russian Wasyl Semen was positioned as commander). Olgierd was introduced at the request of the Commission for the Evaluation of Scripts as the grandchild of a Polish migrant who moved to Siberia in 1863. His role was to personify the friendship between Russians and Poles. It also meant that a Polish-speaking person could thus be placed in the position of tank commander, a position that was exclusively reserved to Soviets during the war.

The Commission initiated changes that diluted the Russian identity of the crew in order to bolster its Polishness, thereby overcoming the unpopularity of the Soviet-controlled Berling Army in post-war Polish society.[61] At the same time, it was essential to gloss over the fact that people like Olgierd's grandfather were sentenced to expulsion because of their anti-Tsarist behaviour after the January Uprising of 1863 in the former Polish-Lithuanian Commonwealth against the Russian Empire.

The four tank-men come together in the Polish First Armoured Brigade symbolically called the defenders of Westerplatte, as it never fought in Westerplatte. This Brigade was a Polish military unit within the Soviet-controlled Berling Army. The series neglects to mention the fact that the Berling Army was composed of Polish war deportees to the Soviet Union who had not made their way earlier to the bigger army of General Władysław Anders set up under Allied command in the 1941–1942 period, which had left the Soviet Union for Iran and Palestine in March 1942 and was put under British supervision following a British-Soviet-Polish understanding.[62]

Rewriting history at the bug

The series' content is the result of a compromise between what Polish producers were allowed to achieve within the constraints of the state-controlled broadcasting system and what the young audience expected. This compromise can be seen most clearly in scenes that take place at the borders, namely on the Bug and Oder rivers. The second episode of the series features Janek Kos sitting in his tank in the vicinity of the eastern bank of the Bug on 22 July 1944 and listening to a message on Radio Moscow informing listeners that the Polish Army had crossed Poland's eastern border at the Bug a day earlier, on 21 July 1944, and had just liberated the Polish people.[63] The problem with this is that the Bug was not the Soviet-Polish border in the interwar period: it became so only after the war.[64] The date 21 July 1944 refers to the establishment in Moscow of a provisional Polish government, an important source of legitimacy for communist power in Poland in the post-war period. The news was announced in Moscow and reached Poles via Radio Moscow.

In contrast to the portentous words of the Radio Moscow newsflash, the camera reduces the action in the next scene to a tank crew subversively crossing the Bug. The camera zooms in on the four soldiers in their tank – a boy's archetypal favourite toy – and their dog – a child's faithful friend – reaching the river bank.[65] Whereas in the initial version Gustlik, upon seeing the river, exclaimed: 'We'll soon be in Poland, guys!', the censors required this to be changed to: 'Isn't that the Bug?' in order to provide this new propaganda piece with authenticity, as soldiers of the Berling Army would not have associated the Bug with the Polish border.[66]

As a female Red Army soldier orders the crew to wait while a convoy of Soviet soldiers crosses, Janek and his dog Szarik start to distract the Soviets with tricks.[67] The soldiers laugh and stop to watch them, creating a traffic jam. The rest of the tank crew then take advantage of the commotion and swiftly cross the river without waiting for permission, blowing kisses to the female border guard. The four men thus outsmart the Soviets, thanks to their Zorro-like escapades, and it is as if their disobedience is justified because they are Poles and therefore are the 'real' liberators. While the Polish vice-minister of culture, Tadeusz Zaorski, called the dog scene absurd, because 'one dog would never be able to hold up a convoy', another member of the Commission pleaded for the scene not to be deleted so as to keep children's attention.[68]

Subsequent research conducted in America has shown that a child's attention is indeed triggered by signals associated with child-oriented content. As children know that these will lead to enjoyable content, they are willing to watch scenes they do not understand or to continue watching when a particular scene does not seem to appeal at first glance.[69] The waiting and the sulky border guard enforcing unfair rules stress the importance of the border line, but there was little here for a child to enjoy. The Commission members decided to conduct a test screening of the episode, giving children the final say on whether the dog scene would stay in or not.[70] Now established as co-decision-makers as to how propaganda content was to be consumed, the children voted to keep the scene. The decision-making process behind the dog scene thus shows that a majority of adults involved in the broadcasting decision were so concerned about making television enjoyable for children that they were willing to give them a decisive voice.

On the other side of the bridge, ecstatically happy civilians await the arrival of the crew. Their presence is no accident. It is the result of an intervention from the Commission, which had lamented a 'lack of emotions' in the welcoming party and demanded more enthusiasm from the crowd.[71] As a result, Polish-speaking civilians offer flowers to their liberators and the main characters rejoice in being home. The scriptwriter even introduced a joke so as to optimize Grigorij's Georgian background: he has darker skin because his Polish father was a chimney sweeper, a joke that the Commission members particularly liked.[72] Janek, in turn, asks around whether anybody has heard of his father. He discovers that all 7,000 Westerplatte soldiers have died. Not only does this discovery ascribe an artificial significance to a battle in which, in reality, only fifteen Polish soldiers died,[73] it also creates an artificial continuum between the soldiers who had defended Polish freedom in 1939 and the tank crew restoring it, thanks to their crossing of the Bug in 1944.

Although it is never mentioned that there is a border at the Bug, the whole scene is built on contrasting the two banks of the river. Viewers are expected to laugh at and admire the actions of the tank crew, but not to give a second thought to the notion of the Bug as an incontrovertible border. Throughout the Bug episode, the young public's identification with the heroes of the tank crew and their sympathy for the dog render the occasionally incongruous historical setting somewhat more digestible. But the latter was not without ideological meaning. By ensuring that this backdrop had little in common with history, and much more with the nation's imaginary history, the scriptwriters were able to situate the television series in a Polish context and to encompass in the show expressions of nationalism that reminded viewers of their place in the world.[74] Raising this new official narrative beyond the level of conscious awareness accelerated its absorption, as if it were a banal phenomenon that no longer needed to be discussed.[75]

Stabilizing the consciousness of the Western Polish border: The Oder River

The three episodes that take place at the Oder River stage a battle reminiscent of a *Zorro* episode between the good guys (the tank crew) and the bad guys (the eternal German enemy).[76] In the thirteenth episode, our Polish tank crew operating under Soviet supervision repairs its cannon barrel on the eastern bank of the Oder and tests it by firing off random shots across the river towards the Germans; they hit an ammunition station.[77] This places their leading Soviet officer in a difficult position, because he is supposed to punish his crew, all the while handing them a medal.[78]

The second scene takes place the following day, when the tank crew erects a wooden pole marking the border on the river bank. This activity answers to an order sent to all members of the Polish People's Army two weeks after the Yalta Conference. However, there is a twist: although this activity aimed to show its support of the 1945 Yalta Treaty, for the benefit of viewers watching in the late 1960s, it also unwittingly brought to attention the western Polish borderlands' insecure post-war status. Grigorij designs a pole representing a Georgian mountain – a symbol from Stalin's native state – and a Polish eagle – the symbol of the Polish state since the Piast dynasty. Grigorij's action has a twofold meaning: to show that the Polish territory encompasses anew the western lands where the Polish state had once arisen and that in the 1960s its security was guaranteed by the Soviet Union.

The message from the first scene is that the tank crew members are spontaneous social actors who are not under the thumb of their Soviet superiors; they are allowed a degree of subversiveness when it comes to defending the motherland. The second scene is considerably more propagandistic, but in combination with its predecessor does not seem quite so out of place. What might appear crudely doctrinaire on its own becomes much more acceptable when viewed directly after a scene depicting charming escapades. The first scene may even grant significance to the second. Viewers could transfer the message from one to the other and be left with the impression that the tank men's initiative to erect a border pole had come straight from the heart and was not just the implementation of an order. The intention informing such a juxtaposition of scenes seems to transform what might initially have appeared to be propaganda into cowboy tricks. Such a representation designed for children seems all the more obvious since such 'spontaneous' practices on the tank crew's part are omnipresent throughout the show.[79] Later research on children's comprehension of television has indeed revealed that a repetition of practices influences the children's meaning-making process and facilitates their ability to memorize a programme.[80]

Finally, the Battle of the Oder begins. The tank is positioned on a wooden raft and Polish soldiers drag it by hand, holding onto a cable attached to both sides of the river. But the cable snaps and the tank crew is dragged by the current right into the hands of a German commander, with only the dog being able to swim back. Recognizing the cannon barrel with which he had been attacked the day before, the commander makes a bet with them: if the tank-men are able to drive with their tank through a German firing line, they will be set free. Although the tank doesn't survive the ordeal, the crew does, and the four men make their getaway into a wood.[81] Later, they overpower a German watch tower at a water dam and take the watchmen as prisoners of war.[82]

Surprisingly, one local German watchman, Kugiel, informs the crew that German soldiers are planning to flood the city at the river in order to defend it against the advancing Soviet and Polish troops. The reason for Kugiel's betrayal of his fellow Germans is that he does not want his house to be flooded.[83] After a number of skirmishes between the good guys and the bad guys, the tank crew is able to beat the Germans and reach the western bank of the river, thanks to an inspiring combination of courage, ingenuity and sense of fraternity.[84]

The presentation of the character Kugiel is particularly significant. Because of the general emphasis on the irredeemable wickedness of Germans, the depiction of Poland's supposed ideological allies from East Germany proved problematic in the film, as in real life.[85] In the entire audiovisual collection of the Polish People's Republic, we can find only one movie besides this television series that features a positive East German character.[86] Kugiel is thus intended to serve as a sympathetic representation of the people of the GDR. Although he lives on the western bank of the Oder, he speaks Polish because he fell in love with a Polish-speaking woman from the city of Piła, who was singing in a Polish church choir. Piła, situated on the eastern bank of the Oder, was part of Germany in the interwar period. It became Polish only in 1944–1945. In contrast to other cities with a similar history, a significant portion of Piła's inhabitants spoke Polish, and the town even had a Polish church choir.[87] Piła was chosen for the series because it could create the erroneous impression that the Polish western borderlands had always been inhabited by a large number of Catholic Poles. In this way, one could gloss over an unpleasant truth concerning the mass expulsion of Germans in the early post-war years. Kugiel is portrayed as an opportunist, who decides to help Poles because he is sure there is something in it for him. The message for Polish children was that you could cooperate with your East German neighbours, as long as you watched out.

The series' public impact

Four Tank-Men premiered on 9 May 1966 on the commemoration day of the Soviet victory over Nazi Germany and became an instant hit. A 1968 opinion poll indicated that 70 per cent of Polish viewers liked the series,[88] and that by the end of 1974, 7,109,000 individuals had seen it.[89] The series was also shown in the cinema, with four episodes bundled together; in this format, it attracted 8,343,912 viewers in 1968. It was ranked twenty-fourth on the list of the fifty biggest box-office hits on Polish screens from 1945 to 2000. This is an impressive result, considering that only five movies from this or an earlier period finished in a higher position – out of these, only three were Polish, and all were made for adults.[90]

The hype it must have created can be felt while reading articles in weeklies such as *Polityka* (Politics), as well as children's magazines such as *Walka Młodych* (The Fight of the Young). From the end of the 1960s onwards, many children from Poland and other Eastern Bloc countries were brought up watching the series. Recently, the series has become a nostalgia consumer product. Many who had been materially better off before the transformations of the 1990s have started to look back fondly to cultural productions from their childhood in search of familiarity and safety.[91] Andrzej Skłodkowski directed a documentary about the staging of the series, Marek Łazarz summarized the fictional content of the series in a book, a privately owned museum was opened and DVD box-sets have been released.[92] The series has also found a devoted international fan base. The Wikipedia page of the series is accessible in thirteen languages, the Internet Movie Database has a popular fan page and YouTube enables viewers to watch the series at any time.[93] The fact that Polish public television has shown the series again in the early afternoon since 2010 proves that Polish children continue to enjoy it.

After 'all those Zorros and Robin Hoods', Polish children in the 1960s finally found their own Polish hero.[94] The series became a point of reference in children's games: after having played Zorro, children now either wanted to be 'Janek' or were 'in love with Janek'.[95] Furthermore, it was not only in the living room and schools that children expressed their admiration.[96] Around 20,000 children joined the newly established *Kluby Pancernych* (Armoured Children's Clubs), which engaged their members in social actions dedicated to the series. Football stadiums were packed with people wanting to meet the actors, and 'hundreds' of letters were written to them.[97]

Television influences social interaction. Whereas some sociologists point to increased cohesion among family members gathered in front of the television, others state that watching television has replaced family interaction and conversation, leading to a swifter exposure of children to the moral values expressed by the television industry.[98] Watching television also leads to sociological standardization and homogenization. By the end of the 1960s, most Polish children were able to recognize Szarik, the dog.[99]

The life of the series after 1989

Four Tank-Men was shown on a regular basis until 2006, when the director of the National Polish Broadcasting Corporation, Bronisław Wildstein, acceded to the request of a veteran organization (Porozumienie Organizacji Kombatanckich i Niepodległościowych) to stop airing programmes that falsified history. Despite the controversy, private television channel Kino Polska showed the series again in 2007. In 2008, TVP broadcast the series again, now accompanied by a talk show in which film critic Krzysztof Kłopotowski discussed the falsifications with, more often than not, nationalist-conservative historians.

Kłopotowski invited a Russian PhD student from Warsaw University, Viktoria Dunaeva, to discuss the third episode. When she attempted to downplay the propaganda's role by saying that it was merely an 'adventure film for children', Kłopotowski replied that 'the best propaganda (was) adventure for children'. After a heated discussion, he bade Dunaeva farewell with the following words: 'So, all those years of Soviet indoctrination must have had some effect.'[100] Kłopotowski firmly believes that a united Polish society existed during and after the war, which suffered under the yoke of German and Soviet oppression, both occupying forces being equally iniquitous. He and his right-wing allies grumble over the show's heinous propaganda without bothering to examine the reasons for the show's success, nor to look beyond the show's flagrant inaccuracies. Kłopotowski was heavily criticized; one of his articles received more than 78,000 negative reactions online, conclusive proof if it were needed that the series remains immensely popular.[101] Fans continue to take pleasure in the show's subversive and adventurous appeal, even while acknowledging that it was a communist television production.[102]

Conclusion

The Polish children's television series *Four Tank-Men and a Dog* first aired in 1966, stimulated feelings of belonging, along with a shared history and set of values, through the fictional adventures of Berling Army soldiers during the Second World War. The dominant paradigms in the historiography of children's television, centralizing the importance of genre in the West and of propaganda in the East, do not enable us to understand the popularity of this state-controlled television series. This popularity extended both in space, that is, throughout the Soviet Bloc, and in time, with the series being shown in Poland almost without interruption from its release until today.

Researching the series with a transnational cultural lens, however, reveals that television codes and conventions from the West were integrated in this communist production. The series' content is the result of a compromise between what Polish children, who were enthusiastically watching the imported American children's Western *Zorro*, expected and the degree of freedom television producers could negotiate within the constraints of the censored, state-controlled broadcasting system.

The insights this chapter offers into that negotiation mechanism are eye-opening. Not only do they depict television producer Konrad Nałęcki as a creative co-author of a narrative on Polish national ideology, they also show that adults in power, concerned about providing children with successful entertainment, gave the latter freedom of choice concerning the editing of a crucial border scene. As a result, communist children's television is both specific and universal, and both propaganda and genre are key concepts needed to analyse its meaning.

The depiction of borders at the Bug and Oder rivers in *Four Tank-Men*, which played a quintessential role in the legitimation of the Polish People's Republic, is clearly propagandistic. While the crossing of the imagined eternal Soviet-Polish border at the Bug symbolized the transformation from Polish captivity to Polish freedom, the fighting at the Oder warned viewers of the perennial threat of German revisionism, from which Poland would only be protected through securing friendship with the Soviet Union. Another specificity of *Four Tank-Men* lies in the irony, inconsistency and internal contradictions of the plot that corresponded to the way Polish society was organized, insofar as Polish borders needed to be kept in place, and national identity celebrated under the acceptance of Soviet hegemony. The joke that tank-man Grigorij had a darker skin because his Polish father was a chimney sweeper, which serves to gloss over his Georgian background once he finds himself on Polish soil, showcases the volatility of historical meanings.

However, since they consumed the series as an entertaining adventure, young viewers considered its historical content largely irrelevant, in the same way that an American child would enjoy the narrative plot of a Western. The universality of this communist children's television series lay in the fact that the historical content functions only as a backdrop against which the heroes can present themselves as a cowboy gang undertaking subversive activities during their journey to the West. To that end, television producer Konrad Nałęcki borrowed enthusiastically and intensively from different genre codes and conventions: the road movie, the comedy, the war movie and, above all, the Western. While the depiction of the crossing of the Bug River was based on a gross historical falsehood, the Oder River scenes employ the tropes of a Western battle: good guys versus bad guys. These adaptations grant the series its universal appeal. Packaging ideology at the margins of, or beyond, conscious awareness was nonetheless meaningful, as the representation of borders reminded Polish children of their place in the world. To an extent, enjoying the series meant endorsing its ideological content and accepting its stance on the nation's territory.

Is adventure for children the best type of propaganda, as right-wing conservative television critic Krzysztof Kłopotowski remarked of *Four Tank-Men* in 2008? Now grown-up and resentful or ashamed to have been 'deceived',[103] some ex-devotees criticize *Four Tank-Men* for its inaccuracies. What they forget is the extent to which children, just like their parents, were willing to accept political ambiguities in exchange for entertainment. Its subversive merit lay in the fact that the series transformed a dominant narrative of the past based on forgery into a charming communist fairy tale in which children wanted to believe. In the end, children under communism were already consumers of mass media content and, therefore, also ought to be studied as such.

Notes

1   This work was supported by the Austrian Science Fund (FWF) under Grant number V 360- G 22 (Elise Richter Fellowship). I thank Thomas Lindenberger, Libora Oates-Indruchová and Krzysztof Marcin Zalewski for their comments on an earlier version of this text, and Izabela Mrzygłód and Wojciech Diduszko for their research assistance. The author has no financial interest or benefit arising from the direct applications of her research.
2   Alexander Badenoch, Andreas Fickers, and Chistian Henrich-Franke, eds. *Airy Curtains in the European Ether: Broadcasting and the Cold War* (Baden-Baden: Nomos, 2013).

3   *Czterej Pancerni i Pies* (Four Tank-Men and a Dog), [TV programme]. Poland: TVP, 1966–1970.
4   Hannah Arendt, *The Origins of Totalitarianism* (San Diego: Harcourt Brace Jovanovich, 1979), 387.
5   Susan Hayward, *Cinema Studies: The Key Concepts* (London: Routledge, 2006), 185.
6   Karen Stoddard, 'Children's Programming', in *TV Genres*, ed. Brian G. Rose (Westport: Greenwood Press, 1985), 353–365.
7   'Genre', in *Harpers Collins English Dictionary*, https://www.collinsdictionary.com/dictionary/english/genre (accessed 13 July 2017).
8   Stephen Neale, *Descriptions* (Cambridge: MIT Press, 1990), 46–48.
9   Hayward, *Cinema Studies*, 187, 217.
10 For an interpretation of ideology as consensual, see: Louis Althusser, *Essays on Ideology* (Greek Street London: Verso Editions, 1984), 37.
11 Krzysztof Kosiński, *Oficjalne i prywatne życie młodzieży w czasach PRL* (Warsaw: Rosner & Wspólnicy, 2006).
12 Garth Jowett and Victoria O'Donnell, *Propaganda and Persuasion* (Beverly Hills: Sage Publications, 2006), 7.
13 Błażej Brzostek and Marcin Zaremba, 'Polska 1956–1976. W poszukiwaniu paradygmatu', *Pamięć i Sprawiedliwość* 2, no. 10 (2006): 25–37.
14 The series consists of twenty-one episodes in total and was shown on television in three series, which were first broadcast in 1966, 1969 and 1970.
15 Kosiński, *Oficjalne i prywatne*, 92.
16 Charles Ford and Robbert Hammond, *Polish Film. A Twentieth Century History* (Jefferson: McFarland & Company, 2005), 104.
17 Patryk Pleskot, *Wielki mały ekran. Telewizja a codzienność Polaków w latach sześćdziesiątych* (Warsaw: Trio, 2007), 19–20.
18 Eugeniusz C. Król, 'Gesellschaftliche und politische Grundlagen des Bildes der Deutschen im polnischen Spielfilm nach dem Zweiten Weltkrieg', in *Deutschland und Polen. Filmische Grenzen und Nachbarschaften*, eds. Konrad Klejsa and Schamma Schahadat (Marburg: Schüren Verlag, 2011), 41.
19 Jerzy Rudzki, 'Wpływ telewizji na aktywność kulturalną młodzieży wiejskiej', *Biuletyn Telewizyjny*, no. 1 (1964): 30–51 (31).
20 Jerzy Rudzki, *Zafascynowani telewizją: socjologiczne studium o telewizji wśród młodzieży* (Wrocław: Zakład Narodowy im. Ossolińskich Wydawnictwo PAN, 1969), 72.
21 Tadeusz A. Kisielewski, *Janczarzy Berlinga: 1. Armia Wojska Polskiego 1943–1945* (Poznań: REBIS, 2014).
22 'Czterej pancerni, pies i co dalej? Rozmowa z Januszem Przymanowskim' *Płomyczek*, no. 10 (1967): 282–283
23 Krzysztof Tyszka, *Nacjonalizm w komunizmie: ideologia narodowa w Związku Radzieckim i Polsce Ludowej* (Warsaw: Wydawnictwo Instytutu Filozofii i Socjologii PAN, 2004), 141.
24 Andrzej Sakson, 'Odzyskiwanie Ziem Odzyskanych – przemiany lokalnej i regionalnej tożsamości mieszkańców Ziem Zachodnich i Północnych a rewindykacyjne postulaty niemieckich środowisk ziomkowskich', in *Ziemie Odzyskane 1945–2005. Ziemie Zachodnie i Północne 60 lat w granicach państwa polskiego*, ed. Andrzej Sakson (Poznań: Instytut Zachodni, 2006), 267.
25 Miloš Řezník, 'Transformations of Regional History in the Polish "Western Territories" since 1945: Legitimization, Nationalization, Regionalization', in *Frontiers,*

Regions and Identities in Europe, eds. Steven G. Ellis and Raingard Eßer (Pisa: Plus-Pisa University Press, 2009), 228–229.

26 Archiwum Akt Nowych (Archive of New Records, Warsaw; AAN). Uchwała Sekretariatu KC w sprawie wzmożenia walki z dywersyjną antypolską działalnością zachodnioniemieckich rewizjonistów, KC PZPR, 237/VIII/718.

27 The Oder-Neisse border was finally accepted in 1990 in the Treaty between the Federal Republic of Germany and the Republic of Poland on the confirmation of the frontier between them. Available online, https://www.un.org/Depts/los/LEGISLATIONANDTREATIES/PDFFILES/TREATIES/DEU-POL1990CF.PDF (accessed 12 July 2017).

28 Władysław Gomułka is quoted in Tomasz Żukowski, 'Współzawodnictwo w nacjonalizmie. Spór między partią i Kościołem w roku 1966', *Kwartalnik Historii Żydów*, no. 4 (2008): 415–426 (423).

29 Włodzimierz Borodziej, *Geschichte Polens im 20. Jahrhundert* (Munich: C.H. Beck Verlag, 2010), 301 and further.

30 Wanda Królikowska, 'Codzienność zorganizowanego wypoczynku dzieci i młodzieży w Polsce w latach 1956–1970: program i realizacja', in *Życie codzienne w PRL (1956–1989)*, eds. Grzegorz Miernik and Sebastian Piątkowski (Radom-Starachowice: Radomskie Towarzystwo Naukowe, 2006), 96. On difficulties in pinpointing differences between educational and propagandistic aims, see Benita Blessing, 'Happily socialist ever after? East German children's films and the education of a fairy tale land', *Oxford Review of Education* 36, no. 2 (2010): 233–248 (236).

31 Łukasz Polniak, *Patriotyzm wojskowy w PRL w latach 1956–1970* (Warsaw: Trio, 2011), 209.

32 Ibid., 178.

33 C. Dziekanowski, 'Czterej pancerni chcą spać', *Kierunki*, no. 44 (1969): 7.

34 Ewa Gębicka, '"Obcinanie kantów", czyli polityka PZPR i państwa wobec kinematografii w latach sześćdziesiątych', in *Syndrom konformizmu? Kino polskie lat sześćdziesiątych*, eds. Tadeusz Miczka and Alina Madej (Katowice: Wydawnictwo Uniwersytetu Śląskiego, 1994), 23–34.

35 Ibid., 39; Pleskot, *Wielki mały ekran*, 121.

36 Andrzej Duma, 'Struktura audytorium telewizyjnego w Polsce', *Biuletyn Telewizyjny*, no. 1 (1963): 1–50 (43–44).

37 Pleskot, *Wielki mały ekran*, 66.

38 Edward Zajiček, *Poza ekranem: kinematografia polska 1896–2005* (Warsaw: Stowarzyszenie Filmowców Polskich Studio Filmowe Montevideo, 2009), 242.

39 Dina Iordanova, *Cinema of the Other Europe. The Industry and Artistry of East Central European Film* (London and New York: Wallflower Press, 2003), 48.

40 Paulina Bren, *The Greengrocer and His TV. The Culture of Communism After the 1968 Prague Spring* (Ithaca, NY: Cornell University Press, 2010), 202.

41 Polniak, *Patriotyzm wojskowy*, 209.

42 Ibid., 234. Examples are: *Daleka jest droga* (Far Is the Road), dir. Bohdan Poręba, 1963; *Westerplatte*, 1967, *Zamach* (Assassination Attempt), dir. Jerzy Passendorfer, 1959; *Barwy walki* (Battle Colours), dir. Jerzy Passendorfer, 1964.

43 'Czterej pancerni', 282–283.

44 Jerome K. Jerome, *Trzech starszych panów w jednej łódce (oprócz psa)* (Warsaw: Księgarnia nakładowa M. Szczepkowskiego, 1912); Jerome K. Jerome, *Three Men in a Boat / Trzej ludzi w jednej łodzi* (Warsaw: Nakładem Lingwisty, 1922), Jerome

　　K. Jerome, *Trzech panów w łódce (nie licząc psa)* (Warsaw: Iskry, 1956); Jerome K. Jerome, *Three Men in a Boat. To Say Nothing of the Dog* (Warsaw: Iskry, 1958).

45　Steven Cohan and Ina Rae Hark, 'Introduction', in *The Road Movie Book*, eds. Steven Cohan and Ina Rae Hark (Milton Park: Taylor & Francis, 2002), 1.

46　Henry Jenkins and Kristine Brunovska Karnick. 'Introduction', in *Classical Hollywood Comedy*, eds. Kristine Brunovska Karnick and Henry Jenkins (London: Routledge, 1995), 11.

47　Hayward, *Cinema Studies*, 205.

48　Robert Eberwein, *The Hollywood War Film* (Chichester: Wiley-Blackwell, 2010), 11–12.

49　Zbigniew Mitzner, 'Liczby, procenty i "Czterej pancerni"', *Ekran*, no. 24 (1968): 10.

50　John Saunders, *The Western Genre: From Lordsburg to Big Whiskey* (London: Wallflower Press, 2001), 6. Saunders refers to the 1893 lecture of the historian Frederick Jackson Turner, *The Significance of the Frontier in American History*.

51　Pleskot, *Wielki mały ekran*, 176.

52　Katarzyna Pokorna-Ignatowicz, *Telewizja w systemie politycznym i medialnym PRL. Między polityką a widzem* (Kraków: Wydawnictwo Uniwersytetu Jagiellońskiego, 2003), 74.

53　Maciej Łukowski, *Film seryjny w programie telewizji polskiej (lata 1959–1970)* (Warsaw: Wydawnictwa Radia i Telewizji, 1980), 16–18.

54　Bogumił Drozdowski, 'Kino na raty', *Kino*, no. 4 (1968): 12.

55　Marek Haltof, *Historical Dictionary of Polish Cinema* (Lanham: The Scarecrow Press, 2007), 57–59.

56　Tomasz Izajasz, Magdalena Jurczyk, and Karolina Glabus, *Czterej pancerni i pies: śladem filmowej sagi w Bydgoszczy* (Bydgoszcz: Wydawnictwo Pejzaż, 2013), 66.

57　Stanisław Ciesielski, Grzegorz Hryciuk, and Aleksander Srebrakowski, *Masowe deportacje radzieckie w okresie II wojny światowej* (Wrocław: IH UW, 1994).

58　For example, the song 'Płynie Wisła płynie po polskiej krainie (…) Dopóki płynie Polska nie zaginie' [The Vistula flows, flows through the Polish land. As long as it flows, Poland will not perish].

59　Filmoteka Narodowa (National Film Archive; FN). A-216 poz. 79, Stenogram z posiedzenia komisji kolaudacyjnej o polskim serialu 4 Pancerni i pies z dnia 29.03.1966., 1.

60　Ibid., 10.

61　Ibid., 1.

62　Norman Davies, *Trail of Hope. The Anders Army, an Odyssey Across Three Continents* (Oxford: Osprey Publishing, 2015).

63　*Czterej pancerni i pies*, episode 2, dir. Konrad Nałęcki. 13:28–14:11.

64　The Molotov-Ribbentrop Pact of August 1939 initially placed the border between the German and Soviet occupation zones of Poland at the Vistula River. The demarcation line was placed more to the East at the Bug River in the autumn of 1939, and was crossed by the German Army during Operation Barbarossa on 21 June 1941.

65　*Czterej pancerni i pies*, episode 2, dir. Konrad Nałęcki. 21:30–29:12.

66　Stenogram z posiedzenia, 2.

67　Over 3 per cent of the people serving in the Soviet Armed Forces were women. Their amount surpassed 800,000. See Reina Pennington, 'Offensive Women: Women in Combat in the Red Army in the Second World War', *The Journal of Military History* 74, no. 3 (2010): 775–820.

68　Ibid., 5, 12.

69   Aletha C. Huston et al., 'From Attention to Comprehension: How Children Watch and Learn from Television', in *Children and Television: Fifty Years of Research*, eds. Norma Pecora, John P. Murray, and Ellen Ann Wartella (New Jersey: Lawrence Erlbaum Associates Inc., 2007), 50.

70   Stenogram z posiedzenia, 9.

71   Ibid., 6.

72   Ibid., 10.

73   Zbigniew Flisowski, ed. *Westerplatte. Wspomnienia, relacje, dokumenty* (Warsaw: Wydawnictwo Ministerstwa Oborny Narodowej, 1960), XXVI–XXVII.

74   Bren, *The Greengrocer*, 202.

75   Michael Billig, *Banal Nationalism* (London: Sage Publications, 1999), 8–12.

76   KOSc's censorship reports about these episodes seem to be lost. They could not be found in the National Film Library Archive, the National Digital Archives, or the Archive of New Records.

77   *Czterej pancerni i pies*, episode 13, dir. Konrad Nałęcki. 13:40–15:00.

78   *Czterej pancerni i pies*, episode 13, dir. Konrad Nałęcki. 13:40–27:30.

79   Three examples are Janek's decision to kill a sniper in the fifth episode, the tank crew inventing creative ideas in order to take a German group of soldiers into captivity in the seventh episode and Janek and his girlfriend interrupting a kiss in order to capture German soldiers in the sixteenth episode.

80   Brian R. Clifford, Barrie Gunter, and Jill McAleer. *Television and Children: Program Evaluation, Comprehension and Impact* (Hillsdale: Lawrence Erlbaum Associates, 1995), 53.

81   *Czterej pancerni i pies*, episode 13, dir. Konrad Nałęcki. 35:00–42:00.

82   *Czterej pancerni i pies*, episode 14, dir. Konrad Nałęcki. 06:45–13:01.

83   *Czterej pancerni i pies*, episode 14, dir. Konrad Nałęcki. 22:00–26:00.

84   *Czterej pancerni i pies*, episode 15, dir. Konrad Nałęcki.

85   Ingo Loose, 'Hans Kloss – ein "roter James Bond"? Deutsche, Polen und der Zweite Weltkrieg in der Kultserie "Sekunden Entscheiden"', in *Deutschland und Polen. Filmische Grenzen und Nachbarschaften*, eds. Konrad Klejsa and Schamma Schahadat (Marburg: Schüren Verlag, 2011), 48.

86   Król, 'Gesellschaftliche und politische', 35. The movie *Dwoje z wielkiej rzeki* (Two from the Big River) was directed in 1958 by the same director as *Four Tank-Men and a Dog* – Konrad Nałęcki.

87   Zygmunt Boras and Zbigniew Dworecki, *Piła: zarys dziejów (do roku 1945)* (Piła: Urząd Miejski, 1993), 111–112.

88   Albin Kania, 'Film fabularny w telewizji w opinii odbiorców', *Biuletyn Radiowo-Telewizyjny*, no. 8 (1970): 5–14 (7).

89   The only more popular series was *Stawka większa niż życie* (More Than Life at Stake), directed by Andrzej Konic and Janusz Morgenstern. See Stanisław Janicki and Irena Nowak-Zatorska, *Film polski od A do Z* (Warsaw: Wydaw. Artystyczne i Filmowe, 1977), 152–153.

90   The Polish movies were: *Zakazane piosenki* (Forbidden songs), dir. Leonard Buczkowski, 1947; *Skarb* (Treasure), dir. Leonard Buczkowski, 1949; *Faraon* (The Pharaon), dir. Jerzy Kawalerowicz, 1966. See Haltof, *Historical Dictionary*, 220.

91   Julia Banaszewska, 'Powtórka, tęsknota czy zapośredniczenie… Skąd się bierze moda na PRL?', in *Zanurzeni w historii – zanurzeni w kulturze: kultowe seriale PRL-u*, eds. Marek Karwala and Barbara Serwatka (Kraków: Śródmiejski Ośrodek Kultury, 2010), 14.

92   Marek Łazarz, *Czterej pancerni i pies. Przewodnik po serialu i okolicach* (Wrocław: Torus Media, 2006); Documentary *My czterej pancerni* (We Four Tank-Men), dir. Andrzej Słodkowski, 2009; for the private museum see http://www.muzeumczterechpancernych.pl; *Czterej pancerni i pies* (Four Tank-Men and a Dog), [DVD]. Dir. Konrad Nałęcki. Warsaw: Telewizja Polska S.A., 2006.

93   International Movie Database, http://www.imdb.com/title/tt0120948/ (accessed 30 June 2015).

94   Stanisław Dygat, "'Ścigany', "Pancerni" i inni', *Polityka*, no. 8 (1970): 12.

95   Łukowski, *Film seryjny*, 16.

96   Archiwum TVP (Polish Television Archive; ATVP). Talk shows moderated by film critic Krzysztof Kłopotowski following episodes 3 and 4, 2008.

97   Piotr Ambroziewicz, 'Czterej pancerni i Orodziński', *Prawo i Życie*, no. 21 (1969): 5; Włodzimierz Stępiński, 'Uczyłem się wojska. Rozmowa z Romanem Wilhelmem', *Walka Młodych*, no. 47 (1966): 11;
Zdzisław Ornatowski, 'Klub pancerny znowu w akcji', *Ekran*, no. 12 (1970): 22.

98   Marcin Czerwiński, *Przemiany obyczaju* (Warsaw: Państwowy Instytut Wydawniczy, 1972), 123; Rudzki, *Zafascynowani telewizją*.

99   Ambroziewicz, 'Czterej pancerni', 283.

100   ATVP. Talk show following episode 3.

101   Krzysztof Kłopotowski, 'O czterech panzerfaustach a polskim psie' [On four panzerfausts and a Polish Dog], *Salon 24*, 9 May 2011, https://www.salon24.pl/u/klopotowski/304988,o-czterech-pancerfaustach-i-polskim-psie (accessed 8 November 2017).

102   Example: 'It was not as if there was a steadfast Polish nation with a pure Polish Home Army identity, and (the tank – MV) Rudy 102 had demolished this identity and changed Varsovian insurgents into grotesque homos sovietici'. See Paweł Skwieciński, 'Pancerni u źródeł Sierpnia' [Tank-Men at the sources of August], *Rzeczpospolita*, 9 May 2011, www.rp.pl/artykul/153227,654831.html (accessed 22 December 2014).

103   Kłopotowski, 'O czterech pancerfaustach'.

10

Between Censorship and Scholarship: The Editorial Board of the Czechoslovak Academy of Sciences (1969–1989)

Libora Oates-Indruchová

A variety of censorship forms pervaded not only cultural and political discourses and production in the Eastern Bloc but also scholarly publishing. This chapter is concerned with the activities of the Editorial Board of the Czechoslovak Academy of Sciences (*Ediční rada Československé akademie věd*; hereafter, Editorial Board or Board) between 1969 and 1989 vis-à-vis knowledge production and censoring mechanisms. I draw on the holdings of the Editorial Board in the Archives of the Czech Academy of Sciences, catalogued by Alena Míšková in 1990.[1]

Censorship in the Eastern Bloc has been largely studied as something that institutions and state actors employed in order to constrain the creative spirit of individuals and to pursue ideological goals, as has been pointed out most recently by Samantha Sherry.[2] That is certainly the case when studying the discourse of power, although it must be said that the communist power was exceptionally prone to flattering itself about its reach and strength. Sara Jones, in her study of GDR writers, belongs to the minority of censorship researchers who emphasize negotiation rather than repression with respect to communist cultural institutions.[3]

With respect to scholarly censorship, I have studied both science policies, that is, the discourse of the hegemonizing power[4] – the 'rulers', and that of the authors and researchers themselves – the 'ruled'. These two narratives ran almost counter to each other: the policy documents seemed to reveal the increasing domination of political institutions over scholarship, while the researchers' narratives about their experience speak of a great deal of agency and negotiation. So I chose as my third source the records of the Editorial Board of the Czechoslovak flagship research institution: the Academy of Sciences, an actor in an intermediary position between the two poles of power. Its members were positioned as censors, but at the same time they were also creative individuals, scholars. As Board members they had to answer for their decisions to the institutions above them; as authors they were subject to the same ideologies they were bringing to bear upon those below. I was interested in the balance between these two roles played by the Editorial Board, in order to gain an insight into the participation of smaller actors in the system of state-socialist scholarly publishing. I focus my inquiry on the period of normalization (1969–89), because during that time no formal censoring institution existed that would include science and scholarship, insofar as this area was specifically exempt from the law regulating access to information – the so-called Press Law [*tiskový zákon*].[5]

What was the Editorial Board of the Academy of Sciences?

In her introduction to the inventory of the holdings, Míšková provides a valuable summary of the Board's function and activities. The Board was established in October 1961 by a decree of the Central Committee of the Communist Party of Czechoslovakia and held its first meeting in February 1962. Its mandate and scope of responsibilities were considerable: they ranged from the evaluation of publishing plans for books and periodicals of Academia, the publishing house of the Academy of Sciences, through the decisions on all stages of the publishing process (approving proposals and manuscripts, determining the length of publications, setting authors' honoraria), to the impact of the publications and marketing issues, such as sales, stock, profit and losses. It reported to the presidium of the Academy of Sciences, who also appointed senior academic managers (and trusted party members) as the Board members.

The first Editorial Board comprised eleven members and was chaired by the historian Josef Macek. It was disbanded and reappointed several times and the number of its members fluctuated due to resignations and new appointments. In total, there were four Boards: the first lasted from January 1962 to June 1970, the second from October 1970 to December 1979, the third from January 1980 to September 1983 and the fourth from October 1983 to December 1989.[6] The Board held monthly meetings, whose agenda typically included decisions concerning publishing proposals and manuscripts submitted by the Scientific Committees [*vědecká kolegia*] for the various disciplines of the Academy, discussion of editorial issues with their representatives and tasks assigned by the presidium (Míšková 1990). The Board's archives hold the minutes from the meetings, as well as the briefing materials provided to the members.[7]

Periodization of publishing practice

Despite normalization being treated as a homogenous period of state socialism, it had its own internal dynamics and turning points. Political and economic development together with generational exchange structured the conditions of scholarly research and publishing over these twenty years. The repressive measures introduced in the first years of normalization, which aimed at cleansing academia of any traces of the reform process that had led to the Prague Spring, have been extensively researched.[8] So have been various aspects of the impact of the Charter 77.[9] Perestroika as a distinct period, by contrast, has received much less attention, as has an internal chronology of the two decades of normalization.[10] My own research of science policies has shown that the momentum that resulted in the fast and dramatic transformation of academia between

1969 and the early 1970s may have abated, but did not peter out completely. Scholarly research and publishing received new restrictive impulses from above throughout the entire period, including perestroika. These aimed at subsuming all spheres of academia under a centralized party control – an aim that was never fully accomplished, although the policy instruments to achieve it were in place.[11]

The year 1977 is the first significant turning point in science policies. They instated further ideological tightening, probably linked to the publication of the Charter 77. Interestingly, the argumentation of these new directives was much more abstract and diffuse. The concrete and even logically formulated verbal attacks against fairly precisely defined enemies that were present in the early normalization documents disappeared. Documents from the late 1970s onwards increasingly consisted of empty ideological phrases.

The impact of this discursive environment could have been twofold. First, if the language of the policies and, by extension, the limits of permissibility were obscure, then everything and everybody was potentially ideologically precarious. Second, however, the lack of clarity also allowed for creative interpretations of the policies and therefore for negotiation of discursive spaces by the various actors. Moreover, the language that ceased to name blurred the dividing line between the previously unambiguous 'us' and 'them', in which 'them' connoted the Prague Spring reformists. This heralded the beginning of a gradual generational change: young people, unconnected with the events and personages of 1968, began to enter the normalized academia – whether as primarily researchers or primarily apparatchiks.

The record of publication approvals and rejections in the minutes from the Editorial Board's sessions mirrors the evolutionary curve observed in the general science policies: 1977 appears to have been a turning point also in scholarly publishing. Ideological pressure and budgetary issues, including paper quotas, worked in concert, resulting in stricter limitations on who and what was published. The argumentation for decisions also changes from concrete to vague, from more information to less as the years went by. At the beginning of normalization, the Board's minutes relatively honestly cited emigration or ideological reasons, if those were the case, for withdrawing a book from publication or rejecting a publishing proposal or manuscript, and the grounds for the decision were detailed in the briefing materials. From the late 1970s onwards, political reasons are no longer recorded; the minutes list plain 'approved', 'rejected' or 'put on hold' pending such and such supplementary information. Only apparently non-political reasons continue to be given, such as budgetary constraints and thematic divisions among publishing houses.

Yet, in 1977 new grounds for rejecting proposals appear. These could be grouped under the following official headings: 'Recycling', that is, a substantial part of the proposed manuscript has already been published in journals; 'Per author allocation', that is, the author has already published a book recently either in the publishing house Academia or elsewhere; 'Not ours', that is, that the authors are not employed at the Academy of Sciences but at another research institute or university that has their own publishing house; 'Market saturation', that is, a publication on a similar topic is already available; and 'No PhD theses, new editions or studies not resulting from projects conducted within the State Plan of Basic Research'.[12] The recommendation to favour the employees of the Academy was issued in November 1972 as an economizing measure, and it became a regular ground for rejecting publishing proposals towards the end of the decade.[13] The argumentation that authors should publish with their home institution was added as another sieve for considering manuscripts and publishing proposals to the policy of a thematic narrowing of Academia that already existed since 1972. Then a directive from above divided the territory of scholarly publishing into specializations. The publishing house Academia was to publish basic research and selectively also textbooks, manuals, popular science and encyclopaedias, while the publishing houses Svoboda and Pravda were to focus on the history of the Communist Parties and labour movement, as well as on political literature.[14] The requirement that Academia should publish only work resulting from the State Plan became a policy in 1977 and thereafter a regular ground for turning proposals down.[15]

Political reasoning, when it appears, is shrouded in vague formulations, for instance 'Such and such proposal has to be consulted with "bodies" [*s orgány*]'.[16] A direct request for ideological conformity seldom appears. One rare example involves a manuscript on ecology whose printing was postponed until the authors rewrote the text to render it 'consistent with the Marxist understanding of the substance of the ecological issue, while its conceptual solution would be grounded in the Marxist-Leninist scientific world view, as well as in the practice of building a socialist society'.[17] However, this unusually frank formulation appears only in the draft of the minutes and is crossed out in pencil, while the finalized document was not preserved in the archives. The briefing materials were rarely preserved between 1979 and 1982.

Sifting through the Editorial Board's archive, no dramatic changes during perestroika are discernible. Nonetheless, minor reform tendencies had already begun in the early 1980s. They did not necessarily point to any ideological relaxation, but to an emergence of new, if tentative and limited, spaces for scholarly expression. In 1982, the Board received an impulse from above to discuss the possibility of creating new journals for the first time since the onset of normalization,[18] although nothing came of it till the regime change. In 1987, a reform of the peer-review system was proposed, and in 1988 approved. From then on, the authority to choose peer reviewers was delegated from the Editorial Board to the editors-in-chief, with the exception of social sciences and humanities.[19]

Material conditions of publishing progressively worsened throughout normalization – perestroika certainly did not bring any improvement in that respect. In the Academia publishing house, a three- to four-year production time *after* the manuscript had been accepted became the rule rather than the exception and would not necessarily imply protractions due to political difficulties. The delays were caused by at least three structural factors that essentially functioned as censoring mechanisms: fixing the publishing plan a long time ahead, backlog in the printing house and paper quotas. Academia's publishing plan was fixed two years in advance.[20] After it was proposed by the Editorial Board, it had to be approved by the presidium of the Academy,[21] and at least at the beginning of normalization also by high party 'bodies'.[22] Academia's contractual printing house had at least a three-year backlog[23]; if the annual reports on the activities of Academia call the situation at the printers' 'unfavourable' [*nepříznivá*] in 1972,[24] by 1989 they use the attribute 'catastrophic' [*havarijní*].[25] Finally, Academia had the same paper quota for books in 1983 as it did in 1953.[26]

Despite the perennial complaints about the paper quotas in the minutes, decisions on the size of print runs are sometimes telling (such as the refusal to reduce the print run of the journal *Social Sciences in the Soviet Union* (*Sociální vědy v SSSR*) from 6,000 to 5,400),[27] but more often mind-boggling from the perspective of today's academic book market. The Editorial Board became first concerned with the demand versus print run issue as late as in 1984 when it began to require quarterly reports from Academia on pre-orders of its books. The table accompanying this request reveals a peculiar production planning: for example, the print run of *Lexikon české literatury* (Lexicon of Czech Literature), a reference book likely to be used by a wide audience including secondary school students, was set at 5,000 copies, while the pre-orders reached 21,711; by comparison, the specialized historical study *Vývoj uhelného průmyslu v českých zemích po průmyslové revoluci* (Coal Industry in the Czech Lands since the Industrial Revolution) was to be printed in 1,000 copies, with a preliminary demand of eighty-six copies.[28]

Levels of approval and restrictive editorial policies

It is difficult to reconstruct the exact practice of the hierarchy of approvals at Academia from the archival holdings of the Editorial Board, because these procedures are not always fully recorded and, anyway, social sciences and humanities were always placed into a separate category, to which exemptions from the general rule applied.[29] What is clear, however, is that Academia had little publishing autonomy: it functioned as a service to the Academy of Sciences that executed the decisions of its Scientific Committees and the Editorial Board. As a publisher it did not even have as much decision-making independence as other state publishing houses or, indeed, as scholarly publishers in other state socialist countries – a complaint expressed already in 1971.[30] Academia requested – in vain – a share in the formulation and implementation of the editorial policy of the Academy of Sciences.[31] Only as late as in May 1987 did the Editorial Board discuss the possibility to entrust editors-in-chief of Academia's publishing departments with appointing peer reviewers from the approved Peer Reviewers Pool, independently.[32] An additional approval level was formalized a few years into normalization, in 1976, when Academia was assigned to request a written review on publication proposals from the authors' heads of department 'in justified cases' [*v odůvodněných případech*]. However, the minutes do not list the criteria for this justification.[33] Still, Academia did have a place in the hierarchy of freedoms and privileges: an author, at least if employed at the Academy of Sciences, could offer a manuscript to a foreign publisher only if Academia was not interested in publishing it.[34]

In the light of this curtailment of authors' agency, it may appear somewhat surprising that the Editorial Board cared whether the authors gave written consent to the publication of their work. How consistently this was observed and whether only in politically sensitive cases cannot be established from this archival source. The minutes do record one case from early normalization when a co-author who had emigrated in 1965 threatened to sue if the botany book to which he had contributed about 30 per cent was going to be published without his name. The Editorial Board feared legal issues and put the publication on hold; it then tasked its chairman with seeking the approval of the president of the Academy.[35] The book was published the same year, citing a collective authorship (*kol.*). Even the name of the (politically non-controversial) lead author was removed and listed only as the author of the Introduction.[36]

The content of journals published by the Academy of Sciences was even more carefully monitored than the content of books. The Editorial Board conducted an annual review of all the journals as to their scientific, as well as ideological, content; also their size and structure (such as the number of pages of individual journal sections) was closely watched. The Academy published sixty-seven journals throughout the period, all of which had a strictly prescribed length, which means that their editors did not have any flexibility as to the number of pages per issue.[37] The paper allocation and therefore also the decision on the size and structure of the journals came from outside of the Academy, from the Czech Bureau for Press and Information (Český úřad pro tisk a informace; ČÚTI), although the Academy had its representative there.[38] As in other instances, the dual pressures of structural and political censorship are difficult to separate: when, in 1977, the Editorial Board recommended that articles by international authors be allocated a maximum of 15–20 per cent of the overall journal content, was it motivated by increasing budgetary difficulties and the paper quota, or by the growing political pressure following Charter 77? The former can be traced in the archives throughout the entire period, while one of the most salient instances of the latter is recorded in 1977: in the name of making the 'ideological and propagandist work of the Academy of Sciences more effective', the Editorial Board assigned the Academia publishing house to compile a list of topics 'suitable for ideologico-educational uses'; these were to include political anniversaries and Academia was to recruit the authors.[39] To be fair, the Board issued recommendations concerning also the scientific quality of the journals, such as the criterion in 1980 that Academia's journals published in foreign languages should not be accepting articles by Czech authors that had been rejected by international journals.[40]

Peer reviews

The Academia publishing house sent both book and article manuscripts for peer review before they were accepted for publication. The process, however, was only partially akin to the scholarly peer review as we know it today. Academia had a special body, the Peer Reviewers Pool [*lektorský sbor*], whose status was instituted in 1972 and revised in 1978. It was obliged to recruit all peer reviewers from within this pool.[41] The names on the list were drawn from the Academy, universities and other research institutions. Every member had to be vetted by their head of department and by the party, as well as by the appropriate Scientific Committee of the Academy of Sciences. In social sciences and humanities, almost all of the reviewers were party members, only fine arts and linguistics included a significant proportion of non-members.[42] The Academia publishing house, however, did not appoint the reviewers, that privilege belonged to the Editorial Board on the basis of a proposal from the relevant Scientific

Committee. The latter could suggest a peer reviewer outside of the pool only if they presented a successful argument that the list did not include a suitable specialist. The appointment was conditioned on the consent of this reviewer's head of department. This mechanism implied that – for better or for worse – a relatively small group of people (several dozen, depending on which Scientific Committee) acted as both scholarly and ideological gatekeepers at Academia.[43] So, on the one hand, if an author or a manuscript aroused the ire of a particular individual, there was little chance of seeing the manuscript in print in this publishing house. On the other hand, if a Scientific Committee befriended a peer reviewer from the list, it acquired a channel for shepherding manuscripts towards successful publication. Even so, the Editorial Board insisted on partially external peer reviews: it reminded the Scientific Committees – supposedly repeatedly – that if an author was not an employee of the Academy, at least one of the two reviewers had to be an employee and vice versa, manuscripts by the Academy's employees had to be assessed by at least one reviewer from the outside.[44]

Briefing materials for the December 1985 Editorial Board meeting suggest that peer reviewing could be a lucrative side job. The Academy had to implement an internal regulation on the remuneration of peer reviewers, following Government Decree [*Usnesení vlády*] no. 298 from 1983 that placed restrictions on side employment contracts. The briefing materials include a detailed analysis of the implications of the new financial regulations for the entire peer-reviewing process. One person could now perform activities under simplified tax conditions of only up to ninety hours for all employers combined outside of their regular employment contract. More work hours required a regular employment contract, which was subject to the main employer's consent and to full taxation. The practice in publishing houses, and not just in Academia, was (and largely remains today) to contract peer reviewers under the simplified arrangement, stipulating the number of hours per item. Often, as the briefing materials state, journals made only a verbal agreement for article reviews and paid the authors for their compounded work once or twice a year. The complaints now expressed were that the obligation to conclude individual written contracts exponentially increased the administrative load in the publishing house, endangered the quality of the peer-review process and put peer reviewers from the Academy of Sciences at a disadvantage. The latter claim was based in that the employees of the Academy could not sign side contracts with their own institution according to the new rules. Neither was it viable for them to do this work without payment, because that supposedly presented too many legal complications. The intriguing underlying assumption here is that the peer reviewers often exceeded the ninety-hours-per-year limit. That was perhaps natural, given that only those listed in the approved pool could act as peer reviewers. However, it also testifies to the not-insignificant financial incentive to oblige the publishing house, to be cooperative and write the peer review in a manner that the publisher desired.[45] That could mean both to write a scathing condemnation of a manuscript on political grounds and, the opposite, to facilitate publication by praising the manuscript's scholarly and ideological merits.

The case of Daniela Hodrová's manuscript *Pohyb románu* (The Movements of the Novel) offers a glimpse of a rather shady peer-reviewing practice – shady by today's standards and hard to tell how routine at that time. The manuscript was based on the author's doctoral (i.e. 'CSc', *candidatus scientarium*) thesis defended in 1980 and submitted as a publishing proposal to Academia in 1982. The Editorial Board approved the proposal in November 1982, but withdrew its approval in May 1983. What happened was that the person appointed as the lead of the two reviewers declined the job (citing other commitments and health issues). The manuscript was sent to the chair of the Fine Arts Scientific Committee [*Vědecké kolegium věd o umění*] for preliminary assessment. He returned a negative report, from which the briefing materials include a quotation. It is worth pointing out that it was one of the rare instances of providing an extract from any reader's reports in the briefing materials or, indeed, fragments of these reports preserved in the Editorial Board archive: 'This is certainly not a step forward with regards to Marxist research, but a step backward. I consider this work as ideologically and methodologically very harmful, it would lead literary interpretation toward a relapse into total ahistoricity and deideologizing.'[46] The Editorial Board scrapped the proposal, but was aware that to do so only on the grounds of a preliminary assessment was at odds with legal procedures. A new lead reviewer had to be appointed, a formal peer review had to be written and the author was to be acquainted with the peer review and given the chance to rewrite and resubmit her manuscript.[47] Predictably, the author of the negative preliminary assessment was appointed lead reviewer in November 1983.[48] The work was not published until ten years later, after the regime change.[49] The Hodrová example illustrates the power fiat that could be deployed to bend any regulations to its will when a piece of writing aroused the displeasure of the gatekeepers. If the authors were not able to draw on their own social capital, this mechanism rendered them powerless, offering them only sham recourse.

Conclusion: Censors or rigorous scholars?

On the example of the Editorial Board of the Czechoslovak Academy of Sciences, I tried to illustrate the complexity of normalization scholarly publishing. Central planning and party leadership determined not only the political line of editorial policies, but also editorial plans and the scope of publication activities and sometimes even of individual publications. That constrained the manoeuvering room of individual actors, even an actor as privileged as the Editorial Board of the Academy. The directives changed with the sways of the political climate and progressive economic difficulties. The Board was answerable to the presidium of the Academy regarding the compliance of all publications with the policies and with the party line. Still, it was not just an instrument of the regime but an actor with agency. If the Board's political function curtailed its agency, its professional function allowed it to accrue agency. It vouched for the scientific quality of the publications, a responsibility that connected scholarship with politics, namely international politics. The argument that science and scholarship were important instruments in the Cold War competition was on hand if the Board chose to push a publication through, emphasizing its scientific importance within the political context. This duality of the Editorial Board's functions opened a space for negotiation between the rulers and the ruled.

The Board's members were politically powerful men and (occasionally) women, but they were also senior scholars who, despite their party allegiance, had genuine professional concerns. Perhaps some, or even most, of them were more apparatchiks than scholars, but the minutes from the meetings provide ample evidence of efforts towards retaining and improving the scientific standards of the Academy's publications. The political argument could be used to support these initiatives just as readily as to justify rejections of non-conformist publications. The refusal to publish 'recycled' texts, raw texts of PhD theses or articles by Czech authors that were rejected abroad demonstrates this endeavour. Such practices would perhaps bewilder many a young scholar today, when not only PhD theses, but often also MA dissertations are seen fit for publication as soon as they are defended.[50]

The Editorial Board of the Academy of Sciences was just one actor on the map of the normalization scholarly publishing landscape, but a crucial gatekeeper guarding access to the most prestigious Czech scientific publishing house. Yet its role should not be seen as straightforwardly censorial, but as ambivalent. At least to some extent, it served the profession, rather than just the party.

Notes

1   Alena Míšková, 'Ediční rada ČSAV 1962–1989: Soupis dílčího archivního fondu (Editorial Board of the Czechoslovak Academy of Sciences, 1962–1989: Inventory of the Archival Holdings)', in *Ediční rada ČSAV [Editorial Board of the Czechoslovak Academy of Sciences]*, holdings of Archiv AV ČR (Czech Academy of Sciences Archive), Prague, 1990.

2   Samantha Sherry, *Discourses of Regulation and Resistance: Censoring Translation in the Stalin and Khrushchev Era Soviet Union* (Edinburgh: Edinburgh University Press, 2015).

3   Sara Jones, *Complicity, Censorship and Criticism: Negotiating Space in the GDR Literary Sphere* (Berlin: de Gruyter, 2011).

4   Libora Oates-Indruchová, 'The Limits of Thought?: The Regulatory Framework of Social Sciences and Humanities in Czechoslovakia (1968–1989)', *Europe-Asia Studies* 60, no. 10 (2008): 1767–1782.

5   Act No. 127/1968 Sb. of 13 September 1968, by which the Bureau for Press and Information and the Slovak Bureau for Press and Information [*Úřad pro tisk a informace* and *Slovenský úřad pro tisk a informace*] were established and which reinstituted censorship after it was briefly abolished in June 1968, states in Section 6 that '[T]he freedom to publish the results of scientific and artistic work is not affected by this law'. However, this declared 'freedom' was then compromised when the Federal Bureau for Press and Information [*Federální úřad pro tisk a informace*] was established in 1981 and was given mandate over all periodicals (Act 180/1980 Sb.).

6   In 1983, the Editorial Board comprised twenty-eight members, a number that was criticized in the draft of a document detailing the Academy's long-term editorial policy. The criticism targeted the inefficiency of the Board. It was too big, and only half of the members attended the monthly meetings; a new Board should therefore be appointed. Holdings of the Ediční Rada ČSAV (Editorial Board of the Czech Academy of Sciences; EBAS). Box 14. 'Upřesnění dlouhodobé koncepce ediční

politiky ČSAV'; Minutes from the 108th session of the 3rd Editorial Board [EB], 24 March 1983.

7   The briefing materials are not preserved for the years 1979–1982.

8   Milan Otáhal, Alena Nosková and Karel Bolomský, ed., *Svědectví o duchovním útlaku (1969–1970): Dokumenty* (Prague: Maxdorf and Ústav pro soudobé dějiny AV ČR, 1993); Antonín Kostlán, ed., *Věda v Československu v období normalizace (1970–1975). Práce z dějin vědy*, vol. 4 (Prague: Výzkumné centrum pro dějiny vědy, 2002); Milan Otáhal, *Normalizace 1969–1989: Příspěvek ke stavu bádání* (Praha: Ústav pro soudobé dějiny, 2002).

9   Markéta Devátá, Jiří Suk and Oldřich Tůma, ed., *Charta 77 – od obhajoby lidských práv k demokratické revoluci 1977–1989: sborník z konference k 30. výročí Charty 77, 21–23 March 2007* (Prague: Ústav pro soudobé dějiny AV ČR and Oddělení edice FF UK, 2008); Jouni Järvinen, *Normalization and Charter 77: Violence, Commitment and Resistance in Czechoslovakia* (Helsinki: Kikimora Publications, 2009).

10 Michal Pullmann's book is the first attempt at a systematic assessment of the societal changes during the perestroika years, while my own early work was concerned with cultural continuities and discontinuities from perestroika to the split of Czechoslovakia in terms of gender. See Michal Pullmann, *Konec experimentu: Přestavba a pád komunismu v Československu* (Prague: Scriptorium, 2011); Libora Oates-Indruchová, *Discourses of Gender in Pre- and Post-1989 Czech Culture* (Pardubice: Pardubice University, 2002).

11 Oates-Indruchová, 'The Limits of Thought?'.

12 EBAS. Box 12 and 13. Minutes from the 55th, 56th, 63rd–64th, and 69th–71st sessions of the 2nd EB, 19 May 1977, 23 June 1977, 18 May 1978, 29 June 1978, 25 January 1979, 22 February 1979, and 22 March 1979.

13 EBAS. Box 10 and 13. Minutes from the 17th and 70th session of the 2nd EB, 23 November 1972 and 22 February 1979.

14 EBAS. Box 14. Minutes from the 108th session of the 3rd EB, 24 March 1983.

15 EBAS. Box 12. Minutes from the 55th session of the 2nd EB, 19 May 1977.

16 EBAS. Box 13. Minutes from the 77th session of the 2nd EB, 20 December 1979.

17 EBAS. Box 15. Minutes from the 12th session of the 4th EB, 24 January 1985.

18 EBAS. Box 14. Minutes from the 97th session of the 3rd EB, 18 February 1982.

19 EBAS. Box 16 and 17. Minutes from the 35th and 41st sessions of the 4th EB, 14 May 1987 and 18 February 1988.

20 EBAS. Box 11. Minutes from the 33rd session of the 2nd EB, 19 December 1974.

21 EBAS. Box 9. Minutes from the 9th session of the 2nd EB, 28 September 1971.

22 EBAS. Box 10. Minutes from the 14th session of the 2nd EB, 7 April 1972.

23 EBAS. Box 9. Minutes from the 3rd session of the 1st EB, 24 March 1970.

24 EBAS. Box 10. Minutes from the 14th session of the 2nd EB, 7 April 1972.

25 EBAS. Box 17. Minutes from the 52nd session of the 4th EB, 16 March 1989.

26 EBAS. Box 14. Minutes from the 108th session of the 3rd EB, 24 March 1983.

27 EBAS. Box 12. Minutes from the 47th session of the 2nd EB, 3 June 1976.

28 EBAS. Box 15. Minutes from the 8th session of the 4th EB, 13 September 1984. Only the first volume of the *Lexicon*, covering letters A–G, came out during the state socialist period, the size of the print run stated in the colophon was 17,000; Matějček's *Vývoj uhelného průmyslu v českých zemích po průmyslové revoluci (do roku 1914)* (Praha: Academia, 1984), was published in 700 copies in the end. On the political tussles surrounding the content of the *Lexicon,* see the study by Zdeněk Pešat, 'Normalizační praxe a Lexikon české literatury', in *Normy normalizace,*

Opava, 11–13 September 1995, ed. Jan Wiendl (Prague and Opava: Ústav pro českou literaturu AV ČR and Slezská univerzita, 1995).

29 Political proclamations and policy documents singled out social sciences and humanities as having a special role and objectives, because the Party leadership defined them explicitly as belonging to 'the ideological sphere'. See e.g. J. Fojtík, 'Situace na společenskovědním úseku a úkoly společenských věd po XIV. sjezdu KSČ', *Nová mysl*, no. 2 (1972): 147–169.

30 EBAS. Box 9. Minutes from the 9th session of the 2nd EB, 28 September 1971.

31 Ibid.

32 EBAS. Box 16. Minutes from the 35th session of the 4th EB, 14 May 1987.

33 EBAS. Box 11. Minutes from the 43rd session of the 2nd EB, 29 January 1976.

34 EBAS. Box 11. Minutes from the 35th session of the 2nd EB, 27 February 1975.

35 EBAS. Box 9. Minutes from the 3rd and 5th sessions of the 2nd EB, 13 January 1971 and 24 March 1971.

36 kol. *Rybízy, angrešty, maliníky a ostružiníky* (Prague: Academia, 1971).

37 This figure 67 is mentioned in the draft of a 1983 document detailing the Academy's long-term editorial policy, and is corroborated by the annual journal evaluations conducted by the Editorial Board ('Upřesnění dlouhodobé koncepce ediční politiky ČSAV'; EBAS. Box 14. Minutes from the 108th session of the 3rd EB, 24 March 1983).

38 EBAS. Box 11. Minutes from the 25th session of the 2nd EB, 28 March 1974.

39 EBAS. Box 12. Minutes from the 56th session of the 2nd EB, 23 July 1977.

40 EBAS. Box 14. Minutes from the 81st session of the 3rd EB, 22 May 1980.

41 EBAS. Box 16. Minutes from the 14th session of the 2nd EB, 7 April 1972, EBAS, box 10; and 35th session of the 4th EB, 14 May 1987.

42 EBAS. Box 16. Minutes from the 35th session of the 4nd EB, 14 May 1987.

43 The minutes from the May 1974 Editorial Board meeting suggest that the interests of the Academy of Sciences and the interests of the Party 'bodies' ran sometimes against each other, although the decision-makers at the Academy were also Party functionaries: the list of reviewers proposed by the president of the Academy at the recommendation of its Scientific Committees was not approved on the grounds that it was too long and 'numerous candidates did not meet all the criteria'; the Scientific Committees were to resubmit a much shorter list. Predictably, it was the social sciences that were to be brought to order first, followed by life and technical sciences (EBAS. Box 11. Minutes from the 27th session of the 2nd EB, 30 May 1974).

44 EBAS. Box 13. Minutes from the 76th session of the 2nd EB, 25 October 1979.

45 EBAS. Box 15. Minutes from the 19th session of the 4nd EB, 17 October 1985.

46 EBAS. Box 14. Minutes from the 110th session of the 3rd EB, 26 May 1983.

47 Ibid.

48 EBAS. Box 15. Minutes from the 2nd session of the 4nd EB, 17 November 1983.

49 Daniela Hodrová, *Román zasvěcení* (Jinočany: H&H, 1993).

50 Today's prestigious American and UK academic presses stipulate frequently in their editorial policies that they do not publish the defended texts of PhD theses, but require their significant expansion and rewriting to consider them worthy of printing.

11

'How Many Days Have the Comrades' Wives Spent in a Queue?' Appealing to the Ceaușescus in Late-Socialist Romania

Jill Massino

The title of this chapter is taken from a line in a letter written by Elena Negru, a longtime party member, to First Lady Elena Ceaușescu in February 1988 – less than two years prior to communism's collapse in Eastern Europe.[1] The letter, which is fifteen pages long, is at once a complaint, denunciation, request for assistance and a warning. Ms Negru does not condemn the Ceaușescus themselves but instead targets the 'bad apples' (e.g. high-ranking functionaries), who she claims are responsible for the injustices suffered by her son and other Romanians. At the same time, she expresses continued support for communism, emphasizing her long-standing membership in the party. Such cautious criticism illustrates the strategic and savvy way individuals highlighted deficiencies, aberrations and abuses within the system without identifying Ceaușescu per se as the cause of the problem. In this way, Ms Negru sought to express her discontent without provoking the ire of the Securitate, the Romanian political police.

Scholars have offered complex analyses of East German *Eingaben* (petitions) and letters written by ordinary individuals to the Soviet leadership; however, the Romanian case has only recently become a site of inquiry–these files becoming available to most researchers only in 2007.[2] Drawing on letters from the archive of the Central Committee of the Romanian Communist Party (CC al PCR; Partidul Comunist Român), this chapter explores how ordinary Romanians petitioned, appealed and complained to the Ceaușescus in the 1970s and 1980s[3] – the height of the officially proclaimed "Golden Era" (*epoca de aur*) when nationalism and the Ceaușescu cult reached epic proportions, while the material circumstances of ordinary Romanians continued to decline.

The correspondence housed in the Central Committee archive ranges from requests for housing, travel visas and new medical technologies, to denunciations of corrupt officials and incompetent co-workers, to allegations of medical malpractice, to complaints about consumer shortages, adulterous husbands and neglectful fathers.[4] While typically grievances, some letters were adulatory in nature with individuals expressing fidelity to communist ideology, loyalty to the party and, in some cases, even inviting Ceaușescu himself to family celebrations such as christenings and weddings.[5]

In other cases, they were enraged criticisms of state policies and outright threats against the regime.

Just as the subject matter of the letters varied, so too did their language and tone. Some authors drew on articles of the Romanian Constitution, civic rights and communist values; others employed maternal, familial or nationalist tropes. Meanwhile, some wrote in a pleading or supplicating tone, while others were more critical, and even sarcastic or mocking in character. Additionally, many referenced their personal lives, foregrounding requests or demands within their larger, biographical narrative of professional achievement, family status and contributions to the building of socialism.

On a basic level, these letters offer insight into people's everyday lives: their needs, desires and hopes, as well as their struggles, misfortunes and frustrations, illuminating the manifold challenges experienced by ordinary individuals during late socialism. As such, they provide rich portraits of daily life under Ceaușescu. Moreover, because these letters were a primary way for individuals to interact with the communist leadership, they shed light on how people conceived of the state and their rights within socialist society. Indeed, they demonstrate that far from being naïve or passive subjects, some Romanians were highly astute and active citizens, cleverly employing official tropes and socialist parlance to vent, appeal to or make demands of the state. As a corollary, those who included their actual name in the letters demonstrate a surprising level of courage and boldness. Clearly, then, Romanians were not as helpless or inert as totalitarian scholars would have us believe.

However, letters were not simply a medium for requesting favours, righting wrongs and venting frustrations; they were also useful tools of the state. As Paul Betts notes about East Germany: 'Complaints variably served as barometers of common hopes and expectations, individual investment in the state, as well as a controlled and controllable outlet of everyday discontent.'[6] Thus, letters served as a de facto opinion poll, enabling the state to gauge, however imperfectly, popular opinion, root out corrupt officials, make relevant policy changes and, if need be, enhance repressive measures. As such, letters could serve as forms of intelligence, which, along with the Securitate, aided in the surveillance of the population and in identifying sources of popular discontent. At the same time, the state regarded ordinary correspondence as a safety valve, a mechanism for expressing frustration and resentment with the system and for providing individuals with the illusion that the party-state was genuinely concerned with their needs and interests. In such a capacity, letters could help forestall – or at least postpone – more active dissent.

The letters examined in this chapter constitute a small sampling of those received by and archived in the Department of Letters and Audiences, which was a section within the Central Committee of the Romanian Communist Party (hereafter, CC al PCR) from the 1960s through 1980s.[7] Individuals typically appealed to high-ranking leaders at the Central Committee in Bucharest as a last resort, after having unsuccessfully sought redress of an issue through the party at the local or regional level. Thus, the letters featured here do not include those received by local officials but not forwarded to the Central Committee.

The regime produced annual statistical reports detailing the number of letters submitted, the nature of the complaints and the status of the complainant (labourer, agricultural worker).[8] The figures far surpass the letters that are archived today, indicating that many letters were 'lost' or discarded, or that the figures in statistical reports were inflated. Also, these reports do not encompass letters that were destroyed or discarded, a phenomenon that certainly occurred on the local or regional level as party officials hoped to suppress knowledge of illicit or incriminating behaviour that either they were engaged in or that occurred in their regions. Moreover, regulations regarding county archives stipulated that some types of documents, including correspondence, did not have a permanent retention period. Therefore, many letters were purged in accordance with these regulations. Additionally, most letters found in the archives today are not accompanied by official responses, as many of them, especially requests for housing and material assistance and grievances about workplace graft, would have been sent back to local authorities where they would have been resolved (favourably or not), after which the local department would send a report to the Department of Letters and Audiences of the Central Committee. Finally, after 1989, some of the documents that had been saved were deemed unimportant and were destroyed, misfiled or went missing during the reorganization of the party archive. The cache of available correspondence is thus incomplete and should not be considered representative of the range of letters written during the period. Readers are therefore forewarned that they will be left in suspense as to the outcome of some cases analysed here.

As with all sources produced in authoritarian states with invasive surveillance apparatuses and repressive police (particularly security police) forces, these letters must be approached with caution. Fear of interrogation, job loss or even imprisonment prevented Romanians from fully speaking their minds. Consequently, these letters do not, in most cases, reflect the extent of people's sentiments at the time. Instead, most individuals couched their criticism within a larger story of personal suffering or injustice, and deflected blame onto a lower-ranking bureaucrat as a means of ensuring that they would not attract the ire of the authorities. They also often expressed themselves in the language of the regime, what Stephen Kotkin refers to as 'speaking Bolshevik'.[9] That said, in certain instances the content of the letters was exaggerated, embellished and even fabricated, as some authors were motivated by a desire to settle scores or by more nefarious motives.

Given that the communist leadership received tens of thousands of letters per year, this chapter only provides a snapshot of the letters of appeal and complaints that were addressed to the Ceaușescus and were selected for archiving by functionaries working at the Central Committee.[10] By the mid-1970s, the public sphere was saturated with the Ceaușescus, their photos appearing on the walls of workplaces, schools and other official buildings, as well as on the cover or first page of a wide variety of publications from the daily newspapers, to scholarly texts, to children's magazines. In addition, Nicolae Ceaușescu could be frequently seen (either indirectly via television or directly in workplace visits) and heard on the radio.[11] Meanwhile, poets wrote paeans to the Ceaușescus in the press, and the couple either inspired or 'authored' books and articles on a wide range of topics and pressing issues. Given their omnipresence, the solidity of their cults of personality by the 1980s and their roles as national patriarch and matriarch, it is unsurprising that individuals regarded the Ceaușescus as the most appropriate recipients of their letters and thus addressed their correspondence to them. Moreover, addressing state leaders in correspondence was practised in the interwar period, and the socialist leadership encouraged individuals to share their views and critiques of the system, presenting letter writing as a form of civic engagement.[12]

No place like home

Requests for new or improved lodging constituted one of the most common appeals made by letter writers. As Romania modernized in the 1950s and 1960s, industrial production took precedence over other entitlements such as consumer goods and housing. The problem of housing newly arrived peasants in cities and burgeoning industrial centres was particularly acute in the 1950s, though apartments were perennially in short supply throughout the socialist period, particularly in urban areas. These shortages were exacerbated by the privileging of the communist elite and, to a lesser extent, skilled workers for housing and by individual gaming of the system through connections and bribery. For those lacking such status, networks and means, bartering, illicit trading or appealing to the authorities was their only recourse for procuring an apartment or seeking a larger one as their family increased in size.

Appeals for housing were usually penned by women since they were responsible for household management and had to contend with cooking, cleaning, storing food and caring for their families in often less-than-favourable conditions. Women's pleas for lodging were often highly emotional in tone, reading like desperate appeals from mothers at their wits' end. For example, in 1973 Floarea Berendei penned a letter to Elena Ceaușescu requesting a larger dwelling for her family, which included herself, her husband and her two daughters aged twelve and twenty. She appealed to Mrs Ceaușescu with the 'conviction of a poor mother, so you will understand the difficult situation I find myself in, and so that you can give me some comradely assistance.'[13] Explaining that her retired husband has a neurological disorder and needs a quiet place to rest (lest he become abusive towards the family), and that her daughters need a decent place to study, her plea is an impassioned one, made by a 'simple' subject as she writes: 'With tears in my eyes, I come to you, comrade Elena Ceaușescu, as a simple, woman worker, with the hope that you'll give me some support so I can be happy, too.'[14] Of note is that Mrs Berendei used socialist parlance, along with maternal tropes, appealing to Elena as a fellow comrade and mother to issue her a larger apartment. Moreover, she referenced the issue of domestic violence, emphasizing its deleterious effect on children. Finally, by noting that her children lacked sufficient study space, she intimates that the state could not provide her with the necessary conditions for nurturing a new generation of well-educated citizens about which the regime endlessly boasted. It is unknown if Mrs Berendei's pleas were heard, as no response to her letter can be found in the file; however, her case might have been settled by local authorities and not recorded. Regardless, Mrs Berendei clearly viewed the first lady as the appropriate recipient for her letter and most likely to come to her aid.

Individuals frequently mobilized the trope of family to request a larger dwelling or relocation to a different city. Moreover, age and ailing health were also invoked in making the case for living near one's family, appeals which could prove successful. For instance, 58-year-old Georgeta Miahi, who cited hypertension, a nervous disorder and heart and severe liver problems, was granted permission, in 1986, to exchange her apartment for one owned by her daughter.[15]

In some cases, a relative's ill health and the author's (or their family's) essential role in their care, was part of a larger, complex story of what they perceived as personal or civic injustice. Such was the case of Olga Tudorache, an actress who wrote at least three letters to the authorities in the late 1980s requesting that the two-room apartment of her recently deceased brother-in-law – which, she notes, 'he devoted 55 years of his hard work and savings to' – be transferred from a state agency (that had taken possession of it) to her 27-year-old son, Alexandru. She places her request within the context of her ex-husband's flight from the country in the 1970s, a move, which, according to Ms Tudorache, left her son effectively fatherless while also scarring his professional trajectory as he was denied party membership because of his illicit departure. Thus, she asserts, her son not only suffered from 'not having a father' but is now forced to 'pay for the sins of a father that he didn't have'.

To convince the authorities that her son is deserving, Ms Tudorache details his educational and professional achievements, emphasizing that he was a 'good child': serious, mature, hard working and thoughtful, who attended university and completed his *repartiție* (state-assigned first job).[16] Additionally, she stresses his filial piety, noting that he (along with his fiancée) had been caring for his aunt, who, until her recent death, was suffering from brain cancer and paralysis. In order to further curry favour with the authorities, she adds that if her son does receive the apartment, he intends to care for his 83-year-old grandmother. She closes with 'you are the only person who can help me. I appeal to your understanding, Madam, as a person, a mother, and a woman'.[17]

In a follow-up letter in October 1989, Ms Tudorache thanked Elena Ceaușescu for her intervention, writing: 'Even if we never receive this house (legal channels told me "it's not legal" – "you don't have the right" – "you cannot") the fact that you, Our Lady, intervened and said "yes" … and wanted well [for him], I thank you! From the depths of my soul, I thank you! With all my tears that I have yet to cry out, I thank you!' From this letter it can be gathered that local officials did not favourably resolve her case, and that she hoped that through persistence, in this instance in the form of lavish gratitude, Elena Ceaușescu would intervene on her behalf and positively resolve her situation. It can be safely assumed, then, that Ms Tudorache's sentiments are more strategic than genuine.

Alongside ill health, one woman referenced her relationship to the Ceaușescu children in the hopes of securing approval for her housing request. A retired teacher, Elena Munteanu, who taught both the Ceaușescu sons, Valentin and Nicușor, and who, at the time of writing, had sustained two liver operations and lived alone in Bucharest, appealed to Elena Ceaușescu in 1986 for permission to move to Constanța, near her family. To arouse nostalgic sentiments within Elena, her letter is accompanied by a newspaper clipping featuring a photo of Elena Ceaușescu's youngest son, Nicușor, on his first day of school in 1958.[18]

Justice for all

Alongside housing, many individuals sought redress for a particular injustice. These letters ranged from requesting a review of a Baccalaureate exam that had allegedly been graded in error to demanding an autopsy of a loved one to identify the cause of death. This latter request was made by Viorel, a 27-year-old carpenter from Sălaj County, whose wife died after giving birth in 1972.[19] Forced into early retirement due to ill health and garnering a pension of a mere 497 lei (the equivalent of $15.84 at the time) per month, he addressed Nicolae Ceaușescu as a fellow parent, hoping to arouse sympathy for his situation as a widower with three children and a debt of 15,000 lei that he owed to the CEC (Casa de Economii și Consemnațiuni), the state bank.

In the letter, Viorel attributes his wife's death to medical malfeasance, claiming that her previous birth involved no complications. In particular, he emphasizes that her death was not natural but, in his estimation, a crime, revenge for a previous run-in he had with a doctor when his wife was rushed to the hospital in an ambulance during perinatal haemorrhaging. At that time, Viorel had repeatedly beseeched the doctor, who was chattering in the hall with some women, to attend to his ailing wife. Growing annoyed, the doctor allegedly grabbed Viorel by his coat collar, to which Viorel, in turn, responded by slapping the doctor. The event culminated with the *miliția* (police) being called in and Viorel's forced escort out of the hospital. After giving birth to another child at the same hospital the following year, Viorel's wife died, for which he blames the aforementioned doctor. Requesting a full autopsy in the presence of a specialist authorized by the Ministry of Health to 'determine the cause of death', Viorel insists on the need for punishment of the doctor if found guilty. In this case, the authorities were swift in their follow-up: a letter sent to the Central Committee that June by Prosecutor L. Tamaș indicated that the wife's death could have been prevented had she been given the correct blood type during a blood transfusion. As a result of such negligence, the doctors who oversaw the procedure, including the one singled out by Viorel, were charged with the crime of wrongful death, punishable under Article 178 of the Penal Code.[20] Given that the death occurred shortly after the introduction of pronatalist policies (under Decree 770) and the concomitant glorification of mothers, and given that Viorel's wife had borne three children, an incident that may have previously been excused as an accident was considered a form of medical malpractice and thus a felony.

Individuals also appealed to the Ceaușescus for other legal interventions, including paternity tests. Such was the case of a 30-year-old mother from Argeș County who, along with her infant son, was thrown out of her husband's apartment shortly after their wedding. Like other letter writers, the woman uses maternal discourse, addressing Elena Ceaușescu as 'the mother of all [Romanians]', as well as a mother with [her own] children, for help, which the woman claimed should make her more receptive to her own suffering as a mother.[21] The woman portrays herself as an unassuming country girl wronged by a greedy city boy, noting that upon receiving 100,000 lei for their wedding and buoyed on by his parents – who regarded her as a poor girl who wasn't good enough for their son – her husband initiated divorce proceedings and denied paternity. Claiming that she was forcibly taken to a hospital where 'experts' determined that her husband was not the father of the child, she rhetorically asks: 'I wonder how they could prove this to be wrong since he was the only man who had ever touched me, and he cheated on me after three months of living together, then decided to marry me.' Thus, she implies that the test results were falsified, ostensibly through the bribery of medical staff by her husband so that he could be free of all legal responsibility for her and their son. Emphasizing her desperate material situation and her son's poor health (he required blood and gamma globulin transfusions and two operations on his ears), she appeals to Elena Ceauşescu for another paternity test so that the child's father can be legally identified and she can be granted the support she desperately needs and deserves. She closes by mentioning her own ill health as well as her concern about the stigma her child will face as a result of being fatherless:

> Comrade Elena Ceauşescu, please keep in mind that my son is the only child in Romania born of an official marriage whose father will not recognize him. He is a child without a father in this world ... I cannot tolerate my child being a 'bastard' thrown in the middle of the street without any kind of support ... I am sick and cannot do very much for him.

By addressing Elena Ceauşescu, this woman most likely believed she had a better chance of having her appeal taken seriously. Moreover, by referencing her husband's abandonment of her and their son and, indeed, his outright denial of paternity, she placed her story within broader socialist discourses on the family, morality and the healthy and harmonious development of the child.

Buffoonery, bribery and thievery

While most letter writers requested improved housing or the redress of a disservice or injustice, some called out incompetent, corrupt or degenerate bosses and functionaries. Historian Sheila Fitzpatrick refers to denunciation letters as 'multi-purpose tools', used variously to settle scores, express party loyalty or ideological fidelity, profit from someone else's misfortunes and flag illicit, dangerous or antisocial behaviour. Accordingly, bringing the misdeeds of others to the attention of the authorities may have been rooted in a genuine belief in socialist ethics (e.g. the sense that socialist values had been compromised and that the targeted persons should be brought to justice), or in a desire to settle scores, seek revenge, or curry favour with the authorities and profit from another individual's fall from grace. These denunciation letters were written either by an individual or a group (e.g. the work collective), who sometimes signed their names to the document and at other times remained anonymous. Despite this, it should be noted that even anonymity did not always insulate individuals from detection as the Seucritate was often able to discover the letter writer's provenance.

An issue that frequently provoked people's ire was corruption. Thus in 1989, an anonymous resident of Botoşani condemned the former mayor for 'not doing anything for the community', using state funds to rebuild her apartment and amass a number of cars, and for 'selling refrigerators, freezers, televisions, coffee and other imported goods on the black market'.[22] Since, already by the mid-1980s, these goods had become scarce commodities, the former mayor's illicit procurement and sale of them, along with her alleged "use" of local funds–a charge referenced later in the letter–was clearly a source of frustration for this individual. In other letters to the authorities, ordinary Romanians similarly expressed indignation about local elites and factory bosses who not only personally enjoyed a range of consumer goods, but were able to profit materially from their illicit sale.

The advancement of individuals lacking the requisite skills, experience or education for their position also prompted letters of complaint. In March 1977, an anonymous employee at Agerpres, Romania's national news agency, submitted a scathing critique of party activist Avram, employed at the time in the Press and Radiotelevision Section of the Central Committee. He writes:

> In all his time working at Agerpres he has engaged only in buffoonery, being known as the clown of this institute. He never once wrote anything on his own. He lifted phrases from the Romanian press that he cited word for word, turning them into minor pieces of news. The rest of the time he engaged in intrigue, gossiped about everyone, and sent more anonymous letters to different Party comrades from Agerpres than anyone else. He has never led a collective, he has never been elected, not even for an office of the main organization … and overnight he became an activist of the Central Committee! … How is it possible that the likes of such an individual, whose life and comportment do not even remotely correspond to the ethics and rigours of the Party, being [in fact] a negative example, made it this far?[23]

The writer then goes on to mention that the man didn't do a *repartiție*, and that it was only 'through flattery, servility and bribery on the part of his father that he managed to convince leading comrades at Agerpres to hire him', inferring that his professional trajectory was due to graft, not merit. Finally, the author claims that the man is an insult to honest and accomplished journalists, denigrating, in front of his old drinking buddies, 'people who had advanced and were promoted through their hard work, through their prestige', and forcing esteemed journalists to leave their jobs altogether. The letter closes with: 'It is distressing to see how a person of such abject character can be promoted. A person who has no moral, professional or political authority and who for this reason cannot enjoy the esteem and respect of journalists'.

The claims made in the letter were by no means alien to Romania at the time, as personal relations and connections were often mobilized for securing work and being promoted, especially in the case of PCR activists. Meanwhile, reference to socialist morals, including the code of socialist ethics, could be used as a basis for demotions.[24]

Other individuals also wrote to the Ceaușescus about corrupt, incompetent and depraved functionaries and activists, similarly expressing amazement and shock that 'such people were being promoted' or being 'admitted to a position of responsibility'.[25] A particularly powerful – and lengthy – denunciation was penned by Ms Negru, the woman referenced at the beginning of this chapter. Her letter discusses the challenges faced by her son, a lawyer, who, because of the heavy snowfall in winter 1984–1985, was unable to travel to work. This, in turn, led to a suspension of legal cases and a reduction of his salary by 50 per cent, even though, as Ms Negru notes, 'the pretty women lawyers, simple-minded, with loose morals, did not face a similar reduction'.[26] After bribing an official at the Ministry of Justice (an expected practice, she infers, by using the term 'requisite bribe'), her son was forced to use the 2,800 lei – given to him by a client for the stamp tax – to pay his bills, and, as a result, was sentenced to a year and a half in jail for fraud and to another seven months for embezzlement. Finally released in July of 1986, and, according to the amnesty law of June 1986, eligible for employment, 'to this day' – February 1988 – Ms Negru writes, her son 'is still unable to find work'. She places the blame for this not on Ceauşescu – who she credits for the amnesty – but on the officials at the Ministry of Justice, which she refers to as a 'nest of abuse and inequity, marred by corruption'. Such corruption included, according to her, debauchery of high-ranking officials and exaction of money from lawyers to support such vices, as well as adulterous behaviour between employees, one of whom, she emphasises, could not have 'attracted women by his looks since he weighs over 120 kg'; a man who is clearly 'taken care of by the Party and does not wait in line an entire week for a bag of chicken legs and heads' (a reference to the typical meat selections acquired after waiting hours in a queue in the 1980s). All this occurs, she notes, 'despite the recent enactment of a Central Committee resolution which requires high-ranking officials to act reputably and ethically, both in public and in private'. She then discusses the bribes that are taken in exchange for admission to the Bucharest Bar, which, in one case, involved the exchange of a large catfish and 20 litres of 'excellent wine'. In the latter part of her letter she asks:

WHO, IN REALITY, IS THE PRESIDENT OF THE SOCIALIST REPUBLIC OF ROMANIA? Comrade Nicolae Ceauşescu or the three louses in the Ministry of Justice? … You, Comrade Nicolae Ceauşescu, are the target of these virulent acts of political sabotage, which are intended to libel you in the eyes of the people. These same people rubbed their fat bellies, grinning when, in Craiova, graffiti appeared on the walls that read: DEATH TO THE TYRANT! … Finally, now, at the twelfth hour, be aware of who holds your power: us, the hungry, the cold and the scared, or that gang of career-driven, fat adventurers who blinded you with flattery … and used their demagogical speeches to sweet-talk you? … Get rid of these adventurers of low morals and think about these people who have nothing to eat, no jobs … If this was wartime and we were under enemy occupation and the people were subject to the suffering I have told you about, the enemy country would be held responsible for crimes against humanity, genocide. But you take no measures to ensure that these serious injustices and abuses are dealt with. This is why you must – because if it had not been for me and my husband who took the bullets for you in '44 and '45, you would not be here today – resolve my son's situation and punish the guilty ones at the Ministry of Justice.

Accompanied by a newspaper photo of the Ceauşescus at a banquet table and signed 'yours faithfully (depending on your answer), Elena Negru', the letter is simultaneously a complaint, denunciation, request for assistance and a warning. It is also rather prophetic given that Ceauşescu was indeed tried for, and found guilty of, genocide at his hasty trial in December 1989. More powerfully, by contrasting the privileged lifestyles of the nomenklatura with the desperate situation of ordinary Romanians, the letter stands as a voice of courage in a time of fear and hopelessness. Amazingly, Ms Negru's scathing criticism of high-ranking communists did not result in serious retribution, such as arrest, although she was questioned by the Securitate.

Rather than 'read the graffiti on the wall' and reform the system, Ceauşescu responded to complaints of consumer shortage by blaming officials for not obeying orders and rationing continued. Instead of feeding the people, he continued to feed his cult of personality. Indeed, rather than any consumer, let alone political, relaxation Ceauşescu emphasized the dangers of reformist movements elsewhere in the bloc to the integrity of socialism, condemning the liberalizations initiated by Soviet leader Mikhail Gorbachev, all the while praising Romanian workers for their high rates of productivity.

Complaints of personal aggrandizement and illicit exchanges by state and local officials, factory bosses and other 'respected' party members were common in the letters surveyed. In his study of popular opinion in Fascist Italy, Paul Corner interprets such letters as exaggerations, if not wholly suspect, rooted in jealousy and revenge rather than justice and political integrity.[27] However, given the frequency of such letters in the folders I consulted, dismissing them simply as exaggerations or vehicles for revenge might miss the mark. Instead, such letters should be considered within the larger context of graft, material deprivation and injustice that existed in Romania at the time. While letters of denunciation may have served the author's self-interest (job promotion, settling scores), they may also have served the collective good (removal of a corrupt boss or local official; increased access to food and other goods). Some were also clearly rooted in notions of fairness, socialist ideology and ideas about proper socialist behaviour. Accordingly, by calling out graft, debauchery and other unprincipled behaviour, individuals were attempting to hold officials accountable to the communist code of ethics, to which all Romanians were expected to adhere.[28]

Give us our daily bread

With the onset of the 1980s and especially Ceauşescu's decision to pay off the foreign debt in 1982 – at the expense of adequately provisioning the population – letters about consumer shortages and rationing (including heat, water, electricity and gasoline) became more common. Either as a protective measure or due to naïveté, many writers don't blame the Ceauşescus outright for the situation, but instead cloak their critiques in the Ceauşescus' lack of knowledge about the living conditions of ordinary Romanians. Like Ms Negru, they emphasize that leading functionaries were concealing the truth from – and even manipulating – the Ceauşescus through flattery and praise, which enabled them to stay in the Ceauşescus' good graces and maintain their privileged position. Unlike Ms Negru's letter, these letters are often written in a servile tone, beginning with salutations such as: 'Dearly beloved comrade, academician, doctor, and engineer Elena Ceauşescu. It is with profound respect and the full belief and hope that you will favourably resolve my problems that I write to you.'

As paternalism was an important component of Nicolae Ceaușescu's cult of personality, individuals appealed to him as 'father'. Similarly, they appealed to Elena as a 'mother'. An anonymous letter written by a group of women in 1982 to Elena Ceaușescu about the 'misfortune that had befallen' them is illustrative.[29] Identifying themselves as workers, mothers and homemakers, they outline their struggles in securing food, beseeching Elena to reverse the measure requiring that enclosed balconies be dismantled because it will exacerbate heating problems and cause canned foods, which are typically stored on balconies, to freeze and become ruined. They claim that while they are used to living on less food, their children are growing and need more and thus they do not know what to do if their food is spoiled. Given the amount of time women (as well as other family members) devoted to procuring food in the form of going from shop to shop or queuing-up for hours, for these women the prospect of food spoilage was nothing short of catastrophic.

For their misfortunes, the women blame not Elena Ceaușescu, but the comrades who do not know what it is like to live in an apartment block 'because they probably live in houses, in great comfort, they have real rooms. They do not know the experience of waiting in endless lines for hours day to day and often not getting a hold of anything', adding: 'Madam, you are misinformed; you don't know how hard life is … Madam, no longer believe the fake praises of those around you … You are considered a loving parent of children and the people are waiting for you to make their lives easier so we can work with enthusiasm.' The women close by imploring Elena: 'Take mercy on us and our children. With tears in our eyes, we beg you to end this measure to dismantle the balconies, which is of no use and only arouses hatred and despair and disapproval.'

Other letter writers used less servile language, criticizing the gulf between socialist rhetoric and everyday life. As the aforementioned Ms Negru stressed in another part of her letter:

> I would like to mention that my son and I eat one loaf of bread a day – yet this one loaf a day seemingly is the cause for the remaining bread throughout the country to be rationed like during the war, even though there has not been a harvest as bountiful as last year's. Well, if all these endless millions of tons of wheat were harvested, where is the bread, in what African countries is it eaten since we are allowed only 300 grams a day, and it is mainly chaff and dirt rather than flour?[30]

Ms Negru was not some lone voice in the wilderness, but represented the sentiments of millions of Romanians who were desperate for basic foodstuffs, frustrated by endless queues and cold apartments, resentful of elite privilege and weary of the empty rhetoric celebrating the bounties of socialist harvest, all the while subsisting on stale or ersatz bread and scrawny chickens and pork hooves.[31] Their discontent with life and the socialist system was evident in daily grumblings, cursings, jokes and eventually and more explicitly in the mass protest that erupted in Brașov in 1987 and the Romanian Revolution of December 1989.[32] It was also evident in the thousands of letters written by ordinary Romanians to Radio Free Europe during the final decade of communist rule. As a group of women poignantly conveyed in 1984:

Mrs Ceauşescu: Why don't you want to understand that we have had enough of so many lies and that we wake up at 3–4 in the morning to wait in line and after that go to work, and when we leave work we try out another line, just to get a little something … to continuously not have hot water, to not have heating in our apartments in winter, at work, to have electricity cut off in apartments, not to be able to change our gas canister when it's empty, to see only preserves and drinks in the stores, to procure our rationed food – especially sugar – at outrageous prices, to be required to work when ill – if we don't have a fever above 40 [degrees Celsius] – etc. etc. … In order to personally convince us of the optimal conditions for "The Protection of Mothers and Children" and how impressively the healthcare system has grown across the country, you make a few 'unannounced' visits to hospitals, creches. … Unfortunately, you are not at all interested in what we Romanian women endure and we ask you why. If you had been born in a palace, we would understand. Have you actually forgotten where you came from and what you fought for in your youth? If it's true that you are the dearest mother, you should understand Romania's children, not only your own … we also believe that our children have the right to a civilized life.[33]

Drawing on maternalist and nationalist discourse, these women underscored the hypocrisy between official pronouncements about protecting mothers and children and the everyday realities of food, heat and electricity shortages. They also point to the gulf between the communist leadership and ordinary Romanians by referencing Elena Ceauşescu's early days as a socialist revolutionary, rhetorically asking how a woman who had been born into modest means could have strayed so far from earlier ideals. Finally, they address her as a mother, both to her own family and to all Romanian children, inquiring why she has neglected her maternal responsibilities to protect and care for her Romanian subjects.

As Ms Negru did, these women explicitly contrasted the lavish lifestyles of the communist leadership with the penury of the masses. However, in comparison with Negru's letter, this one reached a wider audience, being broadcast on Radio Free Europe, to which Romanians themselves tuned into at this time.[34] Yet, Ceauşescu's megalomania, as well as his relentless determination to pay off the country's $10 billion debt, left him blind or indifferent to the daily struggles and frustrations of his people. Indeed, Ceauşescu had no intent of honouring the socialist social contract for even after the letters flowed in, penury continued to characterize Romania throughout the 1980s.

Conclusion

Collectively, these letters speak to Romanians' discontent about their living situation, government policies and the communist leadership. They also testify to the privilege, corruption and inequality that characterized the system. As in other countries, including non-communist ones, such letters provided the state with insight into popular opinion, ostensibly enabling them to identify problems before popular discontent erupted in a more public, mass fashion and alter policy accordingly. Yet, in Romania these letters had little, if any, effect on policy. While a few of the letter writers cited earlier, notably the bereaved husband seeking to discover the cause of his wife's death and the retired woman who requested to move closer to her daughter, received favourable resolutions, those issues at the fore of most Romanians' minds in the 1980s – food, heat, electricity shortages – were of little concern to the state as no policy change was implemented. Thus, desperate pleas to increase food rations fell on deaf ears.[35] This suggests that the state viewed public correspondence primarily as a safety valve and surveillance mechanism, which, from time to time, enabled it to identify corrupt officials, note reports of bribery, theft and other illegalities, and investigate further cases as they saw fit.

In this respect, Romania was not dissimilar from other repressive neighbours in the bloc. For instance, the East German state received millions of letters of complaint over the course of the 1980s, and while some were resolved favourably – in some cases leading to minor policy change – in the end no effort was made to liberalize policy.[36] Along with other neo-Stalinists, such as East Germany's Erich Honecker and Czechoslovakia's Gustáv Husák, Ceauşescu was wholly allergic to systemic reform. With a repressive police apparatus, the Securitate, that relied on the assistance of a large portion of the population, active dissent could be quashed, while more passive forms, such as those that appear in some of these letters, could be simply ignored or be followed up by an interrogation or demotion.[37]

Yet if letters did not lead to substantial policy or systemic change, this begs the question of why? Why did people continue to write letters, and what can these letters tell us about everyday life and socialist citizenship under the Ceauşescus? One answer is desperation. Another reason is a belief in 'rights' and 'justice' – or the lack thereof. In comparison to the 'desperate letters', which were written in the vein of the supplicant appealing to the benevolent mother or father, these letters are written in the form of the socialist citizen who stated opinions, criticized policies, denounced people's illicit activities and suggested improvements to the system.[38] In addition, they often discard with niceties and get straight to the point: 'We are simple but honest people and we cannot overlook the many abuses of those who claim to lead us.'[39]

Finally, we might conceptualize these letters as forms of everyday resistance, coping mechanisms or 'weapons of the weak'.[40] Letters could serve manifold purposes as is clear in Elena Negru's case. Or they could simply serve as a means of blowing off steam, airing one's frustration or taking a cheap shot at those in power. Such was the case of a letter written to Elena Ceauşescu in 1978 by an individual identified as Margareta Oancea, part of which is quoted here:

> Dear Comrade Elena Ceauşescu ... You are an especially fortunate woman with an exceptional destiny ... You are incredibly ugly and despite this so loved by your husband. His example should be followed by the thousands of husbands that neglect, cheat on, lie to, and mock their beautiful wives. If they were somehow brought up, educated in this way, to be thoughtful men with generous souls, unselfish and without pettiness, there wouldn't be so many divorces, broken families, psychiatric hospitals.[41]

The author then inquires why more ready-made foods are not available to Romanian women – as they are to women in the West – and asks: 'Why haven't you done, and why don't you do, something to make yourself pretty? There are aesthetic operations. How are you not embarrassed to present yourself with such an ugly face and so unkempt?' Ms Oancea closes by criticizing Elena's lack of sartorial sophistication, stressing that she must wear a hat and gloves during her upcoming visit with Queen Elizabeth II, lest she look like a 'wild peasant'. Powerless, in this case the author's only weapon was to insult Elena's looks and style.

Although some of the letters I consulted were rooted in the belief that shortcomings in state policy would be resolved and incidents of corruption would be punished, many more were rooted in desperation, disgust and outrage over injustices. Yet, while the letters did not have policy implications, they did provide ordinary people with a medium for articulating their grievances and frustrations – both towards the system itself and the people within it. As such, they offer important insight into the everyday realities of ordinary Romanians – their needs, desires and hopes, as well as their challenges and frustrations. They also offer insight into how Romanians regarded and related to their government, revealing that rather than being naïve or passive dupes of the regime, they understood how power operated: that the elections and unending reports of abundant harvests and overfilled plans were simply part of a larger façade. Finally, many of the grievances conveyed in these letters – continual food and heating shortages, widespread corruption and the glaring gulf between socialist rhetoric and daily life – underscored the hypocrisy and ideological bankruptcy of the system. The regime's neglect of these issues, combined with the repression of the Braşov revolt in November 1987 and later, and more brutally, the peaceful protests in Timişoara in December 1989, ultimately led to the Ceauşescus' demise. Perhaps had they paid a little more attention to these letters (which would have required reading them) their ends might not have been so violent.[42]

Notes

1   This chapter has benefited greatly from the insights and suggestions of Manuela Marin and the participants of the conference 'Party, Security Services, and Government Archives in International Perspective: Perceptions of Society at the Top in East Central Europe, 1945–1981', held in Prague in December 2016.

2   For the Soviet Union, see, for instance, Sarah Davies, *Popular Opinion in Stalin's Russia: Terror, Propaganda, and Dissent, 1934-1941* (Cambridge: Cambridge University Press, 1996); Sheila Fitzpatrick, 'Supplicants and Citizens: Public Letter Writing in Soviet Russia in the 1930s', *Slavic Review* 55, no. 1 (1996): 78–105; Vladimir A. Kozlov and Sheila Fitzpatrick, eds., *Sedition: Everyday Resistance in the Soviet Union Under Khrushchev and Brezhnev* (New Haven: Yale University Press, 2011); Lynne Attwood, *Creating the New Soviet Woman: Women's Magazines as Engineers of Female Identity, 1922-1953* (New York: St. Martin's Press, 1999). For East Germany, see Mary Fulbrook, *The People's State: East German Society from*

Hitler to Honecker (New Haven: Yale University Press, 2005); and Paul Betts, *Within Walls: Private Life in the German Democratic Republic* (Oxford: Oxford University Press, 2010); For Bulgaria, Martin K. Dimitrov, 'What the Party Wanted to Know: Citizen Complaints as a "Barometer of Public Opinion" in Communist Bulgaria', *East European Politics and Societies* 28, no. 2 (2014): 271–295. For Romania, see Mioara Anton and Laurențiu Constantiniu, ed., *Guvernați și Guvernanți: Scrisori către putere, 1945–1965* (Bucharest: IICCMER, 2013) and Mioara Anton, '*Ceaușescu și poporul!' Scrisori către 'iubitul conducător'*, *1965–1989* (Târgoviște: Cetatea de Scaun, 2016). On popular opinion, including analyses of correspondence of ordinary citizens, under dictatorships, see Paul Corner, *Popular Opinion in Totalitarian Regimes: Fascism, Nazism, Communism* (New York: Oxford University Press, 2009), 137; Manuela Marin, *Intre prezent și trecut: cultul personalității lui Nicolae Ceaușescu și opinia publică românească* (Cluj-Napoca: Editura MEGA, 2014) and Corina Doboș, 'Ceaușescu Was My Father! Letters About the Children of the Decree at the End of the 1960s', *International Journal of Humanistic Ideology* 4, no. 1 (2011): 67–80.

3   Individuals also addressed local and regional party leaders; however, due to space constraints and because I was most interested in how citizens appealed to the leader and his wife, they are not included here.

4   Types of correspondence included 'scrisori' (letters), the content of which could vary greatly, 'plângeri' (grievances), 'petiții' (petitions) and 'memorii' (statements or declarations).

5   In addition, Ceaușescu received gifts and thousands of greeting and birthday cards from ordinary individuals during this time. See Marin, *Intre prezent și trecut*.

6   Betts, *Within Walls*, 176.

7   These letters were found in the Chancellery Section and Organizational Section [Secția Cancelarie and Secția Organizatorică] of the Central Committee of the Communist Party of Romania archive. While many are catalogued under files identified as correspondence, others are interspersed with Central Committee meeting minutes and letters from foreign dignitaries. The archive of the Central Committee of the Romanian Communist Party is currently housed at the National Archives in Bucharest.

8   For instance, in 1974 Elena Ceaușescu received 14,809 letters, about ten times the number she received in 1968–1969, and five times more than she received in 1971–1972. Of these, 14,327 were documented as 'researched and resolved'. Most of the letters from 1974 dealt with general or personal problems: over 4,000 were in regards to housing, over 4,000 about civil and penal issues (e.g. securing a divorce from spouses who fled the country), 2,641 dealt with work-related issues, 1,411 with educational problems, particularly re-examination of Baccalaureate exams (BAC; required for a high school diploma and progressing to the university level); 1,000 regarding recalculation of pensions or other types of social assistance; and fewer than 500 related to agricultural issues. Some of the correspondence also included invitations to wedding ceremonies or newborn celebrations (e.g. christenings). See Arhivele Naționale ale României (National Archives of Romania; ANIC), CC al PCR, Secția Organizatorică, dosar 191/1972 vol, 2.

9   Stephen Kotkin, *Magnetic Mountain: Stalinism as a Civilization* (Berkeley: University of California Press, 1995).

10   Nicolae Ceauşescu served as General Secretary of the PCR (1965–1989), President of Romania (1974–1989) and President of the State Council (1967–1974), while his wife, Elena, served as Vice Premier of the Government, Member of the Executive Committee of the Central Committees and President of the National Council for Science and Education.

11   For the most comprehensive examination of the Ceauşescu cult, see Manuela Marin, *Nicolae Ceauşescu: Omul şi Cultul* (Târgovişte: Cetatea de Scaun, 2016).

12   It should be noted that other Romanian dignitaries also received correspondence from ordinary Romanians.

13   ANIC, CC al PCR, Secţia Organizatorică, 1921–1975, dosar 1973/213, f., 48–50. Letter from Floarea Berendei to Elena Ceauşescu.

14   Ibid.

15   ANIC, CC al PCR, Secţia Cancelarie, dosar 101/1986, f. 55. Letter from Georgeta Mihai to Elena Ceauşescu. Approval of her request is filed alongside her letter.

16   Those with connections or money often succeeded in evading their *repartiţie* through bribery, favouritism or some type of exchange, or were assigned to or close to the city in which they had studied.

17   ANIC, CC al PCR, Secţia Cancelarie, dosar 96/1985, f. 63–64. Letter from Olga Tudorache to Elena Ceauşescu, 13 September 1989.

18   ANIC, CC al PCR, Secţia Cancelarie, dosar 101/1986, f. 32. Letter from Elena Munteanu to Elena Ceauşescu, 7 April 1986.

19   ANIC, CC al PCR, Secţia Cancelarie, dosar 173/1972, f. 36–37. Letter from Viorel Bălănean to Nicolae Ceauşescu, April 1972.

20   ANIC, CC al PCR, Secţia Cancelarie, dosar, 173/1972, f. 35. Letter from Prosecutor L. Tamaş to the CC al PCR. See 'Codul Penal din 21 iunie 1968' at http://www.monitoruljuridic.ro/act/cod-penal-din-21-iunie-1968-emitent-marea-adunare-na-ional-publicat-n-buletinul-oficial-nr-38070.html (accessed 3 November 2017). Under this article, those who, in their professional capacity, were responsible for a wrongful death could be imprisoned from two to seven years.

21   ANIC, CC al PCR, Secţia Cancelarie, dosar 96/1985, f. 76–77. Letter to Elena Ceauşescu, 28 September 1989.

22   ANIC, CC al PCR, Secţia Cancelarie, dosar 191/1972–1989, vol. 2. Anonymous letter to Elena Ceauşescu, 12 August 1989.

23   ANIC, CC al PCR, Secţia Cancelarie, dosar 157/1977, f. 153. Anonymous letter to Elena Ceauşescu.

24   See 'Codul principiilor şi normelor muncii şi vieţii comuniştilor, ale eticii si echităţii socialiste', Editura Politică, 1974. Adopted at the Eleventh Congress of the PCR, the code advocated the development of conscientious and morally upright citizens, who would dedicate themselves to party, work and family and contribute to the construction of a multilaterally developed socialist society.

25   ANIC, CC al PCR, Secţia Cancelarie, dosar 191/1972, vol. 1, f., 109–110. Anonymous letter to Elena Ceauşescu.

26   ANIC, Secţia Cancelarie, dosar 191/1972–1989, vol. 2, f., 164–178. Letter from Elena Negru to Elena Ceauşescu, 8 February 1988.

27   Corner, *Popular Opinion in Totalitarian Regimes*, 137.

28   'Codul principiilor şi normelor muncii şi vieţii comuniştilor, ale eticii si echităţii socialiste', 1974.

29   ANIC, CC al PCR, Secţia Cancelarie, dosar 191/1972, vol. 1 f. 42–43.

30   Such criticisms became increasingly common as the 1980s wore on and basic
      foodstuffs became increasingly difficult to acquire. As one merchant noted in 1980:
      'As usual, they spoke very much and with much pomposity, but in reality they are
      only words and empty promises; people can nourish themselves with neither slogans,
      nor talk'. Marin, *Intre prezent și trecut*, 161.
31   For recollections of daily struggles in procuring goods in the 1980s, see Smaranda
      Vultur, 'Daily Life and Constraints in Communist Romania in the Late 1980s: From
      the Semiotics of Food to the Semiotics of Power', in *Remembering Communism: Private
      and Public Recollections of Lived Experience in Southeast Europe*, eds. Maria Todorova,
      Augusta Dimou, and Stefan Troebst (Budapest: Central European University Press,
      2014) and 'Țara umilinței în Templele Foamei; cum ne-am bătut pe un ou, pe "Frații
      Petreus," de pe cartelă sau pe o sticlă cu lapte. Lumina, butelia, și căldura la porție',
      Historia, https://www.historia.ro/sectiune/general/articol/tara-umilintei-in-templele-
      foamei-cum-ne-am-batut-pe-un-ou-pe-fratii-petreus-de-pe-cartela-sau-pe-o-sticla-
      cu-lapte-lumina-butelia-si-caldura-la-portie (accessed 15 March 2016.)
32   On 15 November 1987, several thousand workers walked off their jobs at the Steagul
      Roșu (Red Flag) factory in Brașov to protest wage cuts and food shortages. Among
      the chants of the marchers were, 'Thieves … we want our money back', 'We want
      Sunday back', 'We want food for our children', and 'Down with Ceaușescu! Down
      with communism! 'Down with the Golden Era… down with tyranny'. See Ruxandra
      Cesereanu, 'Revolta muncitorilor din Brașov, 1987', *Revista 22*, no. 14 (2003),
      retrieved at: https://www.revista22.ro/revolta-muncitorilor-din-brasov-1987-702.
      html. (12 March 2018).
33   '"Un grup de femei," [aprilie-mai] 1984, difuzată la 27 mai 1984' cited in Gabriel
      Andreescu and Mihnea Berindei, *Ultimul deceniu comunist: Scrisori către radio
      Europa Liberă vol 1 (1979–1985)* (Iași: Polirom, 2010), 261–262.
34   It is believed that Radio Free Europe's audience in Romania grew considerably under
      Ceaușescu, and by the final decade of communist rule most of the population –
      including members of the police and security services – tuned in.
35   In the folders I consulted, most letters are not accompanied by a response or report.
      This indicates that the authorities did not respond, or did not archive their response.
36   See Paul Betts, 'Socialism, Social Rights, and Human Rights: The Case of East
      Germany', *Humanity* 3, no. 3 (2012): 407–426.
37   For instance, Radu Filipescu, an electronics engineer, was sentenced to ten years
      imprisonment in 1983 for distributing anti-Ceaușescu leaflets. Meanwhile, Doina
      Cornea, Professor of French at the University of Cluj, and her son, Leontin, were
      placed under house arrest for distributing pamphlets in support of the Brașov strike.
      Others who engaged in anti-state activities were imprisoned or forcibly committed to
      psychiatric wards or institutions.
38   Fitzpatrick, 'Supplicants and Citizens', 103–104.
39   ANIC, CC al PCR, Secția Cancelarie, dosar 191/1972, vol. 2, f. 26. Anonymous letter
      to Elena Ceaușescu, 6 March 1988.
40   On everyday resistance, see the classic work by James C. Scott, *Weapons of the Weak:
      Everyday Forms of Peasant Resistance* (New Haven: Yale University Press, 1987) and,
      for the Soviet context, Kozlov and Fitzpatrick, *Sedition*.
41   ANIC, CC al PCR, Secția Cancelarie, dosar 191/1972, vol. 1, f. 69–71. Letter from
      Margareta Oancea to Elena Ceaușescu, 31 May 1978.
42   See Kozlov and Fitzpatrick, *Sedition* on the role of popular resistance in contributing
      to the collapse of the Soviet system.

12

Authenticating the Past: Archives, Secret Police and Heroism in Contemporary Czech Representations of Socialism

Veronika Pehe

The late 2000s in the Czech Republic saw a trend of increased interest in the archival document as a means of historical authentication. This chapter examines two parallel developments of this preoccupation on the discursive level and analyses their occasional intersections: in public debate and in cultural representations. With the establishment of the Institute for the Study of Totalitarian Regimes (Ústav pro studium totalitních režimů; ÚSTR) in 2007, an institution dedicated to examining the archives of the Security Services during the Nazi occupation and the period of Communist Party rule,[1] the topic of the archive reanimated public debate. As was the case in the 1990s, when various memory activists took it upon themselves to publically disclose names of alleged former secret police collaborators, thus tarnishing the reputation of a number of people,[2] information emerging from the institute sparked discussions on the supposed collaboration of several prominent public figures with the communist secret services.

At the same time, popular representations of the past adopted the archive as a theme and motif. As I show in this chapter, the presumed credibility of archival documents allowed cultural producers to introduce moral categories in fictional narratives. The figure of the compiler of the archival document – the secret police officer – became the ultimate villain. Focusing on examples from literary and film production, my contention is that this trend of 'authenticating the past' arose in a definite context: it bolstered a politicized memory of the socialist period at a time when the latter seemed to be increasingly receding into the past. This trend was mirrored by a heightened preoccupation on the part of distinct state and NGO actors with manufacturing a national memory of anti-communist heroic resistance.

Institutional interventions

The opening of ÚSTR in 2007, after heated discussions in Parliament[3] and accompanying controversies in the public sphere, has been the most visible marker in a changing memory landscape in the Czech Republic. Throughout the 1990s and the early 2000s, the Czech memory of socialism had been marked by, on the one hand, an anti-communist consensus in the public sphere, instrumentalized by political actors as a means of legitimization, and, on the other hand, by a preponderance of comedies in literature and film. The latter were characterized by small, private stories of everyday life, in which protagonists performed futile gestures of fleeting resistance with little resonance.[4] While the cultural producers producing these representations ranked among a cultural elite, their more lenient and conciliatory assessment of the past regime resonated with audiences and contrasted with the condemnation of the past by the political elite.

But in the mid-2000s, representational and institutional culture began to evince a new 'search for heroes'. This trend consisted in promoting 'positive models' who lived in a repressive regime, whether they engaged in active resistance or adopted a strong moral standpoint. The activities of the institute constituted a turning point in state efforts to gather, preserve and guard the memory of oppression under the Nazi occupation and communist rule in the Czech Republic.[5] Although the law which brought the institute into being did not employ the term 'national memory' [národní paměť], with its investment in the study of anti-authoritarian resistance, the state was clearly involved in manufacturing a patriotic and democratic national memory and identity[6] and equating the Nazi and communist regimes as 'totalitarian', a view that has been challenged by a number of historians.[7]

The problems surrounding ÚSTR's opening were manifold. Hundreds of press articles have been published every year on the subject of the institute. Criticism focused, among others, on the following issues: the capability of a state-controlled institution to carry out independent scientific research; the question of whether or not the previous regime was totalitarian being already answered in the institute's name and thus a presupposition rather than result of its research; doubts about whether some of the institute's aims, such as academic research and the promotion of a particular historical memory and national identity, are not at odds with one another.[8]

The extent and vigorousness of the debate demonstrates that efforts to reach an official memory politics did not meet with unanimous approval in the public sphere. Michal Uhl, as of 2013 a member of ÚSTR's board – a body appointed by the upper chamber of the Czech Parliament and thus consistently under criticism for being susceptible to political pressures – summarized this effectively in an interview: 'The value consensus about the criminal nature of the previous regime has disintegrated. If it still existed, Czech society would not be debating ÚSTR.'[9] This chapter will not analyse the whole range of positions and opinions surrounding the institute's birth, nor describe the increasing public contestation of the national memory ÚSTR attempted to project. Instead, it focuses on debates surrounding the Security Services Archives (Archiv bezpečnostních složek or ABS, an independent institution, whose collections ÚSTR is dedicated to studying) and the manufacturing of a heroic memory. Such a topic is relevant because these two issues were simultaneously picked up by literature and film.

Critics cited the misappropriation of the archive at the hands of scholars with a politically preordained agenda as the chief problem faced by the institute.[10] The archival document thus emerged as a tool of both legitimating claims about the past and casting doubt on past events. The latter is the case particularly as the reliability of secret police materials is subjected to resolving, among others, the following methodological issues: false information provided by informants; the artificial 'recruitment' of collaborators (who were later surprised, if not astonished, to find their names on secret collaborators' lists) in order to meet quotas; the manipulation of information by secret police officers to fulfil ideological requirements; the shredding of files after 1989, leading to incomplete information; and last but not least, the lack of contextual information on the circumstances in which an informer had either willingly or unwillingly collaborated.

Although the preamble to the Act that brought the institute into being paraphrased George Santayana, 'Those who do not know their past are doomed to repeat it',[11] the political skirmishes surrounding ÚSTR would rather suggest that those who control the past also control the present. Apart from high personnel turnover in its early years, ÚSTR had to deal with accusations of sensationalism and critique regarding several high-profile affairs, the most prominent being the accusation that novelist Milan Kundera had denounced a Western agent to the security services.[12] Another criticized, and later contested, 'finding' of the institute included information about plans to assassinate President Klement Gottwald. These were supposed to have been hatched by the Mašín brothers, members of an anti-communist resistance group and sons of the prominent anti-Nazi underground resistance fighter Josef Mašín, who was executed in 1942.[13] Allegations of such plans were immediately denied by one of the brothers, Ctirad Mašín, in an interview he gave to the daily *Mladá Fronta Dnes*.[14] Another surprising piece of information emerging from ÚSTR was that Joska Skalník, an artist imprisoned for anti-regime activities in the 1980s and one of Václav Havel's close collaborators during the time of his election and first months as Czechoslovak president, had in fact reported information to the secret police. Criticism of this incident focused mainly on the fact that ÚSTR had published this claim without asking Skalník for comment.[15]

Turning victimhood into resistance: A political project

But the state was not the only actor purporting to be a caretaker of memory. The 'fortification' of the memory of resistance was promoted through several interconnected institutions and organizations that came together in a complex web of state-sanctioned and grass-roots culture of memorialization, which aimed to introduce notions of heroism into public discourse. The organization Post Bellum was founded in 2001 at the outset of this development. It records oral histories with war veterans, as well as victims of injustice during the socialist period, and those who actively opposed the previous regime. Launched at the initiative of a few journalists who intended to document the fates of war veterans after the Second World War (hence the Latin name *Post Bellum* – Post-War),[16] it has since grown into a large NGO with a number of significant media and institutional partners which have promoted its projects (including ÚSTR). Since 2006, journalists from Post Bellum have been airing the regular program *Příběhy dvacátého století* (Stories of the Twentieth Century) on

Czech public radio. The organization's other main project is the building of an online oral history archive called *Paměť národa* (Memory of the Nation), but their activities have also included organizing exhibitions on Václav Havel, the meetings of Czech and Polish dissidents and the assassination of Reinhardt Heydrich, to name just a few.[17] Further projects include a graphic novel,[18] educational workshops for schools,[19] a phone app called 'Places of the Memory of the Nation' – an interactive guide to places connected to twentieth-century history and, since 2010, the awarding of the Memory of the Nation Prize.[20] Post Bellum can be seen to actively promote a heroic discourse, which they believe is missing in the Czech public sphere – their very first oral history project was called *Hlasy hrdinů* (Voices of Heroes), before being renamed Memory of the Nation.[21]

This memorialization of heroes was granted an official seal of approval in 2011, when the centre-right dominated Parliament with Petr Nečas as premier passed the Act on Third Resistance.[22] The Act defines an anti-communist resistance fighter as anyone who carried out armed struggle against the communist regime, as well as anyone who contributed to destabilizing or overthrowing this regime through written and editorial work, including by working from abroad. It also grants the right to a financial reward and pension benefits.[23] The law thus updates and gives practical impact to an earlier resolution of 1993, which stated that opposition to the communist regime was 'legitimate, just, morally justified, and … worthy of respect'.[24] The 2011 Act clearly prescribes a vision of heroism and represents a shift in emphasis from the previous accent on victimhood, promoted by organizations such as the Confederation of Political Prisoners (Konfederace politických vězňů; KPV), a successor organization of the short-lived club K231 of 1968, which gathered together those imprisoned for political reasons during the first years of Communist Party rule. Since 1990, the KPV has been fighting for the recognition, judicial rehabilitation and monetary compensation of those abused by communist authorities.[25]

Yet the Act on Third Resistance revealed that there was no public consensus on the existence or legitimacy of armed resistance against the communist regime, let alone on whether it should be officially commended. The most divisive case is that of the resistance group of the Mašín brothers, who, in their subversive activities and eventual armed flight from the country in 1953, killed several people, including police officers and, even more controversially, at least one civilian.[26] Reactions in the press, opinion polls and television debates have shown that this case has highly polarized the public; it remains unclear whether the Mašíns' actions should be lauded or condemned.[27]

When the Mašín brothers' close collaborator Milan Paumer died in 2010, journalist Zbyněk Petráček wrote that in recent years the 'relationship towards ambiguous heroes' has 'certainly' begun to 'evolve'.[28] Indeed, as he reminded his readers, former premier Mirek Topolánek had declared the Mašín brothers 'heroes' in 2007 and granted them special recognition in the form of a 'Prime Minister's Plaque' in 2008, while the defence minister honoured the Mašíns' sister in 2009. During Paumer's funeral, the cabinet stopped its session and Premier Nečas stated: 'We have the right to fight enslavement with all necessary means.'[29] Paumer's death in fact accelerated the efforts to codify the Third Resistance in law, which resulted in the 2011 Act.

From the second half of the 2000s, the coming together of several state and non-governmental institutions to generate a national memory has represented an increasing effort to hold onto a narrative that was falling apart. The anti-communist consensus that had played such a role in public discourse in the immediate aftermath of the 1989 revolution was increasingly challenged, as demonstrated not only by the wave of criticism surrounding ÚSTR and the Third Resistance Act but also through the emergence of new press platforms outside of the traditional right-wing dailies and weeklies. With the rise of the internet, blogging platforms attached to the online news sites of the major dailies have given voice to opinions spread across the political spectrum. Since 2005, new left-wing print and online platforms[30] have contributed to diversifying the political range of the Czech media and have voiced stark criticism of the dominant anti-communist discourse. These developments suggest that a wholesale condemnation of the socialist past has become less automatic.

The lack of consensus around ÚSTR and the Third Resistance issue points to a discursive shift in the Czech public sphere: anti-communism is no longer as convenient a tool with which to demonstrate allegiance to the new elite as it was in the 1990s. The condemnation of the past serves to stifle critique of the present. Increasing disagreement with this preordained narrative also shows that positions on the socialist past in the Czech public sphere have become more pluralized. In a climate of rising contestation, official memory politics is used ever more strongly as a legitimating mechanism for the path that Czech society took after 1989. The evolution of the discursive level in reaction to several interventions into the memory landscape has been the topic of public debate; what has been less discussed is how the cultural memory of socialism has been simultaneously restructured by changes in representational strategies.

The archival turn

The archival document, rather than personal memory, has become the privileged medium to provide access to the past. It is now both a feature of institutional discourse and a representational strategy. Alongside the evolution of public discourse on the socialist past, representational culture saw a shift away from comedy and towards drama as the genre of choice. Narratives that portrayed the previous regime with humour as coming-of-age tales had gained cult status in the 1990s, among them Michal Viewegh's 1992 novel about late socialism *Báječná léta pod psa* (Bliss Was It in Bohemia),[31] whose jocular tone was welcomed by critics,[32] or director Jan Hřebejk's 1999 hit film comedy *Pelíšky* (Cosy Dens), which was seen in cinemas by over 10 per cent of the population.[33]

The shift from comedy to drama was not abrupt, nor can it be interpreted as a direct reaction to the developments in the public sphere. Rather, both representations of the past and public debates began to explore new topics in relation to socialism in the second half of the 2000s in ways that ran parallel to one another, and at times intersected explicitly. The new turn was not absolute; in this section, I do not review all the representations of socialism that arose in this period, which played out in a variety of genres and broached a number of thematic concerns, but rather I attempt to outline one specific, distinctive trend of dramatic, even tragic narratives among these representations. The preoccupations of this representational trend gathered around core themes that echoed the debates around ÚSTR and Third Resistance.

First, historical documents gained a new importance in narratives about socialism in this period. In parallel to discussions of the appropriateness of the State Security (StB) archives as a means of shedding light on historical events, the 'archive' emerged as a motif and metaphor in fictional accounts. Arguably, this move signals an increased sense of distance from the past – it is only through letters and files rather than their own memories that audiences can now, with the increasing time-gap since the demise of the previous regime, access the past. The shift of the late 2000s suggests that memory is less reliable; where the former comic narratives were able to recount personal tales without additional means of authentication, the new turn requires historical validation of this new vision of the past.

Second, the new archive-inspired representations evinced a new 'search for heroes' and grand narratives. Stories about the socialist past no longer found their locus in the everyday occurrences that structured comedic representations. Instead, alongside the Act on Third Resistance, which attempted to stamp an official label of heroism on those who had previously been largely seen as victims, representations increasingly turned to large-scale historical events, traumatic episodes and heroic actions which overcame the small-scale resistance of the everyday. Not all the works discussed later in the chapter feature all of these elements; the thematic and generic repertoire of this literary and cinematic production is quite varied. However, they are all characterized by what I term here a 'dramatic turn' away from comedy.

The new 'new novel'

In the second half of the 2000s, literary efforts at depicting the socialist period often operated in a genre that could be described as 'intimate tragedy' – they focused on the private and on the family, but these spheres were encroached upon by traumatic historical events. The corpus of texts – largely novels and novellas – that are set in or otherwise deal with the socialist period has grown quite large. I will not map here all literary works that touch upon this theme, but will discuss several texts that were published at approximately the same time as the new trend in memorialization took off and gained institutional validation. The award of a range of literary prizes[34] serves as an indication of the topics the cultural elite was interested in promoting. An indication that said elite is small but influential is given by the accumulation of acclaimed titles concerning the state socialist past published by the Brno-based publishing house Host (Guest), which has a strong record of bringing out young contemporary Czech authors. What unites this body of literature is the archival document as a key means of accessing, while also often obscuring, the past. The newly found concern of this literary production thus resonated with the ways in which information emerging from ÚSTR's archives revealed, but at the same time further tangled, the histories surrounding individuals such as the Mašín brothers or Milan Kundera.

An early example is Jiří Hájíček's 2005 novel *Selský baroko* (Rustic Baroque),[35] which inaugurated this 'archival trend' in depicting the socialist past. In this text, set in the present, archivist and genealogist Pavel Straňanský returns to the traumatic history of the 1950s and the forced collectivization of Czechoslovak agriculture. He is commissioned to find a denunciation letter written by one-time village beauty Rozálie Zandlová, which had been used as a pretext by local authorities to create a case against several successful farmers. Thanks to this ploy, the latter were labelled 'kulaks' and forced to leave their village. *Selský baroko* is a novel of the unspoken – Hájíček resorts to a framing narrative in which we follow the silent and meditative Straňanský as he uncovers snippets of the past to form a jigsaw puzzle that can never be fully reconstructed. The text builds a contrast between Straňanský's trustworthy laptop, which holds his own archive of collected data, and faulty human memory, which cannot or does not want to remember how events really unfolded. In the end, the opening up of the past does not lead to greater understanding or redemption; the letter that Straňanský searches for is used to discredit a political opponent by a local politician. The only use of the past is a political instrumentalization in the present.

As is the case in *Selský baroko*, contemporary or archival documents emerge in Tomáš Zmeškal's *Milostný dopis klínovým písmem* (A Love Letter in Cuneiform),[36] Jan Balabán's *Zeptej se táty* (Ask Dad)[37] and Kateřina Tučková's *Žítkovské bohyně* (The Goddesses of Žítková).[38] These textual traces of the past disrupt or change the lives of the characters in the present. In these novels, the past is no longer an object of amusing memories of childhood or adolescence, the former structuring mechanism of comic portrayals. The subject position of the protagonists and reader is that of an adult, and moreover an adult who is willing to reflect critically upon the past. While in comedic representations a child's perspective allowed authors to adopt a deliberately naïve view of political events and focus instead on private joys and 'small' histories, here the mature perspective is prepared to face trauma. Even Věra Nosková's *Bereme, co je* (We Take What Comes),[39] though a straightforward memoir that eschews a double time frame of past and present, recounts its heroine's childhood years from a perspective that ascribes the child an adult distance and political awareness: 'Now I'm ten, I know many things about life and falsehood,'[40] states the main protagonist, Pavla. She can decode the political situation from the outset, and already in the opening of the novel passes judgement on her grandfather, who is 'a so-called honest communist or rather communist-idiot.'[41]

Almost all of these works implicitly or explicitly value the present perspective from which they are written as superior to the past that they deal with: in *Žítkovské bohyně*, ethnographer Dora is grateful that she no longer has to accommodate her work to the empty political demands and meaningless materialist phrases that the pre-1989 period asked for; in Jiří Hájíček's *Rybí krev* (Fish Blood),[42] the characters place high hopes in the new democratic political representation in order to address environmental concerns in their region. Yet the judgement passed on the socialist period is not unequivocal. The motivations of characters are complex, and clear heroes or role models appear only seldom. For instance, Josef, the hero of Zmeškal's *Milostný dopis klínovým písmem*, does not fit into any of the established vocabularies that circulated in contemporary public debates; he is a former political prisoner, but unwilling to think of himself as a victim or hero: 'He, a victim? That didn't go well with him or his profession. He always thought of himself as someone who had had something resembling an accident, an unpleasant political accident, which had had permanent consequences, but it never occurred to him that he was a victim.'[43] However, it is ever clearer who the villains are. Both *Milostný dopis klínovým písmem* and *Žítkovské bohyně* demonize the figure of the StB officer, a trope that also appears frequently in film production. Officials in power are thus clearly condemned, but positive examples are harder to come by. The period is depicted as producing some form of character flaw in most protagonists.

The new 'new wave'

The turn away from comedy is even more apparent in cinema. In particular, I am here concerned with the films *Pouta* (Walking Too Fast, dir. Radim Špaček, 2009),[44] *Kawasakiho růže* (Kawasaki's Rose, dir. Jan Hřebejk, 2009),[45] *Ve stínu* (In the Shadow, dir. David Ondříček, 2012),[46] the HBO mini-series *Hořící keř* (Burning Bush, dir. Agnieszka Holland, 2013)[47] and *Fair Play* (dir. Andrea Sedláčková, 2014).[48] A number of strategies contribute to this demarcation: the different generic repertoires they invoke (drama, thriller, neo-noir, courtroom drama), their evocation of fear as a dominant mood, but also their desire to depict Czechoslovak history as grand narrative with a large social trajectory, expressed through the protagonists' efforts to undermine and stand up against the communist regime.

The complex epistemology of the notion of hero as it has been mediated by the archival document is taken up explicitly in *Kawasakiho růže*. In the manner of several literary examples, events from the socialist past are framed by a present-day narrative. The film echoes the themes central to the debates around ÚSTR and Third Resistance: the psychiatrist and former dissident Pavel Josek is meant to receive a 'Memory of the Nation Prize' in an oddly prescient move on the part of the film-makers (as the organization Post Bellum only began to award eponymous prizes a year after the film's release, in 2010). The central plot revolves around the appearance of an StB file which documents that prior to his dissident activities, Josek had informed on his future wife's boyfriend in order to rid himself of his rival. The archival document thus emerges, as in *Žítkovské bohyně*, as an intrusion of the past.

The main topic of the film clearly resonated with contemporary 'agent scandals'; revelations about Milan Kundera and Joska Skalník's possible involvement with the secret police had circulated in the press only weeks before the film's premiere and became part of the journalistic discourse around the picture.[49] Indeed, as Sune Bechmann Pedersen has observed, the film-makers consciously drew inspiration from the Kundera affair for their story. For instance, the real-life Western agent Kundera allegedly denounced ended up emigrating to Gothenburg in Sweden after 1968. So too the man whom Josek informs on in *Kawasakiho růže* was forced to emigrate by the secret police and starts a new life in Gothenburg.[50]

Kawasakiho růže directly thematizes and explores memory. The film does not contain any flashbacks; the past emerges only as documents or in the spoken word. The main protagonist is a psychiatrist specializing in human memory; thus, the film's exploration of the ways in which the past affects present lives is tackled explicitly. Who can be considered a hero and what counts as failure is problematized; the identity of the villain, on the other hand, remains clear – as was the case in some of the literary productions discussed earlier. The StB officer who stepped into the lives of the young Josek and his rival, forcing the latter to emigrate, is portrayed as a demonic, sadistic man who maintains a cool, professional detachment from his past activities. The final scene depicts him, his loving family and his friends celebrating his birthday; this is a way for film director Hřebejk to comment on the lack of public condemnation and ostracization of those who used their status and power to inflict repression on others.

The character embodies the evolution of the secret policeman figure in Czech cinema. Jaroslav Pinkas, a historian at ÚSTR, sees this as part of a discursive shift whereby protagonists are repositioned as social actors who participate in shaping their own fate.[51] This comes in opposition to the largely passive characters of comedies, whose individual agency was limited to a few, fleeting private gestures. In Jan Svěrák's Oscar-winning 1996 film *Kolja* (Kolya),[52] the StB officers who interrogate the protagonist, Louka, are mostly pathetic and at times comic characters whom Louka more or less outwits; while the 'good cop' doesn't get Louka's jokes, the 'bad cop' turns out to be clumsy rather than threatening when he gets his hand stuck to a roll of sellotape. In the films of the dramatic wave such as *Pouta*, *Kawasakiho růže*, *Ve stínu*, *Hořící keř* and *Fair Play*, the figures of StB officers are far from the incompetent characters in *Kolja*; rather, like *Pouta*'s anti-hero Antonín Rusnák, they are cruel and despicable, even sadistic.

Authenticating the villain: The archival document in fiction

In the original comedies, the 'regime' was often 'someone else', an absent Other hovering in the background. The rulers were quite often ridiculed, while 'evil' remained vague and depersonalized. The new dramatic wave shifted the figure of the enemy from an abstract regime to individual actors who implement the rulers' domination. Evil is now concretely embodied in specific characters. By employing the archival document as a means of historical authentication, these narratives have switched to playing out their conflicts in strongly moral terms, where perpetrators and victims are clearly identified. And yet, not even written documents necessarily provide moral clarity about the past. *Kawasakiho růže* uses the archival document as a mechanism to simultaneously give past events a seal of approval and question their veracity, in a similar way to the public debates which cited the Security Services Archive as a tool of both shedding light on the past and misusing it. Is Josek ultimately a villain or someone who deserves our sympathy for displaying weakness? *Kawasakiho růže* does not guide the viewer towards an unequivocal answer. Similarly, scandals such as the one surrounding Milan Kundera show how difficult it is to establish any kind of definite narrative about the past based on archival documents; indeed, the question of Kundera's alleged collaboration was never satisfactorily resolved. The nature of the archive is such that despite the assurances of memory activists, it often just adds more troubling layers to an already-complex construction.

Kawasakiho růže thus shows that while a moral fuzziness surrounds the question of collaboration with the secret police, those formerly in the services of this body are, in retrospect, presented as the real culprits. In comedies, the question of collaboration was dismissed as an understandable, if hardly commendable, human failure. As previously mentioned, Michal Viewegh's *Báječná léta pod psa* had set a new comic standard when the main protagonist's father developed an exaggerated paranoia of the secret police after attending an interrogation; here, on the contrary, all humour is gone. Some mitigating circumstances can be applied to the distinction between the portrayal of regular police (SNB) and secret police (StB). While SNB officers can sometimes be upright characters fighting for justice in a corrupt system, such as Captain Hakl in *Ve stínu* or Major Jireš in *Hořící keř* (both played by popular actor Ivan Trojan, typecast as a positive hero), the StB officer lacks any redeeming features.

Literary works can use reprints of archival documents – whether real or fictional. Reproductions of the fictional StB file of the aunt of the main heroine in *Žítkovské bohyně* allow the reader to follow how the communist authorities built a case against the aunt's practice as a healer, which they construe as 'anti-state activities'. These excerpts, complete with graphic layout resembling actual typewritten documents, are interspersed throughout the text. Similarly, films have resorted to inserting archival footage into their narratives and thus generate authenticity through colour schemes resembling those employed by film-makers during the time represented. For instance, Agnieszka Holland's mini-series *Hořící keř*, which recounts the aftermath of Jan Palach's self-immolation in January 1969 in protest of the Warsaw Pact invasion, occasionally inserts black-and-white footage into the narrative (otherwise shot in colour). Indeed, the use of archival footage as a historical anchor was already present in the serial production *Vyprávěj* (Tell Me a Story, Czech Television, 2009–2013).[53] Recounting the story of an 'ordinary family' from the 1960s to the present, the series framed each episode in several minutes of clips from the archives of Czechoslovak Television, most often reminding viewers of period products or popular culture; at the end of the first round of archival footage, the scene would fade from black and white into full colour, signalling the beginning of the fictional narrative. Within the genre of a retro soap opera, these archival documents served as a contrast with the stylized portrayal of the past, while the project of *Hořící keř* is to match its visuals as closely as possible with period footage. But the visual identity of the mini-series does not make it inherently more authentic than *Vyprávěj*; as Christoph Classen argues, "'Authenticity' has to be historicized and contextualized. It goes without saying that the quality of things that people take to be true – the presentation techniques and iconography a display has to use to be accepted as a "true" representation of reality – changes over the course of time.'[54] In the case of *Hořící keř*, its basis in true historical events and real personages is the most obvious authenticating mechanism:[55] also, it chimed in with the changing discursive context, which saw a greater interest in grand narratives, heroism and trauma, as opposed to making light of the past.

Epistemology of the hero category

As I have suggested, the use of archival materials in fictional narratives led to an increased concern with moral categories. If villains are to be found in the secret police, dramatic narratives have tended to pitch them against heroes that are more sharply defined. While the more intimate settings of literary production had somewhat problematized the notion of hero, large-scale films searched for positive heroes to drive their narratives. *Ve stínu, Hořící keř* and *Fair Play*, all consciously present heroic role models: director David Ondříček described detective Hakl in *Ve stínu* as a '[morally] clean hero', and it is in this key component that *Ve stínu* departs from its noir models with their flawed and outcast protagonists.[56] For Czech cinema, this was an untypical move. Clear-cut heroes are hard to come by within the Czech cultural tradition. When it comes to heroism, scholars often cite Jaroslav Hašek's canonical First World War novel about the good soldier Švejk, a tale of a would-be simpleton who always manages to trick his superiors, as a significant cultural model and expression of a decidedly unheroic Czech national tradition.[57]

Part of the discourse around *Ve stínu* and *Hořící keř* consisted of a comparison of Czech and Polish traditions of heroism. Polish director Agnieszka Holland, who had herself been a witness to the events portrayed in *Hořící keř* as a student at Prague's Film Academy, called Jan Palach 'a rather Polish hero:'[58] she corroborated this idea with the cultural stereotype that the Czechs have a much more tortured and self-conscious relationship to their heroes than the Poles, who celebrate theirs wholeheartedly.[59] Ondříček, the director of *Ve stínu*, agreed with this distinction, suggesting that 'in Poland, the Mašín brothers would have been declared national heroes long ago, while we are still musing about the opportuneness of assassinating Heydrich'.[60] Clearly, these film-makers aimed to introduce a corrective to what they perceived as an insufficiently heroic narrative in Czech culture.

Apart from celebrating Palach's heroic act, *Hořící keř* also tells the story of a morally upright heroine, lawyer Dagmar Burešová, who defends Palach's family in a defamation case. This is the point where these narratives resonate best with the new discourse on resistance and heroism in the public sphere: the new heroes qualify as anti-communist resistance fighters in their own right and are not afraid to state this explicitly. In *Fair Play*, the athlete Anna refuses to take part in the Olympic Games despite having qualified, because she 'simply will not represent this system',[61] as she tells her trainer and a high-up party official in a scene shot in dramatic close-up.

While the heroism in comedies was petty and destined to fail, the heroism of the dramatic mode is meant to be genuine; yet here, too, its results are not taken for granted. In *Ve stínu*, this message is made particularly clear when detective Hakl attempts to reassure his small son about an 'invincible monster' he is fighting: 'If we fight with it often enough, it will get tired and weak. And perhaps then someone will beat it someday.'[62] The vision of heroism these films promote is founded on the notion of sacrifice: both Burešová in *Hořící keř* and Hakl in *Ve stínu* engage in fights which they reckon will fail; in *Fair Play*, Anna's mother prefers to be sentenced for copying illegal printed material rather than to become an StB informer, thus cutting short her daughter's career as a professional athlete. In this way, the image of the hero resonates with what scholars working on Czech national identity have identified as a cult of victimhood in the Czech historical imaginary.[63] As journalist Zbyněk Petráček points out, the heroes of anti-communist resistance are figures like army general Heliodor Píka or social democratic politician Milada Horáková, that is, people who were unjustly persecuted and executed in show trials (in 1949 and 1950, respectively), rather than those who actively fought back, like the much-disputed Mašín brothers.[64] The Third Resistance narrative, Petráček further suggests, turns both groups into heroes by co-opting the victims of the communist regime into the category of resistance fighters. But despite institutional attempts to promote an image of active or even armed resistance, this effort remains fraught and is still awaiting its cinematic depiction.

Conclusion: Memory shifts

With the increasing challenge to the dominant post-1989 anti-communist narrative and the growing plurality of opinions in the public sphere, state actors and cultural elites have felt an evermore pressing urge to introduce strong models about the past. Throughout the 1990s and early 2000s, the anti-communist consensus within Czech public discourse did not require the manufacturing of big heroes or culprits. But this consensus increasingly came under attack through a diversification of the media, especially with the advent of online journalism. New critical voices have sought to problematize the blanket rejection of the socialist past and its interpretation as 'totalitarian', within both the media and the historical profession.

A similar trend can be observed in popular culture. Alongside a preoccupation with the archival document, which has occasionally helped to problematize categories of heroism and collaboration, particularly in literature, large-scale film production has also embarked on an expanded 'search for heroes' in narratives about socialism. While public discourse tended to revolve around sensationalist 'agent scandals', the StB officer has emerged as the real culprit in cinematic representations, be it in *Kawasakiho růže*, *Milostný dopis klínovým písmem* or *Pouta*. These new narratives have sketched a polarized, moral map of socialism, in which evil StB officers are pitched against heroes who are not afraid to confront state power upfront, be it with courageous lawyer Dagmar Burešová in *Hořící keř*, the 'good cop' Hakl in *Ve stínu* or the athlete Anna in *Fair Play*.

The official efforts to promote an active memory of resistance and the narratives featuring characters that embodied evil both used ethical categories to construct exemplary tales. They aimed to project a democratic national identity for a people who know who its heroes are and can pinpoint perpetrators. This intensified preoccupation with heroes, villains and morality from the mid-2000s onwards can thus be interpreted as an ever-increasing effort at manufacturing not only a national but also a nationalist historical memory. The latter has since been gaining increasing prominence in Czech public discourse. Indeed, the Czech Republic, too, has been swept up in wider European and North American developments. Since about 2015, in response to a number of political crises, the political mainstream has increasingly shifted towards populism, conservatism and nationalism. While these changes may have appeared swift, they did not occur out of the blue and need to be understood in historical context; this chapter has been a contribution to the exploration of their longer genesis in the field of culture and memory politics.

Notes

1   The terminology used to refer to the pre-1989 regime in this chapter distinguishes between the ideological project of the Czechoslovak Communist Party (communism, communist regime and Communist Party rule) and its practical, day-to-day implementation (state socialism).

2   For an overview of various 'collaboration scandals', see Muriel Blaive, 'Zpřístupnění archivů komunistické tajné police: případ České republiky – od Zdeny Salivarové k Milanu Kunderovi', *Souvislosti: 'Kauza Kundera' rok poté* 20, no. 4 (2009): 158–173.

3   The final debate on the Institute lasted five hours. See ČTK, 'Ústav paměti národa bude zkoumat i protektorát' [Institute of the Memory of the Nation will also study the Protectorate], *Týden.cz*, 16 March 2007, http://www.tyden.cz/rubriky/domaci/ustav-pameti-naroda-bude-zkoumat-i-protektorat_6023.html (accessed 12 December 2016).

4   For more on what I term 'petty heroism' in representations of socialism, see Veronika Pehe, 'Drobné hrdinství: vzdor jakožto předmět nostalgie v díle Petra Šabacha a Michala Viewegha', *Česká literatura* 63, no. 3 (2015): 419–434.

5   Until then, the Security Services archives fell under the remit of the Office for the Documentation and Investigation of the Crimes of Communism (Úřad dokumentace a vyšetřování zločinů komunismu; ÚDV), a department of the police. ÚSTR's competencies are however much wider, aimed not only at investigation, but also towards research, education and commemoration.

6   For an analysis of the issues at stake in the legal framework under which ÚSTR was set up, see Tomas Sniegon, 'Implementing Post-Communist National Memory in the Czech Republic and Slovakia', in *European Cultural Memory Post-89*, eds. Conny Mithander, John Sundholm, and Adrian Velicu (Amsterdam: Rodopi, 2013), 97–124.

7   The historiographical framework of totalitarianism, which interprets the communist regime through a binary of oppression and resistance, has increasingly fewer adherents among academic historians also in the Czech context, not only through the increased study of leisure, popular culture and everyday life under socialism, but also on the level of social history. Perhaps the most significant work to emerge from Czech academia posing a theoretical challenge to the 'totalitarian paradigm' is Michal Pullmann's *Konec experiementu: přestavba a pád komunismu v Československu* (Prague: Scriptorum, 2011).

8   For a summary of the arguments against the institute's early incarnation from the perspective of historians, see Michal Kopeček and Matěj Spurný, 'Dějiny a paměť komunismu v Česku' [History and memory of communism in Czech Republic], *Lidové noviny*, 9 January 2010, 24; see also Martin Hekrdla, 'ÚSTR v době ústrků' [ÚSTR in a time of machinations], *Týden*, 2 April 2013, 61; Michal Kopeček, 'ÚSTR lépe a vědecky. Ale jak?' [A better and more scholarly ÚSTR. But how?], *Lidové noviny*, 8 April 2013, 13.

9   Marek Švehla, 'Ke slovu musí přijít levicoví historici' [Left-wing historians must be heard], *Respekt* 24, no. 16 (2013): 38–43.

10   See, for example, Vít Smetana, 'Vznikne orwellovský ústav?' [Will there be an Orwellian institute?], *Právo*, 20 March 2007, 6; Kopeček and Spurný, 'Dějiny a paměť komunismu v Česku', 24; Lukáš Jelínek, 'Ústav totality si libuje v přítmí' [Totalitarian institute relishes semi-darkness], *Právo*, 27 October 2011, 6.

11 Act 181/2007 Coll. The full text is available on ÚSTR's website: https://www.ustrcr. cz/o-nas/zakon-c-181-2007-sb/. Santayana's original aphorism is slightly different to the version in Act 181: 'Those who cannot remember the past are condemned to repeat it.' George Santayana, *The Life of Reason: Reason in Common Sense* (New York: Scribner's, 1905), 284.

12 Adam Hradilek, 'Udání Milana Kundery' [Milan Kundera's denunciation], *Respekt* 19, no. 42 (2008): 38–45. Available in English at https://www.respekt.cz/respekt-in-english/milan-kundera-s-denunciation (accessed 27 October 2017). For in-depth analysis of the 'Kundera Affair', see the special issue of *Souvislosti: 'Kauza Kundera' rok poté* 20, no. 4 (2009): 140–180.

13 See 'Bratři Mašínové prý chtěli zabít i Klementa Gottwalda' [The Mašín brothers allegedly wanted to also kill Klement Gottwald], *Novinky.cz*, 4 April 2008, https:// www.novinky.cz/domaci/136857-bratri-masinove-pry-chteli-zabit-i-klementa-gottwalda.html (accessed 10 September 2017).

14 Luděk Navara, 'Atentát na Gottwalda? Pouhé úvahy, říká Mašín?' [A plan to assassinate Gottwald? Mere contemplation], *iDnes.cz*, 5 April 2008, http:// zpravy.idnes.cz/atentat-na-gottwalda-pouhe-uvahy-rika-masin-feq-/domaci. aspx?c=A080405_114528_domaci_jan (accessed 10 September 2017).

15 Patrik Eichler, 'Dialog o Ústavu?' [Dialogue about the Institute?], *Literární noviny*, 3 November 2008, 3; drv, 'Hlasy za odvolání Žáčka sílí. Přidal se i Havel' [More voices call for Žáček's removal. Havel has joined them], *Lidové noviny*, 20 November 2009, 1.

16 Jiří Kubík, 'Muž, který založil banku vzpomínek' [The man who founded a database of memories – interview with Mikuláš Kroupa], *Mladá fronta Dnes*, 16 November 2013, 13.

17 An overview of past exhibitions organized by Post Bellum can be found at https:// www.postbellum.cz/co-delame/vystavy/ (accessed 30 August 2017).

18 Jana Fantová and Jan Palouček, ed., *Ještě jsme ve válce: Příběhy dvacátého století* (Prague: Argo; Post Bellum; ÚSTR: 2011).

19 For an overview of workshops organized by Post Bellum, see https://www. postbellum.cz/co-delame/workshopy/ (accessed 30 August 2017).

20 For an overview of the organization's activities, see http://www.postbellum.cz/ (accessed 30 August 2017).

21 Miloš Kozumplík, 'Mikuláš Kroupa: Hrdinové nejsou', *Instinkt* 7, no. 45 (2008): 68–69.

22 Act 262/2011 Coll. https://www.vlada.cz/cz/ppov/eticka-komise-cr/dokumenty/ zakon-c-262-2011-sb–98376/ (accessed 30 August 2017).

23 Luděk Navara and Jan Gazdík, 'Byli jste hrdinové. První odbojáři to uslyší už (až) dnes' [You were heroes. The first resistance fighters will hear it already (only) today], *Mladá fronta Dnes*, 10 April 2012, 4.

24 Available on the website of the Chamber of Deputies of the Parliament of the Czech Republic: http://www.psp.cz/sqw/sbirka.sqw?cz=198&r=1993 (accessed 12 December 2016).

25 For more on the activities of the KPV and their claims to a memory of victimhood, see Chapter 6 of Françoise Mayer, *Les Tchèques et leur communisme* (Paris: EHESS, 2003), 167–194.

26 For an overview of the Mašín case and accompanying debates, see Josef Švéda, *Mašínovský mýtus: ideologie v české literatuře a kultuře* (Příbram: Pistorius & Olšanská, 2012).

27   A 2011 poll conducted for Czech Television showed that only 15 per cent of
      respondents considered the Mašín brothers' actions 'heroic', 27 per cent perceived
      them as 'unjustifiable criminal acts', while 41 per cent were undecided. Statistics cited
      in Švéda, *Mašínovský mýtus*, 224. See also, Naďa Adamičková and Marie Königová,
      'Třetí odboj: Mašínové rozdělili sněmovnu' [Third resistance: the Mašín brothers
      have divided the parliament], *Právo*, 11 June 2011, 4.

28   Zbyněk Petráček, 'Kdo ocení Paumera?' [Who will award Paumer?], *Lidové noviny*,
      27 July 2010, 10.

29   Luděk Navara, 'Pohřeb Paumera mění pohled na odboj' [Paumer's funeral changes
      view of resistence], *Mladá fronta Dnes*, 5 August 2010, 1.

30   These include the initially weekly and later biweekly critical magazine *A2*, and later
      its online daily platform *A2larm*, as well as the mid-2000s incarnation of *Literární
      noviny* (Literary News) before some of its editorial staff went on to found the online
      daily *Deník Referendum* (Referendum Daily) in 2009.

31   Wherever possible, official translations of film and novel titles are used. Where no
      English version exists, translations are my own.

32   See, for example, Pavel Janáček, 'Groteska o velké lásce' [A grotesque about great
      love], *Nové knihy*, 25 November 1992, 1; Jiří Tyl, 'Autorský subjekt jako osvoboditel
      (sebe sama)', *Iniciály* 4, no. 36 (1993): 25–26.

33   For box office statistics, see http://lumiere.obs.coe.int/web/film_info/?id=13559
      (accessed 30 August 2017). Taking into account the film's wide availability on DVD
      and frequent repeats on television, its penetration is exceptional in the Czech
      context.

34   Among these prose works are Jiří Hájíček, *Selský baroko* (Brno: Host, 2005, Magnesia
      Litera prize 2006); Věra Nosková, *Bereme, co je* (Prague: Abonent ND, 2005,
      nominated for Magnesia Litera prize); Věra Nosková, *Obsazeno* (Prague: MozART,
      2007, nominated for Josef Škvorecký prize); Petra Soukupová, *K moři* (Brno: Host,
      2007; Jiří Orten prize 2008); Tomáš Zmeškal, *Milostný dopis klínovým písmem*
      (Prague: Torst, 2008; Josef Škvorecký prize 2009); Jan Balabán, *Zeptej se táty* (Brno:
      Host, 2010; Magnesia Litera prize 2010); Kateřina Tučková, *Žítkovské bohyně* (Brno:
      Host, 2012; Josef Škvorecký prize 2012), *Jiří Hájíček, Rybí krev* (Brno: Host, 2012;
      Magnesia Litera prize 2013).

35   Hájíček, *Selský baroko*.

36   Zmeškal, *Milostný dopis klínovým písmem*.

37   Balabán, *Zeptej se táty*.

38   Tučková, *Žítkovské bohyně*.

39   Nosková, *Bereme, co je*.

40   'Teď je mi deset, o životě a falši leccos vím.' Nosková, *Bereme, co je*, 60.

41   '...... takzvaný poctivý komunista neboli komunista blbec'. Ibid., 10.

42   Hájíček, *Rybí krev*.

43   'On, oběť? To nešlo dohromady ani s ním, ani s jeho profesí. Vždy o sobě smýšlel
      jako o člověku, který měl takřka nehodu, nepříjemnou politickou nehodu, po které
      byly trvalé následky, ale že by byl oběť, to ho nikdy nenapadlo.' Zmeškal, *Milostný
      dopis*, 173.

44   *Pouta* (Walking Too Fast), [Film]. Dir. Radim Špaček, Czech Republic: Bionaut, 2009.

45   *Kawasakiho růže* (Kawasaki's Rose), [Film]. Dir. Jan Hřebejk, Czech Republic: In
      Film Praha, 2009.

46   *Ve stínu* (In the Shadow), [Film]. Dir. David Ondříček, Czech Republic, Slovakia,
      Poland, Israel: Lucky Man Films, 2012.

47 *Hořící keř* (Burning Bush), [Film]. Dir. Agnieszka Holland, Czech Republic: HBO Europe, 2013.

48 *Fair Play*, [Film]. Dir. Andrea Sedláčková, Czech Republic, Slovakia, Germany: Czech Television, 2014.

49 Vojtěch Rynda, 'Lidé se "škraloupem" s tím musejí ven' [People with a 'blot' on their reputation must come out], *Lidové noviny*, 30 December 2009, 7.

50 Sune Bechmann Pedersen, *Reel Socialism: Making Sense of History in Czech and German Cinema Since 1989* (Lund: Lund University/Media-Tryck, 2015), 245.

51 Jaroslav Pinkas, 'Nenápadný půvab normalizace – její sociální realita optikou tehdejší a dnešní filmové kamery', in *Film a dějiny 4: Normalizace*, ed. Petr Kopal (Prague: Casablanca and ÚSTR, 2014), 479.

52 *Kolja* (Kolya), [Film]. Dir. Jan Svěrák, Czech Republic, UK, France: Biograf Jan Svěrák, 1996.

53 *Vyprávěj* (Tell Me a Story), [TV programme]. Czech Republic: Czech Television/ Dramedy Productions, 2009–2013.

54 Christoph Classen, 'Balanced Truth: Steven Spielberg's Schindler's List among History, Memory, and Popular Culture', trans. Kirsten Wächter, *History and Theory* 48, no. 2 (2009): 77–102 (88).

55 Kamil Činátl, *Naše české minulosti, aneb, jak vzpomínáme* (Prague: Nakladatelství Lidové noviny, 2014), 138.

56 Mirka Spáčilová, 'Lampa, klobouk, dlouhý plášť. Vítejte v temném světě Ve stínu' [Lamp, hat, long overcoat. Welcome to the dark world of Ve stínu – interview with David Ondříček], *Mladá fronta Dnes*, 13 September 2012, 2.

57 See, for instance, Ladislav Holý, *The Little Czech and the Great Czech Nation: National Identity and the Post-Communist Transformation of Society* (Cambridge: Cambridge University Press, 1996), 72–73; Radko Pytlík, *Jaroslav Hašek a Dobrý voják Švejk* (Praha: Panorama, 1983).

58 Mirka Spáčilová, 'Nemusí jít o život. Hrdina nelže, nekrade a chodí k volbám' [It doesn't have to be a matter of life and death. A hero does not lie or steal and votes in elections], *Mladá fronta Dnes*, 25 January 2013, 53.

59 Ibid.

60 Spáčilová, 'Lampa, klobouk, dlouhý plášť', 2.

61 'Já prostě tenhle systém reprezentovat nebudu', *Fair Play*, 2014.

62 'Když se s ní často budeme prát, tak se unaví a zeslábne. A třeba jí někdo jednou porazí.' *Ve stínu*, 2012.

63 Robert Pynsent, *Questions of Identity: Czech and Slovak Ideas of Nationality and Personality* (Budapest: Central European University Press, 1994), in particular 190–21; Holý, *The Little Czech and the Great Czech Nation*, 72–73.

64 Zbyněk Petráček, 'Od obětí k odboji' [From victims to resistance], *Lidové noviny*, 12 August 2013, 8.

Bibliography

Abrams, Bradley F. *The Struggle for the Soul of the Nation: Czech Culture and the Rise of Communism*. Lanham: Rowman & Littlefield Publishers, 2004.

Adorno, Theodor. 'Cultural Criticism and Society'. In *Prisms*, edited by Theodor Adorno, translated by Samuel Weber and Sherry Weber. Cambridge: MIT Press, 1982.

Aleksandrov, Valentin. *Ungarskata revoliutsiia 1956: Vutreshnopoliticheski i mezhdunarodni aspekti*. Sofia: Voenno izdatelstvo, 2007.

Althusser, Louis. *Essays on Ideology*. London: Verso Editions, 1984.

Alton, Thad P., ed. *Personal Consumption in Hungary, 1938 and 1947–1965*. New York: Research Project on National Income in East Central Europe, 1968.

Andreescu, Gabriel, and Mihnea Berindei. *Ultimul deceniu comunist: Scrisori către radio Europa Liberă vol 1 (1979–1985)*. Iaşi: Polirom, 2010.

Anton, Mioara. '*Ceauşescu şi poporul!' Scrisori către 'iubitul conducător', 1965–1989*. Târgovişte: Cetatea de Scaun, 2016.

Anton, Mioara, and Laurenţiu Constantiniu, eds. *Guvernaţi şi Guvernanţi: Scrisori către putere, 1945–1965*. Bucharest: IICCMER, 2013.

Arendt, Hannah. 'The Ex-Communists'. *Commonweal* 11 (1953): 595–598.

Arendt, Hannah. *The Origins of Totalitarianism*. New York: Harcourt, Brace, 1951.

Attali, Jacques. *Noise: The Political Economy of Music*. Minneapolis and London: University of Minnesota Press, 1985.

Attwood, Lynne. *Creating the New Soviet Woman: Women's Magazines as Engineers of Female Identity, 1922–1953*. New York: St. Martin's Press, 1999.

Bachmann, Klaus, and Jens Gieseke, eds. *The Silent Majority in Communist and Post-Communist States. Opinion Polling in Eastern and South-Eastern Europe*. Vienna: Peter Lang, 2018.

Badenoch, Alexander, Andreas Fickers, and Chistian Henrich-Franke, eds. *Airy Curtains in the European Ether: Broadcasting and the Cold War*. Baden-Baden: Nomos, 2013.

Bakhtin, Mikhail. *Speech Genres and Other Late Essays*. Austin: University of Texas Press, 2006.

Balabán, Jan. *Zeptej se táty*. Brno: Host, 2010.

Banaszewska, Julia. 'Powtórka, tęsknota czy zapośredniczenie … Skąd się bierze moda na PRL?' In *Zanurzeni w historii – zanurzeni w kulturze: kultowe seriale PRL-u*, edited by Marek Karwala and Barbara Serwatka. Kraków: Śródmiejski Ośrodek Kultury, 2010.

Bárta, Milan. 'Akce "Isolace": Snaha Státní bezpečnosti omezit návštěvnost zastupitelných úřadů kapitalistických států'. *Paměť a dějiny*, no. 4 (2008): 41–50.

Bárta, Milan. 'Přestaňte okamžitě rušit modré'. In *Paměť a dějiny*, no. 3 (2012): 45–54.

Barth, Bernd-Rainer, and Werner Schweizer, eds. *Der Fall Noel Field: Schlüsselfigur der Schauprozesse in Osteuropa*. Berlin: Basisdruck, 2005.

Bartošek, Karel. *Les aveux des archives. Prague, Paris, Prague (1948–1968)*. Paris: Le Seuil, 1996.

Bechmann Pedersen, Sune. *Reel Socialism: Making Sense of History in Czech and German Cinema Since 1989*. Lund: Lund University/Media-Tryck, 2015.

Betts, Paul. 'Socialism, Social Rights, and Human Rights: The Case of East Germany', *Humanity* 3, no. 3 (2012): 407–426.

Betts, Paul. *Within Walls: Private Life in the German Democratic Republic.* New York: Oxford University Press, 2010.

Bieberle, Josef. 'K politickým procesům (Olomoucký případ 1949–1950)'. *Slezský sborník* 88, no. 3 (1990): 167–182.

Billig, Michael. *Banal Nationalism.* London: Sage Publications, 1999.

Blaive, Muriel. 'České Velenice, eine Stadt an der Grenze zu Österreich'. In *Grenzfälle. Österreichische und tschechische Erfahrungen am Eisernen Vorhang,* Muriel Blaive and Berthold Molden. Weitra: Bibliothek der Provinz, 2009.

Blaive, Muriel. 'The Czech Museum of Communism: What National Narrative for the Past?' In *Museums of Communism: New Memory Sites in Central and Eastern Europe,* edited by Steven Norris. Bloomington: Indiana University Press, 2018.

Blaive, Muriel. 'Discussing the Merits of Microhistory as a Comparative Tool: The Cases of České Velenice and Komárno', *East Central Europe* 40, no. 1–2 (2013): 74–96.

Blaive, Muriel. *Une déstalinisation manquée: Tchécoslovaquie 1956.* Brussels: Complexe, 2005.

Blaive, Muriel. 'La police politique en action: les Tchécoslovaques et la révolution hongroise de 1956', *Revue d'histoire moderne et contemporaine* 49, no. 2 (2002): 176–202.

Blaive, Muriel. *Promarněná příležitost: Československo a rok 1956.* Prague: Prostor, 2001.

Blaive, Muriel. *Scénario du film '1956, le rendez-vous manqué de l'histoire'.* Prague: Cefres, 1997.

Blaive, Muriel. 'Zpřístupnění archivů komunistické tajné police: případ České republiky – od Zdeny Salivarové k Milanu Kunderovi'. *Souvislosti: 'Kauza Kundera' rok poté,* no. 4 (2009): 158–173.

Blaive, Muriel, and Berthold Molden. *Hranice probíhají vodním tokem. Odrazy historie ve vnímání obyvatel Gmündu a Českých Velenic.* Brno, Barrister & Principal: 2009.

Blažek, Petr et al. 'Tváře vyšetřovatelů Státní bezpečnosti'. *Pamět a dějiny,* no. 4 (2012): 66–75.

Blessing, Benita. 'Happily socialist ever after? East German children's films and the education of a fairy tale land. *Oxford Review of Education* 36, no. 2 (2010): 233–248.

Bloch, Marc. *The Historian's Craft.* Manchester: Manchester University Press, 1954.

Boras, Zygmunt, and Zbigniew Dworecki. *Piła: zarys dziejów (do roku 1945).* Piła: Urząd Miejski, 1993.

Borodziej, Włodzimierz. *Geschichte Polens im 20. Jahrhundert.* Munich: C.H. Beck Verlag, 2010.

Bourdieu, Pierre, and Lutz Raphael. 'Sur les rapports entre l'histoire et la sociologie en France et en Allemagne'. *Actes de la recherche en sciences sociales* 106, no. 1 (1995): 108–122.

Brabec, Václav. 'Vztah KSČ a veřejnosti k politickým procesům na počátku padesátých let'. *Revue dějin socialismu,* no. 3 (1969): 363–385.

Brecht, Bertolt. *Buckower Elegien, 1953. Ausgewählte Werke in sechs Bänden.* Dritter Band: Gedichte 1. Frankfurt: Suhrkamp, 1997.

Bren, Paulina. *The Greengrocer and his TV. The Culture of Communism After the 1968 Prague Spring.* Ithaca, NY: Cornell University Press, 2010.

Bren, Paulina, and Mary Neuburger, eds. *Communism Unwrapped: Consumption in Cold War Eastern Europe.* New York: Oxford University Press, 2012.

Brownlee, Jason. *Authoritarianism in an Age of Democratization*. New York: Cambridge University Press, 2007.

Bruce, Gary. *The Firm. The Inside Story of the Stasi*. Oxford: Oxford University Press, 2010.

Brzostek, Błażej, and Marcin Zaremba. 'Polska 1956–1976. W poszukiwaniu paradygmatu'. *Pamięć i Sprawiedliwość* 2, no. 10 (2006): 25–37.

Bucur, Maria. *Heroes and Victims. Remembering War in Twentieth-Century Romania*. Bloomington: Indiana University Press, 2009.

Bunce, Valerie J., and Sharon Wolchik. *Defeating Authoritarian Leaders in Postcommunist Countries*. New York: Cambridge University Press, 2011.

Cârjan, Mihai-Dan, and Adrian Grama. 'Șerban Voinea/Lotar Rădăceanu'. In *Plante Exotice. Teoria și practica marxiștilor români*, edited by Andrei State and Alex Cistelecan. Cluj: Tact, 2015.

Černý, Jindřich. *Osudy českého divadla po druhé světové válce: Divadlo a společnost, 1945–1955*. Prague: Academia, 2007.

Certeau, Michel de. *L'invention du quotidian. 1. Arts de faire*. Paris: Gallimard, 1990.

Cesereanu, Ruxandra. 'Revolta muncitorilor din Brașov, 1987'. *Revista 22*, no. 14 (2003).

Chiper, Ioan. 'Oragnizarea comitetelor de fabrică (23 August – Octombrie 1944)'. *Studii. Revistă de istorie* 17, no. 4 (1964): 809–834.

Christian, Michel. *Camarades ou apparatchiks? Les communistes en RDA et en Tchécoslovaquie (1945–1989)*. Paris: PUF, 2016.

Ciesielski, Stanisław, Grzegorz Hryciuk, and Aleksander Srebrakowski. *Masowe deportacje radzieckie w okresie II wojny światowej*. Wrocław: IH UW, 1994.

Činátl, Kamil. *Naše české minulosti aneb, jak vzpomínáme*. Prague: Nakladatelství Lidové noviny, 2014.

Classen, Christoph. 'Balanced Truth: Steven Spielberg's Schindler's List Among History, Memory, and Popular Culture', translated by Kirsten Wächter. *History and Theory* 48, no. 2 (2009): 77–102.

Clifford, Brian R., Barrie Gunter, and Jill McAleer. *Television and Children: Program Evaluation, Comprehension and Impact*. Hillsdale: Lawrence Erlbaum Associates, 1995.

Clybor, Shawn. 'Laughter and Hatred Are Neighbors: Adolf Hoffmeister and E.F. Burian in Stalinist Czechoslovakia, 1948–1956'. *East European Politics and Societies* 26, no. 3 (2012): 589–615.

Cohan, Steven, and Ina Rae Hark. 'Introduction'. In *The Road Movie Book*, edited by Steven Cohan and Ina Rae Hark. Milton Park: Taylor & Francis, 2002.

Combe, Sonia, ed. *Archives et écriture de l'histoire dans les sociétés post-communistes*. Paris: La Découverte, 2009.

Combe, Sonia, ed. 'Figures de l'officier traitant à travers les archives de la Stasi'. *Cultures et Conflits* 53, no. 1 (2004): 99–112.

Combe, Sonia, ed. *Une société sous surveillance: les intellectuels et la Stasi*. Paris: Albin Michel, 1999.

Combe, Sonia, ed. *Une vie contre une autre. Echange de victime et modalités de survie dans le camp de Buchenwald*. Paris: Fayard, 2014.

Connelly, John. *Captive University: The Sovietization of East German, Czech, and Polish Higher Education, 1945–1956*. Chapel Hill: University of North Carolina Press, 2000.

Cook, Linda J. *The Soviet Social Contract and Why It Failed: Welfare Policy and Workers' Politics from Brezhnev to Yeltsin*. Cambridge: Harvard University Press, 1993.

Cook, Linda J., and Martin K. Dimitrov. 'The Socialist Social Contract Revisited: Evidence from Communist and State Capitalist Economies'. *Europe-Asia Studies* 69, no. 1 (2017), 8–26.

Corner, Paul, ed. *Popular Opinion in Totalitarian Regimes: Fascism, Nazism, Communism.* Oxford: Oxford University Press, 2009.

Czerwiński, Marcin. *Przemiany obyczaju.* Warsaw: Państwowy Instytut Wydawniczy, 1972.

Dale, Gareth. *Popular Protest in East Germany, 1945–1989.* London: Routledge, 2005.

Dallin, Alexander, and George W. Breslauer. *Political Terror in Communist Systems.* Stanford: Stanford University Press, 1970.

Daskalova, Krassimira. 'Audiatur and altera pars: in response to Nanette Funk'. In 'Ten Years After: Communism and Feminism Revisited'. *Aspasia* 10, no. 1 (2016): 102–168.

Davies, Norman. *Trail of Hope. The Anders Army, an Odyssey Across Three Continents.* Oxford: Osprey Publishing, 2015.

Davies, Sarah. *Popular Opinion in Stalin's Russia. Terror, Propaganda and Dissent 1934–1941.* Cambridge: Cambridge University Press, 1997.

Deutscher, Isaac, ed. *The Non-Jewish Jew and Other Essays.* Oxford: Oxford University Press, 1968.

Devátá, Markéta, Jiří Suk, and Oldřich Tůma, eds. *Charta 77 – od obhajoby lidských práv k demokratické revoluci 1977–1989: sborník z konference k 30. výročí Charty 77, 21–23 March 2007.* Prague: Ústav pro soudobé dějiny AV ČR and Oddělení edice FF UK, 2008.

De Mesquita, Bruce Bueno, Alastair Smith, Randolph M. Siverson, and James D. Morrow. *The Logic of Political Survival.* Cambridge: MIT Press, 2003.

Dimitrov, Dimitur. *Suvetska Bulgariia prez tri britanski mandata (1956–1963): Iz arkhiva na Foreign Office za subitiia i lichnosti v Bulgariia.* London: BBC, 1994.

Dimitrov, Martin K. *Politika na sotsialisticheskoto konsumatorstvo.* Sofia: Ciela Publishers, 2017.

Dimitrov, Martin K. 'Tracking Public Opinion Under Authoritarianism: The Case of the Soviet Union Under Brezhnev'. *Russian History* 41, no. 3 (2014): 329–353.

Dimitrov, Martin K. 'What the Party Wanted to Know: Citizen Complaints as a "Barometer of Public Opinion" in Communist Bulgaria'. *East European Politics and Societies and Cultures* 28, no. 2 (2014): 271–295.

Dimitrov, Martin K. 'Zhalbite na grazhdanite v komunisticheska Bulgariia'. In *Da Poznaem Komunizma: Izsledvaniia,* edited by Ivailo Znepolski. Sofia: Ciela Publishers, 2012.

Dimitrov, Martin K., and Joseph Sassoon. 'State Security, Information, and Repression: A Comparison of Communist Bulgaria and Ba'athist Iraq'. *Journal of Cold War Studies* 16, no. 2 (2014): 4–31.

Dimitrova, Nina. 'Rolia na sotsialnite uslugi v Bulgariia v perioda 1944–1989 g.: Trudoviiat kolektiv kato razshireno sotsialistichesko semeistvo'. In *Da poznaem komunizma: Izsledvaniia,* edited by Ivailo Znepolski. Sofia: Ciela Publishers, 2012.

Doboş, Corina. 'Ceauşescu was my father! Letters about the Children of the Decree at the end of the 1960s'. *International Journal of Humanistic Ideology* 4, no. 1 (2011): 67–80.

Doktorov, Mikhail. *V skhvatka s oktopoda: 'Vtoriiat tsentur' v borbata sreshtu zhivkovistite, 1965–1968 g.* Sofia: Ares Press, 1993.

Dorůžka, Lubomir, and Miloslav Ducháč. *Karel Vlach: 50 let s hudbou.* Prague: Ekopress, 2003.

Drozdowski, Bogumił. 'Kino na raty'. *Kino,* no. 4 (1968).

Duma, Andrzej. 'Struktura audytorium telewizyjnego w Polsce'. *Biuletyn Telewizyjny,* no. 1 (1963): 1–50.

Dvořáková, Jiřina. 'Bedřich Pokorný - vzestup a pád'. *Sborník Archivu Ministerstva vnitra,* no. 2 (2004): 233–279.

Dvořáková, Jiřina. *Státní bezpečnost v letech 1945–1953*. Prague: Úřad dokumentace a vyšetřování zločinů komunismu, 2007.

Eberwein, Robert. *The Hollywood War Film*. Chichester: Wiley-Blackwell, 2010.

Engelstein, Laura. 'Combined Underdevelopment: Discipline and the Law in Imperial and Soviet Russia'. *The American Historical Review* 98, no. 2 (1993): 338–353.

Epstein, Catherine. *The Last Revolutionaries*. Cambridge: Harvard University Press, 2003.

Fair-Schulz, Axel. *Loyal Subversion. East Germany and Its Bildungsbürgerlich Marxist Intellectuals*. Berlin: Trafo, 2008.

Falk, Barbara J. 'Resistance and Dissent in Central and Eastern Europe: An Emerging Historiography'. *East European Politics and Societies* 25, no. 2 (2011), 318–360.

Fantová, Jana, and Jan Palouček, eds. *Ještě jsme ve válce: Příběhy dvacátého století*. Prague: Argo; Post Bellum; ÚSTR, 2011.

Faure, Justine. *Americký přítel: Československo ve hře americké diplomacie 1943–1968*. Prague: Lidové noviny, 2006.

Feiwel, George R. *Poland's Industrialization Policy: A Current Analysis Sources of Economic Growth and Retrogression*. New York: Praeger, 1971.

Feld, Steven. 'Waterfalls of Songs: An Acoustemology of Place Resounding in Bosavi, Papua New Guinea'. In *Senses of Place*, edited by Steven Feld and Keith H. Basso. Santa Fe: SAR Press, 1996.

Festinger, Leon, Henry W. Riecken, and Stanley Schachter. *When Prophecy Fails*. Minneapolis: University of Minnesota, 1956.

Fitzpatrick, Sheila. *Everyday Stalinism. Ordinary Life in Extraordinary Times: Soviet Russia in the 1930s*. Oxford: Oxford University Press, 1999.

Fitzpatrick, Sheila. 'Popular Opinion in Russia Under Pre-War Stalinism'. In *Popular Opinion in Totalitarian Regimes: Fascism, Nazism, Communism*, edited by Paul Corner. Oxford: Oxford University Press, 2009.

Fitzpatrick, Sheila. 'Supplicants and Citizens: Public Letter Writing in Soviet Russia in the 1930s'. *Slavic Review* 55, no. 1 (1966): 78–105.

Flisowski, Zbigniew, ed. *Westerplatte. Wspomnienia, relacje, dokumenty*. Warsaw: Wydawnictwo Ministerstwa Oborny Narodowej, 1960.

Fojtík, J. 'Situace na společenskovědním úseku a úkoly společenských věd po XIV. sjezdu KSČ'. *Nová mysl*, no. 2 (1972): 147–169.

Ford, Charles, and Robbert Hammond. *Polish Film. A Twentieth Century History*. Jefferson: McFarland & Company, 2005.

Foucault, Michel. *Discipline and Punish: The Birth of the Prison*, translated by Alan Sheridan. New York: Vintage Books, 1979.

Foucault, Michel. *History of Sexuality. An Introduction*, vol. 1, translated by Robert Hurley. New York: Vintage Books, 1980.

Friedrich, Carl J., and Zbigniew K. Brzezinski. *Totalitarian Dictatorship and Autocracy*, 2nd rvsd. ed. Cambridge: Harvard University Press, 1965.

Frolík, Jan. 'Nástin organizačního vývoje státobezpečnostních složek sboru národní bezpečnosti v letech 1948–1989'. *Sborník archivních prací*, no. 2 (1991): 447–510.

Fulbrook, Mary. 'The Concept of "Normalisation" and the GDR in Comparative Perspective'. In *Power and Society in the GDR, 1961–1979: The Normalisation of Rule?*, edited by Mary Fulbrook. New York: Berghahn Books, 2009.

Fulbrook, Mary. *The People's State: East German Society from Hitler to Honecker*. New Haven: Yale University Press, 2005.

Fulbrook, Mary, ed. *Power and Society in the GDR, 1961–1979. The "Normalization of Rule"?* New York: Berghahn Books, 2009.

Gębicka, Ewa. "'Obcinanie kantów", czyli polityka PZPR i państwa wobec kinematografii w latach sześćdziesiątych'. In *Syndrom konformizmu? Kino polskie lat sześćdziesiątych*, edited by Tadeusz Miczka and Alina Madej. Katowice: Wydawnictwo Uniwersytetu Śląskiego, 1994.

Gieseke, Jens. 'Auf der Suche nach der schweigenden Mehrheit Ost. Die geheimen Infratest-Stellvertreterbefragungen und die DDR-Gesellschaft 1968–1989', *Zeithistorische Forschungen*, no. 1 (2015): http://www.zeithistorische-forschungen. de/1-2015/id%3D5182 (accessed 1 March 2018).

Gieseke, Jens. 'Opinion Polling Behind and Across the Iron Curtain: How West and East German Pollsters Shaped Knowledge Regimes on Communist Societies'. *History of the Human Sciences* 29, no. 4–5 (2016): 77–98.

Ghodsee, Kristen. 'Pressuring the Politburo: The Committee of the Bulgarian Women's Movement and State Socialist Feminism'. *Slavic Review* 73, no. 3 (2014): 538–562.

Gieseke, Jens, ed. *Staatssicherheit und Gesellschaft: Studien zum Herrschaftsalltag in der DDR*. Göttingen: Vandenhoeck & Ruprecht, 2007.

Goffman, Erving. *The Presentation of Self in Everyday Life*. Garden City: Anchor, 1959.

Goldman, Wendy Z. *Inventing the Enemy: Denunciation and Terror in Stalin's Russia*. Cambridge: Cambridge University Press, 2011.

Goldman, Wendy Z. *Terror and Democracy in the Age of Stalin: The Social Dynamics of Repression*. Cambridge: Cambridge University Press, 2007.

Graf, Jan de. 'More than Canteen Control: Polish and Italian Socialists Confronting Their Workers, 1944–1947'. *International Review of Social History* 59 (2014): 71–98.

Grama, Adrian. 'Labouring Along. Industrial Workers and the Making of Postwar Romania'. PhD diss., Central European University, Budapest, 2016.

Gregory, Paul. *Terror by Quota: State Security from Lenin to Stalin*. New Haven: Yale University Press, 2009.

Grift, Liesbeth van de. *Securing the Communist State: The Reconstruction of Coercive Institutions in the Soviet Zone of Germany and Romania, 1944–1948*. Lanham: Lexington Books, 2012.

Haggard, Stephan, and Robert R. Kaufman. *Development, Democracy, and Welfare States: Latin America, East Asia, and Eastern Europe*. Princeton: Princeton University Press, 2008.

Hájíček, Jiří. *Rybí krev*. Brno: Host, 2012.

Hájíček, Jiří. *Selský baroko*. Brno: Host, 2005.

Haltof, Marek. *Historical Dictionary of Polish Cinema*. Lanham: The Scarecrow Press, 2007.

Hanzlík, František. *Únor 1948: výsledek nerovného zápasu*. Prague: Prewon, 1997.

Harrison, Erica. 'Radio and the Performance of Government: Broadcasting by the Czechoslovaks in Exile in London, 1939–1945'. PhD diss., University of Bristol, 2015.

Hauslohner, Peter. 'Gorbachev's Social Contract'. *Soviet Economy* 3, no. 1 (1987): 54–89.

Havel, Václav. *The Power of the Powerless*. Armonk: M. E. Sharpe, 1985.

Hayward, Susan. *Cinema Studies: The Key Concepts*. London: Routledge, 2006.

Hein, Christoph. *Der Tangospieler*. Berlin: Aufbau-Verlag, 1989.

Hein, Christoph. *The Tango Player*, translated by Philip Boehm. Evanston: Northwestern University Press, 1994.

Hellbeck, Jochen. 'Of Archives and Frogs: Iconoclasm in Historical Perspective'. *Slavic Review* 67, no. 3 (2008): 720–723.

Helmreich, Stefan. 'An Anthropologist Underwater: Immersive Soudscapes, Submarine Cyborgs, and Transductive Ethnography'. *American Ethnologist* 34, no. 4 (2007): 621–641.

Hirschman, Albert. *Exit, Voice and Loyalty. Responses to Decline in Firms, Organizations and States*. Cambridge: Harvard UP, 1970.

Hodos, George. *Show Trials: Stalinist Purges in Eastern Europe*. New York: Praeger, 1987.

Hodrová, Daniela. *Román zasvěcení*. Jinočany: H&H, 1993.

Holt, Robert. *Radio Free Europe*. Minneapolis: University of Minnesota Press, 1958.

Holý, Ladislav. *The Little Czech and the Great Czech Nation: National Identity and the Post-Communist Transformation of Society*. Cambridge: Cambridge University Press, 1996.

Hopkin, David. *Voices of the People in Nineteenth-Century France*. Cambridge: Cambridge University Press, 2012.

Hradecký, Tomáš. 'Hodnocení činnosti krajského tajemníka KSČ Mikuláše Landy pohledem regionálních politických složek z doby před procesem'. *České, slovenské a československé dějiny 20. století*, 8 (2013): 343–354.

Huguenin, Duane. 'Mutations des pratiques répressives de la police secréte tchécoslovaque'. *Vingtième siècle: Revue d'histoire*, no. 96 (2007): 163–177.

Huguenin, Duane. 'Youth, the West, and the Czechoslovak Secret Police: Immaturity or Ideological Diversion?' *Vingtième Siècle: Revue d'Histoire* 1, no. 109 (2011): 183–200.

Huston, Aletha C. et al. 'From Attention to Comprehension: How Children Watch and Learn from Television'. In *Children and Television: Fifty Years of Research*, edited by Norma Pecora, John P. Murray, and Ellen Ann Wartella. New Jersey: Lawrence Erlbaum Associates Inc., 2007.

Inglot, Tomasz. *Welfare States in East Central Europe, 1919–2004*. New York: Cambridge University Press, 2008.

Ionescu, Ghiţă. *Communism in Romania, 1944–1962*. Oxford: Oxford University Press, 1964.

Iordanova, Dina. *Cinema of the Other Europe. The Industry and Artistry of East Central European Film*. London and New York: Wallflower Press, 2003.

Ivanov, Dimitur. *Politicheskoto protivopostaviane v Bulgaria 1956–1989 g*. Sofia: Ares Press, 1994.

Izajasz, Tomasz, Magdalena Jurczyk, and Karolina Glabus. *Czterej pancerni i pies: śladem filmowej sagi w Bydgoszczy*. Bydgoszcz: Wydawnictwo Pejzaż, 2013.

Janicki, Stanisław, and Irena Nowak-Zatorska. *Film polski od A do Z*. Warsaw: Wydawnictwo Artystyczne i Filmowe, 1977.

Jarausch, Konrad, 'Au-delà des condamnations morales et des fausses explications. Plaidoyer pour une histoire différenciée de la RDA'. *Genèses* 52, no. 3 (2003): 80–95.

Jarausch, Konrad. ed. *Dictatorship as Experience: Towards a Socio-Cultural History of the GDR*. New York: Bergahn Books, 1999.

Järvinen, Jouni. *Normalization and Charter 77: Violence, Commitment and Resistance in Czechoslovakia*. Helsinki: Kikimora Publications, 2009.

Jelínek, Václav. *Skandál v obrazárně: Komedie nanesená v rámci linie se zvláštním přihlédnutím k otázkám současnosti*. Unpublished Manuscript no. 6108. Prague: Československé divadelní a literární jednatelství, 1953.

Jenkins, Henry, and Kristine Brunovska Karnick. 'Introduction'. In *Classical Hollywood Comedy*, edited by Kristine Brunovska Karnick and Henry Jenkins. London: Routledge, 1995.

Jerome, Jerome K. *Three Men in a Boat. To Say Nothing of the Dog*. Warsaw: Iskry, 1958.

Jerome, Jerome K. *Three Men in a Boat/Trzej ludzi w jednej łodzi*. Warsaw: Nakładem Lingwisty, 1922.

Jerome, Jerome K. *Trzech panów w łódce (nie licząc psa)*. Warsaw: Iskry, 1956.

Jerome, Jerome K. *Trzech starszych panów w jednej łódce (oprócz psa)*. Warsaw: Księgarnia nakładowa M. Szczepkowskiego, 1912.

Ješutová, Eva, ed. *Od Mikrofonu k posluchačům*. Prague: Český rozhlas, 2003.

Jones, Sara. *Complicity, Censorship and Criticism: Negotiating Space in the GDR Literary Sphere*. Berlin: de Gruyter, 2011.

Josten, Josef. *Oh, My Country*. London: Latimer House, 1949.

Jowett, Garth, and Victoria O'Donnell. *Propaganda and Persuasion*. Beverly Hills: Sage Publications, 2006.

Kalinova, Evgeniia, and Iskra Baeva. *Bulgarskite prekhodi 1939–2005*. Sofia: Paradigma, 2006.

Kalous, Jan, ed. *Biografický slovník představitelů ministerstva vnitra v letech 1948–1989*. Prague: Ústav pro stadium totalitních režimů, 2009.

Kalous, Jan, ed. *Instruktážní skupina StB v lednu a únoru 1950 – zákulisí případu Číhošt*. Prague: Sešit ÚDV, 2001.

Kalous, Jan, ed. 'Karel Černý – neznámý personální architekt Státní bezpečnosti'. *Pamět a dějiny*, no. 4 (2010): 70–79.

Kalous, Jan, ed. *Štěpán Plaček - Život zpravodajského fanatika ve službách KSČ*. Prague: Ústav pro studium totalitních režimů, 2010.

Kania, Albin. 'Film fabularny w telewizji w opinii odbiorców'. *Biuletyn Radiowo-Telewizyjny*, no. 8 (1970): 5–14.

Kanushev, Martin. 'Postoianen nadzor i infranakazatelnost: bulgarskoto nakazatelno pravo prez perioda 1957–1969 godina'. *Sotsiologicheski problemi* XLI, no. 3–4 (2009): 175–199.

Kaplan, Karel. *Dans les archives du Comité Central: 30 ans du secrets du Bloc soviétique*. Paris: Albin Michel, 1978.

Kaplan, Karel. *Nebezpečná bezpečnost*. Brno: Doplněk, 1999.

Kaplan, Karel. *Pět kapitol o únoru*. Brno: Doplněk, 1997.

Kaplan, Karel. *Report on the Murder of the General Secretary*, translated by Karel Kovanda. Columbus: Ohio State Press, 1990.

Kaplan, Karel. *Short March: The Communist Takeover in Czechoslovakia 1945–1948*. London: C. Hurst, 1987.

Kaška, Václav. *Neukáznění a neangažování: Disciplinace členů Komunistické strany Československa v letech 1948–1952*. Prague and Brno: Conditio Humana and Ústav pro studium totalitních režimů, 2014.

Kavan, Rosemary. *Freedom at a Price: An Englishwoman's Life in Czechoslovakia*. London: Verso, 1985.

Kershaw, Ian. *Popular Opinion and Political Dissent in the Third Reich: Bavaria 1933–1945*. Oxford: Clarendon Press, 1983.

Kisielewski, Tadeusz A. *Janczarzy Berlinga: 1. Armia Wojska Polskiego 1943–1945*. Poznań: REBIS, 2014.

Knabe, Hubertus. *Die Mörder sind unter uns*. Munich: Propyläen Verlag, 2007.

Knapík, Jiří. *V Zajetí moci: Kulturní politika, její systém a aktéři 1948–1956*. Prague: Libri, 2006.

Kocka, Jürgen. 'The GDR: A Special Kind of Modern Dictatorship'. In *Dictatorship as Experience: Towards a Socio-Cultural History of the GDR*, edited by Konrad Jarausch. New York: Berghahn Books, 1999.

Koenker, Diane. *Club Red: Vacation Travel and the Soviet Dream*. Ithaca, NY: Cornell University Press, 2013.

Kolář, Pavel. *Der Poststalinismus: Ideologie und Utopie einer Epoche*. Cologne: Böhlau, 2016.

Kopecký, Václav. *Proti kosmopolitismu jako ideologii amerického imperialismu*. Prague: Orbis, 1952.

Kornai, János. *The Socialist System: The Political Economy of Communism*. Oxford: Clarendon Press, 1992.

Kosiński, Krzysztof. *Oficjalne i prywatne życie młodzieży w czasach PRL*. Warsaw: Rosner & Wspólnicy, 2006.

Kostlán, Antonín, ed. *Věda v Československu v období normalizace (1970–1975). Práce z dějin vědy*, vol. 4. Prague: Výzkumné centrum pro dějiny vědy, 2002.

Kotkin, Stephen. *Magnetic Mountain. Stalinism as a Civilization*. Berkeley: University of California Press, 1995.

Kott, Sandrine. *Le communisme au quotidien: Les entreprises d'Etat dans la société est-allemande*. Belin: Paris, 2001.

Kott, Sandrine. *Communism Day-to-Day. State Enterprises in East German Society*. Ann Arbor: The University of Michigan Press, 2014.

Koudelka, František. *Státní bezpečnost 1954–1968. Základní údaje*, vol. 13. Prague: Sešity ÚSD, 1993.

Kovanič, Martin. 'Institutes of Memory in the Slovak and Czech Republics – What Kind of Memory?' In *Secret Agents and the Memory of the Everyday Collaboration in Communist Eastern Europe*, edited by Sándor Horváth, Péter Apor, and James Mark. London: Anthem Press, 2017.

Kovanda, Karel. 'Works Councils in Czechoslovakia, 1945–47'. *Soviet Studies* 29, no. 2 (1977): 255–269.

Kozlov, Vladimir A., and Sheila Fitzpatrick, eds. *Sedition: Everyday Resistance in the Soviet Union Under Khrushchev and Brezhnev*. New Haven: Yale University Press, 2011.

Kramer, Mark. 'Stalin, Soviet Policy, and the Establishment of a Communist Bloc in Eastern Europe, 1941–1948'. In *Stalin and Europe: Imitation and Domination, 1928–1953*, edited by Timothy Snyder and Ray Brandon. Oxford: Oxford University Press, 2014.

Król, Eugeniusz C. 'Gesellschaftliche und politische Grundlagen des Bildes der Deutschen im polnischen Spielfilm nach dem Zweiten Weltkrieg'. In *Deutschland und Polen. Filmische Grenzen und Nachbarschaften*, edited by Konrad Klejsa and Schamma Schahadat. Marburg: Schüren Verlag, 2011.

Królikowska, Wanda. 'Codzienność zorganizowanego wypoczynku dzieci i młodzieży w Polsce w latach 1956–1970: program i realizacja'. In *Życie codzienne w PRL (1956–1989)*, edited by Grzegorz Miernik and Sebastian Piątkowski. Radom-Starachowice: Radomskie Towarzystwo Naukowe, 2006.

Kuczynski, Jürgen. *Ein linientreuer Dissident. Memoiren 1945–1989*. Berlin: Aufbau-Verlag, 1992.

Kula, Marcin. 'Poland: The Silence of Those Deprived of Voice'. In *Popular Opinion in Totalitarian Regimes: Fascism, Nazism, Communism*, edited by Paul Corner. New York: Oxford University Press, 2009.

Kunze, Rainer. *Deckname 'Lyrik'. Eine Dokumentation*. Frankfurt: S. Fischer Taschenbuch, 1990.

Landsman, Mark. *Dictatorship and Demand: The Politics of Consumerism in East Germany*. Cambridge, MA: Harvard University Press, 2005.

Łazarz, Marek. *Czterej pancerni i pies. Przewodnik po serialu i okolicach*. Wrocław: Torus Media, 2006.

Lazitch, Branko. *Les partis communistes d'Europe 1919–1955*. Paris: Les îles d'or, 1956.

Lebow, Katherine. *Unfinished Utopia: Nowa Huta, Stalinism and Polish Society*, 1949–1956. Ithaca: Cornell University Press, 2013.

Levitsky, Steven, and Lucan A. Way. *Competitive Authoritarianism: The Origins and Evolution of Hybrid Regimes in the Post-Cold War Era*. New York: Cambridge University Press, 2010.

Lindenberger, Thomas. 'Der ABV im Text. Zur internen und öffentlichen Rede über die Deutsche Volkspolizei der 1950er Jahre'. In *Akten. Eingaben. Schaufenster. Die DDR und ihre Texte: Erkundingen zu Herrschaft und Alltag*, edited by Alf Lüdtke and Peter Becker. Akademie Verlag, 1997.

Lindenberger, Thomas. 'Creating State Socialist Governance: The Case of the Deutsche Volkspolizei'. In *Dictatorship as Experience. Towards a Socio-Cultural History of the GDR*, edited by Konrad Jarausch. New-York: Berghahn Books, 1999.

Lindenberger, Thomas. 'Die Diktatur der Grenzen. Zur Einleitung'. In *Herrschaft und Eigen-Sinn in der Diktatur. Studien zur Gesellschaftsgeschichte der DDR*, edited by Thomas Lindenberger. Cologne: Böhlau, 1999.

Lindenberger, Thomas. 'Eigen-Sinn, Domination and No Resistance'. In *Docupedia-Zeitgeschichte*, https://docupedia.de/zg/Lindenberger_eigensinn_v1_en_2015.

Lindenberger, Thomas, ed. *Herrschaft und Eigen-Sinn in der Diktatur: Studien zur Gesellschaftsgeschichte der DDR*. Cologne: Böhlau 1999.

Lindenberger, Thomas. 'La police populaire de la RDA de 1952 á 1958'. *Annales* 53, no. 1 (1998): 119–151.

Lindenberger, Thomas. 'Tacit Minimal Consensus: The Always Precarious East German Dictatorship'. In *Popular Opinion in Totalitarian Regimes: Fascism, Nazism, Communism*, edited by Paul Corner. Oxford: Oxford University Press, 2009.

Lindenberger, Thomas. *Volkspolizei: Herrschaftspraxis und öffentliche Ordnung im SED-Staat 1952–1968*. Cologne: Böhlau, 2003.

Lindenberger, Thomas, and Alf Lüdtke, eds. *Eigen-Sinn. Sprawowanie władzy jako praktyka społeczna*. Poznań: Wydawnictwo Nauka i Innowacje 2018.

Loose, Ingo. 'Hans Kloss – ein "roter James Bond"? Deutsche, Polen und der Zweite Weltkrieg in der Kultserie "Sekunden Entscheiden"'. In *Deutschland und Polen. Filmische Grenzen und Nachbarschaften*, edited by Konrad Klejsa and Schamma Schahadat. Marburg: Schüren Verlag, 2011.

Lovejoy, Alice. *Army Film and the Avant-Garde: Cinema and Experiment in the Czechoslovak Military*. Bloomington: Indiana University Press, 2015.

Lovell, Stephen. *Russia in the Microphone Age: A History of Soviet Radio, 1919–1970*. Oxford: Oxford University Press, 2015.

Lüdtke, Alf. 'Arbeit, Arbeitserfahrungen und Arbeiterpolitik. Zum Perspektivenwandel in der historischen Forschung'. In *Eigen-Sinn. Fabrikalltag, Arbeitererfahrungen und Politik vom Kaiserreich bis in den Faschismus*, edited by Alf Lüdtke. Hamburg: Ergebnisse Verlag, 1993.

Lüdtke, Alf, ed. *The History of Everyday Life: Reconstructing Historical Experiences and Ways of Life*. Princeton: Princeton University Press, 1995.

Lüdtke, Alf. 'Kolonisierung der Lebenswelten oder Geschichte als Einbahnstraße?' *Das Argument* 140 (1983): 536–542.

Lüdtke, Alf. 'Polymorphous Synchrony: German Industrial Workers and the Politics of Everyday Life'. *International Review of Social History*, no. 3 (1993): 39–84.

Lüdtke, Alf. 'La République démocratique allemande comme histoire. Réflexions historiographiques'. *Annales* 53, no. 1 (1998): 1–39.

Lukács, Georg. *History and Class Consciousness: Studies in Marxist Dialectics*. London: Merlin Press, 1971.

Lukes, Igor. 'The Birth of a Police State', *Intelligence and National Security* 11, no. 1 (1996): 78–88.

Lukes, Igor. 'Rudolf Slánský: His Trials and Trial'. CWIHP Working Paper No. 50, 1–79.

Łukowski, Maciej. *Film seryjny w programie telewizji polskiej (lata 1959–1970)*. Warsaw: Wydawnictwa Radia i Telewizji, 1980.

Machcewicz, Paweł. *Poland's War on Radio Free Europe, 1950–1989*. Washington, D.C. and Stanford, CA: Woodrow Wilson Center Press, 2014.

Madarasz, Jeannette. 'Economic Politics and Company Culture: The Problem of Routinisation'. In *Power and Society in the GDR, 1961–1979. The 'Normalisation of Rule'?*, edited by Mary Fulbrook. New York: Berghahn Books, 2009.

Magaloni, Beatriz. *Voting for Autocracy: Hegemonic Party Survival and Its Demise in Mexico*. New York: Cambridge University Press, 2006.

Major, Patrick. *Behind the Berlin Wall: East Germany and the Frontiers of Power*. Oxford: Oxford University Press, 2010.

Maňák, Jiří. *Komunisté na pochodu k moci 1945–1948*. Prague: Studie ÚSD, 1995.

Maňák, Jiří. *Proměny strany moci*. Prague: ÚSD, 1995.

Maňák, Jiří. *Proměny strany moci III: Početnost a složení pracovníků stranického aparátu 1948–1968*. Prague: ÚSD, 1999.

Mark, James. *The Unfinished Revolution: Making Sense of the Communist Past in Central-Eastern Europe*. New Heaven: Yale University Press, 2010.

Marin, Manuela. *Intre prezent și trecut: cultural personalității lui Nicolae Ceaușescu și opinia publica româneasca*. Cluj-Napoca: Editura MEGA, 2014.

Marin, Manuela. *Nicolae Ceaușescu: Omul și Cultul*. Târgoviște: Cetatea de Scaun, 2016.

Mayer, Françoise. 'Individus sous contrôle dans la société tchécoslovaque de 1945 à 1989'. *Cahiers du CEFRES*, no. 32 (2012): 5–13.

Mayer, Françoise. *Les Tchèques et leur communisme*. Paris: EHESS, 2003.

McDermott, Kevin. 'A "Polyphony of Voices"? Czech Popular Opinion and the Slánský Affair'. *Slavic Review* 67, no. 4 (2008): 840–865.

McDermott, Kevin, and Klára Pinerová. 'The Rehabilitation Process in Czechoslovakia: Party and Popular Responses'. In *De-Stalinising Eastern Europe: The Rehabilitation of Stalin's Victims After* 1953, edited by Kevin McDermott and Matthew Stibbe. Basingstoke: Palgrave Macmillan, 2015.

McDermott, Kevin, and Vitězslav Sommer. 'The "Club of Politically Engaged Conformists"? The Communist Party of Czechoslovakia, Popular Opinion and the Crisis of Communism'. *Cold War International History Project*, Working Paper No. 66, 2013.

Meyer, Peter. 'Czechoslovakia'. In *The Jews in the Soviet Satellites*, edited by Peter Meyer et al. Syracuse: Syracuse University Press, 1953.

Mickelson, Sig. *America's Other Voices: Radio Free Europe and Radio Liberty*. New-York: Praeger, 1983.

Migev, Vladimir. *Kolektivizatsiiata na bulgarskoto selo (1948–1958)*. Sofia: Universitetsko izdatelstvo 'Stopanstvo', 1995.

Migev, Vladimir. 'Nasiliia, reformi i kompromisi: Kum vuprosa za otrazhenieto v Bulgariia na krizisnite protsesi v suvetskiia blok (1953–1981 g.)'. In *Istoriiata – profesiia i sudba: Sbornik v chest na 60-godishninata na chlen-korespondent d. ist. n. Georgi Markov*, edited by Vitka Toshkova, Vasilka Tankova, and Nikolai Poppetrov. Sofia: Tangra TanNakRa, 2008.

Migev, Vladimir. *Prazhkata prolet '68 i Bulgariia*. Sofia: Iztok-Zapad, 2005.

Migev, Vladimir. 'Za Aprilskiia plenum – 1956 godina i za liberalizatsiiata na rezhima v Bulgariia prez 50-te i 60-te godini na XX vek (Opit za istoricheska eseistika)'. *Istoricheski pregled* LXV, no. 1–2 (2009): 187–199.

Mikhailov, Stoian. *Sotsiologiiata v Bulgariia sled Vtorata svetovna voina*. Sofia: M8M, 2003.

Millar, James R. 'The Little Deal: Brezhnev's Contribution to Acquisitive Socialism'. *Slavic Review* 44, no. 4 (1985): 694–706.

Mitter, Armin. 'Die Ereignisse im Juni und Juli 1953 in der DDR'. *Aus Politik und Zeitgeschichte*, no. 5 (1991): 31–41.

Mitzner, Zbigniew. 'Liczby, procenty i "Czterej pancerni"'. *Ekran*, no. 24 (1968).

Mlýnský, Jaroslav. *Únor 1948 a akční výbory Národní fronty*. Prague: Academia, 1978.

Mólnár, Miklós. *De Béla Kun à János Kádár. Soixante-dix ans de communisme hongrois*. Paris: FNSP, 1987.

Mrňka, Jaromír. *Svéhlavá periferie: Každodennost diktatury KSČ na příkladu Šumperska a Zábřežska v letech 1945–1960*. Prague: Ústav pro studium totalitních režimů, 2015.

Neale, Stephen. *Descriptions*. Cambridge: MIT Press, 1990.

Neumayer, Laure. 'Integrating the Central European Past into a Common Narrative: The Mobilizations Around the "Crimes of Communism" in the European Parliament'. *Journal of Contemporary European Studies* 23, no. 3, 2015: 1–20.

Niri, Carol. *Frontul unic muncitoresc în perioada 23 august 1944 - februarie 1948*. Bucharest: Academia de Ştiinţe Social-Politice 'Ştefan Gheorghiu', 1968.

Nosková, Věra. *Bereme, co je*. Prague: Abonent ND, 2005.

Oates-Indruchová, Libora. *Discourses of Gender in Pre- and Post-1989 Czech Culture*. Pardubice: Pardubice University, 2002.

Oates-Indruchová, Libora. 'The Limits of Thought?: The Regulatory Framework of Social Sciences and Humanities in Czechoslovakia (1968–1989)'. *Europe-Asia Studies* 60, no. 10 (2008): 1767–1782.

Onişoru, Gheorghe. *Pecetea lui Stalin. Cazul Vasile Luca*. Târgovişte: Cetatea de Scaun, 2014.

Orlow, Dietriech. 'The GDR's Failed Search for a National Identity, 1945–1989'. *German Studies Review* 29, no. 3 (October 2006): 537–558.

Ostermann, Christian F., ed. *Uprising in East Germany, 1953: The Cold War, the German Question, and the First Major Upheaval Behind the Iron Curtain*. New York: Central European University Press, 2001.

Otáhal, Milan. *Normalizace 1969–1989: Příspěvek ke stavu bádání*. Prague: Ústav pro soudobé dějiny, 2002.

Otáhal, Milan, Alena Nosková, and Karel Bolomský, eds. *Svědectví o duchovním útlaku (1969–1970): Dokumenty*. Prague: Maxdorf and Ústav pro soudobé dějiny AV ČR, 1993.

Oushakine, Serguei. '"Red Laughter": On Refined Weapons of Soviet Jesters'. *Social Research* 79, no. 1 (2012): 189–216.

Oushakine, Serguei. 'The Terrifying Mimicry of Samizdat'. *Public Culture* 13, no. 2 (2001): 191–214.

Paczkowski, Andrzej. *The Spring Will Be Ours: Poland and the Poles from Occupation to Freedom*. University Park: Pennsylvania State University Press, 2003.

Palmowski, Jan. *Inventing a Socialist Nation: Heimat and the Politics of Everyday Life in the GDR, 1945–90*. Cambridge: Cambridge University Press 2009.

Patten, Alan. '"The Most Natural State": Herder and Nationalism'. *History of Political Thought* 31, no. 4 (2010): 657–689.

Patzelt, Eva. *Un haut fonctionnaire est-allemand aux prises avec l'intelligentsia (1963-1989). Kurt Hager face aux écrivains Volker Braun, Stefan Heym, Helmut Sakowski et Erwin Strittmatter*. Paris: L'Harmattan, 2014.

Pavka, Marek. *Kádry rozhodují vše!: Kádrová politika KSČ z hlediska teorie elit (Prvních pět let komunistické moci)*. Brno: Prius, 2003.

Pažout, Jaroslav, ed. *Informační boj o Československo/v Československu (1945-1989)*. Prague: Ústav pro studium totalitních režimů, 2014.

Pehe, Veronika. 'Drobné hrdinství: vzdor jakožto předmět nostalgie v díle Petra Šabacha a Michala Viewegha'. *Česká literatura* 63, no. 3 (2015): 419–434.

Pennington, Reina. 'Offensive Women: Women in Combat in the Red Army in the Second World War'. *The Journal of Military History* 74, no. 3 (2010): 775–820.

Pernes, Jiří. 'Dělnické domonstrace v Brně v roce 1951'. *Soudobé dějiny* 3, no. 1 (1996): 23–41.

Pernes, Jiří. *Krize komunistického režimu v Československu v 50. letech 20. století*. Brno: CDK, 2008.

Pernes, Jiří. 'Mládež vede Brno: Otto Šling a jeho brněnská kariéra 1945-1950'. *Soudobé dějiny* 11, no. 3 (2004): 45–46.

Pernes, Jiří. *Snahy o překonání politicko-hospodářské krize v Československu v roce 1953*. Brno: Prius, 2000.

Pernes, Jiří. 'Únor 1948 jako významný mezník ve vývoji československé společnosti'. In *Únor 1948 v Československu: Nástup komunistické totality a proměny společnosti*, edited by Jiří Kocián and Markéta Devátá. Prague: Ústav pro soudobé dějiny AV ČR, v. v. i., 2011.

Pernes, Jiří, and Jan Foitzik, eds. *Politické procesy v Československu po roce 1945 a případ Slánský*. Brno: Prius pro ÚSD AV ČR, 2005.

Pernes, Jiří, Jaroslav Pospíšil, and Antonín Lukáš. *Alexej Čepička. Šedá eminence rudého režimu*. Prague: Brána, 2008.

Peroutka, Ferdinand. 'Projev při zahájení vysílání Rádia Svobodná Evropa'. In *Ferdinand Peroutka pro Svobodnou Evropu*, edited by Jan Bednář. Prague: Radioservis, 2013.

Persak, Krzysztof, and Łukasz Kamiński, eds. *A Handbook of the Communist Security Apparatus in East Central Europe*. Warsaw: Institute of National Remembrance, 2005.

Pešat, Zdeněk. 'Normalizační praxe a Lexikon české literatury'. In *Normy normalizace*, Opava, 11–13 September 1995, edited by Jan Wiendl. Prague and Opava: Ústav pro českou literaturu AV ČR and Slezská univerzita, 1995.

Pfaff, Steven. *Exit-Voice Dynamics and the Collapse of East Germany: The Crisis of Leninism and the Revolution of 1989*. Durham: Duke University Press, 2006.

Pinkas, Jaroslav. 'Nenápadný půvab normalizace – její sociální realita optikou tehdejší a dnešní filmové kamery'. In *Film a dějiny 4: Normalizace*, edited by Petr Kopal. Prague: Casablanca and ÚSTR, 2014.

Pittaway, Mark. *The Workers' State: Industrial Labor and the Making of Socialist Hungary 1944-1958*. Pittsburgh: University of Pittsburgh Press, 2012.

Pleskot, Patryk. *Wielki mały ekran. Telewizja a codzienność Polaków w latach sześćdziesiątych*. Warsaw: Trio, 2007.

Pokorna-Ignatowicz, Katarzyna. *Telewizja w systemie politycznym i medialnym PRL. Między polityką a widzem*. Kraków: Wydawnictwo Uniwersytetu Jagiellońskiego, 2003.

Polniak, Łukasz. *Patriotyzm wojskowy w PRL w latach 1956-1970*. Warsaw: Trio, 2011.

Pons, Silvio. *The Global Revolution. A History of International Communism, 1917–1991.* Oxford: Oxford University Press, 2014.

Pravda, Alex. 'East-West Interdependence and the Social Compact in Eastern Europe'. In *East-West Relations and the Future of Eastern Europe: Politics and Economics,* edited by Morris Bornstein, Zvi Gitelman, and William Zimmerman. London: George Allen and Unwin, 1981.

Pucci, Molly. 'Security Empire: Building the Secret Police in Communist Eastern Europe'. PhD diss., Stanford University, Stanford, California, 2015.

Pullmann, Michal. *Konec experimentu: Přestavba a pád komunismu v Československu.* Prague: Scriptorium, 2011.

Pynsent, Robert. *Questions of Identity: Czech and Slovak Ideas of Nationality and Personality.* Budapest: Central European University Press, 1994.

Pytlík, Radko. *Jaroslav Hašek a Dobrý voják Švejk.* Prague: Panorama, 1983.

Reynolds, Jaime. 'Communists, Socialists and Workers: Poland 1944–48'. *Soviet Studies* 30, no. 4 (1978): 516–520.

Řezník, Miloš. 'Transformations of Regional History in the Polish "Western Territories" Since 1945: Legitimization, Nationalization, Regionalization'. In *Frontiers, Regions and Identities in Europe,* edited by Steven G. Ellis and Raingard Eßer. Pisa: Plus-Pisa University Press, 2009.

Rosenfeldt, Niels Erik. *The 'Special' World: Stalin's Power Apparatus and the Soviet System's Secret Structures of Communication,* translated by Sally Laird and John Kendal. Copenhagen: Museum Tusculanums Forlag, 2009.

Rudzki, Jerzy. 'Wpływ telewizji na aktywność kulturalną młodzieży wiejskiej'. *Biuletyn Telewizyjny,* no. 1 (1964): 30–51.

Rudzki, Jerzy. *Zafascynowani telewizją: socjologiczne studium o telewizji wśród młodzieży.* Wrocław: Zakład Narodowy im. Ossolińskich Wydawnictwo PAN, 1969.

Rychlík, Jan. 'Komunistická propaganda v Československu 1945–1989 z tematického hlediska'. In *Informační boj o Československu/v Československu (1945–1989),* edited by Jaroslav Pažout. Prague: Ústav pro studium totalitních režimů, 2014.

Sabrow, Martin. *Das Diktat des Konsenses: Geschichtswissenschaft in der DDR.* Munich: Oldenbourg, 2001.

Sabrow, Martin. *Erich Honecker – Das Leben davor, 1912–1945.* Munich: C.H. Beck, 2007.

Sakson, Andrzej. 'Odzyskiwanie Ziem Odzyskanych – przemiany lokalnej i regionalnej tożsamości mieszkańców Ziem Zachodnich i Północnych a rewindykacyjne postulaty niemieckich środowisk ziomkowskich'. In *Ziemie Odzyskane 1945–2005. Ziemie Zachodnie i Północne 60 lat w granicach państwa polskiego,* edited by Andrzej Sakson. Poznań: Instytut Zachodni, 2006.

Şandru, Dumitru. *Comunizarea societăţii româneşti în anii 1944–1947.* Bucharest: Editura Enciclopedică, 2007.

Saunders, John. *The Western Genre: From Lordsburg to Big Whiskey.* London: Wallflower Press, 2001.

Scott, James C. *Domination and the Arts of Resistance. Hidden Transcripts.* New Haven: Yale University Press, 1990.

Scott, James C. *Weapons of the Weak: Everyday Forms of Peasant Resistance.* New Haven: Yale University Press, 1987.

Sewell, William H. Jr. 'The Concept(s) of Culture'. In *Beyond the Cultural Turn. New Directions in the Study of Society and Culture,* edited by Victoria E. Bonnell and Lynn Hunt. Berkeley: University of California Press, 1999.

Sherry, Samantha. *Discourses of Regulation and Resistance: Censoring Translation in the Stalin and Khrushchev Era Soviet Union*. Edinburgh: Edinburgh University Press, 2015.

Shore, Marci. "'A Spectre Is Haunting Europe ... ' Dissidents, Intellectuals and a New Generation'. In *The End and the Beginning. The Revolutions of 1989 and the Resurgence of History*, edited by Vladimir Tismaneanu and Bogdan C. Iacob. Budapest: CEU Press, 2012.

Siegelbaum, Lewis H. *Cars for Comrades: The Life of the Soviet Automobile*. Ithaca, NY: Cornell University Press, 2008.

Simpson, Christopher. *The Science of Coercion: Communication Research and Psychological Warfare, 1945-1960*. New York and Oxford: Oxford University Press, 1996.

Šlouf, Jakub. *Spřízněni měnou. Genealogie plzeňské revolty 1. června 1953*. Prague: FF UK, 2016.

Sniegon, Tomas. 'Implementing Post-Communist National Memory in the Czech Republic and Slovakia'. In *European Cultural Memory Post-89*, edited by Conny Mithander, John Sundholm, and Adrian Velicu. Amsterdam: Rodopi, 2013, 97–124.

Stanoeva, Elitsa. 'Organizirane na sotsialisticheskata turgoviia v Bulgariia (1954–1963): doktrinalni protivorechiia i mezhduinstitutsionalni naprezheniia'. *Sotsiologicheski problemi* XLVII, no. 1–2 (2015): 111–133.

Sterne, Jonathan. *The Audible Past: Cultural Origins of Sound Reproduction*. Durham and London: Duke University Press, 2003.

Stoddard, Karen. 'Children's Programming'. In *TV Genres*, edited by Brian G. Rose. Westport: Greenwood Press, 1985.

Stoianova, Penka, and Emil Iliev. *Politicheski opasni litsa: Vudvoriavaniia, trudova mobilizatsiia, izselvaniia v Bulgariia sled 1944 g.* Sofia: Universitetsko izdatelstvo 'Sv. Kliment Okhridski', 1991.

Švéda, Josef. *Mašínovský mýtus: ideologie v české literatuře a kultuře*. Příbram: Pistorius & Olšanská, 2012.

Svolik, Milan W. *The Politics of Authoritarian Rule*. New York: Cambridge University Press, 2012.

Taylor, A.J.P. *The Course of German History*. London: Hamish Hamilton, 1945.

Taylor, Frederick. *Exorcising Hitler: The Occupation and Denazification of Germany*. London: Bloomsbury Publishing, 2011.

Tomek, Prokop. *Československá redakce Radio Free Europe: Historie a vliv na československé dějiny*. Prague: Academia, 2015.

Tomek, Prokop. 'Rádio Svobodná Evropa a jeho československá redakce'. In *Svobodně! Rádio Svobodná Evropa 1951–2011*, edited by Marek Junek et al. Prague: Radioservis, 2011.

Tomek, Prokop. 'Rušení zahraničního rozhlasového vysílání pro Československo'. *Securitas Imperii*, no. 9 (2002): 334–367.

Tomek, Prokop. *Život a doba ministra Rudolfa*. Prague: Vyšehrad, 2009.

Totok, William, and Elena-Irina Macovei. *Între mit și bagatelizare. Despre reconsiderarea critică a trecutului, Ion Gavrilă Ogoranu și rezistența armată anticomunistă din România*. Iași: Polirom, 2016.

Tríska, Jan F. 'Czechoslovakia and the World Communist System'. In *Czechoslovakia Past and Present I*, edited by Miloslav Rechcígl. The Hague: Mouton, 1968.

Tučková, Kateřina. *Žítkovské bohyně*. Brno: Host, 2012.

Țurlea, Petre. *8 Noiembrie 1945*. Bucharest: Institutul Național pentru Studiul Totalitarismului, 2000.

Tyl, Jiří. 'Autorský subjekt jako osvoboditel (sebe sama)'. *Iniciály* 4, no. 36 (1993): 25–26.

Tyszka, Krzysztof. *Nacjonalizm w komunizmie: ideologia narodowa w Związku Radzieckim i Polsce Ludowej*. Warsaw: Wydawnictwo Instytutu Filozofii i Socjologii PAN, 2004.

Vaughn, David. *Battle for the Airwaves: Radio and the 1938 Munich Crisis*. Prague: Radioservis, 2008.

Veber, Václav. *Osudové únorové dny 1948*. Prague: Nakladatelství Lidové noviny, 2008.

Verma, Neil. *Theater of the Mind: Imagination, Aesthetics and American Radio Drama*. Chicago: University of Chicago Press, 2012.

Volokitina, T.V., T.M. Islamov, G.P. Murashko, A.F. Noskova, and L.A. Rogovaia eds. *Vostochnaya evropa v dokumentach rossiiskikh arkhivov 1944–1953*. Moscow: Sibirski khronograf, 1997.

Vultur, Smaranda. 'Daily Life and Constraints in Communist Romania in the Late 1980s: From the Semiotic of Food to the Semiotics of Power'. In *Public and Private Recollections of Lived Experience in Southeast Europe*, edited by Maria Todorova, Augusta Dimou, and Stefan Troebst. Budapest: Central European University Press, 2014.

Werth, Nicolas. 'Une source inédite: les *svodki* de la Tchéka-OGPU'. *Revue des études slaves* 66, no. 1 (1994): 17–27.

Wolf, Christa. *Was bleibt*. Berlin: Aufbau, 1990.

Wolf, Christa. *What Remains*, translated by Heike Schwarzbauer and Rick Takvorian. New York: Farrar, Strauss & Giroux, 1993.

Yurchak, Alexei. *Everything Was Forever Until It Was No More: The Last Soviet Generation*. Princeton: Princeton University Press, 2006.

Zajiček, Edward. *Poza ekranem: kinematografia polska 1896–2005*. Warsaw: Stowarzyszenie Filmowców Polskich Studio Filmowe Montevideo, 2009.

Zmeškal, Tomáš. *Milostný dopis klínovým pismem*. Brno: Torst, 2008.

Żukowski, Tomasz. 'Współzawodnictwo w nacjonalizmie. Spór między partią i Kościołem w roku 1966'. *Kwartalnik Historii Żydów*, no. 4 (2008): 415–426.

Index